"With All Your Possessions"

And you shall love the Lord your God . . . with all your might—that is, with all your material possessions.

—Rashi on Deuteronomy 6:5

"With All Your Possessions"

Jewish Ethics and Economic Life

MEIR TAMARI

THE FREE PRESS
A Division of Macmillan, Inc.
NEW YORK

Collier Macmillan Publishers
LONDON

The Free Press
A Division of Macmillan, Inc.
866 Third Avenue, New York, N.Y. 10022

Collier Macmillan Canada, Inc.

Printed in the United States of America

printing number
1 2 3 4 5 6 7 8 9 10

Library of Congress Cataloging-in-Publication Data

Tamari, Meir.
  With all your possessions.

  Bibliography: p.
  Includes index.
  1. Commercial law (Jewish law)   2. Judaism and economics.   3. Ethics, Jewish.   I. Title.
LAW   346′.07′089924   86-22964
ISBN 0-02-932150-6   342.67089924

To my wife Devorah
without whom this book
would never have been completed

Contents

Preface

The idea for this book arose during the early years of my teaching at the Bar Ilan University in Israel. Although the university is an Orthodox Jewish institution, I found myself teaching courses in corporate finance in exactly the same way I would have done in any other university in the world, with the content completely divorced from a Jewish value system. While nobody wanted to detract in any way from the quality of the professional training afforded to the students, nevertheless this divorce from the religious values of the university troubled me and other members of the faculty. After much debate, I created a special course that would attempt to present to the students this value system and its practical application to economics. That course, which is still offered at that university, inevitably led to this book.

In studies of this nature, it is extremely difficult, perhaps even impossible, not to inject one's personal economic or religious philosophy into the discussion and thus distort the source material. Since I do not belong to a particular school of economic thought, I would like to assume that I have not been guilty of such distortion; yet it would be arrogant to assume this, and so the reader is asked to see this book as the presentation of a possible economic system determined by the demands of Jewish morality and faith.

In order to ensure that the book is readable for scholars and laymen alike, I have tried to keep it as free from technical terms as possible. For the same reason, the hebraic texts are my own translation except where quoted from English language sources.

Over the years, the issues dealt with in the book have been discussed with my colleagues in the Research Department of the

Bank of Israel (Israel's central bank) and at the Faculty of Economics at Bar Ilan University. Deserving of special mention are Professors Yehuda Don and Shlomo Eksteen, who were largely instrumental in having the course included in the curriculum at Bar Ilan; Professor Yehoshua Lieberman, a former student, who is today making a major contribution to research in this field; and to the governor of the Bank of Israel, Dr. Moshe Y. Mandelbaum.

In addition, I have benefited much from the reactions and comments both of the students who participated in the course at the university, and of the audiences that I addressed at various forums in Israel and the United States. Of particular importance were the participants at the Conference on Decision Making in Business at Nijenrode, the Think Tank on Religion and Social Issues at the Fraser Institute in Vancouver, and the National Havurah Institute held at Hartford University in 1980–1981. Chapters 1, 2, and 5 of the book are expanded versions of the paper I presented at Vancouver.

The rabbis in Israel and abroad with whom I have discussed and studied the subject matter of the book over the past fifteen years are too numerous to be mentioned. This is my opportunity to thank them for the many hours they spent helping me to understand the relevant halachic material. Their opinions and ideas have helped to shape the book, while their criticisms have, I hope, kept the errors and misconceptions to a minimum.

My personal thanks are also due Rabbi Sholem Lipskar and the Aleph Institute of Miami for the sabbatical, funded by them, that enabled me to initiate a major portion of this book.

Special thanks are also owed to Martha Moradi and my secretary Esther Peterman of the Bank of Israel, whose technical skills at both deciphering and typing the complicated material of the book have been an important contribution. My editor at The Free Press, Edward Rothstein, has my profound appreciation for his understanding of the importance of this subject.

The book is not intended to provide authoritative rulings on specific issues; for such decisions one must turn to the rabbinic authorities. The twin purpose of the book is to provide an authentic and balanced view of Jewish economic life and to focus attention on the issues involved in its conduct.

CHAPTER 1

Introduction

PURPOSE OF THE BOOK

Economic decisions, both on the part of an individual and of a society, do not take place in a vacuum. The spiritual, moral, and cultural structure of the society and the individual underlies economic conduct just as it is in turn affected by economic success or failure. The economic life of the Jew, then—his attitude to material assets, his conduct in buying and selling—is a reflection of the ethical and moral principles of Judaism. The object of this book is to show that there does indeed exist, as a result of the Jewish value system, a separate and distinct "Jewish economic man," molded by religious law and communal practice. My primary purpose in writing the book is to provide authentic Jewish answers to the challenge of wealth. The terms "he" and "man" are used throughout this book in the generic sense to refer to people regardless of gender.

Jews and non-Jews alike frequently disassociate Jewish economic behavior from the practices of Judaism and its ethical and moral codes. It is as though the Jew has been living an economic existence divorced completely from his religious and cultural milieu. This leads to uncritical acceptance of various theories that bear no relationship to the economic behavior developed by the Jew in his independent homeland and in the many countries of his exile. So, for example, we find champions of capitalism using the Jew as a role model for private enterprise. Sombart,[1] like

1

Weber[2] a proponent of the free enterprise system, saw the Jew—with his frugality and hard work, his devotion to family and community, and his high level of literacy and education—as a positive force in the emergence of modern capitalism. He characterized the Jew as one of the prime creators of modern market economies, which he attributed to his need for political freedom, his ability to transcend national boundaries, and Judaism's legitimization of the profit motive in the accumulation of capital. Given Tawney's essays[3] on the connection between Protestantism and the development of capitalism, it is very easy to show the relationship between these Jewish traits and the emerging capitalism of the eighteenth century. Present-day sociologists have added the effects of minority-group status—the need to excel and the lack of security—to this link between the Jew and capitalism.

The problem with these arguments is that they divorce Jewish economic practices from Jewish sources. These sources impose important restraints on the free market model, restraints that derive from peculiarly Jewish concepts of mutual responsibility, the sanctification of everyday living and God-given absolute morality. Even though the free market economies have historically been very beneficial to minorities, including Jews, nevertheless, many minorities in the world have developed in a radically different pattern. The Jewish economic man looks different from his Armenian, Gypsy, or Southeast Asian counterpart.

At the other end of the spectrum were those who viewed socialism as a modern expression of the Mosaic code and the moral teachings of the bibical prophets. Thus, A. S. Lieberman, one of the fathers of Jewish socialism, wrote, "For us, socialism is not strange. The community is our existence, the revolution our tradition, the commune the basis of the Torah, which has been made concrete in the laws that land is not to be sold in perpetuity, in the law of the Jubilee and Sabbatical years, a system of equality and tranquility."[4] But despite Judaism's insistence on economic justice, charity, and mutual assistance, it also recognizes the legitimacy of private property, the profit motive, and market mechanism.

External historical forces on Jewish economic life have also not been analyzed clearly. Secular ideologists of the Zionist movement in the nineteenth century, for example, saw the major cause of anti-Semitism in the inverted economic pyramid, wherein Jews, lacking a base of farmers, artisans, and workers, concentrated in the liberal professions, commerce, and finance. They viewed this as an unnatural situation which created hate and persecution, as exemplified in Eastern Europe, where the Jew, trapped between the feudal nobility and the impoverished masses, became the archetypal exploiter.[5] This was not the fault of the Jew, they argued, but rather the result of historical events that deprived him of land and forced him into money lending and rent collecting. Unknowingly, this view accepted the analysis of the anti-Semite. Most scholars have followed the same line, seeing the economic lifestyle of the Jew as something caused solely or primarily by extraneous factors. This view basically accepts Toynbee's thesis of the fossilization of Jewish civilization—its attitudes and practices[6]—which are regarded as simply a reaction to external factors and the acts of others, and lack any independent ideological framework or value structure. Undoubtedly, external factors created new situations and affected the economic life of the Jew. However, to attribute these external factors primacy in the collective shaping of attitudes and practices makes Jewish history merely a reaction to outside pressures and denies it an intrinsic and independent value system.

What is common to all these attitudes and their innumerable variations is a complete detachment from Jewish source material, a lack of data on how Jews really lived, and an ignorance of how Jewish economic societies actually operated over the past 4,000 years. This book will use legal, historical, and religious sources in an attempt to present a balanced and correct evaluation of the relationship between the Jew and economic activity. My purpose is to show, through these sources, how economic activity was traditionally guided and determined by the teachings of Judaism and its religious law.

For centuries, Jews enjoyed autonomy in many countries and maintained rabbinic courts of law which regulated and governed their economic activity, thereby preserving its specifically Jewish characteristics. The Bible and the homiletical literature established an ethical and moral framework within which Jewish communities operated, introducing nonmaterialistic considerations, a unique social structure, and distinctive role models, which together tempered and restrained the excesses of more egostic economic activity.

Thus while economic activity is considered by Judaism a legitimate pursuit in the normal world, nevertheless, there exists a distinctly Jewish framework within which this activity may take place. This framework seeks to sanctify man's everyday actions in this field, in exactly the same way as it introduces holiness into the domain of other basic needs, like sex, food, shelter, and social organization. The same specific and characteristic attitudes of Judaism that determine behavior in other fields apply here as well. Attitudes and behavior with respect to poverty, money, finance, trade, and welfare are determined by Jewish conceptions of man's partnership with God, man's duty and ability to sanctify and save himself through righteous acts, the recognition of the claims of others on one's property, and overriding understandings of the demands of justice, mercy, and righteousness. The result, reflected throughout centuries of Jewish life, is a specifically Jewish economic system. The divorce of Judaism from this sphere of activity introduces a distortion into true Jewish living.

SCOPE OF STUDY

The scope of Jewish concern with economic activities is as wide as the range of those activities themselves. So this book will cover all aspects of economic life—competition and profits, wages and labor, money and banking, taxation and welfare—as these are dealt with in Jewish sources.

Thus, Jewish laws and customs had to address the issues of competition, prices, and profits so that these would not infringe or destroy the moral or ethical structure of Judaism. This meant protecting the weak and ignorant and controlling successful groups or entrepreneurs so that they could not use their economic power to the detriment of society. The wages, rights, and obligations of workers are understood, in Jewish law, to be special cases of laws governing prices and profit; workers are protected from severe deprivation, but incur obligations as well. Judaism's treatment of the market mechanism has implications regarding the free entry of workers and new firms into the market, truth in advertising and marketing, and the effect of major technological changes.

Furthermore, although Judaism recognizes the legitimacy of capital as a factor of production, the Mosaic code forbids the taking of interest, and requires the interest-free loan as part of the economic system. It is necessary, then, to examine the development of Jewish banking to see how it was made harmonious with Jewish law. In modern times, this affects the treatment of bank credit, installment buying, inflation, and exchange rates.

And since Jews enjoyed a great measure of autonomy throughout the centuries, even after they lost political independence in their own homeland, they also enjoyed the sovereign right to tax members of their communities. This system of taxation was not just a method of collecting taxes to be paid to the non-Jewish authorities. It was also, and perhaps first and foremost, a method of financing the needs of the Jewish community, even in earliest biblical times, for defense, health facilities, free education, and charity in its widest sense. The system also took into account the value system of Judaism in defining taxable income, specifying exemptions from the tax burden, and prescribing the duty of the individual to share in the costs of the community. With the emancipation of the Jew in the nineteenth and twentieth centuries, and his inclusion in the general society, this independent taxation system, like all other aspects of coercive communal living, weakened and, in many countries, ceased to exist. Nevertheless, the experience of many centuries provides a prototype of Jewish fiscal philosophy and practice.

Jewish and non-Jewish sources throughout the ages have agreed that charity and social welfare are hallmarks of Jewish life. Individuals and communities alike have been obligated to provide for the needs of society. This obligation has never been left merely to the conscience of the individual Jew, but has been recognized as an area for justifiable communal coercion. Futhermore, as we will discover, this social philosophy covers a wide range of issues from support for the poor and needy to public education and from the prevention of damage to property or person to limitations on the use of natural resources. A comparison between this social philosophy and modern welfare economics will reveal ways of rectifying abuses now suffered in many western economies.

SOURCES

In order to show that this specifically Jewish system goes beyond the theoretical and is not mere wishful thinking, it is necessary to provide data on the existence, nature, and scope of such a system as it operates in all these various aspects of economic life.

Fortunately, such data exist in abundance in three different yet related sources: legal codes, communal legislation, and religious literature.

Legal Sources: Codes and Responsa

Legal tradition, dating back to the earliest days of Jewish national independence, had already been codified in the early years of the Common Era. This tradition, written and oral, covered the economic aspects of life in addition to such areas as ritual observance and marriage and divorce. Through the later codes of Moshe ben Maimon (Maimonides), Ya'acov ben Asher, and Joseph Caro, an authoritative, systemized legal framework was provided covering a multitude of questions related to economic activity, which enabled Jewish societies to operate as independent entities.[7]

It may be argued that the existence of these codes does not prove that a Jewish economic system actually worked or even existed; they might simply represent a utopian model. Why this would be so in regard to economics, when the existence of a Jewish life based on these same codes in the areas of marriage and divorce, ritual obervance, etc., is universally accepted, is very difficult to understand. Be that as it may, there has developed a whole literature which proves that the economic practices prescribed in these codes were—and are—observed.

Throughout the ages, in all the countries of the wide Jewish diaspora, Jews turned to the rabbinic authorities for guidance and judgment in applying the law to problems arising out of all aspects of economic activity. The resulting responsa—rabbinic answers to questions on Jewish law and observance—are not merely theoretical discussions elucidating fine points of law. Primarily they are legal reports of actual cases arising out of the whole gamut of individual and communal activites in the marketplace. There is not a single major rabbinic figure who did not include in his responsa matters dealing with economic issues. Such responsa provide us with a rich source of data and a wealth of detail on the actuality of Jewish economic life in various countries and at various periods of time—and convey, as well, the unity of Jewish economic conduct over time, originating as it does in a common, continous legal tradition. (The responsa continues today, as the rabbinic authorities in Israel, England, and the United States continue to receive and answer such questions.)

Since this book is meant for the general public rather than as a textbook for rabbinic and legal scholars (and since it is in no sense to be taken as itself providing a binding legal code) only a sample of legal decisions is presented here. An effort has been made to present only decisions that express a fundamental principle or represent a particular school of thought, or that are invoked to solve problems arising out of new technological or socioeconomic conditions. In the latter case it has not always been possible to provide the reader with clear-cut decisions, either because the subject has not been discussed by an authoritative source or because conflicting opinions have not yet been resolved into an authoritative ruling. Nevertheless, relevant opinions, even if tentative, are provided so that one may gauge the possible solutions envisaged by Jewish law. In some cases, the questions are discussed but not answered at all, suggesting that there is value even in the discussion per se.

It must be stressed that both the codes of law and the decisions of the responsa are primarily concerned with the legal as distinct from the economic issues at stake. (For example, the exact date and stipulations of a contract are usually important in the settling of a legal claim, yet they may have no significance as economic factors.) Furthermore, they are legal discussions, and like all such discussions, are couched in their special terminology. Since our interest is primarily in the economic aspects, the legal issues per se are not dealt with. Throughout the book, care has been taken to present the rabbinic decisions as free of legal and scholarly discussion as possible, so that the lay reader may follow them without difficultly. In the following chapter the reader is provided with a brief description of the structure and history of the rabbinic law, while in the back of the book, a glossary of terms has been provided.

Communal Enactments

Despite the wealth of rabbinic decisions in both the codes and responsa regarding economic activity, rabbinic authorities tended to leave the market to the customs, practices, and legislation of the merchants and the community. The role of rabbinic courts was primarily to oversee these and to make sure that they did not distort or negate the religious law or the demands of morality and justice. Much of Jewish life until the middle of the nineteenth century was

characterized by communal rule expressed in independent legislative and fiscal authority. So the legislative records, budgets, and
ordinances of the Jewish communities in various countries are an
important source of data with respect to the workings of a Jewish
economic system. They show that the moral tenets of Judaism and
the decisions of rabbinic courts were actually translated into everyday practice. The autonomous Jewish communities must not be
viewed as the voluntary religious or social entities with which we
are familiar today. One must bear in mind throughout this book
that the *kehilah* (community) was comparable to the public sector
of modern times at the local, state or national level. Therefore, the
communal enactments provide some idea of what an independent
Jewish economic society would look like, especially as regards the
role of government—an issue that has assumed major importance
in all modern economies.

Ethical Literature

Legal decisions and legislation are not in themselves sufficient
to maintain the social and economic fabric of a society; that requires a value structure and moral code acceptable to the majority
of that society. In their absence, a schism will develop between the
law and legislation and economic realities. Hence, despite the
centrality of rabbinic law to Judaism, it is essential that attention
be paid to the ethical teachings that constitute the ideological
framework of Jewish society. It is this framework within which the
individual's economic aims, his methods of achieving them, and
the degree of his social responsibility are formed and nurtured, to
be reflected in the application of rabbinic and communal legislation. And in the modern world wherein the Jew lives—in an open
society exposed to non-Jewish cultural and social pressures—this
ethical value structure is perhaps even more important to defining
a Jewish economic personality than it was in the closed, autonomous societies of previous generations.

Hence, although I have tried not to allow this book to become
a moralistic treatise, reference is made to homiletical and agadic
literature as well as to philosophical writings and ethical treatises.
The stories of the Chasidic masters and the lifestyle of the giants
of the Musar movement during the last few centuries have also
been included, since they provide role models for the average in-

dividual. Throughout Jewish history, laymen, as distinct from relatively small groups of scholars, have engaged in the serious study of religious texts and homiletical literature, as constituting a major, obligatory form of religious worship. This "grassroots" study meant that ordinary individuals in Jewish society were continually exposed to this literature, an exposure that provided them with their intrinsically Jewish value structure.

ALLIED STUDIES

In order to enable the reader to pursue his or her own independent study of the issues raised in this book, a special bibliography of modern scholarship in English and Hebrew, over and above the studies referred to in the text, has been provided. At the same time, a word of caution must be raised regarding studies of this nature. It is extremely difficult for a scholar not to inject his or her own economic or religious philosophy into the discussion, yet the bias is not always made clear to the reader. So we find that in the first half of this century many studies in Jewish economic history and behavior were heavily influenced by the socialist or liberal philosophers of the time and tend, therefore, to present a Judaism synonymous with those philosophies.[8] At the present time, the pendulum seems to have swung in another direction, and now scholars tend to equate Judaism with the most extreme free market philosophers.[9]

It should also be borne in mind that most of the publications listed in the bibliography are the work of noneconomists—primarily rabbis, lawyers, and historians. These legal and historical aspects are undoubtedly important and of interest; yet, invariably the economic issues are lost. The studies by Y. Lieberman and A. Levine, on the other hand, are outstanding examples of scholarship conducted primarily from an economist's point of view.[10]

The legal and literary sources do show that there exists a Jewish economic wisdom, and examples of this wisdom will be provided whenever appropriate to the subject matter discussed. It will also be shown that the rabbis of the Talmud anticipated many modern economic theories and gave very sage advice. At this stage, two examples may suffice.

1. We find the following saying in the Talmud: "A man should always keep his wealth in three forms: one third in real estate, another in merchandise, and the remainder in liquid assets."[11] These three forms differ from each other in their degree of liquidity, risk, and short-term profitability—so the rabbinic advice could be construed as a portfolio theory.

2. In the early 1960s, the economist R. Coase propounded a theory that described environmental obstacles such as pollution in terms of economic efficiency, by considering the opportunity cost of correcting the misallocation of resources.[12] Y. Lieberman has subsequently written a paper in which he finds Talmudic support for this theory.[13]

SUMMARY

Judaism does not propose any specific economic theory or system; rather, it proposes a moral-religious framework within which the theory or system must operate. Decisions on investments, on consumption, on rates of growth, on fiscal policy, and on all the other constituents of economic life have to be made on the basis of economic criteria; then they have to be reexamined in light of this religious framework to discover whether or not the proposed choices are acceptable. My thesis in this book is that specifically Jewish moral and religious principles have indeed created a framework within which Jews have operated economically and can continue to operate.

CHAPTER 2

An Overview of Jewish Law

TORAH

Since Judaism is very much a communal and action-oriented religion, necessitating an accepted pattern of everyday behavior, much of the discussion in this book will center on legal opinions and decisions in one form or another. This chapter offers the reader a guide to the structure, methodology, and personalities of the Jewish legal system which constitutes that pattern.

Judaism as a system of living, in the economic as well as in social and ritual spheres, derives from the Torah, which is the foundation of Jewish law. Although "Torah" is sometimes loosely used to describe all the books of the Bible, or even to include the whole scope of Jewish religious learning, for our purpose "Torah" refers solely to the Five Books of Moses.

At Sinai the Jews, according to Judaism, received the Torah through Divine revelation, so that every idea, every sentence, and, for that matter, every word in the Five Books of Moses is of Divine origin. This written Divine law contains 613 commandments (the so-called *taryag mitzvot*), which are binding on the Jews, some of them at the individual level, some at the collective. The rest of the books of the Bible, the prophetic books and holy writings, are supplementary to the Five Books of Moses themselves, and constitute a sort of expansion or derivation of the laws contained therein. However, from a legal standpoint they are not equal, so that rulings in the prophetic books or the holy writings

11

cannot be understood to contradict the demands of the Torah per se.

However, in addition to this written code of laws—the *Torah She-Bikhtav*—the revelation at Sinai included an oral law—or, more correctly, an oral tradition. This *Torah She-B'al Peh* (oral law) was (according to Judaism) given to Moses as well, so that the two, the oral and the written law, form one unit; Jewish law cannot be conceived of, let alone applied, without reference to this unity. Even though this oral law is an integral and equal part of the Jewish legal structure, it must be noted that the authority of the written law is usually superior, legally; but transgressions of the oral law, being considered primarily of the nature of heresy, are sometimes punishable with greater severity. There are, thus, at the basis of the Jewish legal structure, these two concepts—the divinity of the law and the existence of both a written and an oral law.

The nature of this *Torah She-B'al Peh*, or oral law, may be summed up as follows:

1.   The written law is not detailed enough and therefore the oral law is needed to specify its implementation.

2.   There are laws that do not appear at all in the written form. For example, although animals have to be ritually slaughtered for human consumption, it is an oral law flowing from Moses at Sinai that the slaughtering has to take place through the severing of the arteries of the neck.

3.   The rabbis, by using certain clearly defined legal principles and tools, are able to deduce a new law from an analysis of biblical verses relating to other laws.

4.   In order to protect or to enhance religious principles and biblical practices, the rabbis in each generation have the authority to introduce legislation (sometimes of a temporary nature), even though such legislation had no precedent. Much of this legislation may be regarded as constituting a sort of "fence" around the Torah. In other words, in order to prevent the desecration or transgression of recognized and accepted precepts, rabbinic action can be taken to extend or to limit permissible actions.

Throughout Jewish history, new situations and new issues have been handled, and continue today to be handled, within the framework of this oral law, in accordance with the pattern we have just mentioned. It must be stressed that the machinery whereby the decisions of the oral law in new circumstances become binding law is a relatively slow-moving one, so that at any one period of time it is possible to find conflicting opinions existing side by side. Gradually, through the establishment of a consensus, one or another of these opinions becomes binding.

The personality of the particular authority was, as often as not, insufficient to obtain universal acceptance for his opinion. The greatest rabbinic authorities issued rulings that did not become accepted, despite the respect and honor given to their author and despite the acceptance of many of his other rulings. During the years of exile, there was no parliament, so to speak, whereby these matters could be decided, so that the process of generation of authoritative rulings took much longer and involved much greater discussion.

At all times and in all countries, Jews were encouraged, especially in the economic field, to go beyond the letter of the law and to do that which was more merciful than required, even though the rabbinic authorities could not naturally enforce such kindness. This going beyond the letter of the law is found also in the ritual field, where people can sometimes take upon themselves more stringent or more strict practices than are required by the legal authorites.

The legal structure of Judaism has at all times rested primarily on its Divine origin and on its moral claim on the Jew. As often as not, Jewish communities lacked the power of physical force to back up their decisions, which became general practice, rather, as a result of the religious identification of the individual or of the group. Levi Yitschak of Berdichev, one of the early teachers of the Chasidic movement which swept Eastern European Jewry from the eighteenth century onwards, once said,

> Look how powerful is this law of Moses. The Tsar has many policemen and many soldiers and he is alive and well and rules his kingdom with an iron hand. This Tsar has said that one may not import liquor or certain other articles except by license, yet his whole empire is flooded with smuggled goods. The son of Amram (Moses) has been dead for many centuries and has no Cossacks and no divisions, yet he said one may not have leavened bread in one's home for seven days and in all Jewish homes there is no leavened bread during Passover.

In the same way, rabbinic personalities laid down rules within this oral law, and these were translated into practice very often without the physical authority to enforce them or even without those personalities occupying official rabbinic positions. Maimonides, one of the greatest codifiers, was a physician and not the Chief Rabbi of Cairo. And this pattern has been repeated in the whole process of the oral law right down to our own day.

MISHNAH

From the time of Moses to beyond the period of the Second Temple, the oral law remained an oral tradition. For all these centuries, the written law was studied, analyzed, and applied on the basis of oral study, with the prophets seen as part of this oral tradition. With the rebuilding of the Second Temple some six hundred years before the Common Era, prophecy as Jews knew it ceased, and authority moved completely to the interpreters of the oral law. So we find a chain of rabbinic personalities spanning the period of some seven hundred fifty years until the oral law was reduced to writing. First there was the establishment of the Kneset Hag'dolah (the Great Assembly) under Ezra who had returned from the Babylonian exile. Many practices and decisions in Jewish life were finally formulated and defined by this assembly, which, during the period that the land of Israel was part of the Persian and Macedonian empires, was the ruling body in all respects for the Jewish people in the land of Israel and an authoritative religious body for the Jews outside it.

The period of the Great Assembly was followed by one in which the authoritative positions were divided between two people (*zugot*, or "pairs"), one being the head of the rabbinic court (*av bet din*), the other being the patriarch (*nasi*, pl., *nesi'im*). These two were separate and independent from the Hasmonean kings, the High Priests, or the Roman appointees, such as Herod, who ruled the country politically and militarily. This period of the *zugot* continued almost until the destruction of the Second Temple, the last pair comprising Hillel and Shammai, at the beginning of the Common Era. From that period on, authority becomes centered in the *nesi'im*, who were descendants of Hillel. Throughout, authority was shared by the Sanhedrin, a Greek name for the members of the Great Assembly and a continuation of the Seventy Elders, a tradition stretching back all the way to Moses. It was one of the descendants of Hillel who codified for the first time part of the oral tradition.

In the year 188 of the Common Era, Rabbi Yehudah Hanasi wrote down six tractates of the Mishnah, which codified the authoritative opinions in this oral chain. The period of the Great Assembly and of the *zugot* may perhaps be viewed as a transition between the prophetic period and that of the *tana'im*, as the sages of the time of the Mishnah were known.

"Rebbe," the Teacher, as Rabbi Yehudah Hanasi became known, divided his Mishnah into the following six *sedarim* (orders). Each *seder* is further divided in tractates and chapters:

1. *Zera'im*—dealing with the agricultural laws, such as the prohibition of planting of diverse seeds, the sabbatical year, tithing, and gifts to the poor
2. *Moed*—dealing with the yearly cycle and the festivals
3. *Nashim*—dealing with marriage and divorce
4. *Nezikin*—dealing with the criminal, commercial, and civil codes of law. It is this *seder* which forms the legal basis for the treatment of economic matters in Judaism, primarily in the tractates *Baba Kama*, *Baba Metzia*, and *Baba Bathra*
5. *Kodashim*—dealing with the Temple service and sacrifices
6. *Toharot*—dealing with the laws of ritual purity

Yehudah Hanasi's Mishnah was actually compiled shortly after two previous attempts by Rabbi Akiva and Rabbi Meir to systematize in some form the mass of oral tradition that had accumulated. It should be pointed out that the Mishnah did not include all of the oral law; it was only a synopsis of authoritative opinions. The major part of Jewish law continued to exist as an oral tradition.

Alongside the tractates of the Mishnah there was another body of traditional law, the *baraita* (external teaching). These *baraitot* represented those opinions not considered as authoritative as the Mishnah by Yehudah Hanasi, while the *Tosefta* (supplement) was a more intricate and detailed discussion of the subject matter of the Mishnah. They were both used to explain and amplify the teachings of the Mishnah and were incorporated in the rabbinical discussions.

TALMUD

Despite Yehudah Hanasi's codification, the Mishnah itself soon became the subject of intensive oral study. In the academies of the Land of Israel and in those of Babylon, which emerged as the largest center of Jewish life, scholarship now focused on the written law and on the Mishnah. Within a very short time, the need was felt for a further codification of the Jewish legal system. This was done most authoritatively in the Babylonian Talmud but earlier in a more fragmented form in the Jerusalem Talmud (actually compiled in Tiberias). In the middle of the fifth century in Babylon, Ravina and Rav Ashi codified the post-Mishnaic oral tradition in the Gemara, which, together with the Mishnah, constitutes the Talmud.

The rabbis of the Gemara, the *Amora'im*, were active for some three hundred years of Jewish life in the Land of Israel and in Babylon. Since the chain of tradition stretches back to the revelation at Sinai, the further back in time a source goes, the greater the legal authority attributed to that source. This means that the *Amora'im* cannot reject a ruling of the sages of the Mishnah.

Rabbi Yehudah Hanasi had concentrated primarily on codifying legal material. The Gemara comprised both the Jewish legal tradition—the halakhah (literally, perhaps, "road" or "path")—and the agadah. The agadah could probably be classified as the theological, philosophical, and moral literature of the Jewish tradition, from the time of Moses down to the time of its codification. While Yehudah Hanasi had been busy codifying the legal decisions of the rabbis, there had been created a parallel rabbinic literature primarily in the form of homiletic works—translations and commentaries on the Bible. These included the Aramaic translation cum commentary of Onkelos on the Torah and that of the Prophets by Jonathan ben Uzziel; the source book of Jewish mysticism, the Zohar or Book of Splendor by Shimon bar Yochai; and the *Midrash Halakhah*—literature in which halakhah is deduced or supported from the words of the Torah, which constitutes a kind of legal commentary on the biblical material. This literature includes the *Mekhilta* on Exodus (*Sh'mot*), the *Sifré* on Numbers (*Bamidbar*) and Deuteronomy (*D'varim*), and the *Sifra* on Leviticus (*Vayikra*). There were also other collections of *midrashim*—interpretive commentaries and explanations—covering the five books of Moses and other books of the Bible, the major one being the *Medrash Rabbah*.

All these writings were, however, far more than a commentary. They represented the conceptual framework that lay behind the halakhic rulings. It would be a very serious mistake to try and separate these two streams of halakhah and agadah, as any such separation would probably present a distorted view not only of Jewish religious thinking but, for that matter, even of its legal thought. The unity of halakhah and agadah has been maintained throughout the ages, so that most of the great halakhic personalities and codifiers were not only participants in the agadic stream, but considered it as part of the overall process of Jewish legal thought.

Not all of the tractates of the Mishnah have been included in the Talmud; in some cases we are left only with the written version of Yehudah Hanasi's Mishnah. The Mishnah had been written in Hebrew; however, after the destruction of the Temple there was an acceleration in the process existing for may centuries previous to that, whereby, Aramaic became the lingua franca of the Jewish world, so that the Talmud—or more correctly, the Gemara—was therefore written in that language. Certain prayers, like the kaddish, also written in Aramaic, are still included in the prayerbook of the modern Jew. It is not possible in this chapter to describe the structure or thought process of the Gemara. We will have to restrict ourselves to mentioning here that the Gemara is, to all intents and purposes, a written-down oral tradition, if such a thing can be conceived. Punctuation is reduced to a minimum and the subject does not always follow a clearly defined pattern, so that there are constant digressions embracing, for example, other opinions of the sages being discussed or the introduction of agadic material. For many trained in the Greek thought process, the Gemara remains a difficult book to master, even over and above the language problem occasioned by its Aramaic text.

From the time of its compilation down to the present day, the Talmud, especially the Babylonian Talmud, has been the major subject of Jewish study, not only for rabbis and judges but for laymen of all ages. Each generation and each major center of learning produced its commentaries and its notes, many of which are printed together with the text itself.

The reader will notice throughout this book that many halakhic authorities have become known by their Hebrew initials or by the name of the major book they wrote. So, for instance, the most important of the Talmudic commentators, Rabbi Shlomo ben Yitschak, is popularly known as Rashi, from his Hebrew initials.

Rashi, who became the key to the study of the Bible and Talmud, lived in Franco-Germany in the eleventh century. His disciples, down through the end of the fourteenth century in England, France, and the Rhineland, came to constitute a body of scholars known as the tosafists, authors of "additions" to the Talmud. This body of scholars, spiritual descendants of Rabbenu Gershon Me'or Hagolah of the ninth century, generally maintained a common approach to halakhic issues and lived under a particular form of communal organization. Two of the famous tosafists were grandsons of Rashi: Rashbam (the initials of Rabbi Shmuel ben Meir) and Rabbenu Tam (Jacob ben Meir).

Some of the most important legal authorities in Judaism were part of this school, which continued until the later part of the fifteenth century. Within the scope of this overview, those providing either extensive responsa or some form of codification are mentioned. In the thirteenth century, Rabbi Moshe of Coucy and Rabbi Yitschak of Corbeil each authored a compendium of laws—the *S'mag* (*Sefer Mitzvot Gadol*) and the *S'mak* (*Sefer Mitzvot Katan*), respectively—while the Maharam of Rothenburg, Rabbi Meir ben Baruch, was the source of a vast number of responsa subsequently incorporated in halakhic decisions. His pupil, the Mordechai (Rabbi Mordechai ben Hillel), wrote important collections of halakhic rulings, as did the Rosh (Rabbi Asher ben Yechiel).

Just as important to Talmudic scholars as this Franco-German school of the tosafists is the contribution of the Sephardi (Spanish, Italian, North African, and Middle Eastern) scholars. Although historically they followed the period of the *geonim* discussed in the next section, they have been included here because they too constitute part of the published Talmudic editions of our day. Rabbenu Chananel and Rabbi Yitschak Alfass (The Rif) in eleventh-century North Africa and Spain were the mainstays of this school. Like the Germanic school, they too had a specific system of thought and study. They operated in a socioeconomic framework peculiar to the Moslem and Christian Mediterranean countries, which was more mobile and less rigid then that prevalent in the north western countries of medieval Europe. The Rif provided an extensive collection of legal rulings which followed the order of the Talmud, constituting both a codex and a commentary.

Many of the commentaries written by the tosafists and the Sephardi scholars of this period are included in the printed editions of the Talmud together with the original text. And it is important to note that all the major commentaries on the Talmud became themselves the subject of Jewish scholarship throughout the ages. Down to the present time, this scholarship created and continues to create a vast literature of commentary and responsa.

GEONIM

The physical destruction and economic impoverishment of the Jewish settlement in the land of Israel which followed first the Christianization of the Byzantine Empire, and later the Moslem conquest, brought in its wake the eclipse of the scholarship in that country. In Babylon, however, the Jewish community continued as the major center of Jewish learning. The *Rabbanan Savorai*, the successors of the *Amora'im* and their pupils, were, however, no longer permitted to add any halakhic material to the Talmudic text. The following period, that of the *geonim*, the heads of the academies of Sura and Pumbedita, lasted for almost five hundred years and yielded a further codification of the legal structure. From the far-flung corners of the Jewish world came questions of ritual, belief, history, and law, the answers to which have come down to us. These answers, or *t'shuvot*, established a pattern of rabbinic scholarship carried down throughout the ages and continuing in our own times. The author of a *t'shuvah* would take care to mention supporting and opposing authorities in order to provide a basis for his ultimate decision. A number of codes of law were complied during the geonic period before it came to an end in the eleventh century. These, *Halakhot P'sukot* and *Halakhot G'dolot* were quoted extensively in the rabbinic literature of later generations and invoked as a basis for their decisions.

These responsa and codes paved the way for the growth of scholarship in North Africa, Italy, Franco-Germany, and Spain, which, beginning in the tenth centuries, were to replace Babylon as centers of Jewish scholarship.

THE CODES

Just as the Mishnah and Talmud reduced to writing parts of the oral tradition, so they were followed by codes which presented accepted and definite legal rulings. Naturally, these codes were based on the responsa literature and rabbinic commentaries that had preceded them. They were organized not according to the tractates of the Talmud, but rather according to subject matter—which, in any given case, was typically distributed throughout a tractate and, as often as not, even over a number of different tractates. Furthermore, they have to be distinguished from earlier codifications, which primarily enumerated the *mitzvot* (commandments). Each of the codes referred to in this section, on the other hand, are essentially a codex of Jewish Law.

Chronologically, the first and easily the most comprehensive of all the codes is that of the Rambam, Rabbi Moshe ben Maimon (Maimonides) who lived most his life in Egypt in the late twelfth century. Quite apart from his philosophical works, his commentary on the Mishnah, and his responsa, the Rambam's code, *Mishneh Torah*, marks him as almost another lawgiver. The *Mishneh Torah* comprises fourteen volumes (hence its alternate name, *HaYad Hachazakah*, where the numerical value of the Hebrew letters in *yad* equals 14), and it covers every aspect of Jewish life, including those commandments temporarily in abeyance, such as those governing the order of the Temple service and sacrifices. For the purpose of this book, the most relevant sections of *Mishneh Torah* are *Nezikin*, *Mishpatim*, and *Shoftim*—basically the commercial and judicial elements of the codex.

Maimonides presents decisive legal rulings without including opposing opinions or a summary of the Talmudic discussion on which his decisions are based. In Provence, Rabbi Avraham ben David, the Raivad, wrote a critical review of the *Mishneh Torah* which is included in the text of Maimonides' codex. Other classical commentaries of the *Mishneh Torah* are the *Kesef Mishneh* by Joseph Caro and the *Mishneh La-Melech* by Rabbi Yehuda ben Shmuel Rosanes (Turkey, 1655–1727).

Within a half-century of the Rambam, Ya'akov ben Asher (the son of the Rosh, mentioned previously) compiled the *Arba'ah Turim* (Four Rows—referring to the jewels on the breastplate of the

High Priest), based on the work of his father and the Ramban (Nachmanides) (Rabbi Moshe ben Nachman, 1194–1270, Spain and the Land of Israel). Like them, he would seek to synthesize the approach of the Spanish and Franco-German schools. Most of the later codes, commentaries, and responsa adopted the following arrangement of halakhic material in the Tur, which differed from that of the *Mishneh Torah* even though it drew heavily on that work:

1. *Orach Chayim* (Way of Life)—primarily concerned with the Shabbat, festivals, and prayers
2. *Yoreh De'ah* (Teacher of Knowledge)—dealing with the laws of kosher food, ritual purity, and other aspects of forbidden and permitted things
3. *Even Ha'ezer*—concerned with marriage, divorce, and family matters
4. *Choshen Mishpat* (Breastplate of Judgment)—dealing with commercial and criminal law, property rights, and civil law

It is this last part of the Tur and other codes, together with their commentaries, that provides the source material for halakhic decisions in the economic field. The main exception is the laws of interest, which are dealt with in *Yoreh De'ah*, a reflection of the Jewish treatment of interest as being a matter of spiritual purity, rather than a function of borrowing and lending.

Two other important commentaries which became source books on the Talmud were written in the thirteenth century: *Mordechai* (by Rabbi Mordechai ben Hillel of Germany) and the *Bet Hab'chirah* (by Rabbi Menahem Hameiri of Provence).

It is to Safed in the Land of Israel that we have to turn for the codex which forms the culmination of the post-Geonic period, that of the *rishonim*, or first masters. The *Shulchan Arukh*, written by Rabbi Joseph Caro in 1555 after the exile of Jews from Spain in 1492, gradually became the authoritative legal code for all Jews. Following the pattern of the Tur, Caro limited himself to only those aspects of halakhah which applied after the destruction of the Temple and the resultant dispersal of the Jews. Actually, the *Shulchan Arukh* represents a synopsis of his earlier, monumental work, the *Bet Yosef* (House of Joseph), in which he not only commented on the *Tur*, but, more importantly, presented an analysis of his decisions and the halakhic sources for them.

The *acharonim*, or later masters, from the late sixteenth century down to our own day, apart from using the *Shulchan Arukh* in their responsa, and over and above their own Talmudic studies, created a new literature of commentary on the *Tur* and the *Shulchan Arukh*. It was due to the *Mapah* (Tablecloth), which the Rama, Rabbi Moses Isserles, wrote in the sixteenth century as a gloss on the *Shulchan Arukh*, that the latter became universally accepted by world Jewry. Joseph Caro had not included the halakhic decisions of the Ashkenazim (Franco-German school) in his codex; the Rama's gloss, which did so, made it possible for all Jews to follow one codex.

Today, almost all editions of the *Shulchan Arukh* include in addition to the Rama (whose gloss is usually part of the text), the commentaries of the Taz (Rabbi David ben Shmuel [1586–1667, Poland], named, like many rabbis, for his book, *Turei Zahav* [Rows of Gold]); the Shach (Rabbi Shabbtai Hakohen of the same period, author of *Sifsei Kohen* [Lips of the Priest]); and Rabbi Moshe Rivkes, author of the *Be'er HaGolah* (Well of the Exile), written in Amsterdam in the late seventeenth century.

At the beginning of this century, Rabbi Yechiel Michael Epstein produced an *Arukh HaShulchan*, a digest of the *Shulchan Arukh* to which he added the rulings of subsequent *acharonim*. Other codes, such as the *Mishneh Brurah* of Israel Meir Hakohen (the Chofetz Chaim), do not deal with the subject matter of our book and so are excluded from this overview.

The later sages—from the seventeenth century down to today, in all the countries where Jews lived—continued to write responsa along with commentaries on the Codes and on the Talmud incorporating their own decisions, thus creating an ongoing codification of Jewish law.

HOMILETIC AND MORALISTIC LITERATURE

The basis of the Jewish treatment of economic matters is, naturally, the legal decisions of the rabbis. As with any legal system, however, especially a religious and moralistic one, these legal decisions cannot be appreciated nor can they operate without their philosophical and ethical underpinnings. So our overview must, of necessity, include some reference to these sources as well.

Most of the great halakhic authorities were also engaged in

homiletics, biblical commentary, and ethical writings. There were, futhermore, rabbis whose influence on Jewish behavior was primarily exerted through this type of literature. Thus, following the Rambam's system of thought is the *Sefer Hachinukh* (Book of Education), which sought to explain the ideological meaning of the 613 commandments as they appear in the Five Books of Moses. (It is commonly ascribed to Rabbi Aharon Halevi of Barcelona in the thirteenth century). The *Chovot Halevavot* (Duties of the Heart), by Rabbenu Bachya Ibn Pakuda of eleventh-century Spain; *Sha'arei T'shuvah* (Gates of Repentance), by Rabbi Yonah ben Avraham of Gerondi, Italy, in the early thirteenth century; and *Mesilat Yesharim* (Path of the Righteous), by Moshe Chaim Luzzato of eighteenth-century Italy, are classic moralistic works that became part of the curriculum of Torah students.

In addition, some commentaries on the Torah, like those of the Ramban and of Yitschak Abarbanel (financier to the Court of Ferdinand and Isabella of Spain prior to 1492) and like the *Or Chayim* (Light of Life), by Rabbi Chaim Michael, sought to produce a pattern of behavior, not merely to explain texts. The commentaries of Rabbi Shimshon Raphael Hirsch of nineteenth-century Germany are a modern example of this.

In modern times, two movements which appeared in Eastern Europe had an impact on the pattern of Jewish behavior in all spheres, including the economic one. Chasidism, founded by Israel Ba'al Shem Tov (Master of the Good Name) in the early eighteenth century, soon became a mass movement encompassing large segments of Eastern European Jewry. Through the leadership of various dynasties of *Admorim* (acronym for Our Master, Our Teacher), the Chasidim developed into tightly knit groups with distinctive dress and customs. Chasidism stressed the importance of *Klal Yisrael* (the totality of the Jewish people); the importance of deeds, especially acts of righteousness; and the concept of *tikun olam* (perfecting the world).

Although based on earlier Jewish mysticism, Chasidism must be distinguished from the medieval *Chasidei Ashkenas* (pietists), who produced the great moralistic work *Sefer Chasidim*, by Rabbi Yehuda Chasid. The Chasidic masters taught through the media of biblical commentary, Talmudic and halakhic glosses, and storytelling. A *Shulchan Arukh*, structured according to the practices of the Ari Hakadosh (Rabbi Yitschak Luria, the mystic of Safed in the sixteenth century), was authored by Shneour Zalman of Lyady, founder of the Lubavicher (Chabad) Chasidim. Other Chasidic masters wrote responsa and halakhic commentaries.

In the nineteenth century, Rabbi Yisrael Salanter founded the Musar (roughly, "instruction in right behavior") movement, geared to improving the behavior of students of the *yeshivot* (Talmudic academies) in Lithuania, then the "university capital" of world Jewry. The Musar movement stressed the inclusion of moralistic teachings along with the traditional emphasis on halakhic study. Sometimes special *yeshivot* were created for this purpose, while at other times, these teachings were accepted as part of the standard curriculum. Naturally, both these methods involved the application of a strict moral code of behavior in the economic field through dictating minimal levels of consumption, restraints on business activity, and a constant re-examination of one's personal integrity.

CHAPTER 3

The Challenge of Wealth

MATERIAL GOODS IN A RELIGIOUS PERSPECTIVE

Ever since the dawn of history, material possessions and wealth have been seen as posing basic ethical and spiritual problems. All religions, therefore, have had to offer some perspective regarding the scope and legitimacy of economic activity. Judaism is no exception in this respect, though it differs radically from all other religions in the answers it provides to the relevant questions.

Two distinct sets of problems within the general issue of material wealth would seem to require a religious perspective: the proper allocation of time between work and spiritual activity (such as prayer, religious study, or the fulfillment of religious obligations), and the challenges to ethics and morality. Inequalities in wealth have given rise to injustice, theft, and often bloodshed, and the accumulation of wealth often looks as though it is linked to human lust. All of these behaviors are inconsistent with the ethical and moral teachings of almost all religions. In Judaism's approach to these and allied issues, we will be able to discover the foundations for a specific ethical framework with respect to economic activity, on the part of both the individual and society.

Limitations Imposed by Time

Almost all religions place a restriction on the time permissibly devoted to economic activity, and in this respect Judaism is no different. In the cycle of the Jewish year there are periods when one is not permitted to work or to be engaged in the accumulation of economic goods. On these days abstinence from labor, commerce, or any other economic activity is mandatory as a form of religious observance. In this category we include the fifty-two sabbaths of the year and the eight major festivals, along with occasional time periods incumbent on specific individuals, such as the week of mourning usually required for a close relative or the week during which a bridegroom is not permitted to work. Furthermore, in the agricultural sector of the economy, there are the limitations of the sabbatical year (every seventh one) and the jubilee, in the fiftieth year. All of these injunctions restrict the number of days allotted to economic activity, even though it is not simple to measure their quantitative effect. Modern technology has probably made their effect far smaller than it was in ancient times; many industrial plants, for example, are able to operate without any major loss accruing to them as a result of the religious cessation from work, through the use of mechanical devices. Even farming, considered all over the world to be an every-day-of-the-year occupation, has been shown by the religious settlements in Israel to be no less efficient when the religious restrictions on time are observed.

Far more basic and pervasive than the ritual limitations on the time devoted to economic activity is one that is peculiar to Judaism. This limitation is imposed by the obligation to study Torah. Judaism demands, as a positive religious injunction, that each and every individual, irrespective of his level of knowledge or economic status, devote time to the study of Torah. This obligation is laid not only on the priests, rabbis, and scholars, but applies to all. Furthermore, there is no special time span or period in a person's life that is to be set aside for Torah study; rather, one is obligated to study day and night from earliest youth to one's dying day. This means that every portion of a man's life not spent on the learning of Torah is considered to be a waste of time, *b'tul zman*, and is seen as constituting a serious neglect of one's religious duties.

The concept of *b'tul zman* makes it easy to understand that devoting time to economic activity of any kind might be considered a religious shortcoming, even though Judaism might view the activity as such as being legitimate. Proponents of this opinion would argue that the necessities of life would be provided by God while the Jew devoted all his time to studying the Divinely revealed Torah. "This is the way of the Torah, bread eaten with salt, water in measured quantities, and the floor shall be thy bed."[1]

The Talmud modified this notion, as may be seen from the following.[2] For over a dozen years, it is taught, Shimon bar Yochai hid in a cave studying Torah, despite a Roman edict against it. On leaving the cave he saw a man ploughing a field. "What!" he said. "There is so little time to devote oneself to God's words, and you devote your time to insignificant things like the settlement of the world." And in his anger he turned the man into a heap of bones. This incident was repeated when he came across another person engaged in farming activities. Then a heavenly voice said to him: "Bar Yochai, unless you refrain from turning my world into chaos, I will put you back into the cave."

In the ensuing discussion, Rabbi Yishmael says that a man has indeed to study Torah, but the Divine plan for the world makes it continually necessary to devote time to providing for one's material needs. The Talmud sums up by saying that many tried to be like Bar Yochai and were unable to emulate him, whereas many followed the path of Rabbi Yishmael and were successful.

In the *Ethics of the Fathers* (a popular, ethically oriented tractate of the Mishnah), this majority view was summed up as follows: "Where there is no flour [material goods], there is no Torah [because poverty prevents one from studying Torah and carrying out the Divine commandments]; where there is no Torah, there is no flour."[3] [That is, only the Torah, by placing limits on man's needs and the methods of satisfying them, can put the material things of life in their correct perspective; otherwise, no matter what a man has, he never believes he has enough.]

Some six centuries later, when Maimonides codified the law, he set forth his agreement with Rabbi Yishmael's opinion by prescribing that a man should divide his time equally among three activities: studying Torah; earning a livelihood; and eating, sleeping, etc. Maimonides pointed out that throughout the ages many great sages earned their livelihood in a variety of ways; nevertheless, they remained true to the basic principle that devoting time to the Torah was an essential tenet of Judaism, even when it entailed limitations on economic activity. However, Maimonides frowned on the idea of Torah study based on public support, or pursued as a means of earning a livelihood. This opinion regarding what he called the "middle way" he expressed as follows:

> One should not aim first at accumulating wealth and then devoting time to the study of the Torah. Rather, one should see one's study as permanent and dominant and one's economic endeav-

ors as marginal and temporary. This study is not meant, however, to be a means to economic or personal profit; our sages said, "He who benefits [materially] from the study of the Torah forfeits his life. [Indeed] Torah study which is not accompanied by economic activity is liable to end in sin, and those engaged in this form of study will end up by robbing their fellow men."[4]

But if one were wealthy and did not have to devote a third of the day to earning one's livelihood, Maimonides would have no objection to not doing so. We can see this in his recommendation that a man should go into commerce rather than farming because commerce allowed far more time for study of the Torah.[5] A similar opinion, expressed by another sage at a much later period, maintained that banking and finance were satisfactory Jewish occupations as they allowed a lot of time for the study of Torah.[6]

Irrespective of whether one agrees with the way of Shimon bar Yochai or with that of Rabbi Yishmael, the necessity of devoting time to Torah study, and the consequent limitation on permissible economic activity, is a basic and fundamental tenet of Judaism.

In recent years, dating back to the middle of the last century, rabbinic opinion increasingly allowed that although for the majority it was not possible to follow bar Yochai's way of total dedication to the study of Torah, it was essential to create an elite group that did live in this way, even to the extent of negating all economic activity. The *kolel* system, whereby the community supports Torah students even after they are married, represents the practical application of this viewpoint. This viewpoint has gained strength in our own day, especially in view of the destruction of the great centers of Jewish learning in the Holocaust.

It should be obvious that given the complexity of the modern economy, the restriction on time permissibly devoted to economic endeavors occasioned by the obligation to study Torah will always place a brake on the economic development of the individual. Furthermore, it will have consequences for related decisions and behavior—such as the choice of a career that will not conflict with the time to be allotted for studying Torah.

The Spiritual Challenge of Economic Wealth

Judaism acknowledges the legitimate satisfaction of man's basic needs, provided that these needs are fulfilled within the framework of morality and justice set up by religious law. Man's economic desires are treated by Judaism in exactly the same way as all other basic human needs: as legitimate, permissible, and beneficial, but restricted, educated, and sanctified by observance of God's commandments.

Both in the blessing given to Adam and in that later repeated to Noah, the Lord gave man dominion over the world and all its creatures—such dominion to be used for man's material well-being. Adam was placed in the Garden of Eden "to work and guard it." Judaism envisages a partnership between God and man in which man continues the settlement of the world commenced by the Divine creation and God bestows upon him the Divine blessings.

Man's earning of a livelihood and his creation of economic and material assets are seen as reflections of Divine pleasure. Leafing through the pages of the Bible, one is immediately struck by the fact that the observance of God's commandments leads to an abundance of material goods rather than to some ethereal, otherworldly reward.

For example, the Land of Israel, which is the Divinely destined geographic area for the Jews to live in and create a nation of priests, is not a bleak desert area, but a land flowing with milk and honey. A God-fearing man is characterized as one whose flocks and orchards bear their fruit in season and produce a bounty of goods. Indeed, the daily prayers of the Jewish liturgy request, along with Divine forgiveness, peace, and the healing of the sick, a satisfactory livelihood earned through honest and moral means. Contrariwise, in its portrayal of Divine anger and punishment, the Bible (in all its books) depicts starvation, poverty, and drought as the just deserts of sinners, whoever they may be.[7]

Finally, on the holiest day of the Jewish year, Yom Kippur, when the books of judgment are opened in which all people are inscribed and sealed, there is also a book of *parnasah*—of economic and material welfare. After completing the atonement service, perhaps the pinnacle of Jewish religious life, the high priest offered a special prayer in the Temple, the major component of which is a request for a year of bounty, a year in which Jews will not have to be dependent on others for their livelihood. Obviously, economic wealth and prosperity were regarded as a desirable state—in contrast to the glorification of poverty and asceticism in other faiths and creeds.

It is true that there are references in the Talmud to the merits of poverty.[8] Yet, generally speaking, these are marginal to the general trend of Jewish life. The instances of asceticism to be found in medieval Germanic Jewry, and later on in the scholastic circles of Eastern Europe toward the end of the sixteenth and seventeenth centuries, were also outside of the norm.

By and large, there are no vows of poverty in Judaism as a means of achieving a Divinely blessed state of affairs. There are no accusing fingers pointed at those engaged in normal economic activities and the earning of material goods. The priests and Levites in biblical times were, it is true, not allowed to have a portion of the Land of Israel like all the other tribes, except for the small number of designated towns and villages apportioned to them. According to most of the biblical commentators, however, this was done not in order to produce a priesthood living in a state of poverty and devoting themselves solely to God, but rather to ensure the dispersal of the tribe of Levi throughout the country, so that there would be no area bereft of spiritual leaders.[9]

The poet-philosopher of twelfth-century Spain, Yehuda Halevi, in his presentation of Judaism known as the *Kuzari*, described the Jewish attitude to economic activity as follows:

> Nor is the decreasing of wealth an act of piety if such wealth happens to have been gained in a lawful way and its further acquisition does not prevent him from occupying himself with Torah and righteous deeds, especially for one who has family and dependents and whose desire is to spend his money for the sake of God. . . . For you are, as it were, enjoying the Lord's hospitality, being invited to His table, and should thank Him for His bounty, both inwardly and outwardly.[10]

Mainstream Judaism saw man's material welfare as a reward from Heaven, a gift of the Deity, and therefore as something not intrinsically bad, but rather to be valued and prized. (If it were intrinsically bad, we would expect to find constant exhortations against engaging in economic activity, similar to those found in the case of idolatry, a sin such that everything related to it is to be stamped out.) Rabbenu Bachya (in thirteenth-century Spain), writing in *Kad Hakemach*, explained this divine origin of *parnasah* (livelihood) as follows:

> God in His abundant mercy gives food to all flesh and allocates *parnasah* to all creatures. All are fed and sustained by His great and unfaltering mercy. Just as Divine redemption is miraculous,

so is *parnasah*. Rabbi Shmuel bar Nachman said, "*Parnasah* is even greater than *Geulah* [redemption], for the latter is carried out by an angel." [He cites Jacob's reference in Genesis to "the angel who delivered me from all evil."] *Parnasah*, on the other hand, is granted directly by God himself; as Jacob, in the same place in the Bible, refers to "the God who hath been my Shepherd." Furthermore, man's livelihood requires his active participation [it must be earned]. Apart from the period of the wandering in the desert, or [other instances of] miraculous intervention for limited periods, there is no manna from heaven. This active participation of man in the creation of his own wealth is a sign of man's spiritual greatness. In this respect he is, as it were, an imitator of God. "Since man is superior to all the creation, his *parnasah* is not so easily available [as that of the vegetable and animal kingdoms]. [Apart from growing and producing all those things necessary for his physical well-being,] he must even take the trouble to prepare his food by cooking and baking it."[11]

Yet, despite the legitimacy of economic activity and of man's enjoyment of material goods, Judaism does not allow unlimited accumulation of such goods or unlimited use of them.

Thus, the admonition in Ecclesiastes "Go to the ant, you sluggard" is generally regarded as a favorable injunction to industriousness and economic diligence. The rabbis, however, saw the ant's life as the epitome of foolishness and wasted endeavor. "After all," they said, "the ant eats only two grains of wheat and lives for but one season, yet it labors ceaselessly to amass a fortune."[12]

Although it is necessary and legitimate for man to devote himself to the accumulation of material goods, Rabbi Yosef Yitschak of Lubavich taught, "Even with the greatest efforts a man cannot increase his wealth above that which the Almighty has allocated to him. A man has to do what is necessary for his livelihood but has to understand that these efforts are only marginal and that the real source of his wealth is God's blessings."[13]

It was quite obvious to the rabbis that excessive concern for material goods distorted man's spiritual priorities, often in subtle and ingenious ways. Consider Rashi's commentary on the biblical story of the request by the tribes of Reuben, Gad, and Manasseh for an inheritance in Transjordan.

The tribes of Gad and Reuben, because of their vast wealth and cattle, separated themselves from the tribes of Israel and settled outside of the Promised Land [the lands in Transjordan being better suited to large-scale ranching than the Land of Israel].

Therefore, they were exiled before all the other tribes [as they opted out, as it were, of their Divine inheritance]. They made the primary concern [their children] a marginal one and the secondary consideration [their wealth] of major importance. They said to Moses, "we will build stables for our flocks and cities for our children."[14]

As will be shown in the following section, both the achievement of economic wealth and the use thereof are very strictly limited and channeled by Judaism over and above the restraint imposed by the study of the Torah. These limitations do not flow from an exalted view of poverty, however, or from an "otherworldly" philosophy. Rather, all of man's actions, including those involved in the accumulation of material goods, are to be subjected to the ethical, moral, and religious demands of the Torah, so that the individual and society can attain a state of sanctity even while carrying out the most mundane acts.

An expression of this mainstream Jewish attitude may be seen in the rabbinic discussion of the sin of the generation of the Tower of Babel. The book of Genesis is not at all clear as to why this construction should have called down the displeasure of God and led to the dispersal of mankind. Yitschak Abarbanel, court financier and Torah scholar at the time of Isabella and Ferdinand of Spain, expressed a minority view when he related their sin to urbanization and technological progress.

The sin of this generation [the builders of the Tower of Babel] is similar to that of Adam, Cain, and his sons. The latter were not satisfied with the munificent bounty bestowed on them by a generous Deity and the material plenty available through natural means. Instead of using their status of being created in God's image for the perfection of their spiritual aspects, they devoted themselves to the perfection of crafts, animal husbandry, and agriculture. All of these were attempts to improve and exploit the natural order of things, which the Deity, in his wisdom, provided as sufficient for the needs of mankind. To this "sin" the builders of the Tower of Babel added that of urbanization and political organization. They created a kingdom ruled by Nimrod which supplanted their previous egalitarian society and built cities which destroyed their rural environment. In addition to the greed and aggression following the introduction of a class system of ruled and ruling, they pitted men against each other by their rules of private property. It is this absolute view of private property which led men to declare, "What is mine is mine and what is yours is yours." [According to the sages,[15] this insistence on the absolute primacy of property was characteristic of the people of Sodom, since it led them to refuse to share their wealth with others.] By traveling from *Kedem* [East, or antiquity], the builders of the Tower of Babel separated themselves from *Kadmono Shel Olam* [God, the ancient of the world] by their desire for business and artificial goods.[16]

In contrast to Abarbanel is the explanation of Rabbi Yitschak Arama. Presenting what is the attitude of the mainstream of Jewish thought, he observes that "their sin wasn't the idea of the political system [and the technological progress and urbanization which accompanied it]. Rather it was their view that these [social and economic] activities were an end in themselves rather than a limited and marginal pursuit relative to the spiritual success of man."[17]

Jewish legal and philosophical sources and biblical commentaries abound with praise of actions leading to *yishuv ha'olam* (the settlement of the world) and *yishuv Eretz Yisrael* (the settlement of the Land of Israel) which shows Abarbanel's approach to economic matters to be indeed a minority one. It is not possible to present here even a representative sample of such sources, yet it is necessary to at least give some idea of Jewish attitudes toward this basic question of the legality and desirability of creating economic assets and raising the standard of living of society. Jacob Emden, rabbinic authority and scholar of eighteenth-century Germany, comments as follows on the verse "When you come into the land [of Israel] you shall plant all manner of fruit and trees" (Lev. 19:23).

> However, in *Eretz Yisrael* [the Land of Israel] it [building the world] is like a *mitzvah* [incumbent] upon us even as our sages understood from the above verse that man should take planting seriously and take an example from God, whose first act after Creation was planting [the Garden of Eden]. So you, too, when you enter *Eretz Yisrael* busy yourself with planting first of all. . . . Clearly the sages admonished one . . . to increase the settlement of the land, even if one has enough [so that those who follow him will enjoy the fruits].[18]

A legal expression of the importance of *yishuv ha'olam* may be found in the *Mishneh Torah* codex:

> Those who race birds or play games of chance are guilty of theft according to rabbinic law, since they take money belonging to other people illegally [this according to Rami bar Chama in the

Talmud[19]] and without giving anything in return for it. This is so although it is all done with the consent of the owners [who are engaged in gambling of their own free will]. Even in those cases where there is no theft involved, as in the case of gambling with idolators, it is forbidden since one is thereby engaged in idleness, and it is not fitting for a man to busy himself with things that do not contribute to the settlement of the world.[20]

Following this legal ruling it is not surprising to find much anti-gambling legislation in the ordinances of Jewish communities in different periods and in different countries. So we find in the ordinance of the Rhine communities in the thirteenth century that "it is not permitted to play with a gentile, or with a Jew either, for money or for food and drink."[21] Whatever sociopolitical reasons one may offer for such antigambling legislation, it is impossible to sever it from Judaism's positive attitude toward *yishuv ha'olam* and its rejection of idleness.

Miraculous satisfaction of man's wants, such as the manna in the desert or the raven feeding Elijah, is viewed in Judaism as being a departure from the desired and normal events of life whereby one is not allowed to depend on miracles. The Chasidic master Shmuel of Sochochov explains the antagonism of Balak, king of Moab, to the entry of the Jews into the Land of Israel and his subsequent hiring of Bilaam to curse the Jews in a manner which expresses very well this normative Jewish attitude with respect to the sanctity of the everyday vis-à-vis the miraculous: He writes,

> What objection could Balak have to the entry of Israel into the Land of Israel? After all, they were no threat to his kingdom, nor did their entry into the Land harm him in any way. However, Balak's *philosophy* was threatened. It was "normal religion" as long as the Jews lived a miraculous existence, removed from the mundane economic acts of life: their bread given to them from heaven, their water from the well of Miriam, and protected from the elements by the clouds of heavenly glory. Their entry from the desert into the Land of Israel would change all that. In that land, their economic existence and their material wants would be satisfied through the mundane acts of ploughing and sowing, of trade and commerce, of home building and industry. Their Torah laws would sanctify these acts as well, and it is this type of sanctity that the pagan world of Balak could not accept.[22]

The same Chasidic master pointed out elsewhere that:

The *soul* does not need spiritual elevation—since, after all, it was pure when it was created by God. It is the body that needs to be purified by man, and that was God's purpose in creating it. "The heavens are God's domain and the earth was given to the sons of man," the Psalmist sang—given to him so that he could sanctify and elevate it.[23]

It is this view of the role of economic and material goods and their creation, which is typical of Judaism.

That the economic sphere is a major vehicle of achieving this sanctity may be seen in the fact that of the 613 Divine commandments mentioned in the Torah, well over 100 are related to it. This compares with a mere 24 laws which form the basis for the dietary laws that are such a well-known component of Judaism. The sages of the Talmud said, "He who is desirous of achieving sainthood, let him live according to the tractates of the Talmud dealing with commerce and finance."[24] The following legal discussion is a prototype of the kind of thinking that permeates the rabbinic teachings regarding achievement of sainthood in economic affairs.

According to Jewish law, a person whose land and property adjoins that of another person automatically has the first right to purchase such property (the concept of *bar-metzra*). Since the purchase is to be at the market price, the seller suffers no loss; yet at the same time the buyer is gaining, since the enlargement of his property is often an economic consideration. This is a concept of "one loses nothing and the other one gains."

This law of the adjacent owner is probably one of the most impressive ethical concepts translated into legal form. Maimonides rules that:

> If any man sells his land to another, the neighbor whose land is contiguous may pay the buyer the money he paid and evict him. . . .
>
> This law does not apply to minor orphans [purchasers], since the concept of good and right in regard to orphans exceeds that demanded in the case of normal owners. . . . In the case where a woman bought the land, the adjacent owner cannot apply this law. As it is not usual practice for a woman to be a purchaser of land—if she did so—then it is an act of kindness to let her retain what she has purchased.[25]

Dina d'bar metzra is only one example of the application of this specifically Jewish contribution of "one benefits and the other does not lose" to all avenues of economic endeavor. In the Talmud we find another important example of this idea:

> Reuven leased his mill to Shimon on condition that the latter would grind his corn in lieu of rental. Reuven became wealthy and bought another mill. Now he could do the grinding himself, and so demanded a monetary rental from Shimon. [Shimon,] however, preferred the original arrangement. This would apply only if agreeing to Reuven's request would idle the mill and cause Shimon a monetary loss. In those cases where Shimon has ample orders for grinding, so that it is no loss to him to substitute these for Reuven's corn and pay a monetary rent from the proceeds, then Shimon will be compelled to agree. This is to force him not to act in the manner of the people of Sodom, who refused to do favors to others, even if it cost them nothing in money or effort.[26]

DIVINE OWNERSHIP AND DIVINE PROVIDENCE

Since there is no Jewish textbook on economics, we must turn to the ethical and legal literature as well as to biblical commentators, philosophers, and religious leaders for insights into the ideological basis for Jewish economic behavior.

It is not possible to identify or adequately define the underlying reasons behind the various *mitzvot* (commandments), laws, customs, and rabbinic rulings regarding economic behavior. Some of the dictates of Judaism have more than one concept behind them. Sometimes there is more than one dictate with a common reason, and sometimes various rabbinical authorities have adduced different reasons for the same law. Nevertheless, we attempt in the following sections to systematically detail a Jewish economic framework according to its underlying ideological concepts. The point is not to prove that the author's analysis and conclusions are the correct ones or the only ones, but rather to outline a specific Jewish conceptual framework within which Jews have conducted and do conduct their economic affairs.

The Divine origin of wealth is the central principle of Jewish economic philosophy. All wealth belongs to God, who has given it temporarily to man, on a basis of stewardship, for his physical well-being. Since Judaism is a community-oriented rather than an individual-oriented religion, this means that the group at all levels—communally, nationally, and internationally—is thereby made a partner in each individual's wealth.

There are a very large number of *mitzvot* that reflect this notion of joint ownership of wealth by God, the individual owner, and his fellow man. The most important and outstanding are the regulations relating to the sabbatical (or *shmitah*) and jubilee years. In this chapter we will deal only with the ideological aspects of these regulations, since they serve as indicators of a basic Jewish philosophy.

The biblical commandment in this regard reads, "But during the seventh year you shall let [your land] rest and lie fallow" (Exod. 23:11). The *Kli Yakar,* a biblical commentary, comments on this verse that "the purpose of the law is to teach us not to regard man as absolute lord over the produce of the land, and that one is required to have faith in God that he will provide adequate crops in the sixth year not only for that and the seventh year but also for the eighth, until the new harvest is gathered."[27] This idea of trust in God to provide adequately for all of man's needs permeates many *mitzvot,* such as the free loan requirement, the allocation of time for studying Torah, and the extensive obligations of charity. The *Sefer Hachinuch,* explaining the same verse, adds "This teaches us the attribute of voluntary renunciation of property and the resultant generosity which flows from this attribute [since in the sabbatical year the land was ownerless and its fruit public property]. Man learns from this *mitzvah* that there is an owner to the earth who produces its fruits, and at His will they become ownerless. Furthermore, this renunciation of the fruit of the land teaches us faith and trust in God. A man who at the Divine commandment regularly relinquishes his ownership over his land for this year will never lack for trust in the bounty of God."[28]

In the sabbatical year, not only is the land to lie fallow and man forced to eat from the natural produce of the ground, but everything growing is *hefker*—"ownerless"—and therefore available to all and sundry. Thus the *shmitah* year, by denying human ownership to land—which was the major factor of production in ancient days—demonstrates vividly the complete dependence of man on God for his sustenance. Even though the Jew was enjoined to take all the steps humanly possible to earn a livelihood, he was nevertheless taught that his economic welfare was something provided by God, and therefore to be regulated according to the Divine will.

In the jubilee year, this concept was taken a step further. During the time of Moses the Land of Israel was distributed according to tribes, families, and individuals. Any subsequent sale of the land was of a temporary nature only; the land, irrespective of its present ownership, was to be returned to its original owner in the jubilee year. Now, one can find in this legal requirement many social explanations. For example, one explanation may be that the object of the jubilee was to prevent the accumulation of land by a small, monopolistic group of people. A rereading of both the biblical text and the rabbinic authorities, however, shows very clearly that its prime object is to demonstrate Divine ownership.[29] At the command of the real owner, the Lord, the original distribution was to be re-enacted every fifty years.

The import of the jubilee and sabbatical years, however, goes even beyond ownership of land by the Deity. For these observances signify a reaffirmation by the Jew that the Deity is the primary factor in any economic success. A long list of *mitzvot* can be presented to demonstrate this idea, but perhaps the most interesting ones are those of the First Fruits (*bikurim*).[30]

To any farmer, the first fruits are very special, as they represent the beginning of a successful venture. Yet, the Torah obligated the Jew to take these first fruits to Jerusalem each year and present them to the priest. In itself, this presentation may not sufficiently demonstrate the concept of thankfulness. What does underscore it is the confession that accompanied the bringing of these first fruits.

Every Jew was required to recite a confession at the Temple in which he described how an insignificant little family went down to Egypt, grew rapidly, but was enslaved and persecuted. It was only God's love, and His power over the forces of nature and man, that redeemed this family (that is, Israel) from their slavery, carried them through the dangers of the desert, and brought them into the Land of Israel. The thankfulness expressed in the confession was for the God-given land, its fertility, its crops, and its first fruits, all granted simply through the grace of God. Nothing could be more indicative of Judaism's teaching of man's utter dependence upon God for his economic welfare than this confession.

THE HALAKHAH OF ECONOMIC LIFE

In the economic field, just as in all other areas of life, Judaism was never satisfied merely with the adoption of pious slogans or exhortations to be righteous. All the theories, precepts, and concepts flowing from man's dependence on God for his material wealth were translated by Judaism into daily actions through the mechanism of the halakhah. As explained more fully in Chapter 2, the halakhah is a definitive legal system providing parameters for all of man's actions, both personal and collective. It is a confirmation that man's salvation is achieved through his acts and not just through Divine grace or pious beliefs. Thus, halakhah is the practical means of applying to daily life the concepts of God's ownership of material goods, man's stewardship of these goods, and God's active participation in man's economic success. The halakhah provides the Jew with definitions of what is and what is not permissible, and with regulations governing when the permissible acts are to be done and how they may be done. It is, therefore, to these halakhot, these rules and regulations, that we now turn for our analysis of the Jewish parameters of economic activity. These halakhot dealing with economics may be summarized under the following four groupings:

Theft and Exploitation

In the Ten Commandments, "You shall not steal" appears in the singular form and is understood by the sages to refer to the act of kidnapping and the selling of slaves. The injunction against stealing in its usual sense appears in the Bible in Leviticus in the plural. Answering a Chasid's question as to this distinction, a Chasidic master replied, "Kidnapping of men for sale as slaves is a marginal act in our society, whereas common theft and fraud is something we are all too often guilty of."

No functioning economic society can exist for very long without a legal system to prevent fraud. It would be misleading, however, to consider the communal edicts, halakhic decisions, and homiletic literature against theft, in its widest connotations, as simply constituting Jewish interpretations of a universally accepted dictum. Rather, the majority of authorities (in contrast to Maimonides[31]) saw the prevention of theft or dishonesty as part of a distinctly Jewish socioreligious morality based on the notion of the Divine source of wealth.[32]

The Divine source of wealth makes all form of theft and dishonesty religious crimes, over and above their social aspects. Furthermore, society's concepts of morality, economic and otherwise, are flexible, and change from one generation to another and one cultural group to another. However, forbidding stealing as part of a Divinely revealed law makes the injunction definitive and absolute, and provides a yardstick that cannot be blurred by conventionally accepted infringements.

The code of Jewish law, the *Shulchan Arukh*, written some five hundred years ago in Safed, constitutes the authoritative basis of present-day Jewish living. Its author, Rabbi Joseph Caro, summarized three thousand years of legal practice and thought when he wrote:

> In order not to become accustomed to stealing, one is forbidden to steal even as a practical joke or even with the intent of later returning the stolen article. One is not permitted to steal in order to become liable for the fine laid down in the Bible, thus fulfilling a precept of the Torah. One is not permitted to steal in order to annoy or anger the owner. Whoever steals, even an object which is valueless, transgresses the commandment "You shall not steal" and is liable to a fine, this irrespective of whether he steals from a Jew or from a Gentile or from an adult or from a child.[33]*

The Jewish penal code knowingly does not prescribe imprisonment for theft but rather the return of the stolen object plus a fine equal to it. In the case of slaughtered cattle the fine was fourfold, and in the case of sheep it was fivefold. Maimonides explains this increased fine as being commensurate with the crime. Sheep and cattle graze farthest away from home and are less carefully guarded, so stealing them is easier than stealing other property—this calls for an increased punishment, therefore the greater fine.[34] Since the return of the stolen good is a prerequisite for human and Divine forgiveness, the thief is required to go to great lengths to do so. An example of the efforts required may be found in the following Mishnah:

> He who denies under oath the theft of even *shaveh prutah* [an object worth only the minimum measure of value] and then later admits to his crime has to return it to the owner, even if this means following him all the way to Medea [the most distant point in Persia from the Land of Israel].[35]

---

* Crimes against property in Judaism were never punished by death or maiming or even imprisonment, except for a short period in Eastern Europe, when fraud became prevalent. The sanctity of human life is a cardinal and absolute factor in Judaism, whereas, although private property rights exist, they are limited.

The only penance for theft in Judaism is to return a stolen object to the wronged party, irrespective of the cost or trouble involved. It may not be returned to the son or agent of the owner; however, it may be handed over to an agent of the *bet din*. Some commentators see this exception as an amendment made by the sages to encourage robbers and thieves to do penance by making it easier for them to rectify their crimes.[36]

The concept that all theft constitutes a religious sin against the Deity must be stressed. Theft constitutes a double crime, as it were, against one's fellow man and against God, who forbade it. Indeed, Judaism can conceive of stealing from God even where no human owner is involved. The Talmudic discussion of the blessing that a Jew is required to make before eating or drinking makes this clear: "No one should taste anything without first reciting a blessing over it, as it is said, 'The earth is the Lord's and the fullness thereof [Psalms 24].' Whoever enjoys the goods of this world without reciting a blessing is like a thief."[37]

Over and above the economic loss involved in theft and the moral effect on the individuals concerned, the rabbis were clearly aware of its effect on the social and moral fabric of society. Judaism has always maintained that evil actions and wrongdoing, such as theft and robbery (in Jewish legal terms, a thief steals furtively; a robber openly and forcefully) are not only the problem of the parties concerned. Rather, by perverting concepts of what is permitted and what is forbidden, they eventually undermine the whole basis of society. Permissiveness in regard to theft sooner or later affects man's religious behavior, his sexual mores, and even his regard for the sanctity of human life.

This idea is expressed in the commentary of Rabbi Shimshon Raphael Hirsch on the biblical verse "and the earth was full of *chamas*" (Gen. 6:11). He writes as follows:

The Talmud, discussing the biblical description of spiritual conditions prior to the Flood, concludes that the destruction of that generation was finalized only when they were guilty of robbery.[38] It should be noted that the word *chamas*—"wrongdoing"—is understood in halakhic terms as referring to the theft of a marginal item (less than *shaveh prutah*). Pre-Deluge society was to be destroyed because of all-pervasive economic immorality that concerned itself with the theft of even relatively unimportant things.[39]

In our day this could be construed as covering those areas not commonly viewed as criminal, such as exploiting expense accounts, exploiting consumer ignorance by overcharging slightly, or holding back due payments in order to benefit from inflationary price changes.

One of the Chasidic masters, Shmuel of Sochochov, writing in the early years of this century, queried the severity of the Divine punishment for the sin of *chamas*.

> After all, we know that the sin of that generation [of the Flood] included all three cardinal sins—idolatry, adultery, and murder—for which halakhah prescribes the death penalty. Theft, however, would seem to be a lesser crime, since it does not incur the same penalty. Yet, once theft and robbery become normal and accepted patterns of behavior, they bring in their wake all the cardinal sins—so it was *chamas* that sealed the death of the generation of the Flood.[40]

Furthermore, one who buys stolen goods strengthens the hands of the thieves themselves. After all, if a thief is unable to find a market he will not steal. Nominally law-abiding citizens encourage crime when they provide a market. Economic laws that are not enforced or, being contrary to economic reality, are not viable, also contribute to an increase in crime. For example, when tax evasion or smuggling become commonplace because of excessive tax rates or lax supervision, they soon lead to a decline in the general moral stucture. Knowledge of such realities led our sages to say, "It is not the mouse which is the thief but the hole which encourages him."[41] Halakhic sources and communial enactments reflect this understanding.

All the codes of Jewish law are quite explicit and clear in rejecting trade in stolen goods or in goods that are commonly objects of theft. So we find in the *Shulchan Arukh*:

> One may not buy saplings from the watchmen of plantations, nor may one buy milk or lambs from the shepherds [who in those days were hired watchmen for the flocks of other people]. . . . Nor may one buy anything when one is told to hide it on leaving the place of sale. . . . One may buy from the oil press olives and oil in significant measures but not in small quantities that are liable to have been stolen.[42]

Extracts from the communal records of two Jewish communities show how rabbinic rulings and ethical admonitions were translated into everyday commercial practice. Both deal with measures that either closed the trade outlets for stolen goods or made trade in stolen goods less secretive and, therefore, easier to prevent.

In the communal record book (*Pinkas*) of the Jewish community of Padua in Italy, we find the following decision taken at a meeting in 1580, in response to the secret trade in stolen goods conducted when people were not usually present in public places:

> This is to ratify a regulation which appeared in the old *Pinkas* (1562) forbidding the purchase of goods before the end of the prayers. No man or women, young or old, irrespective of who they are, shall buy any goods suitable for sale before the end of the morning prayer, nor after the bell rings to mark the end of the day [referring to the *ma'ariv* or evening prayers]. Neither are they permitted to take any of the goods or articles to their houses and keep them there until after the prayers.[43]

From another enactment, this time from the Council of Jews in Frankfurt, Germany, dated 1603, we learn that:

> We have agreed that anyone who buys any wares from one who is well known as a thief or lends a thief money on any pledge shall be punished in the manner described above [ostracism]. Anyone who borrows money or wares from Gentiles with the intention of failing to pay for them shall also be ostracized in the manner described, and no Jew shall buy any wares from him or have any commerce with him.[44]

Moshe Chayim Luzzato, in his early-eighteenth-century moralistic work *Mesilat Yesharim*, which is to this day one of the most widely studied Jewish ethical texts, notes:

> Most people are not outright thieves, taking their neighbors' property and putting it in their own premises. However, in their business dealings most of them get a taste of stealing whenever they permit themselves to make an unfair profit at the expense of someone else, claiming that such profit has nothing to do with stealing. It is not merely the obvious and explicit theft with which we have to concern ourselves, but any unlawful transfer of wealth from one individual to another that may occur in everyday economic activities. [He then stringently describes the conditions of honest commerce.] You may ask in your heart, how is it possible for us in our commerce not to try and persuade the buyer of the uniqueness of the article and its value? Remember that one must distinguish between two different things in

this respect. It is both good and honest to do everything necessary in order to show the buyer the real value and beauty of the article. However, for one to cover and hide a defect in the article is nothing less than deceit and is forbidden.[45]

To this should be added the comments of the *Sefer Hachinuch*:

> Thus we see that we have to judge matters pertaining to buying and selling as matters commanded us by the Torah. Furthermore, we learn from the verse, "When you come to sell or to buy from one another, you shall not deal fraudulently with each other" [Lev. 25:14], that one may not exploit or oppress the other party in business, neither as regards the price nor the quality of the goods.[46]

The Mishnah objected even to nonmonetary exploitation. "Just as there is exploitation in buying and selling [the reference is to overcharging or exploiting ignorance], so there can be verbal exploitation. So one is not permitted to ask [the seller] 'What is the price of this article?' when one has no intention of buying."[47]

The variations and possibilities of stealing through ordinary everyday economic activities are almost unlimited. Nevertheless, it is essential from a moral point of view to limit them wherever possible. Not to do so not only causes hardship to others, but destroys the moral fabric of society and negates Divine law. So it is natural that halakhic codes and communal enactments sought to minimize the scope of theft and dishonesty in legitimate commerce in many different ways.

Weights and Measures

The *Sefer Hachinuch*, in discussing the ideology behind all biblical precepts, writes: "The Torah tells us [in Lev. 19:36] that 'Just weights and measures shall you have.' Even though this is included in the general commandment not to cheat one another, the Torah mentions each type of weight and measure separately in order to emphasize the enormity of the crime." In the same verse in Leviticus, God reiterates that "I am the Lord your God, who brought you out of the land of Egypt"; explains the *Sifra* (an extended legal commentary on Leviticus), because God took the Jews out of Egypt precisely in order that they should take upon themselves the *mitzvah* of just weights and measures. The sages of the Talmud reiterate the connection: "The God who distinguished between the seed of the firstborn who died in the plague and the other Egyptians, a distinction based on the most intimate knowledge, shall surely punish he who soaks his weights in salt in order to cheat [in secret]."[48]

In the same vein, Rashi, the quintessential commentator on the Bible, linked the abuse of weights and measures to physical calamity of great proportions. Discussing the attack of Amalek on Israel just after leaving Egypt, the first and unprovoked action against Israel after the miracles at the Red Sea, he notes the proximity of the verse obligating the Jew to eternally remember Amalek [Deut. 25:17] to the restatement in Deuteronomy of the above verse prohibiting false weights and measures. "If you falsify weights and measures," notes Rashi, "be concerned about awakening the enemy."

Mere moralizing, however, does not exhaust the Jewish treatment of any problem, so our sources are replete with legal and communal enactments to prevent economic abuse through fraudulent weights and measures. Thus, the later codes through the centuries reproduced the following law from the Mishnah:

> He who sells to retailers has to clean his weights every thirty days; the householder [who sells to the wholesaler] has to clean them once every twelve months. Rabban Shimon ben Gamliel [who claims that the constant use, characteristic of the wholesaler keeps his measures cleaner] says the converse is true. The storekeeper cleans his weights twice a week and the measures of liquids once a week and has to polish his scale [to remove the dirt] every time he weighs something.[49]

Communal authority had to be invoked in order to translate such injunctions into practice. So Maimonides rules that "The rabbinic court is obligated to appoint overseers in every city and in every province who will inspect the stores in order to assay the scales, weights, and measures. . . . They have the right to punish and fine the storekeeper found with faulty weights or scales."[50] It must be pointed out that the obligation on the part of the rabbinic courts to oversee matters of trade and commerce independently of the non-Jewish courts has been insisted upon by all halakhic authorities from the Talmud down to the present day. Furthermore, this autonomous communal authority was recognized by the non-Jewish world from pagan Roman times through the Moslem and

Christian medieval periods until the nineteenth century—and in certain countries even later.

Unlike other forms of theft, errors made with weights and measures have no minimal level, nor a "statute of limitations" restricting the time period within which redress can be sought. Claims which are of insignificant value are usually considered by the rabbis to be waived in the usual course of business; this is not so, however, in the case of weights and measures errors, since they involve a moral and religious infringement, which the parties to the transaction do not have the power to overlook, even if they so desire. Indeed, the above-mentioned portion of Deuteronomy instructs (25:13 15): "You shall not keep in your pocket [both] a large weight and a small one; neither shall you keep in your house [both] a large measure and a small one, [but rather,] one perfect and just weight shall you have; one perfect and just measure shall you have"—the emphasis here being on the crime of even possessing such faulty measures, let alone using them.

Misrepresentation (G'neivat Da'at)

The Torah forbids "stealing another's mind"—representing things to another in a false light, over and above the theft involved in selling defective goods. Jewish law in this respect has much significance for modern issues of truth in advertising and marketing.

The *Shulchan Arukh*, in dealing with the laws of theft, first legislates against blatant fraud, such as putting the good fruit on top. It then continues to legislate against misrepresentations.

> One is forbidden to beautify the article being sold in order to create a false impression. So one is forbidden to dye a slave's hair or beard in order to make him appear young. One is not allowed to give an animal bran to drink which makes her hair brown and upright, thus creating the impression that she is fat and sleek. Nor may one comb her artfully in order to create the same impression. One is not allowed to paint old baskets to make them look new nor is one allowed to soak meat in water to make it white and look fat.[51]

In Mishnaic times, Jewish law forbade the mixing of wine and water (it seems their wine was very strong and, therefore, needed to be diluted) without informing the customers; under no circumstances could such wine be sold to a wholesaler whose whole purpose in buying it would be to defraud. This legal ruling spread beyond the walls of the courts and became part of communal legislation. Many centuries later, for example, the Jewish community of Corfu in 1651 included in its regulations the following:

> In order to remove every suspicion of deception which may occur in selling wine, it is forbidden to mix wines or to sell two or more jars at the rate which the Jewish communal officers fixed for one. . . . Take heed not to do such a thing, for besides being fined in the prescribed manner whoever does so shall be declared excommunicated and anathema.[52]

It is interesting to note that in interpreting the biblical injunction ''You shall not put a stumbling block in the path of the blind'' [Lev. 19:14], the sages did not confine its scope to simply preventing physical obstacles from being placed in the path of a blind man; rather, this category of prescribed behavior—*lifnei iver*—was understood to embrace the giving of unwise business advice to someone, or the provision, through perfectly legal transactions, of goods that are to the buyer's physical or moral detriment. For all those engaged in the professions of advertising, financial counseling, or brokerage, or in the sale of goods that are either physically or morally harmful to the purchaser, such as weapons, drugs, or obscene materials, observance of such religious rulings imposes severe restraints. Rashi, in commenting on the above verse, explains, ''Do not give detrimental advice to one who is blind in a certain matter [ignorant or misinformed]. Do not say to him, 'Sell your field and buy a donkey,' when your whole intention is to circumvent him and obtain possession of his field.'' The advisor is understood here to be presenting himself as a disinterested party.

The sages of the Mishnah were even more explicit when it came to the question of selling goods to a person that were harmful to him in any way. ''One may not sell arms to Gentiles [since the assumption is that they will be used by them for aggression, while Jews would use them only in self-defense.] Nor may one sell arms to another Jew for resale to robbers or other violent men. . . . One may not sell Gentiles sheep or slaves, since they are accustomed to bestiality and homosexuality.''[53] The question as to whether or not ''Gentiles'' applies to all non-Jews today or only to idolators is not relevant here. What is relevant is Judaism's concern with moral and physical injury produced by legal commerce. *Lifnei iver* may have halakhic consequences for modern arms traffic or trade with societies that are morally offensive. A case in point may be the important role played today in Israel's foreign trade by its export of arms. Another one may be the question of the investment by Jews in or trade with South Africa.

Protecting the Weak

For the weak and powerless members of society, theft and fraud are especially injurious because of their lack of knowledge of the law or of their rights and their lack of money or the political power to protect themselves. It is not surprising, therefore, that Judaism found it necessary to extend special protection to them. The classic example, perhaps, is the halakhic championing of the widow, the stranger, and the poor, over and above the demands of the normative rules of morality.

Sometimes, people who in the ordinary run of things are quite able to fend for themselves need, in special circumstances, the same protection as is always offered to the weaker members of society. There are transactions in which duress is applied to one party in order to provide special benefit to the other. Maimonides considers a case wherein Reuven hired a field from Shimon for a period of ten years without the owner retaining a copy of the written lease. After three years—when one in possession of a field could claim he had lost the deed of sale and yet have the sale recognized by halakhah—the tenant Shimon demanded that Reuven sell him the field; otherwise he would destroy his copy of the lease and claim that he had actually bought it. The sages said that this is duress, since the owner stands to lose all of the purchase price if he refuses. So, even if Reuven makes the sale but can later show in court that he was threatened in this way, the sale will be canceled.[54]

In a similar spirit, the *Shulchan Arukh* advises how to handle a lapse of memory on the part of a merchant and the resultant problems caused to those he has dealt with:

> Whoever bought an article from one of five merchants and each claims the purchase price from him, whilst he has forgotten from whom he bought it, the buyer shall place the money in trust with the *bet din* until the claimants admit or until Elijah comes. [But] if the buyer is a pious man, he will pay each of them so as to clear himself before Heaven.[55]

Damages

The whole question of ecology and damages is dealt with at length in chapter 10 of this book. At this stage only certain principles of law need to be mentioned.

One is not permitted to use one's own body, money, or property in such a way as to cause harm or damage to another's body or property. Furthermore, one is not permitted to willfully destory or waste one's own property nor cause harm to one's body or neglect it. Where such damage is caused, Jewish law provides for financial redress and considers the one at fault guilty of a moral and religious sin. Thus, planting anything alongside a neighbor's plot is classified as stealing.[56] Similarly, pollution, noise, and human traffic "steal" peace, quiet, and fresh air.[57] One may not put in a window so that it overlooks another's courtyard, since the sages maintained that this infringement on privacy constitutes material damage.[58] The moral issue is highlighted by the rabbinic law that an animal may not be eaten even when it has been ritually slaughtered if it has gored someone to death.[59]

Further protection against damage is provided by Jewish law's rejection of the Roman concept of "Let the buyer beware." So explicit is the halakhic approach to the responsibility of the seller that there does not seem to be a necessity for warranties or guarantees. The Talmud takes the attitude that "the omission of the clause of guarantee by the seller is merely an error of the scribe. This principle covers all instances where we can reasonably assume that such a guarantee was implied, even though it was not explicitly stated. The responsibility of the seller, therefore, remains even after the sale."[60] (Obviously, the period of the guarantee depends on the nature and quality of the goods sold.)

This matter of the seller's responsibility even led to a Talmudic ruling limiting the rules of sale mentioned in the Torah:

> Actual delivery into the premises or control of the purchaser is necessary to complete the sale of movable goods. This is a rabbinical enactment that was designed to limit to fixed assets the Torah rule that payment of the purchase price is sufficient to complete a sale. . . . The enactment obligates the seller to exercise great care and supervision of the goods sold as long as they are still in his possession. Now, in case of loss or negligence, he will not be able to claim that since payment had been made, the buyer is responsible and must bear the cost.[61]

In the course of commercial transactions, labor agreements, and investments, one or another party frequently inflicts damage by changing their mind, either canceling the transaction completely or partially altering the terms thereof. The rabbis saw such behavior as morally odious: "He who changes his mind [in economic activities] commits as heavy a sin as he who worships idols."[62] Even in cases wherein no legal recourse was open to the injured party, the halakhah could not remain indifferent to the moral cost involved. This may be seen both from the custom existing to this day by which one may stop the reading of the Torah in the synagogue to demand moral redress, and from the ruling of the *Shulchan Arukh* that

> where one paid money for an article but did not take possession, even though no change of ownership has yet taken place, any party who reneges on the deal does an act not befitting a Jew. This applies both to the seller and the buyer. Whoever reneges on an agreed-upon deal, even if he only paid part of the purchase price, is liable to the rebuke of "He who demanded payment."
>
> How is this done? The guilty party is arraigned in the *bet din* and the rabbis publicly rebuke him by saying, "He who demanded payment [for their sins] from the generation of the flood and the generation of the Tower of Babel, and from the people of Sodom and Gomorrah and from the Egyptians who were drowned in the Red Sea, He will repay whoever doesn't keep his word."[63]

This whole network of halakhic rulings exists in order to ensure that the way a man accumulates wealth is neither morally damaging nor physically harmful to his fellow men. It must also be in accordance with the norms of God-given (Torah) morality, even when these run counter to the accepted practice of the particular society in which a Jew might find himself. It is obvious from these examples that these restrictions, if observed, must necessarily limit the scope of a Jew's economic activities, even though such activities may be profitable and viable from a purely economic standpoint.

The Talmud tells us that the stork (in Hebrew *chasidah*) is so named because of the *chesed* (kindness) that she shows to her fellow birds by sharing her food with them—unlike other birds, who snatch their food and eat it in isolation. A *chasid* once asked his rebbe why the same attribution of high moral status on the basis of providing mutual help shouldn't apply to mice, who also share their food with each other. "It's simple," replied the master. "The storks eat that which is ownerless, whereas the mice share stolen wealth."

Limitations on Private Property

The same Jewish law which protects the rights of the individual to his own property in turn limits those rights and grants others, the community and other individuals, moral claims to that property.

The rabbis of the Talmud, reflecting an interpretation that was already hundreds of years old, claimed that the sin of Sodom was its inability to share its wealth with strangers, with the weak, and with the poor—and its insistence on the absolute right of each individual to his own property.

The Mishnah defined one who said, "What's mine is yours and what's yours is mine" as a simple man. He who says, "What's yours is mine and what's mine is mine" is an evil man. He who says, "What's yours is yours and what's mine is yours" is a righteous person. But "What's yours is yours and what's mine is mine—some say this is the mark of Sodom."[64]

The Malbim, a nineteenth-century rabbinical scholar in central Europe, commented on the verse "The cry of Sodom and Gomorah is very great and their sin exceedingly heavy" [Gen. 18:20] as follows:

> It must be remembered that the Bible stresses that Sodom was fertile and rich "as the garden of Egypt" before its destruction. The citizens of Sodom were worried that the desert dwellers or the poor from the surrounding areas would come to their cities in search of a livelihood and wealth. It was in order to prevent others from sharing in the wealth that legislation against strangers—unless they were rich, like Lot—was passed and enforced in Sodom. This jealous protection of their wealth later led to the corrupt laws and practices which characterized Sodom and precipitated its destruction.[65]

There is a story about the Gaon of Vilna—the preeminent Talmudic scholar of eighteenth-century Lithuania—underscoring this idea. In the middle of the eighteenth century there were re-

newed persecutions of Jews in Germany and Poland, which led to
refugees flooding Vilna; the Jewish Council of Lithuania debated
new legislation to prevent their entry. Obviously what bothered
them was the economic burden of providing food and shelter for
the refugees, as well as the economic threat posed by their competition. When the Gaon arrived and was told of the pending legislation he immediately left, saying, "This is considered new legislation? These are the laws enacted already in Sodom."

Charity is not simply an act of kindness but rather the fulfillment of a legal obligation. The "haves" in Judaism have an obligation to share their property with the "have nots," since it was
given to them by God partly for that purpose. Sometimes this
sharing takes the form of individual gifts, but Judaism also provides a moral basis for the power of society to tax its members so
as to provide for the needy and weak. The Jewish concept that the
market mechanism may, legally or morally, be distorted to assist
the poor and weak at the expense of the property rights of the
strong flows from this view of charity.

Furthermore, halakhah introduced the concept of going "beyond the boundary of the Law."[66] This was intended to educate
and train the Jew to voluntarily forego economic gains that were
legally his in order to allow weaker members of society to maintain themselves. For example, many famous rabbinic personalities
closed their stores after only a few hours of trading. Many of their
potential customers would have preferred to do business with
these great rabbinic scholars, seeing this as a form of support for
religious learning; but the closing of these stores forced customers
to patronize (and hence support) other businesses.

Halakhic authorities also objected to the practice of "forestalling," whereby one intervened in commercial negotiations in a
way that caused loss to a party already involved therein. "If one
seeks to buy or rent either land or movables and another comes
and buys it, he is called a *rasha*—a wicked person.[67] (While a nego-
tiation is still continuing, the seller obviously has the right to
refuse to make a sale and then to offer the goods to another.) The
rabbis' moral anger with regard to this behavior was made clear
even by those authorities who felt that legally there was nothing
which could be done against it.

The Talmud, recounts:

> Rabbi Giddal was negotiating for a certain field and Rav Abba
> bypassed him and bought it. When Rav Abba came for the *sukhot*

festival, Rav Yitschak Naphaha asked him, "If a poor man is examining a cake with the intent of buying it, and another comes and forestalls him, what is the law?" Rav Abba answered, "He is called a wicked man." "Then why do you do so?" "I did not know he was negotiating for it." "Then let him have it now." "No, I will not sell it to him," he answered, "Because this is the first field I have bought and it would be a bad omen to sell it, but I will give it to him as a gift." Rav Giddal would not accept it, as it is written in Proverbs [15:27], "He who hateth gifts shall live." Neither did Rab Abba take possession, since Rav Giddal had been negotiating for it. So it was called the "Rabbis' Field" and was used for the students of the academy.[68]

The duties and obligations imposed by Judaism on one's property go beyond the connotations of "charity" and include acts of righteousness. The prime example of this is the commandment to make interest-free loans. This exists as a separate positive commandment, distinct both from the injunction against taking interest as well as from the obligation to give charity. It is an act of righteousness, granted both to the rich man who is temporarily in financial straits and to the poor man trying to improve his economic situation.[69]

Economic Justice

One of the attributes of God is justice, and man, both Jew and non-Jew alike, is commanded by Him to actively pursue justice.[70] Just as God's conduct of the world reflects this attribute, so too is it a prerequisite of man's conduct of his affairs. So it is not surprising to find that this concept permeates all Jewish religious thinking, both that which relates to man's conduct vis-à-vis his fellow man and that which concerns the relationship between the Jewish people and God.

A stable legal system is an essential prerequisite for any economic activity. No commerce or market can exist without a system that will uphold agreements, enforce contracts, and protect the possession of material goods. At the same time, the halakhic rules governing the economic realm provides a specifically Jewish framework for economic activity.

Halakhically, justice knows no class differences, neither favoring the rich or powerful, nor distorting itself for the poor or weak. Legal rights are blind to one's status; judges are not allowed to fear the wealthy, favor the poor, or succumb to bribery, in all its varied and ingenious forms. To compensate for prejudices and social pressures, however, the Torah set itself up as the protector of those on the outskirts of society: the stranger and the convert, the widow and the orphan.

The halakhah is symmetrical, providing rights for the potentially weaker members of society but also imposing obligations on them. So the recipient of an interest-free loan has the obligation to repay the debt and not waste the loan. Maimonides in his code is very explicit (as is the *Shulchan Arukh*), saying that "even if the lender is wealthy and the borrower poor the debtor has to meet his obligations, even at the cost of losing all his property."[71] To rule otherwise would saddle the lender with all the social and economic problems of the borrower.

It must be stressed that the community in which the creditor lives has the religious and legal obligation (which the creditor as a member shares) to help the debtor socially and financially. The requirement of repayment of the loan exists to reinforce the Jewish dictum that people have obligations as well as rights, a consideration often blurred in modern welfare economics.

It is important to note that the Jewish legal system maintains a clear demarcation between crimes against property and capital crimes. According to biblical command, murder, adultery, and idolatry were punishable by death, without any remission by way of monetary settlement. However, ideally, no prisons ever existed for debtors and no jail sentence was imposed for theft or embezzlement; restitution and fines were all that were imposed. Capital punishment, banishment, or bodily mutation for theft were never recognized. While private property has rights, equitably and severely enforced, they never were considered sacred or holy.[72]

Since in many societies the interests of the ignorant and the weak are not always represented in the legal establishment, it is possible that the law itself may become a means of perverting justice. Our sages were always alert to this problem.

God advises in Amos (2:6) that one of the transgressions on account of which He will not revoke Israel's punishment is that "they sold the righteous for silver and the poor for a pair of shoes [na'alim]." The usual interpretation of this verse is that the crime was selling the poor for a trivial sum or, alternatively, down to their last possessions. Rashi, however, understanding that the only crime that could call for the destruction of Israel was something that undermined the fabric of society, sees more in it than that. He comments that their crime was the "closing in" of the poor—*na'al* in Hebrew meaning not only "shoe" but also "locking in." Rich men, by legally buying up the fields around those of the poor, ultimately forced them to sell their own fields—ultimately leading to exploitation, poverty, and the corruption of society.

Recognition that Jewish justice was the result of God-given law meant that abandonment of the Jewish legal system and adoption of another would be tantamount to, in effect, aiding and abetting theft, through transfers of money that might be legal according to other legal systems but were forbidden by the Mosaic code. So Jewish communities throughout the centuries fought arduously to prevent recourse to non-Jewish courts. As we have noted, the autonomy of Jewish courts and their ability to enforce their rulings was recognized by the secular non-Jewish rulers of many countries, until the period of political emancipation which commenced in the nineteenth-century in Western Europe.[73]

The following quotations from the minute books of the Council of Padua in 1577 and from the decision of the Synod of Castilian Jews in 1431 show the extent to which communities were prepared to go to enforce recourse to Jewish courts and the importance they attached to them.

It has become increasingly common for our people to take their personal conflicts and quarrels to the Gentile courts, to use those courts to frustrate the decision of the Jewish communal council and to prevent through them the implementation of the rulings of the rabbinic court of Venice against recourse to the Gentile courts. In view of this we proclaim that any member of the community who uses the Gentile courts will be excluded from all holy things [and hence not be eligible to be included in a *minyan*, or quorum for prayer]; nobody will be permitted to deal with him, as is usual in the case of excommunicated people; it will not be permitted to slaughter ritually or examine food for him [to determine its *Kashrut*].[74]

The Synod of Castilian Jews ruled that

No Jew or Jewess shall bring his or her neighbor, whether a Jew or Jewess, before any judge, ecclesiastic or secular, who is not of our faith. This even though such a judge should decide in accordance with the laws of Israel. The exceptions are the payment of taxes or imports or coinage or other rights of our Lord the King or of Our Lady the Queen or the money or rights of the church or of a lord or lady of a place. Whoever transgresses this law is to be declared anathema and excommunicated, and no one shall have any dealings with him.[75]

The decisions of the Castilian synod might seem to support the common assumption that the reason for the insistence on recourse to the autonomous Jewish legal system was simply to protect the Jewish community from assimilation. That was only a by-product of this demand, however, not its ground—which was the moral-religious conviction that bypassing Jewish courts who would operate according to God-given law would result in moral and ethical damage to the Jewish people. Even today, therefore, it is problematic in all countries for religious Jews to resort to civil courts. This applies even to using the Israeli civil code, which, although the fruit of Jewish legislators, is not based on Torah law.

Patterns of Consumption

Modesty (in Hebrew *tzniyut*) is usually associated with matters of fashion and sex. Yet, Judaism extended it as a moral category, to many other aspects of human behavior, including the economic. Maimonides, in discussing the characteristics of a Torah scholar—the paradigmatic ethical personality in Judaism—lays great stress on moderation in eating, clothing, and personal belongings.

> Just as the Torah scholar is known for his wisdom and his piety, so should his everyday actions be different and elevated above those of the ignorant; he provides for his family according to his means, yet without excessive devotion to this. His clothing should neither be that of kings nor that of poor men, but rather pleasant, ordinary clothing. His commerce shall be conducted in truth and faith. His word shall be his bond, and he shall be scrupulous in his accounting. He shall always be ready to concede to others when he buys from them and should not press his interests on them.[76]

Maimonides' injunctions do not apply only to "spiritual" behavior; they place severe restraints on the demand for material goods and therefore on the time devoted to acquiring them, as well as on the methods used in their accumulation.

In almost every Jewish community throughout the ages, regulations were introduced limiting ostentatious and luxurious living. Cynics may argue that this was simply out of fear of arousing the jealousy of the surrounding Gentile society. Yet, the lifestyle of many religious Jews throughout the centuries—both leaders and ordinary laymen—is proof that such strictures went far beyond the defensive and were an integral part of Jewish living. Simplicity in furniture, clothing, and entertainment was voluntarily observed as an ideal in many homes, while the folk culture handed down tales of a simple lifestyle on the part of the Jewish rabbinic leadership—thus creating a restrained economic role model.

The intrinsically Jewish nature of this religious value judgment may be inferred from the evidence of Talmudic times, when the social factors found in medieval Europe did not exist yet and so could not have inspired defensive Jewish responses. "Rabbi Shimon says, 'A scholar does not have the right to attend public banquets that are not motivated by the fulfillment of a religious precept.' "[77] Maimonides again codified this as binding law, prescribing that "the Torah scholar should eat his normal meals in his own house and shouldn't participate in public feasting, even with scholars. It is fitting for him to eat in public only those meals associated with a religious precept, such as the marriage of a scholar to the daughter of a scholar."[78]

To this day, limitations of this kind are accepted and practiced in those circles that have maintained a consistant *kehilah* system, whereby the synagogue, school system, religious courts, and ritual supervision are all part of an integrated Jewish community.

That modesty in economic affairs was historically not allowed to remain the subject of moralistic texts may be seen from a small sample of communal sumptuary laws. Thus, the Rhine communities in the thirteenth century enacted a regulation that "no man or woman shall prepare a feast except in fulfillment of a religious obligation."[79] The Synod of Frankfurt in the seventeenth century enacted a severe decree against those who "dress themselves and their daughters in costly clothes."

A Castilian communal enactment of the fifteenth century decreed that "no women, except those unmarried or a bride in the first year of her marriage, shall wear costly dresses of gold-cloth or olive-colored material or fine linen or silk, or of fine wool. Nor shall they wear a golden brooch, nor one of pearls, but they may wear jewelry like silver brooches and belts." Similar laws were passed respecting men. Restrictions were also placed on festivities, because "many spend lavish sums, so we agree that every community shall make such ordinances as are compatible with its needs and position."[80]

The Council of Four Lands, *Va'ad Arba Aratsot*—the roof organization of the Jewish communities in Poland (and, part of the time, Lithuania) from the mid-sixteenth to mid-eighteenth centuries—passed the following enactment:

> The leaders of the community have agreed to deal severely with the question of excessive and wasteful spending of money on festive meals. This is in accordance with the communal enactments made in 5419 (1659) at the fair of Gramnitz, Lublin. It is decreed that the number of participants at the *brit milah* [circumcision] be in accordance with one's financial position. One who pays two golden coins [to the community tax collector] can invite 15 people, who pays four coins invites 20 people, and who pays 6 coins may invite 25 people. This does not include secondary visitors to our community. Every ten invitees must include at least one poor person.
>
> The same principle applies with regard to wedding feasts, except that each group may add 5 invitees. In every case no man shall invite more people than befits his financial status.[81]

(In this case, it would seem, excessive spending might either indicate undeclared wealth [that is, wealth unreported to the communal authorities] or could lead to an inability to meet communal responsibilities. So a fiscal aspect existed over and above the general pattern of restricting needless and frivolous expenditures.)

In our own day, the *Admor* (spiritual leader) of Gur, who numbers many thousands of *chasidim* amongst his followers, has recently limited the number of participants at weddings to 300 in order to limit conspicuous consumption, social competitiveness, and, often, financial deprivation on the part of those trying to keep up with their neighbors. He has also forced his followers to move out of Jerusalem, where the high price of dwelling has meant great hardship, family stress, and jealousy, to areas such as Ashdod or Hatzor, where housing is more reasonable and within the reach of the average person.

Finally, there is an important distinction to be made between the economic modesty of the religious Jew and that of non-Jewish groups such as the Puritans. To the latter, economic activity was not restricted by the injunction to study, which we discussed at the beginning of this chapter. To many of them, hard work and frugality were part of man's destiny.[82] This meant that side by side with their modesty in economic affairs one can observe their intensive involvement in economic and commercial affairs over and above their actual needs. In Judaism, however, economic progress and continuous growth are not unlimited but, rather, severely restricted.

SUMMARY

In this chapter we have shown that there exists an ethical and moral framework for economic activity which is intrinsic to Judaism. This framework must not be confused with economic theory, nor must it be seen as promoting a capitalist or socialist economy. Rather, it is argued that it creates a special economy of its own. It must be stressed that this framework does not provide a guide to investment in any form. Such investment has to be analyzed on purely economic grounds; its implementation would have to be considered within the scope of a religious-moral framework.

Within this framework, economic activity is affected at two levels: that of the individual, both as consumer and producer, and that of the community or state. Basically, the framework places severe constraints on all aspects of economic behavior, even while recognizing that there is nothing intrinsically evil or sinful about pursuing the accumulation of material assets and wealth.

We may summarize the limitations placed by Judaism on economic activity as follows:

1. There is a limitation on the time permissibly alloted to economic activity, on account of the obligation to study Torah.
2. The production or sale of goods or services that are harmful to their consumers, either physically or morally, is forbidden.
3. One is responsible for damages caused by one's body or property.
4. Theft, or economic dishonesty in any form or guise, is forbidden.
5. One is required to limit one's appetite for material goods. One's disposable income is also automatically reduced by the de-

mands of *tzedakah* and interest-free loans, and by taxation to finance welfare, education and the physical well-being of the community.

One may well ask how, if all these limitations are in force, Jewish economic activity has been so prominent over the centuries, especially after the Enlightenment. It has been stressed throughout this chapter, though, that Judaism sees nothing intrinsically wrong with increasing economic assets, so the question is not as significant as it seems; we have been discussing limitations on, not abolition of, economic activity. Furthermore, with the emancipation of European Jewry, there occurred a general breakdown of religious discipline in all spheres, including the economic one. This breakdown led not only to the relaxation of the limitations described in our chapter but also to a weakening of the communal discipline essential for their implementation.

Perhaps at this stage it should be noted that the extent of collective Jewish wealth is highly exaggerated, both by Jews and non-Jews. Despite statistical evidence to the contrary, the myth of the great economic power wielded by Jews has persisted from the days of the Romans—who reduced the land of Israel to poverty in search of its rumored wealth—through the Middle Ages, down to the Protocols of the Elders of Zion and present day anti-Semitism. It is difficult to explain the persistence of this myth. In the following chapter an attempt is made to provide a more balanced view of the real economic situation of the Jew, especially in the nineteenth and twentieth centuries, and to discuss the effect of the Emancipation on Jewish economic behavior.

CHAPTER 4

The Economic History of the Jews: An Overview

INTRODUCTION

It is not possible in a study of this nature to describe at any length the economic history of a people covering thousands of years and embracing most of the countries of the world. Yet at the same time, it would seem difficult to gain a correct perspective on Jewish economic life and thought without offering at least a very brief outline of the salient points of this people's economic history. Such an outline should suffice to put into correct perspective the effect of external pressures on Jewish economic life and to demonstrate the continued existence of characteristic trends that are a direct outcome of specifically Jewish religious and ethical factors. Accordingly, this chapter provides a thumbnail sketch of the economic, social, and political characteristics of the various periods of Jewish history.

THE TANAKHIK PERIOD (until 586 B.C.E.)

During the eight centuries after the Jewish conquest of the land of Israel, the Jews enjoyed what might be termed a normal national existence. Except for the latter part of the period, almost all Jews lived in their own country and enjoyed varying degrees of

61

political independence. The reigns of David and Solomon saw the country at its peak, both politically and economically. Its boundaries stretched from the Gulf of Akaba (Etzion Gever) to present-day Syria. Solomon had concluded treaties with many of his neighbors that led to increased international trade and internal prosperity spurred by extensive state construction. The division of the country into two separate monarchies (North and South) did not result in any severe economic dislocation, and sources both biblical and archaeological describe the emergence of wealthy classes adopting the cultural habits of Egypt, Phoenicia, and Babylon.

Although the period (except for the peace of the Solomonic era) saw numerous battles and wars, these did not seem to have seriously disrupted economic development; neither did the periodic successes of neighboring states in extracting tribute from the Jews. One does not find the savage and grinding economic exploitation which characterized Roman rule during and especially after the destruction of the Second Temple.

From accounts in the Bible[1] as well as the results of archaeological excavation,[2] one is able to infer the existence of an economy based primarily on small farms, producing not only for subsistence but also for markets in the large towns. (Jerusalem, it should be pointed out, remains throughout Jewish history the only major city.) The absence of extensive arable landholdings, owing both to religious legislation and geographical factors, prevented the emergence of large-scale farming units employing a mass of slave labor, such as those found, for example, in Egypt or Rome.

(It should be noted that slavery in Judaism was primarily a means of punishing thieves or of providing a way for debtors to pay off their debts, since the penal system did not provide for any form of imprisonment for these "crimes." Slavery was, in effect, a system wherein a man sold the earnings arising out of his labor for a capital sum equal to that of either the debt or the theft. Jewish law frowned heavily on men voluntarily selling themselves as slaves.[3] As a result of warfare, there were foreign slaves who were captured during various campaigns; however, there is no evidence to show the existence of an economy based on slave labor, such as existed in other ancient economies.)

Despite the agrarian nature of Jewish society in this period, there is no reason to doubt the existence of a more sophisticated economy in which Jews were also active. It is true that non-Jews played the major role in trade and commerce. The Hebrew word for trader would seem to illustrate this, since the Jews adopted the name of a non-Jewish tribe, *"Cana'ani,"* to describe those engaged in commerce.[4] Nonetheless, there is reason to believe that Jews played some role in the commercial life of the period. Although the Phoenicians served as the primary merchant adventurers of the Middle East, there is reason to assume that Jews were to be found among the crews of Solomon's fleets. We also know that Jewish artisans and craftmen assisted in the construction of Solomon's Temple and the public buildings of other sovereigns[5]—so that by the time of the first exile (586 B.C.E.), the Babylonians took into exile artisans, merchants, and civil servants in addition to farmers.[6]

Although there is little evidence at this time of any sort of real financial institutions existing in the land of Israel at that period, nonetheless there existed a royal treasury as well as a repository for tithes and offerings in the Temple.[7] Furthermore, from the words of the prophets we know of the existence of a wealthy class[8]—of moneylenders,[9] bankers, and merchants.[10]

There was a highly developed social welfare system which provided for the needs of the poor and weak—orphans, widows, the stranger, and the landless—in accord with biblical law. Other religious injunctions limited the exploitation of laborers and debtors.[11] Education and religious facilities were financed through tithing and free-will offerings.

Archaeological excavations have revealed the existence of special jars that were used to hold grain at various stages of its tithing: grain that had not been tithed, grain that had been partially tithed, and grain that was ready to be consumed or sold after all the required gifts had been allocated to the priests, the Levites, and the poor. These archaeological findings, dating from the days of the Judean Kings, are an exact confirmation of the regulations in the oral law (Mishnah), which was finally codified some 800 years later.[12]

Taxation was an accepted and justified part of Jewish life, reflecting the obligation of the individual to share in all the costs of public policy. The people accepted the king's right to tax them from the outset of the monarchy[13] and rendered such taxes in money, labor, and kind. Military service, too, was part of the tax structure from the earliest days of settlement in the land of Israel,[14] so that a citizen's army, rather than hired mercenaries, was the foundation of the military strength of the country. It was excessive taxation, not taxation per se, against which the people revolted in the post-Solomonic period—a revolt not against their obligations as Jews, but against the misuse of royal powers.[15]

As shown previously, these welfare institutions flowed from the fundamental Jewish attitude that a man's property does not belong to him alone but is held in partnership with God and with the community. Thus, the ramified welfare state of the Jews was never a reaction to the Gentile world, but an institution that was firmly entrenched in Jewish life from the very beginnings of Jewish existence.

Equally entrenched were Jewish moral standards for economic behavior. The prophetic books of the Bible contain a long list of complaints against economic crimes, and it would seem reasonable to view these prophetic standards as representing commonly accepted, though often breached, standards of the community. Just as present-day moral and ethical comment reflects the accumulating of cultural and social mores, so, we can assume, did the prophetic tirades against usury, false weights and measures, dilution of the currency, and nonobservance of the sabbatical and jubilee years.[16]

MISHNAIC AND TALMUDIC TIMES (586 B.C.E. to 500 C.E.)

The Mishnaic period differed radically from the previous era in a number of ways, all of which affected the economic life of the Jews directly and indirectly. There now existed a widespread Jewish Diaspora, actually larger than the Jewish settlement in the Land of Israel. In the latter days of the First Temple (probably the ninth or eighth century B.C.E.), there developed Jewish communities in Babylon, Egypt, and Asia Minor, and subsequently the dispersion continued. Nevertheless, for some eight or nine centuries after the destruction of the First Temple and the subsequent loss of independence in 586 B.C.E., the Land of Israel remained the major center of Jewish life.

The destruction of the Temple had been accompanied by a mass expulsion of the Jewish people to Babylon, while some fled to Egypt and the countries of Asia Minor. There they joined communities that had been established during the latter days of the Jewish monarchies. A small remnant was allowed to return under the Persians, and so a new Temple and Jewish settlement arose. First the country was part of the widespread Persian Empire, which granted full religious and cultural autonomy both to the ever-growing Jewish settlement in the Land of Israel and to the larger Jewish population in Babylon and Persia. This was the period of Ezra and the men of the Great Assembly, who made important decisions with respect to the liturgy, canonization of the Bible, and religious law. Later the country became part of the Hellenic Empire of Alexander and his successors, who, while seeking the cultural integration of the Jews into Greek culture, left them a large measure of legal and social autonomy, so that Jewish law continued to govern economic activity. The independent Hasmonean kingdom made this autonomy even more important. Even the Roman conquerors who finally destroyed the Temple and brought an end to Jewish political independence continued to view the religious leadership as the relevant Jewish authority. After the destruction of the Temple and the cessation of the High Priesthood (recognized as the chief communal authority during most of the period), the heads of the academies, especially the *nesi'im*—descendants of the Davidic dynasty through the family of Hillel—became the religious, cultural, and political center of the Jews not only for Israel but also for the ever-growing Diaspora.

Aided by the persecutions of Herod, the destruction of the Temple, and, finally, the unsuccessful Bar Kochba revolt, this Diaspora became far larger than the Jewish community in Israel itself. By the third century c.e., large communities were to be found throughout the Roman Empire and beyond, extending to Yemen, Saudi Arabia, India, and the Slavic countries. As a result of this Diaspora, Jews were integrated into the sophisticated economies of the various empires within which they lived, so that both the scope and character of their society changed.

During this period of history, the world economy was characterized by extensive foreign trade, a breakdown of national and cultural barriers, and the sophistication of consumer goods. There were relatively long periods of peace—first under the rule of Persia, then under the rule of the Hellenistic Empire, and finally under that of Rome—which encouraged economic activity. As a result, Jews, both in Israel and in the Diaspora, were increasingly engaged in manifold economic activities. Small farms still remained the basis of agriculture, yet now farming in Israel produced goods also for the export market. There is evidence of

Jewish wine, spices, and perfumes, and perhaps textiles being exported to the corners of the Roman Empire.[17] Jewish basket weavers, fishermen, and sailors were to be found in Babylon.[18] A variety of guilds of Jewish artisans were to be found in the Jewish community of Alexandria.[19] In many countries of the Diaspora, the Jewish merchant and banker seem to have made their first appearance at this time. This diversification into crafts, trade, and banking was not a result of any ideological change, nor something forced on Jews by a hostile world. Judaism never had any religious or ethical objection to buying and selling goods for profit, and so this diversification was simply a result of changed economic opportunities.

The main function of Jewish banking in those days was the exchange of coins and the accepting of deposits for safety and investment. It was often linked to the function of buying and selling goods, and the Mishnah employs the term *shulchani* for both a banker and a merchant.[20] We find in the Mishnah, of course, a clear elaboration of the forbidding of interest, so that it seems that the major banking functions were the lending of money free of interest on the basis of pledges (something akin to pawnbroking, except that it was interest-free), and the providing of capital to joint ventures in which the provider participated in the risk.[21]

The welfare system mentioned in the previous section was so deeply rooted in Jewish life and practice that it was able to cater even to the needs of a large, nonagrarian, and mobile population living under conditions of recurrent warfare, expulsion, and slavery. The autonomous Jewish communal structure could easily expand the biblical taxation system, while the acceptance of the religious teaching of mutual obligation and a trustee concept of wealth meant rapid response to new and enlarged needs. So we find mention of funds for the redemption of Jews enslaved by the Romans and Babylonians,[22] together with an elaborate form of communal taxation to provide for welfare and education[23] and the provision of free loans.[24]

The provision of judiciaries in each eligible town or village was a continuation of the system whereby each tribe, each town, and the Temple itself had been a seat of law courts. These *batei din* (courts) provided an independent Jewish legal framework for the conduct of trade and commerce. The *batei din*, however, were engaged not only in settling legal issues but also in such activities as price fixing and control of wages, supervision of weights and measures, and the rights of workers. As these items will be dealt with in the various chapters of this book, it is not necessary at this stage to provide examples; it is sufficient to mention that such institutions already existed in this early period.

Furthermore, the dissemination of religious education which charactertized the whole period played an important part in the retention of Jewish ethical and moral teachings as the ideological framework for economic behavior. The courts referred to above were also centers around which revolved important educational activities, as were the academies that arose in various parts of the Land of Israel and then in Babylon. It was at this time that the communal provision for basic education—at least for males—transformed the existing parental obligation to educate the young into a national concern. The institution of *kallah* months in Babylon—Adar and Elul— during which ordinary men, along with scholars and students, streamed to the academies for study conventions serves as a dramatic example of the extent of adult religious education. The redaction of the oral Mosaic law to writing—first in the form of the Mishnah and then later in the Talmud—together with this learning meant that all aspects of Jewish religious life, including economic activity, continued to be regulated and conducted within the framework of the Torah. The Gentile authorities, whether pagans, Romans, Christian emperors, or rulers outside the Roman Empire (as in Babylon), recognized by and large the autonomy of their Jewish communities, so that Torah law continued to provide the social and economic framework of Jewish life.[25]

Despite the loss of political independence that followed the destruction of the Second Temple in 70 C.E. and the ever-growing worldwide dispersal of population, the ability of Jews to communicate with each other created a framework for continuity in communal living and common religious behavior in economic as in other spheres.[26] During the days of the Second Temple, Jews from distant lands sent to Jerusalem both their obligatory offerings to the Temple and their sons, to study in the academies of Jerusalem. The political delegations sent to Rome from the Land of Israel were received and assisted by their coreligionists just as traders and refugees were by the Jewish communities of Diaspora settlements. Rabbi Akiva traveled easily through the lands of the Middle East to raise funds for the Bar Kochba insurrection. (There were parallel Jewish revolts in many of these countries.) The completion of the Talmud, which marks the conclusion of this period, saw the beginnings of correspondence between the academies of

Babylon and world Jewry regarding religious and philosophical matters. This was paralleled by commercial and social correspondence between widely separated Jewish communities. This ease of communication also facilitated international trading, commerce, and finance, based as these are on interdependence, trust, and compatible, if not common, legal structures. The economic pattern that evolved has been repeated throughout Jewish economic history down to our own day.

Many historians and sociologists either take this communal coherence and ease of communication for granted or tend to view it as merely a social defense mechanism, the reaction of a minority group to a hostile world—taking the form of a subculture replacing the physical and political homeland. It would be naive to ignore any of these factors; yet there is ample evidence that they were only marginal. Rather, what we have here is a development that flows basically and primarily from fundamental Jewish philosophy and religious practices. The concept of a Divinely chosen national entity demanding mutual responsibility; the existence of a common language for study and prayers; and the existence of a national memory integrated into religious observance are fundamental to Judaism and predate the exile. It is impossible, therefore, to view Jewish communal coherence and ease of communication simply as reactions to the anti-Semitism of the alien world.

From the sixth century C.E., it becomes necessary to divide Jewish economic history into two main strands: the Jewry of Europe, and that of Spain, North Africa, and the Middle East. European Jewry lived under the conditions of medieval Christendom and its particular economic realities, whereas the latter lived under Moslem rule, in countries with a radically different economic system. It must be stressed that the basic tenets and premises of Judaism remained the same, so that today, after over a thousand years of separation, the religious differences between Sephardi and Ashkenazi Jews are marginal. Nevertheless, the realities of differing economic systems made their mark in many different ways.

JEWRY IN THE MOSLEM WORLD

The Jews of North Africa and Asia Minor, and even those of India, seemed to have been able to pursue a relatively free economic life, even though they were fettered by the status of second-class citizenship. Throughout the countries of Moslem supremacy, members of other faiths were considered to be infidels, thus, theoretically to be destroyed or converted. Nevertheless, the various Moslem rulers made great use of infidels in their bureaucracy and allowed them relatively free trade and entry into all the various crafts. Thus we find Jewish artisans in Yemen, a diversified economy in Moslem Babylon and Iraq, and a highly developed Jewish mercantile class presiding over the international trade between the Far East, North Africa, Asia Minor, and Europe.

Although Islam, like Christianity, forbade taking interest, Islamic oral law provided a mechanism for banking and credit, so there was no necessity to create a special class of largely Jewish money lenders. At the same time, the mosques, because of the egalitarian nature of Islam and its lack of a clearly defined clergy, never assumed the same economic functions as the Catholic Church of medieval Europe. The mosques served neither as major landowners nor as depositories of wealth, so that there was very little religious incentive for economic discrimination against Jews. Furthermore, Islam, while opposed to nonbelievers, provided for their existence within the body politic, so that the Jew did not have to exist as a chattel of the church or the crown. Naturally, in periods of persecution Jews suffered; their property would be looted and their businesses destroyed. Yet expulsion, relegation to a special economic status, or existence on the periphery of the economic world were never major features of the Moslem world, as they were of Christian Europe.[27]

Because the economic basis for Jewish life in the Moslem world was never as restrictive as in Christendom, Jewish economic life developed parallel to the economic fortunes of the countries in which they lived: rising in expanding economies, declining and contracting amidst economic misfortunes facing the host economy. For example, as economic activity in the countries of North Africa, Asia Minor, and the Far East declined after the sixteenth century, and their role was taken over by the countries of Western Europe, the economic conditions of the Jews in these countries also declined.

Irrespective of changes in economic fortune, the community continued to administer and to control Jewish life with regard to taxation, courts, the legal system, and religious education. Thus even while it was not perhaps as highly organized or powerful as it was in Western Europe, nevertheless, it remained a continuation of the Jewish mainstream dating back to the Jewish settlement in Israel.

With the explosion of world trade that characterized the later Middle Ages in Europe, North Africa, and the Middle East, the Jews of the Moslem world became intimately involved in both trading and financing. Luxury goods from the Far East, Syria, and Persia were transported and sold through caravans making their way across North Africa and Spain into Europe, across the Mediteranean Sea, and even via Eastern Europe.

Furthermore, the universities of the Moslem world, which included for relatively long periods Spain and Southern Italy, attracted scholars who, in addition to their Jewish learning, were proficient in the science, philosophy, and literature of their time. All the great scholars of the Jewish world—Maimonides, Halevi, Abarbanel—shared this common pattern of involvement in the knowledge of their time. Rabbinic personalities were commonly medical men, traders, royal ministers, or financiers; almost none of them occupied official rabbinic positions.

In this relatively open society, Jews fulfilled a wide gamut of economic functions. Some idea of the variety of Jewish economic life in the Moslem world may be gauged from the accounts of Jewish travelers of that time and from letters that have been preserved. In the genizah (repository of religious and communal papers) of the Cairo community, for example, we find a letter from a Jewish merchant in Cairo to a colleague in Syria instructing how he should conduct himself as the agent for a third party in Morocco.

Rabbi Benjamin of Tudela (Spain), a sort of twelfth-century Jewish Marco Polo, described the social, economic, and religious life of the Jews of the Mediterranean countries: "So the Greeks of Constantinople hate the Jews and subject them to great oppression and beat them in the streets. Yet the Jews are rich and good, kindly and charitable."[28] Describing the Jews of Jerusalem, another traveler of the fourteenth century, Rabbi Isaac Hilo, writes:

> Many of them are engaged in handicrafts, such as dyers, tailors, and shoemakers. Others carry on a rich commerce in many different goods and have fine shops. Some are devoted to science, such as medicine, astronomy, and mathematics. But the greatest number of their learned men work day and night in the study of

the Torah and Kabbalah [Jewish mysticism]. These are maintained out of the coffers of the community. The Jews in Hebron
are numerous and do a considerable trade in cotton, which they
spin and dye, as well as in all sorts of glassware made by them.[29]

Owing to the discovery of the New World and the seaway
round the Cape of Good Hope to the Far East, the economic importance of the Mediterranean world declined. The countries of
Western Europe gradually became the primary mercantile powers
and, ultimately, the major industrial nations. This led to a general
economic decline in the countries of the Moslem world and the
stagnation of their Jewish communities. Large pockets of poverty-
stricken and relatively underdeveloped Jewish communities became the norm in North African and Middle Eastern countries. At
the same time, individual Jews continued to play an important
role in the shrunken commerce of these countries.

In the eighteenth and nineteenth centuries, the European colonial powers increased their trade with Far Eastern markets, and
Sephardi Jews played an important role in the resulting expansion. Families like the Sassoons were pioneers in the development
of Indian and Southeast Asian trade and finance. Jews played a
major role in the banking and commercial activities of Egypt,
Syria, Iran, and Hong Kong. They were also an important part of
the professional and bureaucratic structure of these countries. The
Europeanization of the countries of North Africa and the Middle
East at the beginning of this century was accompanied by the
growth in a substantial Jewish mercantile and professional class
as the economies of these countries developed. The weakening of
restrictive Moslem practices that was encouraged by the colonial
powers, primarily France, made this development easier and
quicker.

EUROPEAN JEWRY

The economic history of the Jews of Europe must be understood against the background of developments in the countries in
which they lived. Generally speaking, European economic history
follows a common pattern. With the downfall of the Roman Empire and the resulting political anarchy, physical security and
safety became a prime need. In most of Europe, there existed a se-

vere danger to life and property, and men were therefore prepared to pay heavily for the provision of physical security. In return for this commodity (security), they were prepared to pay with their freedom of movement and freedom of activity. At the same time, the breakdown of Roman law and peace, the decline of international trade, and the necessity for subsistence farming made agriculture the prime economic activity and land the major factor of production. These two factors together gave rise to what is known as the feudal system, whereby in return for security men provided labor and food to those above them in the hierarchy. Those at the top provided land and security in return for manpower and food.

The conversion of the Germanic tribes to Christianity introduced a special Jewish element into this system. The Catholic Church, being the repository of learning, law, and social welfare, became the primary unifying factor, transcending local and tribal loyalties, so that feudalism was based on an international concept of Christendom rather than on national entities.

The Jew had, therefore, no place in the economic hierarchy of a united Christian Europe. He was automatically excluded from the framework of a Europe conceived to be part of a united church culminating in the Holy Roman Empire. Under the influence of the Church, Jewish life gradually became more and more marginal, as Church law restricted the Jewish role socially, economically, and physically. As Jews were not able to bear arms or own land, they had no place in the feudal hierarchy. The Jew became a chattel of the temporal ruler and even of the landowning Church authorities. In return for his security and the right of residence, the Jew had to surrender the right of free movement, the choice of occupation, and even sometimes the right to marry—over and above the forced service required by and tax money paid to the feudal overlords.

Nevertheless, Jews were frequently invited to settle in a city or state when their presence was considered economically beneficial. Invariably their very success soon brought in its wake anti-Jewish legislation, persecution, and often expulsion. The ideological necessity for the Church to persecute the Jew because of his rejection of their messiah, together with the jealousy of Christian leaders and financiers, made such persecution and expulsion a constant practice in European history—aided by the availability of the Jew as a convenient scapegoat for social, political, and economic troubles whenever they appeared.

This pattern basically characterized Western Europe until the French Revolution and Eastern Europe until the end of the nineteenth century. That is, the Jews were a separate factor and fulfilled a peculiar role within the organization of European economic life. He was required to pay for his security in the form of both special services and special taxation. It is true that in the course of time, the reality of economic life produced variations, both fiscal and physical, from country to country and from period to period. Nevertheless, the basic pattern remained operative, and any deviation was either temporary or local.

At the same time, the economic factors that produced feudalism in Christian Europe further emphasized the special position of the Jew in that society—the most glaring example being the gradual emergence of the Jew as the money lender of Europe. It is true that in many parts of Europe the Jews fulfilled the role of banker, as taking interest was forbidden in Christianity. Nevertheless, the period in which the Jew was the prime banker was in reality severely limited to two major periods, the late Middle Ages and the nineteenth century; in the latter period, their role was totally unrelated to religious considerations. The former period saw the rapid growth of international trade and a cash economy partly as a result of the Crusades, and the Jew was a major force as both a banker and trader.

Already, however, in the late thirteenth century, and progressively after, the Italian Lombards, Venetians, and Genoans appeared on the European scene as money lenders and bankers, soon to be followed by the merchants of the Hanseatic cities of Northern Germany and those of Eastern and Central Europe. This competition was aided by cases of the crown confiscating the debts owed Jews, as well as by riots instigated by debtors to rid themselves of their debts. A twelfth-century Christian chronicle written in England describes such a confiscation: ''In the meantime, Aaron the Jew of Lincoln [the greatest Jewish banker in England] died, and we were forced to pay to our Lord the King all that we had owed [to the Jew] on behalf of William of Fossaro.''[30]

In the nineteenth century, the industrialization of Europe and the subsequent colonial expansion called for large sums and an efficient banking system. Famous financial houses in Western Europe, such as the Rothschilds, the Warburgs, and Goldsmith, were especially active as investment bankers in this period.

Even though Jews continued to be financiers to the German

princelings, after the Middle Ages their role, generally speaking, became a limited one. At the same time, we find the emergence of a Jewish role as tax collector, administrator of feudal estates, and economic middleman. This role spread to Eastern and Central Europe, where its influence was far greater than in Western Europe and remained in force until the breakdown of feudalism in the nineteenth century. In Western Europe the early emergence of the national states of France, England, the Netherlands, and Scandinavia restricted this role.

It should be noted that this role of middleman between the feudal nobility and the masses in Eastern Europe made the Jew a perpetual victim of the clashes between these two Gentile classes. As often as not, the feudal lords would direct the anger and envy of both the masses and the commercial classes against the Jew.

The international trade of medieval Europe was primarily of two types: the East–West flow between Europe and the Middle East and the North–South trade between Northeastern Europe and the countries of the Baltic sea and the Mediterranean. The Jews were active and important in both trade currents; it seems that the factors underlying their involvement may be summed up as follows:

1.   The Jew was able to bridge the gap between Christian Europe and the Moslem countries. Contact between the two worlds was generally taboo; only the Jew was nominally accepted by both in substantial numbers. In exactly the same way as they were active in the translation of Greek and Roman manuscripts via Arabic into Latin and the transmission of Arab sciences to Christian scholars, so, too, the Jews were active in the transfer of economic goods from the Far East via the Moslem countries. A major part of this trade was in spices, jewelry, weapons, and slaves, and it seems that the profit margins were so great that they compensated for the high degree of risk involved.

2.   Despite the anarchy and danger which prevailed in feudal Europe, the Jew was able to exploit a cohesive Jewish communal network to facilitate his trade. This network provided security for the traveling merchant, facilitated the movement of funds without the physical transfer of money, and enabled a foreign merchant to obtain information regarding local market conditions and the reliability of the local Gentile suppliers or customers. The existence of travel documents issued to travelers by Jewish communities ask-

ing other communities to protect them and assist their members, together with the provision of community-operated hotels, contrasts strongly with the jealousy and antagonism existing between the Christian citizens of different towns and loyalties. The high level of Jewish education and literacy facilitated the smooth operation of economic ventures. Bills of exchange and letters of credit, often written in Hebrew, made the transfer of funds through the agency of relatives or agents in distant cities possible without exposure to the brigandage common on the roads of Europe.

3.   The autonomy enjoyed by Jewish communities resulted in a extended legal system that provided the Jewish merchant with protection against defaults in debts and compensation for broken contracts on the part of his fellow Jewish trader. Jewish moral, ethical, and religious principles provided a framework of trust and responsibility without which the banking system, or the system of international trade in which the Jews played an important role, would have been impossible.

(These factors operated in the Moslem world as well, so that we find the Jews in North Africa and the Middle East constituting a major element in the trade of these countries with Europe and the Far East.)[31]

The existence of a highly developed legal system and the subjection of the Jew to this system provided the basis and vehicle for the existence of an independent Jewish economic life. This legal system included the power (essential to any form of independence) of taxation, respecting both taxes needed by the community and those special taxes levied by the Christian temporal and religious lords.

But Jewish autonomy permitted the intervention of the communal lay leadership, under the scrutiny of the rabbinic courts, into all economic affairs, over and above the matter of taxation. Such intervention extended to price controls, the supervision of Jewish guilds, or other restrictive practices, and restraints on conspicuous consumption. It goes without saying that Jewish ethical and moral teachings were given practical expression through the power of this autonomy. Obviously, given the variations in sociopolitical structure of both non-Jewish and Jewish societies over long periods of time and over the large geographic area of the Diaspora, the degree of this autonomy and its resultant effectiveness varies from period to period and country to country. By and large, such communal autonomy remained in force in Western Europe until the French Revolution and in Eastern Europe and the Moslem world until the beginning of this century.

From the period of the Middle Ages until the Napoleonic wars, Jewish economic life in Europe was consistently restricted by the biases both of the Church authorities and of Gentile competitors. The economic opportunities available to the Jew were often narrow, his livelihood depending on a small base of restricted activity. Expulsion, persecution, and confiscation led to a highly mobile and unstable life. The excessive risk of everyday living led to the holding of liquid assets and to high-profit ventures. This persecution, however, was often mitigated by the ease of acceptance which one Jewish community extended to the exiles of another Jewish community, even when it endangered their already fragile economic base.

At the same time that banking and commerce were major Jewish economic occupations, it should be pointed out that the separation of the Jew from agriculture, crafts, and manufacturing was not as complete as is often imagined. There is evidence of the existence of Jewish farmers, primarily in Central and Eastern Europe, throughout the period, at the same time as other Jews served as agents of the absentee Gentile landlords. There is also evidence of a widespread Jewish involvement as artisans throughout Europe in textiles, woodworking, metalworking, jewelry, and the working of precious stones. One may find numerous examples not only of individual artisans but also of Jewish guilds engaged in these operations—as, for instance, the tailors' guild of Prague in the seventeenth century, the cobblers' and carpenters' guilds in Spain prior to the expulsion, and the guilds of southern France. The existence of apprenticeship regulations in Jewish court proceedings regarding the infringement of the rights of trainees is added evidence of this.

It is important to remember that in actual fact, the manufacturing activities of Europe as a whole, prior to the seventeenth century, were relatively minimal. Therefore, the limited Jewish involvement was probably primarily the result of the limitations of the entire manufacturing sector prior to the Industrial Revolution in the late eighteenth century. This is substantiated by the emergence of a large Jewish proletariat in Poland when that country entered the Industrial Age.

The modern economic history of the European Jew has to be

viewed in light of the political emancipation which followed the Napoleonic Wars. Political, religious, and legal restraints were gradually relaxed and ultimately abolished. This process began in Western Europe at the beginning of the nineteenth century but was only finalized throughout Europe after World War I. Nevertheless, political freedom, even in its varying stages, enabled the Jew to participate in the Industrial Revolution as it spread throughout Europe and later to the countries of North and South America.

It must be borne in mind that this participation in the economic development of the modern world occurred simultaneously with a decline in the power of Jewish communities. The easing of external anti-Jewish pressures was obviously an important factor in this decline. It seems, however, that the major factor was the rise of secularism and assimilation, which undermined the authority of the halakhic value structure and, hence, the legislative framework that had given the community so much of its power. Communal autonomy was increasingly restricted to the sphere of religious activity and social welfare; the regulation of economic activity was left to secular (non-Jewish) society. Patterns of consumption, limitations on economic activity on account of religious study and observance, and even the assumption of philanthropic obligations became matters solely of individual, voluntary judgment.

Many Orthodox Jews, however, have continued to submit both to the Jewish Codes and to the rulings of the rabbinic courts, so that religious rulings regarding economic activities have continued throughout the nineteenth and twentieth centuries down to the present day. There is no rabbinic personality of any stature, either in Western Europe or in the relatively new communities of the United States and England, whose responsa do not include rulings regarding wages, labor conditions, strikes, interest, repayment of loans, competition, and related matters. That these rulings were often issued in the context of legal action concerning activities either between Jewish merchants or between Jewish employer and employee engaged in a specifically religious activity is irrelevant. They provide evidence of a continued religious involvement in economic matters that can be applied to a much wider set of problems.

This decline in communal autonomy was accompanied by the persistent impoverishment of the Jewish masses of Eastern Europe. The Cossack uprising led by Chmielnicki in 1648 led to a holocaust of famine, murder, rape, and looting from which Polish Jewry did not recover. Later, the Russian Tsars annexed many of the countries of Eastern Europe, and the economic lot of the Jews grew worse. Neither the industrialization of Poland nor the liberal movements of the nineteenth century were able to improve the position of the Jews. The former led to mass migrations to the industrial cities, so that an urban poor replaced part of the rural poor, with the social results found in similar circumstances in other economies. The liberal movements never made much permanent headway against the corrupt and autocratic Tsars, so that many Jews began to emigrate to Western Europe, the United States, and other countries. This emigration, a mass movement of approximately three million Jews over a period of 100 years, was aided by the zeal of the Russian governments to forcibly convert the Jews within their territories. Above all there was the grinding poverty at home and the lure of the streets "paved with gold" abroad.

The First World War brought in its wake the rise of secular nationalist states in Central and Eastern Europe, which led to a certain improvement in the economic position of the Jews. Nevertheless, the majority of the Jews in Poland and the Baltic states were still economically depressed. In the new centers of Jewish life in the Americas, Australia, and South Africa, as with those of Western Europe, Jewish economic fortunes followed closely on those of the host economies as the Jew no longer represented a specific and separate economic entity.

At the same time, certain inbred attitudes remained and the Jewish religious and cultural heritage continued to affect Jewish economic life, even though expressed no longer in organized communal existence but rather as individual voluntary acts.

The emphasis on charity and mutual assistance that had characterized Jewish communal life for centuries continued. The Jewish poor—immigrant communities in the New World or the poverty-stricken masses of Eastern Europe—were looked after through voluntary financial aid. For example, in the report of the Jewish Board of Guardians we find that in 1897, of the 1772 paupers in the slums of Whitechapel, only 9 were Jews. Some fifteen years later, despite the mass emigration of Jews from Eastern Europe that prompted the report, there were 20 Jews among 20,000 paupers.[32] Today, the existence of Jewish poor in New York City is concealed both by their reluctance to ask for charity and by the widespread philanthropy that funds Jewish social services.

The massive financial aid channeled by world Jewry to the State of Israel for humanitarian purposes could never have been raised were it not for this tradition of communal responsibility. And this tradition has extended to host societies as well. Every country in Western Europe and in the Americas bears physical evidence of Jewish philanthropy's financing of health services, social amenities, and educational facilities for the benefit of the general public.

At the same time, it must be stressed that, as in the non-Jewish world, the response to social and economic issues became for the modern Jew a matter of private and individual choice. Where one feels free to observe all, some, or none of the rituals of Judaism, so one will feel free to maintain Jewish attitudes toward economic behavior or not. The giving of charity; the degree of competition; attitudes toward one's employers or employees; the adoption of material goals in life and of noneconomic status symbols—all these are today usually results of Jews' private consciences, modified by their surrounding non-Jewish cultures. It is not surprising, therefore, to find that a distinctly Jewish pattern of economic life does not in fact exist for many Jews in the Western World, any more than does a Jewish pattern of behavior in other fields.

The emergence of political freedom for the Jew permitted him to participate in the expansionary economy which followed the Industrial Revolution in every country. The migration from the backward areas of Eastern Europe to the Western world meant that the bulk of the Jewish people became concentrated in the economically advanced countries. In contrast to the commonly accepted view of the Jews as radical or socialist, historical facts point to their rapid advancement through the capitalist system to become a predominantly middle-class group. An investigator for Charles Booth, of Salvation Army fame, saw the Jewish immigrant masses of Victorian England as prototypes of the capitalist system:

> We have here [in Whitechapel, in London's East End] all the conditions of the [free market] economist satisfied: mobility; perfect competition; . . . modifying conditions almost absent; pursuit of gain an all-powerful motive; combinations [cartels] practically unoperative.[33]

It was this successful integration of the Jew into the booming economy of the nineteenth and twentieth centuries, together with the Jewish identification with social and liberal progressiveness, that enabled the anti-Semitic characterization of them as personifying both communism and capitalism.

Anyone with an insider's knowledge of the reality of Jewish life, however, knows that the Jewish free market was, even without the authority of organized religious communities, tempered with a large infusion of acts of charity and mutual assistance. The same Whitechapel abounded with synagogues and houses of study, a ramified educational system, interest-free loan societies, and philanthropic institutions. Throughout the major cities of the Western world we encounter this amalgam of a free market economy, a pronounced entrepreneurial spirit, and the voluntary assumption of the financial burden of Jewish communal welfare.

SUMMARY

Even though the modern economic history of the Jews of the Western world became integrated into that of their respective countries, nevertheless in certain respects Jewish and general economic history have developed along different lines. It is not at all clear whether this separate development, discussed below, is the result of specifically Jewish characteristics, simply the retention of human characteristics produced by 2000 years of Diaspora, a logical reaction to economic opportunities, or a synthesis of them all. Be that as it may, the differences between the Jewish economic development and that of the general society in the nineteenth and twentieth centuries may be summarized as follows:[34]

1. Jews concentrated in certain industries, such as trade (wholesale and retail), textiles (manufacturing and trading), diamonds (trade, polishing, and cutting), jewelry, and consumer goods (as opposed to heavy industry and transport). These industries had been the basis of the "Jewish economy" since medieval times; in many of them, the proportion of Jews was greater than their proportion in the total population. Furthermore, as often as not these industries were the basis of the Jewish economy, with Jews filling the roles of both employer and employee.

It is interesting to note that the Bolshevik revolution in Russia has not removed the occupational preferences of Jews. Light industry (textiles, food, and machine building), education, and trade still remain the primary occupations of Russian Jews.

2. The Jew played, and continues to play, an important role

in the liberal professions—medicine, law, science, and education—as well as in the publishing and communications industries. The latter were especially important in Germany in the first half of this century and in the present-day United States. Whereas medicine has always attracted Jews, Jewish representation in the other professions may perhaps have been a secular outgrowth of the traditions of Torah study and rabbinic law, and of the centuries-old Jewish involvement with religious publishing.

In the Americas and in Western Europe, first (immigrant) generation involvement with industry gave way to an increased involvement in the professions on the part of their children and grandchildren—a reflection of both the improved standard of living of the second generation and of the increased share of the service sector in the national economies of the Western world.

3. With the exception of Eastern Europe and Israel (including pre-state days) the proportion of Jews engaged in agriculture was marginal, even though the reasons varied. In Israel, the creation of a Jewish working class and an agriculturally based economy derived not from economic necessity but primarily from ideological motives—viz., the reversal of the inverted pyramid of occupations so typical of Jewish history, wherein a narrow apex of workers stood on a broad base of traders, entrepreneurs, and financiers. Countries like Czechoslovakia, Poland, and Romania had relatively large numbers of Jews in farming, though compared with the proportion of the non-Jewish population in farming they would have to be considered only marginal.

4. In most countries only an insignificant proportion of Jews were engaged in construction, the civil service, the military services, and finance. This was partly a result of discrimination, since these fields were closely allied to the national power structure, with which Jews were characteristically not associated. (A parallel situation exists today in the case of the Chinese throughout Southeast Asia.) Thus, the erosion of anti-Semitism in the United States has been accompanied by an increase of Jewish employment in the civil service at all levels.

The employment structure of the Jews worldwide, and their participation in the general economy as described above, must be seen against the background of the overall development of the world economy over the past decades. Throughout the Western world, the importance of "smokestack" (heavy industry) industries has declined and that of the service and high technology industries has risen. In this process, which has been accelerated since the end of World War II, the Jew has played an important part in both the scientific and industrial aspects. The development of the entertainment and leisure industries and of such fields as telecommunications and computer sciences has, because of their relative freedom from inherited ethnic biases and their dependence on educational achievement, provided Jews with an ever-widening scope for economic growth. In part this development enabled the remnants of European Jewry after the Holocaust to integrate themselves economically in Canada, the United States, and South America, just as it enabled the Jews of the free world to partially finance the philanthropy necessary to settle those who emigrated to Israel.

CHAPTER 5

Competition, Prices, and Profits

INTRODUCTION

How does one know which goods to produce, where to market them, and what prices to charge for them? How is society to decide which firms are to be allowed to operate in different industries or locations, which of them are to grow or die, and how to adapt to technological change? These are questions that have to be answered irrespective of the size of an economy or the degree of its sophistication. At the same time, the degree of competition operating in an economy and the profits earned by the various factors will be determined by the type of market mechanism chosen by a particular society. In most countries of the Western world there exists a mixed economy, in which there exist varying degrees of a free market alongside intervention on the part of the central government. In Communist countries the above questions are answered by a central planning authority, even though in some of them, such as Yugoslavia, elements of a free market economy have been introduced.

The results of whichever market mechanism is chosen by a particular society are not purely economic ones. The whole web of social relations is affected by the ability of people to invest money or labor in enterprises that will provide them with their economic needs (irrespective of how these are defined), their material security, and the mobility to benefit from changed technological or commercial conditions.

Pricing policies, rates of profitability, and restraints on competition determine, in no small measure, the distribution of wealth in a society and the changes therein. Such decisions are translated into matters of poverty and welfare, sometimes perpetuating human suffering, sometime alleviating it, and in yet other cases intensifying it. Thus, social equity and economic justice are a direct result of policies affecting the market mechanism. It would be impossible, therefore, to discuss an authentic Jewish economic life unless we were able to provide answers to the questions arising out of such issues.

The role of the marketplace in determining prices through the supply and demand mechanism was recognized by the sages and defined precisely in the Talmud some fifteen hundred years ago. "It is said in the name of Rabbi Akiva that the existing price is the stable one. If more is demanded the customer will refuse to buy, and if the price offered is lower, the seller will refuse to sell."[1] In the Tosefta Demai it is put even more succinctly. "If the supply of fruits (olives) is increased and then decreased, the market will return to its original position."[2] This puts the idea of equilibrium price as determined by supply and demand very simply.

The sages even differentiated between two types of changes in supply which affect the market mechanism differently:

1. *batzoret*: a shortage affecting the distribution of goods but not the total quantity supplied: for example, a breakdown in transport so that one area may have to import goods and pay a higher price as a result of the higher transportation costs. The effect would be similar to that induced by seasonal changes in prices.

2. *kafna*: a decline in the total quantity of goods supplied, due to drought, war, or other catastrophe[3]

In the case of *batzoret*, the market mechanism alone would rectify the imbalance within a short period. In the case of *kafna*, however, society would have to adopt special measures in order to prevent great suffering. Rabbi Hanina defined the difference between them as follows: "If a *se'ah* of grain costs one sela and the sela is easily obtainable—this is *batzoret*. However, when four *se'ahim* cost a sela but the sela is not easily obtainable, then this is *kafna*."[4]

Rabbi Yochanan added, "In *batzoret* money is cheap and only goods are scare, but in *kafna* money is dear and goods are cheap." *Batzoret* would seem to refer to inflationary conditions, whereas *kafna* would correspond to a recession or depression.

These early examples of insight into the workings of the price mechanism are not really of any great significance, since similar insights can probably be found in many other early societies. What is of great importance are the methods by which the forces of supply and demand determining prices and profits are allowed to operate within the value system of Judaism.

In the real world, a constant conflict exists between the interests of the individual and that of other individuals or of society. What is profitable for one may reduce or obliterate the profits of others, and one group of individuals may find profitable something that is detrimental to society as a whole. The market mechanism is often blind to the special needs of weak and deprived groups. At the same time, political power, scarcity, war, and unequal distribution of wealth through inheritance may give an individual or a group of individuals the power to distort the regulatory forces of the competitive markets. Sometimes that which is profitable and expedient to one party in the marketplace is caused by a lack of proper economic information or legal facts on the part of the other.

The purpose of this chapter is to discover to what extent the halakhic sources, assisted by communal enactments throughout the ages, introduced checks and balances in an attempt to regulate market forces in accordance with the tenets of justice and mercy. These checks and balances constantly had to deal with a dynamic economic and social system, which meant that the identity of injured or threatened parties changed along with the nature of the prevalent abuses.

A CONCEPTUAL FRAMEWORK

The ideological framework within which market forces are to operate in Judaism may be summarized as follows:

1. The society is free to choose, through its legislative machinery, any system whereby to allocate its resources, their prices, and the return on them. In the same way, it is free to determine

the degree of competition that it desires, provided that the demands of justice and mercy are met.

2.   Despite this elective freedom, the halakhah tended to prefer a free market mechanism, which would provide for the benefit of the majority of the members of society.

3.   The regulation of prices, profits, and competition was a legitimate concern of the rabbinic courts, as was the judicial treatment of breaches of contract and agreement.

4.   Market forces must be restrained by considerations of justice and righteousness, and the free market mechanism has to be distorted by communal action and by rabbinic decision in order to protect the welfare of the weak and the ignorant, as well as the prosperity of the community.

5.   Factors disrupting the free operation of market forces, such as monopolies, cartels, or restrictive agreements, are disallowed, unless they benefit society or unless they are needed to temporarily ease the disruptive effects of sudden change.

6.   Considerations of morality and kindness are part of the market mechanism, even when they cannot be legally enforced. A broad-ranging religious educational system has to be provided to make such considerations effective.

7.   Each individual has the right to perform with his property and within his legal jurisdiction whatever economic activity he sees as most profitable to him, and others engaged in the same activity cannot prevent him from doing so, except in those cases limited by rabbinic law or communal edicts.

CONTROL OF PRICES AND PROFIT

Throughout history, down to our day, there have been circumstances which generated demands for price controls, which would allow producers and entrepreneurs a "reasonable" profit while enabling consumers to pay a "just" price. Thus, public utilities, where they are in private hands, are regulated by public bodies in order to achieve this balance. And during periods of war, most countries introduce rationing and/or price controls in order to assure a fair allocation of goods and to prevent firms from reaping excessive profits from the shortages resulting from the diversion of resources to the war effort.

Irrespective of the form that price control takes, it always involves distorting the pricing mechanism based on free market forces. The effects of distortion will be the same (given the same degree of control) irrespective of the ideological basis for control. In other words, the economic effects of price control will be the same whether it is instituted for "socialist" reasons or for "liberal" ones—or for religious ones. However, the practical effects depend on public acceptance. Distortion of the price level through control often leads to shortages and may create a "black market." Yet if the general public accepts the morality of the control, the shortages will not create a black market.

The concept of controlling prices and limiting profits in Judaism differs radically from that prevalent in medieval Christendom or in latter-day socialism. Despite certain Talmudic sayings to the contrary,[5] no anticommercial tradition existed in Judaism as existed in Christian social thought. The essence of the early and medieval Christian argument was that payment may be morally demanded only by the craftsmen who make the goods or by those who transport them, not by the entrepreneur. One of the early fathers of the church wrote that, "Whoever buys a thing that he may gain simply by selling it unchanged and exactly as he bought it, that man is like the buyers and sellers who were cast forth from God's temple."[6] Thomas Aquinas held that "the occupation of the merchant and all that surrounds it is to be justly condemned, since it serves only the lust of gain and Mammon."[7] Basically, these medieval churchmen were the precursors of the Marxist Labor Theory of Value, which also denies a legitimate role to capital and therefore regards profit derived from capital as immoral.

In Judaism, the merchant and the entrepreneur play a legitimate and even desirable role in commerce and therefore are morally entitled to a profit in return for fulfilling their function without any need of apology. This acceptance of the legitimate role of traders and merchants is the reason for the Talmudic argument that "he who buys and sells is not called a seller unless he earns a profit from the transaction; the formal transaction alone is not enough to make him a trader."[8]

Not only did the rabbis not see anything wrong with profitable entrepreneurial activity per se, they even appreciated the difficulties that would come upon the whole community should "the bottom drop out of the market." "Our sages taught," it says in the Talmud, that "it is permissible to announce a public fast in the face of an impending recession even on the Shabbat [a day when mourning or expressions of sorrow of any kind are usually forbidden]." Rabbi Yochanan said, "for example in the case of flax in Babylon or wine and oil in Eretz Yisrael." Rav Yoseph added [the indicator of a serious downturn or recession in these leading industries], "when prices drop by forty percent."[9]

Nevertheless, there is a Jewish concept of a just price and a reasonable profit. This concept, however, does not seem to flow primarily from analyses of the costs of production, or the value of labor input, or from utility to the consumer. Rather it is the special character of the Jewish conception of private ownership and economic endeavor, as explained in chapter three, which determines the nature of the Jewish concept of a just price. That we are dealing with a moral or religious issue rather than an economic one can be seen from the fact that the forms of price control discussed here all refer to basic commodities or their ingredients, with investment goods (such as land, slaves, or monetary instruments) excluded. If the rationale behind the Jewish concept of price control were based primarily on economic theory, these goods should have been included. Furthermore, other factors affecting pricing, such as the need for full disclosure, the fulfillment of contractual obligations, and the preservation of the equal rights of the parties concerned, all flow from basic religious teachings and are seen as expressions of moral duties.

Halakhic discussions of just price are couched in legalistic terms, so it is often difficult to understand the underlying thinking and values. Fundamentally, the halakhah provides, in the case of basic commodities, for the negation of abnormal profits over and above the market price (which itself provides for a normal profit); such abnormal profits are seen as imposing duress and as akin to theft. To distort the normal market price and limit individual profits, in the interest of society or sections of it, administrative, judicial, or moral intervention is required.

Trading in Basic Commodities

Although they understood that the same market forces that operate to price all goods apply to basic commodities as well, the rabbis stressed the moral challenge posed by profiting from trade in such goods. These goods, like wine, oil, fruits and vegetables, and bread, were essential to man's existence (or in Hebrew, *chayei nefesh*—things on which life depends); hence they and their ingredients had to be traded in a manner different from other goods in order to prevent suffering, even if this meant a distortion of the market mechanism.

So we find a number of Talmudic statements expressing disapproval of profits earned from trade in these commodities. (The prices of such goods are affected, not only by the normal profits earned by their producers, but also by the extent of the marketing process [even though this may make for greater efficiency in distribution]. Limitations on trading in such essential goods were established, therefore, to minimize the effect on their prices.) These statements were incorporated into the various codes and formed the basis for communal enactments aimed at preventing Jews from acting as middlemen in the distribution of these goods. "One may not earn a livelihood in the Land of Israel in basic commodities. This one brings his produce and sells it and the other brings his produce for direct sale, in order that they may sell cheaply. In those places, however, where oil is plentiful it is permissible to earn one's livelihood from trade therein."[10] Such trade does not lead to an increase in price because of the plentiful supply.

The language of the Talmud led Maimonides to see these limitations as primarily another means of assisting in the perpetual settlement of the Land of Israel, unlike other similar restrictive injunctions that apply to any place in which Jews form a majority group. Many of the authorities in various periods were divided as to whether this injunction referred only to trading in unchanged goods or included middlemen who packaged or transported the goods and were therefore making a real economic contribution which entitled them to trade in these goods.[11]

The Talmud imposes other limitations on trade in basic commodities; thus, "One may not earn twice on the sale of eggs."[12] In the ensuing discussion, there emerges a difference of opinion between the two sages Rav and Shmuel as to whether the word "twice" refers to a 100% rate of profit or to the role of the middlemen in the chain of marketing factors; most authorities held the latter opinion. It should also be noted that Maimonides ruled that this injunction refers specifically to eggs,[13] while the *Shulchan Arukh* followed by the majority of opinions saw eggs as only an example and therefore extended the injunction to all basic foodstuffs.[14]

There is also a general injunction against hoarding, or cornering the market on, basic goods. The economic wisdom of "cornering a market" at a time of excess supply and reselling later when demand increases was obvious to the rabbis; they were concerned solely with the moral problem. So the Talmudic discussion ends by saying that "hoarders of produce, those who lend money at interest, users of false weights, and price gougers are those to whom the prophet refers when Amos says 'The Lord has sworn by the strength of Jacob that He will never forget their actions.'"[15] This being the rabbis' frame of reference, they distinguished between dealers and middlemen, for whom speculation was forbidden, and the producers themselves. The former were simply laying in stocks to benefit from the expected shortage. The latter, under no moral obligation to sell these products to the general public, could withhold their products at times of excess supply in order to benefit from better prices later on. To do otherwise would be to "support," as it were, the buyers of their goods. Both this injunction, originally phrased as relating to Jewish settlement in Eretz Yisrael, and the former one, were regarded by the later authorities as applying to any community where Jews constituted a majority.[16]

Any decline in the supply of basic foodstuffs is obviously tantamount to an increase in their price, so it was necessary for the halakhic authorities to deal with this aspect of the trade in these commodities. Thus, the Talmud rules that "it is forbidden to export from the Land of Israel goods essential to life. . . . Just as one may not export these goods to countries outside the Land of Israel, so one may not export them to Syria [considered in many halakhic decisions to occupy a midpoint between the Land of Israel and other countries]. Rabbi Yehudah Hanasi permits the transfer of these goods from one province in the Land of Israel to another."[17] The Rambam and the *Shulchan Arukh* repeat the language of the Talmud. The former, however, ruled against the opinion of Rabbi Yehudah, on the grounds that the "export" of basic goods within Israel itself would lead to increased prices in the localities in which they were produced. It would seem reasonable to assume, however, that Maimonides would have permitted such sales in those areas where basic goods were plentiful, since they would not lead to a shortage or a price increase. It is interesting to note that Rabbi Yehudah ben Beterah permitted the export of wine, on the basis that the decreased supply lessened the immorality that so often flows from excessive drinking—another example of the constant interplay of general moral considerations and purely economic ones that is so typical of the traditional Jewish treatment of economic questions.

The basic concern behind these injunctions respecting trade that might lead to shortages in, or increased prices for, essential commodities was the welfare of the average consumer. When it came to basic foodstuffs, this welfare had to take precedence over the abnormal profits that might be earned by entrepreneurs. Therefore we find in the source material additional measures to increase the supply of essential goods. Thus, during the year, there are specific periods during which reduced supply and increased demand might lead to acute shortages and speculative hoarding: An example is the major festivals, prior to which the butchers would prefer not to slaughter animals, thus restricting the supply and enabling them to raise their prices. The following mishnah presents the halakhic treatment of this problem: "In these four periods [the last day of Sukkot, Shemini Atzeret; the eve of the first day of Passover; the eve of Shavuot; and the eve of Rosh Hashanah, the New Year] butchers can be forced to slaughter their cattle, even if they have only one buyer who wishes to buy one dinar of meat from an ox which is worth a thousand dinarim."[18] In the subsequent discussion in the Talmud, the sages changed a basic halakhic rule of commerce, thus allowing the buyer to acquire a part of the ox merely by paying his dinar, even though movable goods cannot be purchased by money alone but require an act of possession. By this decision the sages were, in effect, providing for an increase in the supply of meat in order to allow the people to enjoy the festivals, without allowing an increase in price..

A consistent problem in agriculture is that of excess supply. What is one to do with the results of an overabundant yield? If the farmer is unable to sell all his crops or store them at an economical cost, he will restrict the planting of the next crop; then the following year will be one of shortage and hardship for the consumer. In most modern economies, the government usually provides a variety of programs, such as price supports, to iron out these fluctuations and provide a steady and sufficient supply of food. One such method is the destruction of the excess crop. It would seem from the following discussion in the Talmud that there is rabbinic sanction for such destruction in the interests of the consumer.

Some of the good things which [the Talmudic sage] Rav Huna used to do: Every Shabbat eve he would send a messenger to the market who would buy up all the perishable vegetables which the gardeners had been unable to sell. These would then be thrown into the river. "Surely he should have given them to the poor?" [it is asked]. "No," came the rejoinder, "they would then get used to getting it free and would not come to buy in the future." [And a drastic reduction in demand would lead to an equivalent reduction in supply.] [Another questioner asked,] "Perhaps he should feed them to the animals?" "It seems Rav Huna holds that it is not permissible to feed food fit for human consumption to animals" [presumably in order to keep the separation between man and the rest of creation absolute and permanent].[19]

Finally (in the same Talmudic discussion) comes the crucial question from the economic viewpoint: "Perhaps he should not have bought them at all?" "No," comes the answer, from the sage who was repeating Rav Huna's teaching. "If nobody would pay them, then the gardeners would produce less in the future." This would lead to future shortages and higher prices, or at best to constant instability in the production of basic foodstuffs. It is not clear, however, whether such financial measures, aimed at modifying fluctuations in the prices of such goods, are something that can be automatically demanded of the public authorities or whether they are a matter for individual or communal choice.

All these injunctions suggest an active public policy aimed at encouraging direct producer-consumer marketing and shortening the chain of intermediaries in the marketing of basic commodities. However, halakhic intervention in the trading in essential goods was not restricted to the supply side. It is obvious that changes in demand can also lead to price changes, so that a decline in the former will usually lead to a reduction in the later. So halakhic injunctions leading to reduced demand will offset any price increases flowing from artificial or natural intervention in the supply of goods, thus protecting the average consumer. From the various sources it seems that this protection through the demand mechanism has historically been extended beyond basic foodstuffs to include any goods that are considered to be essential to normal Jewish living.

We find the following story, dating back to the last days of the Second Temple period, told in the Talmud. According to the Torah, a woman was obligated to bring an offering of pigeons after birth or miscarriage before she could perform the rites of purification and renew sexual relations with her husband.

> The price of the pigeons offered by women after birth reached one golden dinar [a price which put it far beyond their means]. Rabbi Shimon ben Gamliel announced that he would not leave the *bet midrash* until he reduced the excessive cost of the pigeons. He taught that a woman is obligated to bring only one offering irrespective of the number of births. This [drastic change in demand] led to a decline in price that very same day to a quarter of a silver dinar [one thousandth of a golden dinar].[20]

This method of frustrating high prices and monopolies by changing religious rulings to manipulate demand has continued to serve halakhic authorities throughout the ages. For example, in the sixteenth century, the Gentile fishermen created a cartel which raised the price of fish in Moravia. This caused great distress among Jews, who, in keeping with tradition, insisted on eating fish at their Shabbat meals. The Tsemach Tsedek, the leading halakhic authority at that time, knew that simply releasing the Jews from observance of this tradition would only increase the difficulties of the poor. The rich would simply continue to buy fish irrespective of the cost, while the poor, refusing to acknowledge their limited means, would further impoverish themselves by insisting on eating fish on Shabbat just like the rest of the community. So that week he pronounced all fish ''treifa'' (unfit to eat) and the monopoly disappeared.[21]

This ruling was later incorporated in the twentieth-century code of Jewish law, the Mishnah B'rurah. The same philosophy, whereby changes in ritual are instituted in order to reduce prices, is reflected in the recent rulings by the *bet din* of Jerusalem permitting the joint purchases of *etrogim* (the citrons needed for the Sukkot festival) by partners. (The usual practice requires each person to use an *etrog* which is his own personal property. However, since the demand had led to great increases in price, this requirement was waived.) Another ruling has encouraged the purchase of *etrogim* in sealed boxes (preventing the usual individual examination for minute defects)—all at an equal, fixed price—in order to break the spiral of ever-increasing prices resulting from the desire of people to fulfill the commandment of beautifying (adorning) a ritual *mitzvah*.

Price Controls

In most countries and throughout Jewish history, the appoint-
ing of inspectors to enforce price controls and to reduce profit
margins was a common feature of the Jewish communal structure.
Naturally, the greater the autonomy enjoyed by a community, the
more common were price controls and the greater the ability to
enforce such controls. This communal power was based on the decision in the Talmud enjoining Jewish courts to appoint overseers,
both for prices and for weights and measures.[22] It is interesting to
note that there is an alternative opinion in the Talmud held by
Shmuel, that the efficiency of the market mechanism of supply
and demand would force merchants to automatically offer their
goods at the lowest possible price, thus making the appointment
of such overseers unnecessary. The rabbis, understanding the limitations of the market mechanism, rejected this opinion. Another
Talmudic source tells us that, "These overseers flailed the merchants, saying, 'Sell cheaply, sell cheaply.'"[23]

So Maimonides and Joseph Caro ruled in their codes that imposing such price controls on basic commodities was part of the
obligation of the rabbinic courts. "The Courts are obligated to announce the fixed prices [of basic goods] and to appoint inspectors
for this purpose, so that each one should not earn whatever he
wants. They [the courts] shall only allow a profit rate of ⅙, and the
seller shall not earn more than this." (In this instance the limitation on profits is calculated as a percentage of the seller's costs,
and should not be confused with the general limitation on profits
resulting from charging prices over and above the market price,
referred to in the following section.) Maimonides goes on to restrict the control of prices solely to basic goods: "Luxury items
such as spices are not subject to price fixing, and everyone may
earn whatever he wishes."[24]

In the same chapter, Maimonides rules in accordance with the
opinion brought in the Mishnah, that the people of the city (by
majority vote or through their representatives) "can fix the prices
of goods even of bread and meat [i.e., of basic necessities] at
whatever level they see as being necessary [often leading to sharp
price increases]. Furthermore, anyone not complying with their
ruling may be punished."

Naturally, the seller is bound by these fixed prices as long as they are operative. Should prices rise, as a result of shortfalls in supply, changes in demand, or natural phenomena, the seller is free to charge whatever he wishes until a new communally adjusted price is announced.[25]

The edicts of the various Jewish communities translated these halakhic dicta into everyday practice. Jews who infringed communal price controls were liable to physical punishment, monetary fines, or even excommunication, just as were those who disobeyed all other communal regulations.

In Spain in the fifteenth century, the Synod of Castilian Jewry included the following resolution in its *Pinkas* (communal records):

> Every community of ten families or more shall establish a tavern whose kosher wine may be obtained both for themselves and for travelers. Those who don't already have such a tavern shall appoint one man from the class of wine sellers and another from the class of wine buyers. These shall declare under oath that they will see to it that the wine is sold in accordance with the custom of the place and at the price at which it is sold to Christians [in other words, there is to be no exploitation of the religious need for kosher wine]. They must add to the price the amount paid in taxes for the Talmud Torah [religious education] fund. If they see that the Jewish wine involves greater costs they shall allow the price of the Jewish wine to be revised by just that amount.[26]

The concept of communal price controls, while primarily applied to consumer goods, was sometimes expanded to embrace goods and services other than basic foodstuffs. Thus:

> The minute book of the Council of Four Lands (the autonomous Jewish Council of Great Poland, Lesser Poland, Lvov Land, and Volhynia from the sixteenth to eighteenth centuries) records regulation of the wages of *shadkhanim* (marriage brokers) and teachers, and of the fees paid to judges by litigants.

> We have been made aware once again of the public outcry concerning the exorbitant fees charged by the judges, the fines which they take, and the fact that they ask for fees twice [once at the beginning of the case and once at its conclusion]. So we have ruled that only at the conclusion of the case may they take 1½ large coins. If, however, the litigants wish to each give them one

large coin they may do so. In no case, however, is the fee to exceed this.[27]

An entry in the *Pinkas* of the Va'ad Kehilot Lita in the same period came to restrict the profit margin to be earned from interest: "When the lender comes to claim his profit [interest] from the borrower, the judges are not permitted to allow him more than 20 gulden for each 100 gold coins. In the case of secured loans only 17 out of each hundred." [28]

Ona'ah: A Just Price

Alongside these moral exhortations and administrative actions taken by the halakhic authorities to prevent economic suffering through restraints on the market mechanism, additional redress was provided through the application of the just price—*ona'ah*—limitation. The concept of *ona'ah* does not seem to flow merely from a concept of fraud or theft but rather as a form of exploitation in commercial transactions. It is instructive that the codes deal with it in the laws of buying and selling and not together with those of theft. There is valid ground to consider it primarily as a price different from that of the market price, as a result of lack of knowledge on the part of one of the parties or the use of undue influence by either of them.

The basis for this interpretation lies in these observations:

1.   The rabbinic concept of just price—*ona'ah*—derives from the biblical verse (Lev. 25:14) "When you sell to your neighbor or buy from your neighbor's hand you shall not oppress one another." In most places in the Bible where the word *ona'ah* is used, it refers to the exploitation of status or strength as for instance in the commandments (Exod. 22:20) "And a stranger you shall not oppress" and the parallel injunction in Lev. 19:33.

2.   All the commandments forbidding theft or robbery are understood to include non-Jews as well, whereas *ona'ah* applied only to Jews. Thus, it cannot be understood as fraud or theft, but rather as an extra duty devolving on the Jew to refrain from taking advantage of a position of, say, superior information. This duty could be implemented only in a reciprocal relationship; therefore, it had to be limited to Jews only.

3.   *Ona'ah* exists not only in business transactions but also in speech (*ona'at d'varim*). For instance, one is not allowed to vex a convert to Judaism by saying to him, "Remember the actions of

your idolatrous ancestors.'' The sages of the Talmud, commenting on this example, pointed out that such

> *Ona'ah* in speech is far more serious than *ona'ah* in business, since the latter can be rectified by restitution, whereas the injury inflicted by speech cannot be. *Ona'ah* in business, after all, only affects one's material goods, whereas one's very being is affected by other forms of *ona'ah*. In the bibical text [Lev. 25:17], the name of God is added to the injunction against [i.e., that which is traditionally understood to prohibit] *ona'ah* in speech but not to that [in Lev. 25:14, quoted above] concerning *ona'ah* in business, making it a far more serious crime.[29]

Additional evidence that the concept of the just price is primarily a moral concept, concerned with the exploitation of ignorance or duress, may be seen from some of the halakhot in the codes, which disallow the claim of *ona'ah* in cases of full disclosure. Thus, for example:

> He who buys and sells *in good faith* cannot be guilty of *ona'ah*. If the seller says to the purchaser, ''This article which I am selling at 200 is sold in the market at 100'' there is no case of *ona'ah*. [He may include in his selling price the costs of transportation, porterage, and hotel expenses but not his own wages as a laborer. Now if he publicly declares his profit margin, there is no claim of *ona'ah*].[30]

A just price cannot exist unless there exists a fixed price set through some legislative machinery, as described in the previous section. Where such fixed prices exist, a sale is valid only if the price does not differ from the market price by more than one-sixth. Above that point the sale may be invalidated by the courts. Price differentials below this are considered to be acceptable and therefore need no legal redress. At the one-sixth level, however, even though the sale is valid, the injured party can claim compensation for the differential between the market price and that charged.

Given the centrality of justice and its symmetry in Judaism, it is not surprising to find that the legal protection provided by the concept of *ona'ah* applies equally to buyer and seller. In the case of the buyer, the law applies (and enforcement can be sought) within the time that is needed to show the goods to an expert and have them valued. The seller, however, who no longer has the legal protection of possessing the article sold, was originally permitted unlimited time within which to press the claim of *ona'ah*.

The possibility of a claim of *ona'ah* introduces an element of uncertainty into all transactions, so that the time period involved is of great importance. In the Mishnah, Rabbi Tarfon disagreed with the sages.

> Rabbi Tarfon held that the cut-off point for *ona'ah* was not one-sixth [as ruled by the sages] but one-quarter [which, obviously, enabled merchants more freedom to charge above the market price], but allowed the buyer unlimited time to claim the protection of the law. When the merchants of Lud heard the ruling about the price range of *ona'ah*, they rejoiced. However, when they heard about Rabbi Tarfon's opinion regarding the time allowed [to seek redress and invalidation], they quickly applauded the ruling of the sages.[31]

We find an early application of this ruling regarding the permissible time for enforcement in the following responsum written by Rabbi Meshullam sometime in the tenth or eleventh century in the Rhineland:

> Reuven bought an object, showed it to his partner [who, it is presumed, is the expert]. The partner, Shimon, claims the *din* [judgment] of *ona'ah*, as the price charged is above that of the market price. My answer is that since the purchaser has waited for longer than it should have taken him to show it to an expert or to his relatives, the law of *ona'ah* does not apply, even if the overcharge was more than one-sixth of the market price.[32]

The protection does not apply to slaves, promissory notes, and land,[33] since in halakhic terms, they do not fall into the category of salable goods. In addition, in economic terms it may well be that the reason for their exclusion lies in the difficulty of fixing a market price for these articles in view of the subjective evaluation involved. Two modern scholars, Lieberman and Levine, have offered alternative classifications. Lieberman argues that the halakhah makes a distinction between consumer goods and capital goods.[34] Levine sees the distinction as being between situations of elastic demand vs. unelastic demand.[35] (In the latter—as, say, in the fugitive–ferryman case described below—the buyer will essentially pay any price demanded.)

Irrespective, however, of the economic grounds for these and other exemptions from the law of *ona'ah*, the ethical issue remains clear. Whenever people's basic needs are threatened, it would seem that the majority opinion applies the rule of *ona'ah*.

It is Judaism's concern with the moral questions presented by circumstances such as duress, danger to life, and the maintenance of basic economic existence that in fact determines the scope of the protection of *ona'ah*. Where there is evidence that we are dealing with pure market considerations, there is no moral necessity for this protection. So Levine explains the exemption of barter transactions (except for produce and household goods).[36]

The emergence, however, of nonmarket considerations and the ethical problems posed by them led to an extension of the law of *ona'ah* even to those goods not included by the Mishnah.

Thus, the Rosh (Asher ben Yechiel, of thirteenth-century Spain) was asked a question concerning Reuven, who bought a house from Shimon at twice the market rate. Now Reuven wants to nullify the sale, on the grounds of *ona'ah*. In his responsum, the Rosh writes as follows:

> You must be aware that the law of *ona'ah* does not exist in the sale of land. Rabbi Yitschak Alfasi [of eleventh-century North Africa] has claimed in accordance with the ruling of the Rambam that the sale of land cannot be voided even if the price is 100 percent in excess of the market price. However, Rabbenu Tam [of twelfth-century Franco-Germany] ruled that in such a case *ona'ah* exists in the case of real estate, and we should consider the sale invalid. This is the correct judgment.[37]

In our own day, this opinion of the Rosh was used as the basis for a decision of the Israeli secular courts.

The classic case of duress is the Talmudic discussion of the overcharging of a fugitive by a ferryman.[38] A ferryman transports a fugitive across the river, thereby saving him from immediate danger. Understanding his client's position, the ferryman charges him far more than the usual price. Naturally the fugitive pays, knowing full well that he is being overcharged; he really has no alternative. Despite his agreement, the fugitive is entitled to subsequently claim protection of the law of *ona'ah* and receive the price differential. In accordance with this discussion, Rabbi Joel Sirkis, of sixteenth–seventeenth-century Poland, ruled that even a sale made with full knowledge of the excessiveness of the price paid could be voided by the laws of *ona'ah* if the buyer argued that he needed the goods badly and therefore agreed under duress to the price.[39]

Viewed in the prespective of a modern, sophisticated economy, the law of *ona'ah* would seem to demand a public policy requiring full disclosure of the market prices of basic commodities.

Furthermore, in those cases where a monopolistic situation arises, even a temporary one, legal redress would have to be provided with respect to even those goods not normally considered essential ones, since the community is faced with an economic form of duress.

COMPETITION

The existence of a competitive market—or, contrariwise, of monopolies or other restrictive practices—creates a large number of ethical issues. It is true that the general public usually benefits from competition between sellers of goods and services, in the form of either lower prices or improved goods. The introduction of new technologies or the entry of new firms, also a form of competition, has a similar effect. At the same time, however, some entrepreneurs and some employees suffer a decline in profits or a loss of earnings from this same competition. These losses may be minimal and temporary, until market forces adjust themselves. They may, however, lead to the permanent disappearance of whole industries or large numbers of firms, with resultant unemployment and loss of livelihood for both workers and entrepreneurs. By and large, halakhic sources were primarily concerned with communal welfare and so encouraged a competitive market and opposed the formation of monopolies or cartels, as we will see in this section. Considerations of justice and welfare are symmetrical in Judaism, so that in those cases where a free market became destructive to the community or where great individual suffering was caused, the same sources implemented restrictive practices, which we discuss in the next section.

Price Cutting

In the Mishnah we read that

Rabbi Yehudah said, "The merchant may not distribute roasted wheat or nuts to children or to the servants, since he accustoms them to buy from him [thereby harming the business of the other traders]." However, the sages permit this practice, since the merchant can say to his competitors, "I distribute nuts, you can distribute other gifts." Rabbi Judah added: "Similarly, he may not lower his prices." [But] the sages said, "The memory of the

shopkeeper who lowers prices shall be blessed" [since he benefits the community by lowering prices].[40]

Rashi adds that the hoarders of produce will see that prices are
falling and they will sell their goods cheaply, thus adding to the
public welfare. The sages in the Talmud mention that even if the
same storekeeper suffers losses, it is the communal welfare that
has to predominate. Similarly, the sages permitted the decoration
of the shopkeeper's goods (provided the decoration is known) as a
form of price cutting. The later halakhic authorities ruled like the
sages on all the issues raised in the Mishnah.[41] It must be stressed
that price cutting is not allowed if it does not result from lower
profit margins or reduced production costs, which other firms can
emulate. This can be seen from a question addressed to Rabbi
Shaul Natanson in nineteenth-century Poland, concerning competition which flowed from nonpayment of taxes, and his response.

> *Question:* Reuven has a license to conduct a store and pays
> his taxes accordingly. His neighbor, however, does not have such
> a license, and the public authorities ignore [his nonpayment of
> taxes]. Reuven now wants to prevent his neighbor from selling
> goods.
> *Answer:* It seems to me that Reuven can prevent him if it can
> be shown that the lower prices charged by his competitor flow
> from nonpayment of taxes. Even though the *Shulchan Arukh* has
> ruled that one cannot prevent price cutting, since it is for the
> benefit of the public, this is so because the other producers wish
> to keep their prices high. In our case, however, the sole factor is
> the nonpayment of taxes, which Reuven cannot emulate; and
> therefore no benefit [to the public] accrues from the price cut
> [presumably since they lose the services paid for with the
> taxes].[42]

This general legal support for a competitive market must be
modified by the moral objection cited by the Gemara. "A poor
man was offering a cake for sale; he who offers a lower price [than
him] is called an evil one."[43] Though the sages considered under-
cutting or forestalling a poor man to be morally unjust, an action
that righteous men should avoid, nevertheless, they provided no
legal redress. This is in accord with the general principle in Judaism that distinguishes between justice and righteousness, as explained in chapter 3. We will see, however, in this chapter that
some later authorities quoted the above statement from the Ge-

mara in support of their legal decisions restricting competition, going beyond mere moral disapproval.

Free Entry

Inter-firm competition is often dependent on the right of free entry into the marketplace. This may refer to the ability to practice various professions freely, to open a new business to cater to an expected or actual demand, or to move from one geographic area to another in order to benefit from changed economic conditions. Naturally, such free entry will affect the profits and business prospects of those already established in that area or line of business, who can often earn abnormal profits through restricting supply (and hence raising prices) by, for example, preventing or limiting such free entry. The closed shop principle, licensing arrangements, and immigration laws are all forms of restriction on economic competition.

The Talmud discusses at great length the extent of the rights of house dwellers in a neighborhood to protect themselves and their property from any activity they consider harmful to their interests. While they can prevent the establishment of firms that are ecologically harmful, for example, those causing smoke or noise, they cannot prevent someone from setting up a business venture of a type that already exists, since they have, so to speak, given their consent to this type of activity. (In modern parlance, the zoning laws already provide for them.)

The sages did not accept the argument that the entry of new firms should be forbidden because they would injure existing ones. They conclude this discussion by supporting competition through free entry: "It is permitted for a man to set up shop alongside shop, bathhouse alongside bathhouse, etc., and the existing firms cannot prevent it. The new firm can argue that you conduct your business on your property and I do the same."[44] This Talmudic opinion is repeated in the rulings laid down by most of the later authorities.[45] Throughout the Middle East and Mediterranean countries one can still see similar marketing arrangements—which, apart from being exotic, produce a far more competitive market than the shopping centers common to modern town planning, with their emphasis on one firm for each type of business.

This free entry ruling, however, seems to contradict another Talmudic decision: "A fisherman can force others to withdraw a distance equal to that of a fish's swim from his nets." Similarly, existing firms should be able to prevent others from enticing their customers away by establishing similar businesses. The fisherman incident, however, has been explained as constituting a special case. Rabbenu Tam explains that as the fisherman has already set down his bait, the fish may be regarded as his. Customers, on the other hand, are free to shop wherever they wish to so that nobody can regard them as being "his" until a sale is made.[46]

One could argue that free entry of new firms or workers should be permitted in those cases wherein all concerned are citizens of the town or country concerned. In such cases, stimulation of competition is to the benefit of the whole community. If, however, the new workers or entrepreneurs are foreigners or even citizens of another town, their free entry could be seen as benefiting their home towns or countries rather than the host society. At least it could be argued that such free entry is detrimental to the native population. This question of whether work and business opportunities can be limited to local or national residents is an age-old yet ever timely one. Some Jewish biblical commentators saw the primary sin of Sodom and Gomorrah as being their exclusion of neighboring poor tribes in order to prevent them from sharing in their wealth. Medieval cities limited the movement of citizens of neighboring towns, and today most nations restrict the freedom of non-nationals to work or engage in business.

The primary source for the Jewish treatment of this subject is the Talmudic discussion between Rav Huna the son of Yehoshua and Rav Huna. Rav Huna the son of Yehoshua argued that a foreigner has the full rights of residence, including those of an economic nature, provided he pays the taxes applicable to that community; whereas Rav Huna argued that even payment of taxes did not entitle foreigners to trade.[47] The ruling of Rav Huna the son of Yehoshua became the norm in halakhic sources. To allow freedom of entry without a corresponding tax liability would be immoral as well as unfair. Applied to a contemporary context, this ruling would argue in favor of payment of city taxes by those earning their livelihood in the city but living in the suburbs.

The sages of the Talmudic period, however, allowed certain types of competition to exist even where there was no obligation to share in the tax liability. The previously cited section of *Baba*

Bathra mentions that already in the days of Ezra the Scribe (c. 500 B.C.E.), peddlers were allowed to wander from city to city without paying taxes, so that "the daughters of Israel should not lack for jewelry and cosmetics." On market days, out-of-town merchants were allowed to display their wares without becoming liable for municipal taxes, despite the complaints of local merchants. In view of the special place accorded in the Jewish value structure to the study of Torah, it is not surprising to find the halakhah encouraging similar free movement on the part of rabbinic scholars without the constraint of taxation.

All these Talmudic rulings were repeated by almost all the later codifiers of Jewish laws and form the basis of many responsa throughout the ages. Underlying them all is the basic premise that all entrepreneurs can emulate the price cutting or other forms of competition engaged in by others.[48]

The problem, however, is not only one of being permitted to operate within a community or neighborhood. As often as not the outside entrepreneurs or workers are prepared to offer their goods and services at a lower rate, and it is also this price (or wage) competition to which their local counterparts object. From a legal point of view, the halakhic issue here, too, seems to be whether living in a certain place or being engaged in a certain business creates property rights that others cannot infringe or whether some notion of the public good has to prevail.

We have seen that with regard to other local businesses, there does not seem to be such a property right, since everybody can cut prices or provide other forms of consumer inducement. With regard to "foreigners" this too seems to be the rule, where such competition is to the communal benefit.

Consider the ruling of Rabbi Joseph Ibn Migas, of eleventh-century Spain,

> that local businessmen can prevent outsiders from operating similar businesses [even if the outsiders pay the applicable taxes], provided there is no loss caused to the consumers—for example, if the outsiders sell their goods for the same price as the locals. If, however, they offer the same goods more cheaply or provide goods or services of better quality, then they cannot be prevented from operating. The reason for this is that we cannot make a ruling that will benefit part of the population [the local businessmen] at the expense of the other part [the consumers].[49]

A typical responsum regarding the price competition offered by new "foreign" firms is that of Rabbi Abraham ben Moses di Boton, of sixteenth-century Salonika.

> *Question:* Reuven, a tailor from one of the villages, has come to settle in our town. In the village his expenses were minimal and the average cost of living low, so he is accustomed to working cheaply. Now he undertakes work in our town at prices far below the prevailing price. The other tailors now complain that they are unable to match his prices because their costs are high, and he is therefore stealing his livelihood. Can they prevent him from operating here or force him to charge the same prices as they do?

Rabbi Boton's answer was a negative one.

> *Answer:* From a legal point of view, the people of the town cannot prevent Reuven from lowering his prices to half of what the others are charging. This is the opinion of Rabbi Joseph [Ibn Migas]. Even according to the Nimukei Yosef in *Baba Bathra*, who holds that Ibn Migas' rule applies only where the price differential is great, surely there cannot be a greater one than in our case. It is true that it is arguable that there are authorities who offer an opposing view. . . . Still, the argument is not very clear-cut and is therefore not sufficient to prevent Reuven's competition.[50]

It should be obvious that given the importance attached in halakhic thought to the stringent fulfillment of contracts, both written and oral, competition contrary to such contracts, whether by local newcomers or foreigners, cannot be accepted. Such a case was presented to Rabbi S. M. Shvadron in late-nineteenth-century Galicia by litigants from the Mediterranean island of Rhodes.

> *Question:* Reuven leases from the government a plant for the pressing of wool in which he processes cloth for the textile manufacturers. . . . There is an agreement between him and the manufacturers that the latter may not establish another, similar plant. Now Shimon, not one of the weavers, has gone and bought ground in order to establish such a plant. Can Reuven prevent him from doing so?

"Reuven," wrote the Rabbi in his response,

> is clearly entitled to prevent the establishment of this new plant. The agreement between him and the weavers is valid and binding, so they are obligated to have their wool processed by

Reuven. Furthermore, the plant has been established because of Reuven's initiative, enabling the weavers to increase their output and to continue to do so in the future. He has in a sense acquired rights to the output of the weavers. Shimon has to attract the same weavers to use his plant, in effect stealing from Reuven.[51]

RESTRICTIVE PRACTICES

In a complex economy, unlimited competition in various forms may easily bring human hardship and suffering despite the economic benefits derived. Often the competition is unequal, as in the case of a chain store vs. an individual storekeeper, or a corporate employer vis-à-vis an individual worker. It may well be that the market is not large enough to provide all the factors with a viable return on their investment, so that further entrants may cause widespread depression. Competition may also be unfair when an individual has made an investment in time, money, or knowledge in order to perfect a new process, create a specific article, or create commercial goodwill; the entry of new entrepreneurs exploiting the fruits may be robbing the individual of his investment. In all these cases society may be faced with such undesirable consequences as large-scale unemployment, depressed industry, and widespread bankruptcy.

It is true that in economic theory, human and financial resources adjust themselves, in the long run, to the changes brought about by competition. In reality, though, this adjustment may often take a long time and, if left to ordinary market forces, may actually never be made—and society has to pay the human and moral costs until the adjustment takes place. The social and moral values of each society will prompt legislation striking a balance between the economic loss resulting from restrictive practices and the human suffering arising out of unlimited competition.

So in Judaism, too, provisions were made for restrictive practices in order to alleviate or minimize the suffering and hardships caused by competition. These provisions had to take into account that some of the economic factors discussed earlier might no longer apply. Thus, as economies become more sophisticated, market days disappear, the marketplace becomes more formal and more involved, specialization increases, and the investment involved becomes greater. All these changes will lead to a greater demand for protection on the part of original investors. Naturally, the overall economic conditions of a particular period or community determined the degree of individual or communal hardship as well as the benefits resulting from free competition. These, in turn, defined the ethical and moral issues involved and were reflected in the consequent rabbinic legislation and communal enactments.

Restrictive Trade Agreements

Jewish law recognized as valid and binding agreements reached by the artisans or merchants of a community to restrict competition, fix prices, and determine the quantity of goods produced. We have already discussed the obligation and right of the town authorities to set prices, and it seems to be this right that gives legitimacy to such agreements.

A full discussion of trade associations (guilds), cartels, and labor unions has been postponed to chapter six, where we examine the halakhic treatment of the role of trade unions. Although unions represent employees, they are, from an economic point of view, no different from arrangements entered into by entrepreneurs. At this stage, it is sufficient merely to note the main characteristics of the halakhic attitude toward restrictive associations.

Restrictive practices usually require the agreement of all the artisans or merchants in a city (some authorities accept majority vote). Furthermore, they require the approval of a prominent personality (*adam chashuv*), who can serve as an arbitrator between the interests of the members of the trade association and the general welfare. It is only in the absence of such a person that the community council or trade association can validate a restraint-of-trade agreement.

The Talmud tells us that "some butchers made an agreement between themselves allocating specific days to each one for the sale of meat."[52] When the case came before Rabbah, he annulled the arrangement because it lacked his approval.

Hasagat G'vul

Some of the decisions in favor of restraints on competition were from the biblical commandment (Deut. 19:14) against removing a neighbor's landmark (the stones which served as the boundary markers between fields)—*hasagat g'vul*. The sages queried the purpose of such an injunction, since the Torah had already forbidden theft, which *hasagat g'vul* is. They answered that this injunction taught that whoever annexed his neighbor's domain in the Land of Israel was guilty of two transgressions—theft and *hasagat g'vul*.[53] The rabbinic legislators following this broader application expanded the concept of *hasagat g'vul* to encroachment on another's livelihood.

The moral objection voiced by Talmudic authorities against competition later became built into the legal system. Commenting in the Talmud on a verse in Ezekiel which enumerated the mark of a righteous man, Rabbi Acha, the son of Rav Chanina, saw in fringing on a neighbor's livelihood as the real meaning of defiling a neighbor's wife.[54]

In most cases the limitation on encroaching on the livelihood of one's neighbor did not apply to those cases where such competition would lead only to a decline in profitability, but primarily to cases involving the total destruction of the other's livelihood. Furthermore, the restriction was, as often as not, limited in time, in effect providing a "breathing space" until the market adjusted itself.

In 1955, Rav Yitschak Ya'akov Weiss, then the head of the rabbinic court of Manchester, England, was asked to rule on such an issue.

> *Question:* Shimon was the hired agent of Reuven, who introduced him to all his customers. Later Shimon left Reuven's employment in order to become the agent of Ya'akov, who had always been Reuven's main supplier. Now Shimon does business on his own with all of Reuven's clients. Furthermore, Ya'akov has discontinued the supply of goods to Reuven on the grounds that Reuven, contrary to their agreement, also buys goods from other suppliers. Reuven has asked us to instruct Ya'akov to refrain from supplying goods to Shimon. There exists, he argues, an understanding between Ya'akov and Shimon to deprive him of his livelihood. In his words, "Ya'akov is strengthening the hands of an evildoer [Shimon] who is guilty of transgressing his neighbor's boundary [*hasagat g'vul*]."
>
> *Answer:* You ask me for my opinion regarding the above problem. . . . My answer is as follows: He, Shimon, has eaten of Reuven's bread and knows all his trade secrets, etc., so that he is even like one who takes his very soul. . . . If Shimon refuses to refrain from dealing with Reuven's clients, the court can instruct Ya'akov to cease to supply him with goods. However, in order

not to prevent Shimon's economic advancement permanently, the court must make the restraint valid only for a certain fixed period, at the end of which all the parties are free to operate as they wish.[55]

Of special interest is the application of the concept of *hasagat g'vul* to the law of copyright and the issue of rent control.

The basic problem is that of the intangible asset that an inventor or author or tenant has acquired through the application of his intellect (or through tenure). Society has to choose between the benefits arising out of the proliferation of new technology or new books, or the provision of housing, and the cost involved in protecting the original investor. This problem arose in the Jewish world in the nineteenth century with the invention of machinery that would bake matzot (unleavened bread for Passover). A major schism developed between those rabbis who permitted the use of machine-made matzot and those, primarily the Chasidic masters, who did not—a schism that continues down to today. A main objection was the loss of income suffered by the poor—the widows and orphans who normally found employment baking matzot, thus acquiring, as it were, an interest or asset in the hand-baking process.

Halakhic sources recognized early on that theft could apply to intangible assets like copyright or goodwill or to the products of the mind, so that artists, inventors, and authors could have their property protected.[56]

Copyright

The writing and publishing of books has long been an important Jewish industry. With the invention of printing the reproduction of commentaries on the Torah and other rabbinic literature became cheap and feasible, thus depriving their original authors of a legitimate profit or royalty. On the other hand, there is a rabbinic maxim, "The jealousy of the scribes [scholars] increases knowledge"[57]—so that every step should be taken to enable the general public to obtain books as cheaply and easily as possible. Given the centrality of learning in Judaism and the importance of the publishing industry in Jewish economic life, we are clearly presented with a moral choice between these two conflicting interests.

The ban proclaimed in 1751 by the Council of Four Lands restricting publication of a new Talmud is only one of some fifty similar bans issued by that council concerned with safeguarding the copyright of authors or publishers:

> Praise be to God for the clarity and beauty of the new Talmud published by the illustrious traders Joseph and Jacob Propes Katz [publishers in Amsterdam]. They have emptied their pockets of gold . . . spared no trouble in proofreading, nor in creating a thing of beauty. . . . No man shall dare to print the Talmud before the elapse of twenty-five years from the date of its completion by them. It is true that there still remain a few years of the twenty-year ban issued on behalf of the previous publishers. Just as they encroached slightly on their predecessors, so it is permitted to encroach on them and it is not necessary to insist on the full complement of years.[58]

Such bans had legal force, as may be seen from the responsa literature. It is not clear, however, whether such protection applied where no public ban, either by a communal body or rabbinic personality, existed.

An interesting problem emerges from the responsa literature as to whether the protection is valid for the entire length of the period provided for in the ban on republication or whether the expected loss of the original publisher or author is the paramount consideration. Rabbi Mordechai Bennet (early-nineteenth-century Moravia) is quoted as follows:

> The approval [haskamah] given by the great scholars to publishers, preventing others from reprinting their books, is definitely binding, even though it is not verbal [the usual requirement for a valid oath].[59] However, when the publisher has already sold the whole of the edition, he may not prevent others reprinting the book and thus hinder the work of Heaven [i.e., the spread of learning]. This is true even if the period for which the ban was given has not yet ended, since his not losing anything thereby.[60]

It is true that the publisher could now go ahead and earn extra profits by means of a second or third edition; yet he had to forgo this in the interest of Torah study. The same source, however, quotes the opposing opinion of Rabbi Zalman Margolis (early-nineteenth-century Poland), who maintains that even if the publisher has already sold his complete edition, the ban is valid until the expiration of the original period for which it was given.[61]

Rent Control

From pre-Crusader times down to the end of the nineteenth century, the Jews of Europe were confined either to ghettos or special streets, or were restricted to certain areas of the country, as in the Pale of Settlement in Tsarist Russia. In the Moslem world, too, mellahs, or special quarters, existed, and the ability of the Jew to live where he pleased was curtailed. These restrictions severely limited the supply of houses, making their rents a matter of major communal interest. The natural increase in population, and the pressure of refugees from the periodic expulsions, increased the demand for housing, exacerbating the situation. A constant discrepancy between supply and demand created a spiraling increase in rents and often meant the dispossession of the poor. Jews would vie with one another in offering higher rentals to the Gentile landlords, and the right of occupancy became a valuable economic asset, as did the right to dwell in a certain area.

In some areas the right to marry was rationed temporarily, in view of the scarcity of housing. Sometimes, as in the Italian cities of the sixteenth century, the community would demand from the Gentile authorities a guarantee that rents would not be raised or that dwellings would not be destroyed.

So it is not surprising that the concept of *hasagat g'vul* was invoked to protect the community from the social problems caused by housing shortages. The following enactment, found in the record book (*Pinkas*) of the Jewish community of Padua and dated 1580, is typical of such communal action:

> This is to ratify our agreement to enactments which appeared in the old *Pinkas* [which had been destroyed by fire] in regard to renting houses in the ghetto from the non-Jewish owners. According to that enactment of the community (1540), the *herem* [designation of banned property] of Rabbenu Gershon applies to those who try to rent houses that are already rented to other Jews. This means that for three years after a Jew has been evicted from his house, no Jew may offer to rent the house [thus preventing constant competition between Jews, leading to increased rentals]. At the same time, we also confirm the enactment of 1575 that the legal protection of tenancy from competition only applies to the house in which one lives. In all other cases, every Jew is free to hire a house from a Gentile without fear of sin.

The Maharam of Rothenburg (thirteenth-century Franco-Germany) included at the end of his responsa a similar restriction regarding the competition for houses. He exempts from the restriction, however, those cases where the present tenant has announced his intention not to re-rent the house, or where he tries to reduce the rent. In such cases everybody is free to offer the landlord the same rent. Similarly, houses rented from another Jew are exempt from the restriction on competitive bidding, presumably on the understanding that Jews would not try to extort excessive rentals from other Jews.

Both these examples show how careful the rabbis and communal authorities were to preserve a balance between the real social needs of the community and the freedom of the individual to do with his own property whatever he considered best, within a free market mechanism. A variation dealing with the hoarding of vacant rooms or houses, in order to profit from the spiral of limited supply, constantly increasing demand, and consequent rising rentals, may be found in the communal *Pinkas* of the community of Poznan:

> Concerning the rich who maintain several empty houses and plenty of living space, . . . joining houses to house. . . . so the number of houses declines and the poor cannot find places to live. . . . the *parnassim* [communal wardens] have to prevent this. They also have to supervise and see that the tenancy is fixed and that the rentals should not be allowed to increase too rapidly.[62]

The same community had in its *Pinkas* a number of such regulations, including one in which the *parnassim* are obligated not only to supervise tenancy and rentals but also to be responsible for increasing the supply of houses. The responsa of the Chasidic Rabbi Avraham of Sochochov,[63] in nineteenth-century Poland, those of Rabbi Sasportas of seventeenth-century Amsterdam,[64] and those of Samuel di Medina of sixteenth-century Salonika[65] all dealt with the protection of tenants from rental competition arising out of overcrowding, anti-Semitic landlords, or natural phenomena.

Property Rights

Perhaps the most common and far-reaching source of restrictive halakhic decisions and communal enactments was the acquisition by an individual or a community of a monopoly, either through outright payment or as an acquired right (*chazakah*), through the passage of time or by common agreement, or by implied consent. Where such a property right exists, nobody is allowed to infringe it (by, say, operating a similar business or engaging in price competition). Much of the relevant halakhic discussion seems to revolve around the question of whether such a right actually existed in a specific case, how it may or may not have been acquired, and under what conditions it may be acquired, sold, inherited, or invalidated.

The most important types of monopoly rights are those of settlement, as exemplified by the *herem hayishuv*, and trading, like the *marufiya* or *aronda*.

Settlement Rights: *Herem Hayishuv* and *Hezkat Hayishuv* 66

Every Jewish community has always enjoyed the right to restrict the entry of undesirable or harmful elements. The question is, however, whether an individual can acquire a personal tangible right that can be bequeathed or sold and, more importantly, whether this right can be invoked where the sole issue is that of economic competition. Although the question always exists, it became most pronounced where religious anti-Semitism reduced the economic opportunities open to the Jews. In these circumstances, free entry of other Jews could only bring in its wake ruinous competition and communal suffering—so the *herem hayishuv* emerged.

This was a concept whereby the veteran settlers in a town were considered to have acquired a legal monopoly on residence and trade (*hezkat hayishuv*). Outsiders were prevented from settling and trading under threat of excommunication (*herem*) unless they obtained permission from the community. In contrast to the Talmudic decisions quoted before, willingness to pay taxes was no longer considered sufficient to allow foreigners to settle and trade. The *herem hayishuv* was widely prevalent in medieval Christian Europe (France, Germany, Italy, England) and in Eastern Europe, where it remained until the abolition of anti-Jewish discriminatory legislation at the end of the last century.

The *herem* did not exist in the Jewish communities of Spain, North Africa, and the Middle East. These countries of the Moslem world did not develop the stratified structure of feudal Europe, nor did they place the same economic restrictions on Jews. Here, the Talmudic principle of free entry by residents of foreign towns, provided they paid their taxes, was still upheld.

It must be remembered that Judaism is not an economic system. The purpose of halakhic rulings throughout the ages was to minimize injustice and promote maximum public welfare. Under the conditions emerging in Christian Europe, this could best be done by asserting the monopoly rights of veteran settlers, whereas in Moslem countries competition through free entry was in the communities' best interest.

The scope and severity of the concept of the *herem hayishuv* can be gauged from the edict of the Jewish council of Padua, Italy, proclaimed in 1583:

> Seeing as how the possibilities for earning a livelihood in our town are severely limited and seeing as how the economic facilities to provide for the members of our community are very limited; in addition to this we are worried that some of the people who will come and live here, who are not upright and moral, may, God forbid, destroy our society and cause us embarrassment (with the Gentile neighbors), therefore we have decided that no Jew, from this day on, can come and live here, open a business or earn his livelihood, irrespective of whether he comes as the head of a household or as an individual man or woman [without our permission]. This includes even those who lived here and went away and are now returning. The edict includes the [extended] families of those who are already settled here. All those who will not observe this edict will not be able to participate in the slaughtering of kosher food and will have to be ostracized from the community. We will refuse to circumcise his son, we will not go to his festive celebrations, and in the synagogue on Mondays and Thursdays, he will be announced as a renegade until he repents and observes this edict.[67]

An edict emphasizing the moral and spiritual aspects of free entry, passed in Oxford, England, in the twelfth century, is discussed in the chapter on welfare. That edict has no reference to economic issues; however, almost all of the European communities had restrictive regulations, with additional economic motivations similar to the one of Padua quoted above.

The halakhic treatment of the restrictive regulations of the *herem hayishuv* is not clear-cut. There are supporters and opponents of the economic monopoly rights of veteran settlers. It must

be remembered that, where they existed, these rights were real eco-
omic assets that could be bought and bequeathed. This is quite
clearly stated in a responsum by the Sages of Rome to the heads of
the Paris community. In the case concerned, the injured party
claims, ''I am a citizen of this city, whereas you are a citizen of another one. I am opposed to your engaging in business here any-
more. I only gave you on loan the right to benefit from my inheritance [namely, the right to trade].''[68]

Writing in Germany in the late thirteenth century, Mordechai
ben Hillel Hakohen saw the *herem* as a rabbinical ruling dating
back to Rabbenu Gershon Me'or Hagolah (c. 800 C.E.). Its legitimacy flowed from the authority of the rabbis to make such injunctions, so that the lack of Talmudic sanction was not a detracting
factor.[69] His teacher, Meir of Rothenburg, maintained that custom
(always a powerful factor in Jewish law) and logic (in view of the
narrow basis of Jewish economic life in the feudal system) were
sufficient to give this monopoly legal status.[70]

Other halakhic authorities, however, held that there was actually no basis for a monopoly right belonging to veteran settlers.
The prime objection was that it contradicted the ruling (cited earlier) of Rav Huna the son of Yehoshua, making the right of settlement solely dependent on payment of communal taxes. This
opinion was codified in all the major codes (Rambam's *Mishneh
Torah*, the *Turim*, and the *Shulchan Arukh*); thus: ''The citizens of
a certain community cannot claim to have acquired a legal asset in
the form of the sole right of settlement, and, therefore, they cannot restrict the entry of others. (This is contingent, of course, on
the newcomers' willingness to accept their share of the tax burden.)''[71]

Rabbenu Tam, the grandson of the great medieval biblical and
Talmudic commentator Rashi, objected to the use of a valid *moral*
protective device, the restriction of settlement, for economic purposes.[72] The Rashba, Shlomo ben Aderet, writing in thirteenth-
century North Africa, writes in one of his responsa that ''the new
settler has full rights to housing and a livelihood, provided he participates in the tax burden.''[73] Rabbinic decisions through the centuries continued the controversy regarding the application of the
herem, with some authorities upholding it and others ruling
against it.

There are two categories of would-be Jewish settlers, however,
to whom, there seems to be a consensus, the monopoly rights of
veteran settlers do not apply: viz., refugees and religious teach-

ers. As a result of persecution and expulsion, the refugee has been a common feature of Jewish history, from the feudal period down to the present. Over and above the individual problems involved, Jewish refugees posed a twofold challenge to the host community: (a) the economic problem caused by the need to provide for their welfare, which, as often as not, included their competing with local settlers for a livelihood; and (b) the political and social problems of upsetting the delicate balance vis-à-vis the Gentile surroundings by the admission of large numbers of Jews. Both these factors would make it quite natural for the veteran settlers to try to prevent the admission of refugees.

At the same time, however, the communal orientation of Judaism, with its emphasis on mutual responsibility and acts of loving kindness and mercy, militated against the exclusion of refugees. The common communal practice, in accordance with halakhic rulings, was to freely admit refugees and allow them to trade and earn a livelihood. Nevertheless, they were often restricted, at least temporarily, to a minimal economic existence in order to minimize their competitive impact.

So the Rama writes that "the people who fled from a city because of danger may not be prevented from earning a (minimal) livelihood till the danger passes. The newcomers have to participate in the tax burden according to their minimal trade [and not from their capital]."[74]

The clash between economic self-interest, on the one hand, and the claims of mercy and halakhic rulings, on the other, is reflected in the decisions of the Lithuanian Council in the seventeenth century. In the first decades of the century, the council introduced a number of regulations in the spirit of *hezkat hayishuv* (legal right to settle). These prevented Jews from Poland settling in Lithuania without permission and threatened those entering without such permission with expulsion or invalidation of their acquired rights. Even local Jews were restricted in their movements in order to minimize economic competition. In the middle of the century, however, the Chmielnicki terror destroyed major portions of Eastern European Jewry and caused a flood of refugees. So in 1655 the council ruled that "no community can prevent the refugees from settling nor force them to leave." Later, at the end of the century, the same council admitted refugees from Cracow and released them from all taxes, but did not allow them to settle or trade within the major communities.[75]

Contrariwise, it seems from the sources that the action of the Jewish community of Rome, preventing the settlement of the Spanish refugees after the expulsion in 1492, was a deviation from the Jewish norm.[76]

The treatment of the free movement of rabbis and scholars is another example of where the specific value structure of Judaism limited the protection afforded to local interests. Since study of the Torah is a basic religious precept, obligatory on all and unlimited in time, the spiritual welfare of the community demanded the maximum availability of Torah teachers. Since the rabbinate was an important segment of Jewish economic life, however, economic considerations also arose—such as the effect of the free entry of scholars on the livelihood of the established ones. The communal interest, however, took precedence, since, in the words of the Talmud, "the zealousness of scribes [scholars] increases knowledge."[77]

So we find most authorities disallowing restrictions on the free movement and educational work of rabbinic scholars. At the same time, there were rabbis like the Chatam Sofer, in nineteenth-century Hungary, who prohibited this free competition in those cases where the livelihood of the resident scholar was endangered. This was done in accordance with an accepted principle that ruinous competition, as distinct from lowered profits or reduced earnings, was not to be allowed.[78]

Marufiya and *Aronda*

Until the modern period, much of the economy, both Jewish and general, was conducted under license from the secular or ecclesiastical authorities. Royal charters, feudal licenses, and monopolistic privileges were the basis for most business undertakings. The Jewish economy was especially dependent on such licensing arrangements in the fields of banking and moneylending, tax collecting, equipping and provisioning of armies, and trading in slaves, spices, and luxury goods. Even in more mundane businesses, like textiles, the right to operate was dependent on permission from the local political authorities.

The halakhic authorities saw these monopolistic rights as acquired property rights and therefore as deserving of protection. These rights became known as *marufiya*, from the Arabic meaning literally "a constant friend"—in our context, a permanent business associate. In Eastern Europe, where monopolistic rights existed until the beginning of this century, they were known as *aronda* and became primarily associated with the sale of liquor. Generally speaking, *marufiya* described the relationship between a Jewish entrepreneur and the Gentile authority, not on a racial or national basis, but on the basis of the possession of a monopolistic economic good.

There was a lack of consistency in halakhic cognizance of this monopolistic right, as shown in the thirteenth-century rulings of Mordechai Hakohen. "There are places [in the Jewish world] where the principle of *marufiya* is accepted, as I have seen in the responsa of Rabbi Joseph Tav Elem [Bonfils, an early rabbinic authority in Franco-Germany in the eleventh century], and in others it is not recognized. Where it is not recognized, every Jew may go to the *marufiya* [meaning, here, the source of the monopoly] and lend him money or bribe him to obtain these rights held by another Jew. There is no theft involved, since the property of the Gentiles is available to all [to trade in].[79]

It seems, however, that, by and large, this monopolistic right became the accepted norm in medieval Western Europe and later in the countries of Eastern Europe.

The moral basis for the protection of these monopolistic rights is the objection to forestalling. Since monopolistic rights create abnormal profits, there is a constant incentive for others to approach the source of the right and offer a higher price, thus forestalling the present owner. As explained previously, the rabbis, basing themselves on the Talmudic dictum of "A poor man was negotiating for the sale of a cake, and he who forestalls him is called an evil person,"[80] objected to this practice.

The halakhic principles behind the *marufiya* may be gleaned from a responsum of Rabbi Joseph ben Shlomo Colon, written in Italy in the late fifteenth century in reply to the following question.

> *Question:* Reuven spent money on making arrangements with the ruler of the city in order to be allowed to establish a store and to engage in moneylending. He was delayed for four years and unable to move to that city and operate that business. Now Shimon has also obtained a similar license for the same business. Reuven, as is customary in Jewish communities, has complained in the synagogue against Shimon, claiming that he

is threatening his livelihood. Can he force Shimon to renounce the license?

Rabbi Colon's ruling in favor of Reuven argued that

> Shimon has forestalled that which Reuven is in the midst of purchasing. Shimon can set up a similar business elsewhere without any loss. Unless Shimon can show that his profit margins here are substantially higher than in another city, he can be prevented from operating without Reuven's consent. Reuven has made a considerable investment in time and money. Shimon, by obtaining a permit to lend money, is, in effect, preventing the original investor, Reuven, from conducting his business, thus destroying his livelihood.[81]

The Talmudic case (as explained by Rabbenu Tam) requiring fishermen to move their nets the distance of a fish's swim from one already cast, was the basis for Colon's decision. Rabbenu Tam holds that such restrictions can be applied because the other fishermen are destroying the livelihood of the first (as distinct from reducing it), and because the fish gather on account of an action taken (i.e., an investment made) by the first.[82]

In modern times, these halakhic principles for granting such monopoly rights might serve as a guideline in those industries, such as public transportation, telecommunications, and utilities, that require massive investment and a long period of time for the investment to be recouped.

RESPONSA DEALING WITH COMPETITION

A fuller idea of the currents of halakhic thought regarding the issue of competition may be gained from the following samples of responsa. They represent different degrees of acceptance of the free market mechanism and of the ability of individuals to frustrate free entry of competitors.

Rabbi Meir, Maharam of Rothenburg (Germany, Thirteenth Century)

Question: Reuven and his sons claim to have received permission to settle in town T, and they also show undisturbed settlement for more than three years. Shimon claims that Reuven and his sons received no such permission and that the only reason they were not disturbed was because they were informers and he was afraid of them.

Answer: Since Reuven and his sons claim to have received permission to settle in T, and also show three years of undisturbed settlement, they have the right to dwell in T, and to prevent all newcomers from settling in T without their permission. If, however, Shimon proves that Reuven and his sons are informers, the latter cannot claim undisturbed settlement. If only Reuven was proven to be an informer, his sons may still claim undisturbed settlement for themselves if their claim is entirely independent of that of their father.[83]

David ben Shlomo ibn Abi Zimra (Radbaz) (Egypt, 1479–1573)

Question: The matter concerns Reuven, who rented the monopoly of the local tax collection from the king for a period of three years. After a short period, Shimon came and demanded a share of the monopoly. Otherwise he would add to the price paid to the king, for such is the custom that whoever pays more can dispossess the former monopolist. Reuven, afraid to lose the whole business, agreed to give Shimon a third of his locality. Later Reuven bought Shimon's share at a low price, on the understanding that this sum would be a loan. Now that the loan has reached maturity, Reuven refuses to pay, saying that the whole transaction was conducted under duress.

Answer: It seems clear to me that Shimon did wrong by endangering the livelihood of his neighbor, and is deserving of punishment and of being known as an "evildoer." This is especially so since there exists in Egypt (amongst the Jews) a well-established communal enactment, confirmable by excommunication, that no Jew may rent, or offer a higher rental for, a house or store occupied by another Jew. In those cases where the time for a tax license has elapsed, no one in Israel may make efforts to replace the original owner of the concession. If, however, new conditions are instituted for such a concession, after the elapse of time allotted by the king, another Jew may buy it and not be guilty of evildoing.[84]

Rabbi Joel Sirkis (The Bach) (Poland, 1561–1640)

Question: The case was brought as to who had rights to the wine-selling license granted by the local ruler: the *kehilah* [Jewish community] or the individuals who presently held the license. The individuals had, until then, paid annual license fees to the ruler and a fee to the *kehilah*. The *kehilah* now wished to use the license for the welfare of the community and claimed that they had only "leased" it until then. The present holders of the license claimed that this contravened the laws of the state of Lita [Lithuania] and that the *kehilah* had lost its right to the license by demanding an additional payment, thus infringing an arrangement that had been in force for many years.

Answer: The *kehilah* has the right to the license, since they have always held it from the owner. The principle of not interfering with another's livelihood (*hasagat g'vul*), which may restrain them, applies, however, only to competition between individuals. It cannot be used when weighing the good of the many against that of the few, as in our case. Furthermore, it would be better if the *kehilah* distributed the right to sell wine among a large number of people instead of giving a livelihood only to a few. The laws of the state of Lita in this respect are destructive rather than helpful and therefore cannot be used as a basis for protection.[85]

Rabbi Mordechai Ettinger (Poland, 1804–63)

Question: A complaint was brought by the surrounding villages against the inhabitants of a city who had influenced their ruler to prohibit the "import" of the cheaper wine supplied by the villagers.

Answer: The *din* [judgment] is with the inhabitants of the city. After all, the producers of the wine in the city have to pay a tax to the Jewish community [who leased the wine-making facilities from the overlord and then sublet them for a higher fee], and it is this tax that makes their wine more expensive. In our case, the villagers cannot rely on the ruling of the sages in the Mishnah, who, contrary to Rabbi Yehuda, allowed price competition—even though [generally] the law is according to the sages. The Mishnah is discussing a case where the competitor can say to the other merchants, "If I can reduce prices, so can you." Here, however, the sole cause of the higher prices charged is the tax levied on the city producers, who are therefore not able to reduce their prices to match those of the village wine producers [who are not liable to the tax.][86]

Rabbi Zalman Margolis (Poland, Early Nineteenth Century)

Question: A group of merchants have asked me to order the closure of the new stores that their competitors have opened. These stores are more convenient than those owned by the plaintiffs, and therefore they claim that their livelihood is being reduced.

Answer: There is, however, no reason to restrict the activities of the newcomers. In addition to concerning ourselves about the welfare of the existing firms, surely we are obliged to consider those people whose only opportunity to earn a livelihood is by opening stores for food and allied goods? Surely we cannot prevent them from doing so and thereby cause them to be without a livelihood? The argument that "We came first" is not a valid one, since the competitors cannot be made to lose simply because they came late. Furthermore, according to the law of the country, everybody is free to open a business where he likes, provided the place is suitable.[87]

Rabbi Chaim ben Mordechai Ephraim Fischel Sopher (Hungary, 1821–1886)

Question: The sellers of liquor in two villages complained that a competitor in a nearby village was selling at a lower price, thereby ruining their business.

Answer: If he is selling to all comers at the same price then it is permissible, provided that his lower price is not ruinous [based on the principle that the plaintiff, too, can reduce their prices to meet this competition]. However, he is forbidden to charge some buyers a lower price and others a higher one [thereby financing the price competition as a discriminating monopolist would do].[88]

Rabbi Moshe Feinstein (New York, 1895–1986)

Question: The case concerns some of the founding worshippers of a synagogue in New York, who have left their synagogue in order to start another one nearby. The rabbi, to whom the synagogue belongs, claims that they thereby deprive him of his livelihood and cause him financial loss, since he cannot sell his synagogue except at a great loss. It is now worthless as a synagogue, and its renovation as a dwelling would entail great expense. [The arguments of the worshipers regarding the drawbacks of their former rabbi and synagogue are irrelevant to our discussion.]

Answer: The worshippers [or anybody else, for that matter] had no right to found another synagogue nearby. This is a case of *hasagat g'vul* and of one who infringes his neighbor's livelihood. In a situation where the market is not big enough for both of them, this law applies even to those of the same neighborhood, even according to Rav Huna. [Infringing the livelihood of his neighbor refers not to subsistence earnings, but depends on the socioeconomic status of the plaintiff. Rashi considers that even a reduction in the standard of living of a competitor would not be allowed—not merely a total loss. The Chatam Sofer would prevent the entry of a new firm if it would reduce established firms' earnings below the average earnings of their peer group.]

In our case, the permission granted by the sages to allow such competition on the basis of "I do within my property as I wish, and you may do as you wish within yours" does not apply. That permission is granted in such cases where restriction on competition would result in a loss on the part of the new entrant. However, in our case, no such commercial loss is going to be suffered by preventing the establishment of a new synagogue. In spiritual matters we have a ruling in *Yoreh De'ah* that whereas it is possible for another rabbi to gather pupils, in order to spread Torah, this is restricted to those cases where there is no infringement on the livelihood of the rabbi already entrenched in the community.[89]

Bet Din, Tel Aviv–Yaffo (Israel, 1957)

Question: Reuven has signed an agreement with the newspaper *Yediot Achronot* to reprint and sell books of the Talmud. The newspaper subsequently canceled the agreement and made a similar deal with Shimon. Reuven claims protection against *hasagat g'vul*.

Answer: We have decided against Reuven, as there is no justification for applying the protection of *hasagat g'vul*. We considered the Talmudic case of Reuven, who has a shop in the closed end of a street closed on three sides. When he wishes to prevent Shimon from opening a similar business on the open side, there are two opposing views: Rav Huna, who says he can prevent Shimon, and Rav Huna son of Yehoshua, who says he cannot. The ruling of Aviasef . . . appears to accord with Rav Huna. In that case, while Reuven has a store on the closed end, Shimon wishes to open a store at the open end. This means that customers will pass Shimon's store before reaching Reuven's. Aviasef decided that Reuven could prevent Shimon from opening the store. Rav Huna son of Yehoshua would agree in this case, as Reuven's livelihood is being completely cut off.

The Chatam Sofer, however, interpreted that Aviasef's decision applies only to stores such as those where the storeowner calls out to the customers, enticing them to buy from him, and so cuts off the first storeowner's livelihood completely. In other stores, however, such as tailor shops, where the owner does not call out, the opening of a new store cannot be prevented. Based on the Chatam Sofer, we interpret Aviasef as applying only to cases where there are objective conditions which prevent customers from reaching the other store. It is true that one may see Aviasef's decision as applying to any case where the store-owner's livelihood is cut off and not just reduced, as does the Rama.[90] In that case, argues the Rama, even Rav Huna the son of Yehoshua would agree that the competition can be prevented. The Chatam Sofer also adopts this approach and adds that even if Reuven has an alternative profession or if he is a rich man, he still has the right to stop Shimon.[91]

We have decided, however, that Reuven's case is not similar to a street closed on three sides, and it is not clear that the plaintiff's livelihood is being completely cut off, as in that case. Even if the cases were similar, since the most important *poskim* [rabbinic decisions] do not agree with Aviasef's decision, which is not mentioned in the *Shulchan Arukh*, Reuven cannot prevent the newspaper and Shimon from carrying out their project.[92]

SUMMARY

The major concern underlying the Jewish approach to the question of prices, profits, and competition is the welfare of the community. The free market was generally seen as an efficient and pragmatic mechanism for achieving this. Where this was not so, however, intervention and distortion of the mechanism was insisted upon—despite the legitimacy in Judaism of the profit motive and entrepreneurial activity generally.

Communities were empowered to institute price controls and to shorten the chain of marketing in essential goods. Where an equilibrium price existed, legal redress could be had for overcharging one-sixth above or below the market price. Such redress was available to both buyer and seller. Although applying primarily to essential goods, *ona'ah* was extended, under certain circumstances, to investment and other goods. The "just price" concept in Judaism is primarily concerned with the free flow of information, and many authorities held that if there is full disclosure it does not apply.

Generally speaking, competition between sellers is beneficial, so prizes, advertising, price cutting, etc., are allowed and even encouraged. Other forms of competition, such as free entry for new enterprises, both local and foreign, are also permissible.

In those cases, however, where competition would be immoral

or injurious, the halakhah allowed for restrictive practices. Price agreements, market sharing, and cartels are allowed, provided they are supervised by a distinguished communal personality, if there is one in the community.

Until the modern period, much of the world economy was based on monopoly rights granted by the secular or political authorities. These rights were recognized as real assets and protected by halakhic authorities as such, where the first entrepreneur had made an investment in time, money, or intellect, and provided there was a definite danger of loss of livelihood on the part of the injured party, as distinct from a decline in profitability.

CHAPTER 6

Wages and Labor

INTRODUCTION

Strictly speaking labor is an economic resource, whose price (wages) and use (employment) are fixed by the same laws as govern those of other resources. In reality, however, the fact that labor is a resource consisting of human beings, with all the consequences that flow from that, has not only affected the practical aspects of labor relations and wage policies but has also given rise to special economic theories.

Nowhere else in the whole field of economics is the admixture of psychology, human welfare, and economic self-interest more prevalent than in the matter of labor and wages. Ethical and human issues assert themselves in such a way that what starts out as an exercise in costs, supply and demand, and profits becomes an inseparable compound of morality and economics. A few examples should suffice to illustrate the scope of the problem.

1. Classical economic theory holds that even though there may be disruptions of the economy as a result of changes in demand, supply, or prices, in the long run the various factors of production will adjust themselves to the changed situation. Given the reality, though, of effects on real people, this adjustment period may be far too long and difficult for a society to allow market forces to operate on their own. Thus, workers in an industry that cannot, for technological or other reasons, compete with foreign firms in the same industry or with local substitute industries

could theoretically transfer to other trades or geographic areas. The truth of the matter, however, is that in a democratic society this is not so simple. Moving to another area can often be impossible in human terms, even where it makes sense in economic terms. Retraining or discovering new skills may be impossible owing to age, or to limitations of technical knowledge or intellectual ability on the part of the workers. Naturally, society can ignore these human problems and wait for market forces to finally produce an equilibrium. Whether society does this or not will depend on its ethical and moral framework.

2.   People who lose their jobs through no fault of their own can in most modern economies receive unemployment insurance, sufficient to provide minimally for themselves and their families. Sometimes, it is claimed, these benefits are so high so as to discourage their re-employment. Be that as it may, the reality is that unemployment does not merely mean the loss of an economic asset (namely, income); it also affects people's estimates of their value to society. A man who has to explain to his wife and children that at the age of thirty-five he is redundant faces a human problem far greater perhaps than the material one.

3.   It is simply not true that men work only for the economic benefits represented by their wages. Work often reflects a person's intellectual, emotional, and artistic aspirations, so that the supply of labor is not determined only by wages. Neither, for that matter, is the relationship between worker and employer the result only of buying and selling a factor of production. Terms of employment influence, consciously and unconsciously, the political, social, and educational structure of any society, so that changes in that structure may necessitate changes in labor practice and wages.

Present-day economic thought is very insistent on this aspect of labor relations, as may be seen in the ongoing discussions in most Western countries regarding profit sharing, worker participation in decision making, increasing productivity through reducing boredum, and so on. As a result, we find experiments in Germany with trade union participation in management that reflect the opinion that improvements in wages and working conditions are insufficient to satisfy workers' needs. For the same reason, Sweden's Volvo plants have pioneered a production line involving group participation—a reversal of Henry Ford's assembly line—to cope with boredom and declining productivity. Yugoslavia's worker–management cooperation has been widely studied as reflecting a cross-fertilization of private enterprise and social control. Japan's paternalistic, perhaps almost feudalistic, employment structure, with its assurance of full employment, annual wage-bonus system, and high degree of worker loyalty, is being touted as a reason for the constantly high productivity rates achieved there by industry. The economic effect of these examples is beyond the scope of this book. These examples are presented only to show some effects of social and cultural factors on terms of employment.

The importance of the halakhic treatment of this subject lies therefore not in its determination of wages but in its contribution to the problems of workers' protection and workers' rights and obligations.

Perhaps it is appropriate at this stage to mention that throughout the Jewish Diaspora there has always existed a Jewish working class.[1] Naturally, its size was primarily a function of the size of the local Jewish population and the overall economic development of the surrounding society. Small groups of Jews would tend, as with many marginal minorities, to be heavily represented in commercial, professional, and financial occupations, whereas amongst major concentrations of Jews, workers of all types, skilled and unskilled, were found. One should, however, neither exaggerate the existence of a Jewish working class, as was done by many secular socialist historians (e.g., Mahler), nor negate it, as was done by secular Zionist thinkers (e.g., Borochov). After all, no large concentration of people can exist solely as a mercantile or financial class, and during most periods of Jewish history, this was true of Jewish communities as well. It is obvious that in those countries like Western Europe, where legislation prevented Jews from owning land, farming was not a Jewish occupation. But in Islamic countries and even in Eastern Europe, Jewish farming existed. Furthermore, the autonomy enjoyed by most Jewish communities over long periods of time necessitated a substantial bureaucracy of judges, clerks, tax officers, teachers, etc., in addition to those employed in providing religious services, such as rabbis and ritual slaughterers. Most communities also employed a doctor, watchmen, market officials to supervise weights, measures, and prices, and bookkeepers; the private sector also offered employment and there were always self-employed artisans and professionals. So the occupational distribution of Jews was typically far from stereotyped.

A CONCEPTUAL FRAMEWORK

The basic framework of Judaism's treatment of the array of questions arising out of the employer–employee relationship would seem to be defined on the factors presented below. These factors, I argue, constitute a particularly Jewish approach to labor relations and working conditions.

1. The employer-employee relationship is a specific instance of contractual rights and obligations binding free agents. All legal factors applying to contracts—regarding, e.g., duress, withdrawal, and litigation—apply here. It should be noted that there is no element to the relationship beyond the buying and selling of services. The employer has no political, social, or personal claims on his workers.

2. The worker is entitled to special protection regarding his wages and working conditions over and above the normal legalisms regarding contracts. Halakhic sources understood that as a result of his dependence on his wages, the worker is far more vulnerable to delays, legal snarls, and sudden changes in the marketplace and has to be protected. At the same time, Judaism's symmetry in justice is reflected in its insistence that the worker has obligations as well—primarily, to render honest value for wages received. There is no justification for defrauding an employer—not even that of class struggle.

3. A major form of protection is that granted by custom. Thus, custom usually provides the worker with fringe benefits over and above the wages agreed upon, even where such benefits are not explicit in a contract.

WAGES

There does not seem to be any trace of a Marxist labor theory of value in the Jewish concept of wages. The worker is not seen as the sole contributor to the value of goods or services but as one of the factors of production whose price (wage) is to be determined by a market mechanism. It would seem from the following quotations that the Talmudic sages understood that it is the shortage or availability of workers and the need which the entrepreneur has for them that are the primary factors involved in determining wages.

> The hire of a driver who loads his wagon and delivers it to the proper place is not the same as the hire of one who did not find any load; and the same is the case with laborers who are engaged in work all day compared with those who are idle the whole day.
>
> To what extent may [the entrepreneur] increase the hire? To the amount of forty to fifty *zuz*, provided there are no other laborers to hire for a lower price.
>
> If one hired laborers to wet his fields and in the middle of the day the river from which the water was to be taken ceased to flow, this is an accident the laborers have to suffer [regarding the loss of their wages, since the employer no longer needs them]. If, however, this happens frequently, the employer must suffer.[2]

Actually the rabbis saw the employment of workers simply as a specific example of "hiring" (*s'khirut*)—and, indeed, the discussion of hiring workers in the Talmud precedes those dealing with the hiring of fields, goods, or work animals. This means that all the rabbinic principles concerning cancellation of contracts, duress, prices, etc., apply to the employer–employee relationship, which is seen (all other things being equal) as one entered into freely by both parties. Without getting bogged down in legal details, this contractual character must constantly be borne in mind if we are to understand the nature of Judaism's approach to wages.

At no time is there any concept in Judaism of buying anything but the worker's services. He is not obligated to be servile to his master, nor is there any necessity for loyalty other than the obligation to fulfill honestly what he contracted to do. There is no hint in any of the sources of a class distinction between employer and employee. Even if, in reality, there obviously existed differences between rich and poor, these were not considered intrinsic in a way analogous to the "two nations" of Disraeli's England or the class struggle concept of the Communist philosophers. Rav Kook, the first Chief Rabbi of the Land of Israel, makes this quite clear in his inveighing against the attempt to divide the Jews into proletariat and exploiters—left and right—which characterized the socialist movements during the pre-state days of modern Israel. Such a division, he held, destroyed a basic tenet of Judaism—viz., the unity of the Jewish people.[3]

Indeed, an examination of the status of the Hebrew slave (*eved Ivri*)—one who sold himself because of poverty or was sold in order to repay damages arising out of theft—will show that the purchase of a slave was nothing more than receipt of the capitalized value of his work over a period of time. If this was the Jewish concept of slavery, how much more so must such limits apply to the worker–employer relationship?

Since the basis for wages is a normal contract made by free agents, both sides can withdraw under certain circumstances. In halakhic terms, a contract commences only when some action is performed, so that both sides can retract before the work commences. An act of God, such as a flood, considered to be duress, likewise can invalidate a contract. However, under no circumstances can the breaking of a contract be at the expense of the other party. Furthermore, the sanctity of a contract applies to both verbal and written ones. Where there is no explicit contract, local custom is regarded as the substitute. Jewish law even obligates an employer to pay for work done without his request or knowledge, the only legal issue being the level of wages to be paid.

Even though both sides may, under certain conditions, retract from their contracts without being liable for financial payment, nevertheless the halakhah recognizes the moral issue involved. After all, such retraction means breaking one's word. So the injured party is entitled to *taromet* (resentment), over and above any financial redress. This public sanction of resentment, normally regarded as an evil trait, is Judaism's weapon against the creation of an ideological and spiritual atmosphere in which obligations can be ignored, or discharged merely by a financial penalty. Intangible though it may be, it would seem that such peer group pressure and public disapproval would be a powerful factor in achieving honest business conditions in general, and honest labor relations in particular.

Maimonides codified as law this moral disapproval:

> If the owner hired workers and they wish to withdraw, [each may do so] they have no [financial] claims against each other except *taromet*. . . . [This applies where the work wasn't commenced, since labor contracts in halakhah become valid only upon commencement of work or allied actions such as traveling to the place of work.] In those cases where the workers would have been able to find alternative employment if the owner had not hired them, and now as a result of his retraction they are un-

employed, the owner has to pay them the wages of a *poel batel*
[the amount of money one would pay to enjoy a day of leisure].[4]

Bearing in mind the symmetry of justice in Judaism, it is not
surprising that the same source rules that when workers renege
on a contract the same rule of *taromet,* and financial compensation
when a monetary loss is caused, applies.

It is interesting to note that Maimonides stresses that workers
can stop their work in the middle of the day, since they are not
bondsmen or slaves. Both employer and employee are servants of
the Lord, and therefore the mere act of employment cannot be
construed as a loss of freedom of action. Naturally, *taromet,* in
those cases where no loss is involved, or compensation, where
there is a financial loss, still applies. Maimonides was simply underscoring the Jewish distinction between the status of hired labor
and the condition of servitude.

This distinction is not always to the worker's benefit. For example, the Hebrew bondsman may not be made to perform demeaning tasks, nor may he be subject to "rigorous labour" (Lev.
25:43); perhaps this is an act of *chesed* (lovingkindness) to compensate the bondsman for his loss of freedom. The wage earner,
on the other hand, is a free agent whose labor has been sold according to a contract entered into without duress; he, therefore,
can be made to perform the most demeaning task or to perform
according to the most rigorous standards, if these are agreed upon
in the contract or are part of normal working conditions.[5] (This
does not apply, however, to work that is harmful to his health, as
is explained later in this chapter.)

Nonfinancial Benefits

In addition to monetary wages, remuneration can also take the
form of the nonfinancial benefits accruing to a worker through his
working conditions and fringe benefits. Important as they were
even in early periods of Jewish history, such benefits would seem
to be of greater importance today. In societies providing only a
minimal standard of living, ordinary wages are the essential and
dominant factor. In the modern world, however, considerations
such as vacation, sick leave, and health insurance have become as
important as, if not more important than, wages. This may be

seen from the content of labor negotiations and the cause of strikes in various countries. Actually there seems to be no limit to the forms of nonfinancial benefits, except for the imagination of the workers' representatives.

Halakhic sources see the accepted fringe benefits prevalent at a given time or place, or in a given industry, as having the legal status of part of the total reimbursement of the employee. This understanding is not something special to labor relations but flows from the decisive role of local custom in halakhic decisions regarding all economic activities (taxation, trade, inheritance, etc.), where the rabbinic function was primarily to see that religious and moral principles were not violated. Custom may also be seen as protecting the ignorant, careless, or weaker party.

So we read in the Mishnah that "in those places where it is customary for the workers to eat [at the expense and time of the employer, the employer] must provide for them. [In those places] where it is customary to provide sweetmeats [desserts], [the employer] must provide them."[6] Regarding hours of employment, the same source tells us that "one cannot compel his employees to come earlier or depart later than is customary at that place." The *Shulchan Arukh* ruled that deviations from local customs, in exchange for additional payment, depended on mutual prior agreement.[7]

Perhaps the greatest example of a nonfinancial benefit to which a worker is entitled is the right to eat of the fruits with which he is working. It is true that today's society is primarily a nonagricultural one, which would seem to limit the importance of this right. The extension of this right to many aspects of food production does not do very much to make it applicable to the majority of workers engaged in other forms of manufacturing, trade, finance, and service industries. Nevertheless, even apart from its importance in those industries to which it applies, it would seem that examination of this law yields very important principles that must be applied to labor relations in all industries.

In various places the Torah tells us that one who enters a vineyard or field (and the oral tradition is that this only applies to a worker) may eat of the produce therein. Rabbinic law limited this injunction to include only the produce of the soil, and then only to the extent that it was still in the stages of processing (i.e., not in a completed form). This meant, for example, that grapes could be eaten until they were transformed into wine or that dough could be eaten until baked.[8] Local custom, however, could extend this right.

The limitations on the worker's right to eat of the produce are perhaps more important in the modern period than the right itself. This is especially so since one of the major moral issues in labor relations today (though one rarely raised) concerns the obligations of the worker. Since Judaism is consistently and constantly concerned with the pursuit of justice, it is not surprising to find that the rights of the employer—and, hence, the obligations of the worker—are carefully enunciated even in the discussion of the right of the employee to eat his fill, or for that matter any other benefit, monetary or otherwise, accruing to him. Thus, Maimonides rules that "he who idles away his time by eating [i.e., not during the time allotted to it] or who eats in an illegal fashion or who takes of the fruit and gives it to other people [who are not entitled to it] is guilty. . . ."[9] In the same chapter Maimonides cautions the worker that he may not eat like a glutton, since the Torah granted him the right only to eat his fill. And realizing that defrauding the employer could even take the form of piety, the rabbis instituted a shortened form of grace after meals, "in order that they should not detract from the work of the employer."[10] All these examples are specific extensions and refinements of the general injunction to the worker, as to everybody else, against stealing.

In our day of corporate expense accounts, fringe benefits, and company cars for use on vacation, it is impossible to overemphasize this halakhic insistence on the worker using the benefits allotted to him according to the pertinent conditions. In halakhah, there is no gray area between right and wrong even in this aspect of labor relations.

PROTECTION OF WORKERS' RIGHTS

In view of the Torah's consistent protection of the weak, even beyond the strict requirements of justice, it is not surprising to find a number of halakhic rulings in this vein which serve to protect workers' interests. As workers' welfare was the primary object of such legislation, it should be obvious that when economic conditions changed so that their welfare was best obtained by permitting something that was previously illegal, halakhic authorities would have no objection.

Prompt Payment

According to the codes, the Torah includes four negative precepts and one positive commandment enjoining the prompt payment of wages.[11] Though they were originally phrased in terms of a daily wage, they embrace weekly and monthly payments as these became prevalent.

Withholding of payment of wages causes suffering to the worker, even in today's sophisticated economies. In the sweatshops of New York in the early decades of this century, the subsistence agricultural economies of Southeast Asia, and the factories of some newly developing countries, upsetting fragile family budgets by delaying payment can threaten physical existence by imperiling the essentials of life. Delayed payment of wages may force employees to depend on expensive consumer credit or become entrapped in an unbreakable cycle of usurious loans. These effects are echoed in the peculiar phrase used by the Torah in laying down the obligation of prompt payment: "For he is poor and unto it [the wage] he turns his soul."[12]

By the same logic, Maimomides includes the hire of draught animals, mechanical equipment, and subcontracting within the injunction of prompt payment. The assumption is that the provision of such services was done primarily by small economic units, on whom the disruption of cash flow through delayed or irregular payment would have much the same effect as in the case of an employee. It should be noted that although payment for normal economic transactions is a moral obligation, there is no halakhic injunction, as in the case of wages.

Obviously there would be no objection halakhically to the withholding of part of a worker's salary in the form of investment in mutual funds, government bonds, etc., provided this is with the employee's consent and knowledge. Such withholding is actually a form of enforced saving and is often to the worker's benefit. This may be seen from the schemes for issuing stock to workers as practiced in Western Europe, the automatic participation in consumer index–linked savings schemes prevalent in Israel, and the bonus system prevalent in Japan.

Although most biblical commentators and halakhic authorities saw the worker as the subject of the biblical verse quoted above, there is an opinion that "his soul" actually refers to the employer—an allusion, it seems, to the employer's unholy desire to benefit from the interest-free loan represented by withheld wages, irrespective of the hardship caused to the worker.

Although I was unable to find clear halakhic rulings in this respect, it would seem that the biblical insistence on prompt payment would lead easily to the acceptance of workers as preferred creditors in the case of bankruptcy. Furthermore, in many economies, money withheld from wages for payment of state compulsory loans, social security, or medical benefits is actually never distributed, as the workers are ignorant of their rights or lose evidence of their eligibility. Judaism's insistence on prompt payment would seem to make the employer or public sector agency holding those funds responsible for searching out the beneficiaries and paying them what is actually theirs.

Nonmonetary Wages

From the Talmud, we see that halakhically, a debtor may pay his creditor in kind or near money. "Abbaye questioned Rava: It is written in the Torah that [one who inflicts damages] shall pay from the best of his fields or vineyards [i.e., in real assets]. Does this mean that payment cannot be made in any other form [i.e., in near money]? However we have learned that [returning an object] includes also near money, even bran."[13] The disadvantages to the worker of such forms of payment, however, flow from a number of factors.

1. The worker is often saddled with goods that he has to resell, often after much time and trouble. This represents a loss to him that is especially significant where wages are paid in perishable goods.

2. Payments in kind prevent freedom of choice among economic opportunities. Such a loss of freedom, assuming rational behavior, will lead to a decline in the worker's welfare. The pattern of goods bought and consumed will be dictated by the nonmonetary wages received, which may or may not be the optimum allocation achievable with their monetary equivalent. From a national and individual viewpoint, this constitutes economic waste.

3. The nonmonetary wage may prevent labor mobility and even create political dependence on the employer. As often as not, the nonmonetary wage is not easily transferable to other employers, industries, or geographic areas. Classic examples of the resultant social distortion may be seen in the company towns which flourished in the United States in the nineteenth century or in the immobility of the labor structure in Israel resulting from the inability to transfer pension and other benefits.

It is true that sometimes nonmonetary wages are to the benefit of the worker. In many countries, the high rates of income tax make a raise in the monetary wage unprofitable to the worker. Sometimes, a job may not be possible at all without nonmonetary wages, since the employer doesn't have the financial resources to pay a full monetary wage. The whole institution of indentured servants in the early years of the United States, whereby the employer paid the cost of transport in return for a period of almost free work, is an outstanding example of this. In the modern world, senior executives, rabbis, and government officials are examples of workers whose nonmonetary wages are often in the form of housing, pension plans, job security, etc. Naturally, when the nonmonetary wages are to the benefit of the worker halakhic authorities would raise no objections, regarding them as local custom.

The halakhic status of these nonmonetary wages may be clearly seen in the following ruling of Maimonides. "When one hires a worker to do work for him in hay or straw, etc., and says to the worker, 'Take your wages from what you have worked with [instead of money wages],' we do not pay attention to him [i.e., it has no legal validity]. If the worker accepted wages in kind and then the employer says to him, 'Take your wages [in money] and give me the goods,' we do not pay attention to him."[14] (In the second case, the worker's original acceptance would indicate that the nonmonetary wage was to his advantage.)

Onus of Proof of Payment

There exists in the Jewish legal system a principle that the onus of proof is always on the one who claims money from his neighbor. In other words, if one party (say, to a contract) claims to have paid a debt and the other claims not to have received it, the onus of proof is on the latter. This principle is waived in the case of a worker claiming that he never received his wages. The Mishnah teaches us that "a hired person who claims his wages when they are due [and the employer argues that he has already paid], he takes an oath [that he hasn't received payment] and is entitled to his wages."[15] Even though it is usual practice for the debtor to take an oath that he has paid and then he is released from his debt, in this case the rabbis allowed the claimant to take an oath and collect his wages.

Even where wages are paid through a third party, such as a banker, all that is required is an oath. There are even authorities who claim that in this case even an oath isn't necessary, as it is told in the Mishnah:

> The workers say that they received nothing from the storekeeper [who serves in this case as the agent for the employer]. He [the storekeeper] takes an oath and has to be paid by the employer, and they [the workers] swear by oath and are paid [by the employer]. Ben Nannas exclaimed, "How can this be the rule? One of the parties [i.e., the storekeeper or the workers] is obviously lying, so each of them has to be paid without an oath" [otherwise the name of God will be desecrated by the oath taking. The law, however, is not according to Ben Nannas].[16]

SOCIAL RESPONSIBILITIES OF THE EMPLOYER

We have seen that although Judaism views the worker–employer relationship in the same light as that of any business contract, nevertheless, it understood the human elements involved and therefore took special steps to protect workers. These steps primarily involved protecting the wages of the worker or his working conditions, as determined either by specific contract or by local custom. In this section, however, we consider the question of the social responsibilities of the employer.

In many present-day economies the employer is saddled with the health costs of his employees (even when these are not occasioned by work accidents) and with providing for unemployed or retired workers. Irrespective of whether or not these costs are passed on to the consumer in the form of higher prices, they in effect transfer some of society's welfare obligations to the firm. This means that in addition to being an economic venture conducted for the purpose of earning profits, the firm also acquires social obligations, which may distort its pricing policies and its efficiency. Furthermore, many governments, by making the private corporation responsible for these welfare costs, are able to disguise the real size of public sector spending and remove it from public control. If the private corporation was not required to cover these costs, the government would have to increase its welfare budget and therefore either increase taxation or decrease other expenditures.

In many economies today, the discrepancy between labor costs (including these social benefits) and the formally defined wages received by workers after taxes has ballooned, so that the competitive edge of firms in those economies is blunted even though actual wages are not higher than in other economies.

When we examine Judaism's attitude to these social costs, the primary issue is not whether sick and elderly workers have to be looked after but rather whether this is the responsibility of the employer or of society.

Similarly, we are not concerned here with those services, such as cafeterias, corporate outings, on-site infirmaries, etc., which the employer introduces in order to increase productivity or to achieve smooth labor relations. Such costs are entered into voluntarily as an investment and are therefore not of communal concern. Obliging an employer against his will to assume the costs of health services, severance pay, and pensions, however, is part of the national economic system and as such has to be considered from a Jewish perspective. Such an examination has to maintain a clear distinction between those acts that flow from Jewish law and those which society wishes to take upon itself. Society may obligate employers to accept certain social functions beyond the demands of Jewish law, such obligations then becoming "custom" and therefore taking on the status of law, as has been explained.

The Costs of Injuries and Damages

A clear distinction must be made between those injuries that are caused by defective equipment or some act of negligence on the part of the employer or are the result of his assets or interests and those in which the employer is blameless. In the former type of case, the worker, like any other injured party, is entitled to the fivefold damages awarded by the halakhah. (These damages embrace loss of income, loss of limb, medical expenses, pain incurred, and the shame resulting from the injury.) Our concern here is solely with the employer's responsibility to share in the social and medical costs incurred in the course of his employment of others but for which he is not directly or indirectly responsible. Our question is to what extent is the worker-employer relationship, extended by the halakhah, as distinct from custom or specific contract, to include such costs.

The general halakhic principle seems to be that work, just like any other human activity, has its normal element of risk, which has been considered and accepted by the worker upon his acceptance of employment. In other words, the employer does not have any automatic obligations to shoulder the social costs arising out of such risk. This may be seen from the Talmudic discussion concerning a worker who was injured in a tree during the harvesting of dates and olives. The rabbis in that discussion held that the worker, in his desire to earn the wages offered, knowingly took upon himself this risk.[17] A responsum written in thirteenth-century Spain, rejecting a similar claim for damages, explained that the worker accepted the job despite his knowledge that incidents like this were to be expected in this type of work.[18]

Many avenues of employment, however, present elements of risk far in excess of normal, everyday activities. Workers, like all people, are by halakhic sources forbidden to place themselves in danger, in accordance with the biblical dictum "And thou shalt surely guard yourselves very much" (Deut. 4:15). Understanding that it is not possible to lead risk-free lives, the sages accepted a concept of "normal acceptable risk," beyond which people were not allowed to place themselves in jeopardy. In our own day, such industries as coal mining, with its association with black lung disease, or the asbestos or nuclear industries may present an abnormal risk. A labor contract exposing workers to such risk would seem to be contrary to the obligation to guard one's body against harm and therefore not acceptable, even if the workers agree to it.

That the costs arising out of normal risk do not devolve upon the employer may be seen, for example, from the Rama's ruling, in his gloss on the *Shulchan Arukh,* that "since the employer is liable to pay only for the time worked by a sick worker [and not for the contracted period as a whole], it would seem obvious, therefore, that he should not be obligated to cover the medical costs involved."[19]

Or, consider that the Jewish obligation to redeem captives is univerally accepted both by halakhic rules and by common practice. It was the question of the legitimacy of placing the onus for financing such a redemption on the shoulders of an employer which prompted a referral to Rabbi Joseph Katz of sixteenth-century Crakow.

> You have asked me a question regarding the redemption of Shimon, who was hired by Reuven to travel on his behalf and in the course of these travels was taken captive by bandits. It is obvious that Reuven is not liable to bear the costs of his redemption [which would otherwise have to be covered by the communal treasury]. Since we are dealing with a hired employee, our case is different from that covered by the opinion of the Maharam of Rothenburg, who ruled that the employer was liable. He was dealing with a father–son relationship, wherein the captured agent (the son) was not being paid by his employer (the father). There a dual obligation falls on the employer, that of a father to redeem his son and that of a recipient of a free service. In the case of a hired employee, however, there are no legal opinions that would obligate the employer to redeem his agent. [20]

It is interesting to note that where an employee's travels resulted in his death, the halakhic authorities saw evidence of a moral blemish, which necessitated the employer to do *t'shuvah* (repentance) by compensating the deceased's family.[21] This, however, was not the result of seeing the employer as responsible for financing the normal risk assumed by his worker but rather followed from the Jewish idea that being the cause of damage, however innocently, is a Divine communication of some moral shortcoming, even when it does not involve one in a legal punishment.

Custom, however, as distinct from these legal opinions, seems to have acknowledged the liability of an employer even in those cases where an injury occurs during the normal, everyday activities of the worker. Thus, the Jerusalem Talmud explains that the priests in the Temple suffered from intestinal diseases resulting from their working conditions. These included the drinking of water rather than wine (the latter being considered of medicinal value in those days), working barefooted and dressed only in a single shift, and eating the meat of the sacrifices. The responsibility for their medical care was placed, therefore, on the Temple treasury.[22]

In eighteenth-century Turkey, Rabbi Chaim Pallache was

asked to rule concerning the claim of a worker for medical expenses and wages lost as a result of illness. This worker was hired to accompany his employer on his rounds through the villages to sell articles of glass and such. In his responsum, Rabbi Chaim answered that

> even if the worker became ill, it is the custom to pay him the full salary agreed upon. It is also customary for the employer to pay the full medical costs involved. The reasoning behind the custom is that the probability of the worker becoming ill is increased by the job, which required him to travel away from his city and wander from place to place.[23]

There seems to have been cognizance taken of the difficulties—legal, practical, and perhaps moral—of foisting the medical costs of normal occurrences onto the employer simply because he had hired the sick person. As a feasible and ethical compromise, we find, for example, a communal ordinance issued in Cracow in 1595 related to the care of a domestic servant who became ill. "The householder is required to pay the full costs of hospitalization for the first two weeks. If a longer period is required then the costs shall be shared, half to be paid for by the employer and the rest to be borne by the domestic. Any period after that shall be financed by the charitable funds of the community."[24]

The halakhic attitude toward these employer responsibilities may be summed up by the ruling of the late Chief Rabbi of Israel, HaRav Uzziel.

> Both employer and worker require each other. The worker labors more for his own self-interest than for the benefit of his employer. The law, therefore, does not place any special responsibility on the latter for the worker's welfare or make him liable for injuries suffered [excepting the responsibility placed upon him by custom]. At the same time, however, the Torah obligates him to make every effort to protect his workers from injury; failure to do so makes him liable to the moral crime of "Thou shalt not spill blood in thy house" (Deut. 25:8).[25]

Job Security

Many labor disputes today are vitally concerned with assuring job security and pension payments for workers. Naturally, if a labor contract provides for either of these arrangements, or if they are required by the law of the land, or by custom, the halakhic authorities would enforce them. The question for us, however, is whether they are an intrinsic part of Jewish labor legislation, to be enforced by a *bet din* even where there is no contract or other basis. It seems that the halakhic sources make a clear distinction between the rights of those whose employment is seen to be of a long-term nature and those of others.

In the case of one who is hired on a daily, weekly, or monthly basis, there does not seem to be any responsibility for retaining a worker for longer than the period agreed upon. In other words, workers who are engaged for a fixed period—even as long as a year or two—may be fired at the end of that period without compensation. Where the employer, however, discharges a worker during the period of the contract, without prior notice, he is liable to damages.

Our concern here is with the long-term employee and the obligations of the employer to retain him. Actually these obligations have to be considered under two separate catagories. First, there is the problem of retaining workers who are no longer capable of performing their jobs at the previous or required level, or who are dismissed for other reasons. This will involve questions of severance pay and pensions. In addition, there is the problem of the support of dependents of employees who have died. In contrast to these obligations lies the responsibility of the employer for those workers who have to be fired because the whole business venture is no longer profitable—or not as profitable as it was. This is in reality a question of employment policy and so is discussed in Chapter 9.

Almost all of the halakhic discussions on the rights of no longer productive workers deal with employees of the Jewish public sector: rabbis, cantors, teachers, ritual slaughterers. It is not at all clear whether the rabbinic decisions regarding the benefits due such workers who are no longer able to perform their obligations may be automatically extended to include the employees of private firms. In present-day economies, it is the moral obligation of the private firm with such employees which is the real issue. After all, the welfare paid for by the public sector is the same whether it comes in the form of employee benefits or direct welfare payments. The imposing of such welfare costs on private economic units is a different matter.

Despite the limitation of the halakhic involvement with the

public sector employee, a discussion of the relevant decisions is important, revealing the basic Jewish thinking on this subject. Furthermore, many decisions of the present-day Israeli rabbinate extended the rights enjoyed by such workers to those employed by private firms.

Severance Pay

In many modern economies, workers dismissed for reasons of health, etc., are compensated for the loss of income by severance pay. This is a form of compensation long practiced by Jewish communities.

A modern application may be seen in the case of the principal of the Belz School in Haifa. This school is not part of the state school system, but rather a private institution financed primarily by donations and tuition. After years of service, the principal was dismissed and claimed severance pay. The court upheld his claim, basing its decision on the interpretation of the biblical injunction to grant a terminal payment to the Hebrew bondsman on the conclusion of his services: "You shall surely grant him from your flocks and your granary and your wine-press, of that which the Lord your God has blessed you with" (Deut. 15:14). The *Sefer Ha-chinukh*, which explored the educational, moral, and ethical implications of the laws of the Bible some six centuries ago, comments as follows:

> Even though the law of the Hebrew bondsman applies only to the time in history when the jubilee year applies—that is, when the Land of Israel is divided amongst the twelve tribes— nevertheless, even in our own day the wise man will observe this. He who has employed a fellow Jew for a long period of hire or even for a short-term will, upon termination of the work, grant him some of the wealth which the Lord has blessed him with.[26]

The Israel *bet din* held, therefore, that "we have to reiterate that the *Chinukh* has obligated every employer to make such a grant on the basis of ethical and moral principles, so that the employee should not go empty-handed. Long-term employees, just as the Hebrew bondsman, may [otherwise] find themselves penniless and impoverished at the end of their tenure."[27]

Rabbi Benyamin Rabinowitz, in a contemporary article, expressed it in a different way. "Justice would demand that if as a result of illness or old age, the worker can no longer perform as efficiently as previously or not at all, the employer is obligated to retain him, and not to simply discard him as some used-up article or piece of equipment."[28]

It seems that the codifiers regarded severance pay to the Hebrew bondsman—and, therefore, to the modern worker—primarily as an act of *chesed* (lovingkindness), rather than an obligation of the wage mechanism. So Maimonides placed the obligation of the severance grant in his chapter dealing with *tzedakah*. This would make it something beyond the requirements of law. Nevertheless, there are authorities who maintain that it is the function of the Jewish courts to enforce such righteous acts on the part of the employer. So we find Rabbi Mordechai ben Hillel writing that it is customary in every court in Jewry to force the rich man to perform all those acts that are worthy and just, even if these are not his legal obligations.[29]

Severance pay, however, is only one method of assisting the aged or infirm employee. Another is forcing the employer to retain him on pension or to provide him with assistants who will share the work load with him. We find many examples of both of these solutions in the responsa and communal enactments.

Pensions

An example of the obligation to provide a pension for public sector workers in their old age or in those cases where they are totally disabled is to be found in the minute books of the Community Council of Poznan. Written in Eastern Europe, they contain the following decision, from the year of 1636:

> Seeing as how our teacher, our master, Rabbi Shimon Zusshinder, has sat faithfully in judgment here in our community for many years, and now, due to failing eyesight and age, is no longer able to fulfill this task, it is fitting that the community should see that he is provided for in an honorable fashion.[30]

The basis for such a decision is, again, to be found in the biblical injunction "And thou shalt do that which is righteous and good" (Deut. 5:18); it is an act of kindness rather than a legal obligation. In Jewish law, an employer has the right to fire a worker who is not able to perform the job contracted for, irrespective of the reason. In a responsum written in North Africa we do find, however, a legal basis for retaining workers engaged for life or for long terms.

> Whenever a worker is hired for a lengthy period, everybody knows that it is not possible for one to really work all that time. After all, it is normal for a person to become ill within such lengthy periods. Since the employer did not specify, in their agreement, that he would not retain the worker, even in those conditions that he is not fit to perform his job, so he is obliged to do so.[31]

This argument has been reiterated in the decisions of Rabbi Waldenberg in modern Israel.[32]

It is easy to understand how such obligations to provide for elderly or disabled workers were extended to include their widows and dependents. The element of kindness, as distinct from contractual obligation, in such cases should be noted, since these obligations could be paid from the charitable funds. In reply to a question concerning the widow and orphans of a rabbi, Rabbi Chaim of Tsanz writes, "It is clear that the obligation to provide for his widow and orphans is legally incumbent on the townspeople. They are obligated to support them in a manner suitable to that of a scholar, as is customary in all Jewish communities [not necessarily the equivalent of the salary paid]."[33] The funds for this pension were to be provided from a tax on meat slaughtering. The problem presented to Rabbi Chaim was related to the amount of tax to be levied. The majority wished to impose a tax of 2 to 3 rubles per head of poultry, whereas the minority pressed for a smaller sum. Rabbi Chaim held that, since this is a matter of charity, the majority cannot force their will on the minority.

In the case of communal workers, we find an interesting form of providing for widows and orphans, over and above or instead of a pension. By custom or by law, the sons of communal officials were to succeed their fathers after their death.

This is presented by Maimonides as follows. "The kingship is a hereditary function, as it is written, 'in order that his reign and that of his sons shall be prolonged in Israel' [Deut. 17:20] . . . and not only is this [hereditary] but all communal officials and all appointments in Israel are hereditary."[34]

This succession was seen, then, not only as an expression of honor toward the former officials but also as a means of providing for the maintenance of the widow and other dependents. The son, legally, had the obligation to provide for his mother and younger unmarried siblings, so that providing him with a job enabled him to fulfill this obligation and freed the community from the financial burden.

In order to protect the public from incapable or unsuitable heirs, the halakhah demanded that the successor be fit to fulfill the position. He need not, however, be the most capable or qualified candidate. For instance, the Rama, in his gloss on the *Shulchan Arukh*, writes that sons succeed rabbis "provided they follow their fathers in God-fearingness and even if they are only a little scholarly."[35]

It should be noted that with regard to both pensions and providing for dependents it is not at all clear whether the obligations of the public sector employer can serve as a halakhic model for the private firm. This would seem to be a subject for further research and clear-cut rabbinic decisions.

Provision of Assistance

The halakhic sources provide an alternative to pensions or severance pay as a means of providing for the aged and infirm worker. They ruled that it is possible to force an employer to provide an assistant or assistants for the worker who is no longer able to perform properly. This provision would seem to be a major contribution of Judaism toward solving an important modern problem, which has both economic and social implications. Modern medicine, preventive health care, and improved nutrition have drastically extended the life span and working years of the average person; yet many workers are not able to fulfill their jobs to the same extent as when they were at their physical and mental peaks.

At the same time pressures exist which limit the employment of the aging population. Many labor contracts and business practices are still essentially based on the life expectancy characteristic of earlier decades, so that retirement is mandatory at age 60 or 65 even though people may still be usefully employed beyond that. In attempting to cut production costs, firms endeavor to get workers to accept early retirement. New entrants into the labor market also exert pressure on older workers to retire.

The retirement of such workers because of their age or partial disability involves an economic loss to society, since their skills and accumulated experience are no longer available. Such workers themselves often suffer both physically and mentally from an excess of leisure time, the lack of an organized framework in their life, and the feeling of being redundant. It is true that Judaism's insistence on Torah study may alleviate the problem, yet it is doubtful if this by itself presents a feasible solution to all aspects of the problem.

The communal enactments and rabbinic decisions in this regard would seem to provide a fresh approach that might constitute a viable social and economic solution applicable even to non-Jewish societies.

The halakhic basis for the legal ability to force an employer to provide or finance assistance for an aged or infirm employee may be found in the following responsum of the Rashba, addressed to the Jewish community of Huesca in Spain in the thirteenth century in answer to this query.

> *Question:* The *chazan* [cantor] of our synagogue has served us faithfully for thirty-eight years and now has substituted his son, whose voice isn't so acceptable to some of the members of the community. The *chazan* has argued that even though there are many functions that he can still perform, nevertheless his strength [of voice, presumably] and eyesight have diminished and he is unable to read from the Torah as previously. Therefore he wishes his son to assist him. How are we to decide . . . ?

In his responsum, the Rashba points out that

> it is logical and just to assume that a public official appointed to perform certain tasks has not undertaken automatically to perform all of them unaided at all times. Surely the congregation didn't believe that a man can maintain his strength and ability all his life without sickness or other difficulties suffered by all normal people. So the *chazan* is entitled to have his son assist him, since this was tacitly understood by both parties.[36]

In the absence, therefore, of a contrary clause in a contract an aged employee can demand assistance, the cost of which is to be borne by the employer.[37]

It seems that there is also provision in the halakhic sources for enabling a worker to perform easier tasks as his strength or ability wanes. Rabbi Israel Mavrona ruled that "a teacher who is ill but is able to teach partially [that is, fewer students or fewer hours] is entitled to his full wage, and it is not permissible to dismiss him on these grounds."[38]

In all these cases the assumption is that the worker was hired for all his life or at least for a long period. The casual worker or one hired for a short, specified period does not enjoy any of these rights.

TRADE UNIONS

Legitimacy of Trade Unions and Professional Associations

In the previous chapter, we saw that although the halakhic sources appreciated the benefits of the market mechanism, nevertheless, in certain circumstances restraints on competition were introduced when this was considered to be in the interests of morality or the communal welfare. The same considerations apply to organizations of workers and artisans into professional associations or unions, which may in effect be monopolies or at least act to restrain competition.

Generally speaking, associations of workers, whether hired employees or operating as independent contractors, were already permitted in Talmudic times. "The people of the city are permitted to regulate weights, prices, and the wages of workers. They also have the right to punish those who do not carry out their regulations."[39]

Strictly speaking, this right of regulation applied to "the people of the city," but the commentators understood that in the words of the Rashba, "every association organized for one purpose is to be considered as a 'city' even if the other members of the community are not party to their decisions. Even if only members of one occupation, like the merchants, butchers, or sailors, make regulations and articles of association, their decisions are binding."[40]

All those associations had the right, according to Jewish law, to make bulk purchases on behalf of their members; and to allot specific or restricted times for the selling of goods, according to Maimonides.[41] In modern times, rabbinic opinion has seen trade unions as associations of this type, with recognized rights of organization and penalties for noncompliance with their regulations and decisions. A late Chief Rabbi of Israel, HaRav Uzziel, wrote that "our sages recognized the regulations of craftsmen or of workers' federations, either in the form of one general union or in the form of separate professional ones . . . in order to protect himself, the worker thus had the right to organize, and to enact suitable regulations."[42] In our own day, Rabbi Moshe Feinstein writes: "Regarding the associations of workers known as unions, which make regulations to their mutual benefit, I do not see anything that would seem to be unacceptable."[43]

So we find at various stages of Jewish history examples of such organizations covering many different types of artisans and workers. In Talmudic times, there are references to organizations of weavers and dyers, bakers, drovers, and sailors. The drovers and the sailors provided a form of insurance through a mutual undertaking to provide donkeys or ships in case any of them lost their means of transportation.[44]

In Jerusalem during Temple times there existed special synagogues for each trade and craft, while in Alexandria special sections were reserved in the Great Synagogue for different types of workers. We may assume that there also existed, therefore, some form of economic organization.

Later, in medieval Europe, we find Jewish guilds of artisans parallel to those familiar to us from general economic history; the earliest known one was the Shoemakers Guild of early-fourteenth-century Saragossa, Spain. Evidence of these guilds has been left in the form of membership books and other records. They provided for the care of the sick, made financial arrangements for the families of deceased members, and established regular study groups in Jewish law; they also set standards for the quality of goods produced and the terms of apprenticeship and set aside an address for complaints by the public.

In Eastern Europe, Jewish guilds proliferated in the seventeenth century, spreading rapidly through Poland and Lithuania; they remained in existence until the beginning of this century. Some nineteen Jewish guilds continued to exist in Poland until World War II.

These guilds—like their modern counterparts, the trade unions and professional associations—served a two-fold purpose, with opposite effects on the general public. They benefited society by "policing" the quality of the goods or services provided, through supervision and training of the labor force. At the same time, however, they restrained competition, increasing the cost to the public of their goods and services, and earned monopoly profits for their members. We are primarily concerned here with the economic effects of such associations.

The Talmudic sages were aware of this dual function of the restrictive practices of monopolistic organizations or individuals. In the Temple in Jerusalem, certain families preserved their skills as monopolies, with both economic and religious consequences—an early forebear, perhaps, of present-day restrictive practices and trade unionism.

A distinct lack of approval of such practices is reflected in the Mishnah:

> These shall be remembered for rebuke: the house of Garmu, who refused to teach others how the shewbread for the Temple service was baked; the house of Avtinas, who refused to teach the manner of making the incense; Hugrass ben Levi, who was in charge of the singing in the Temple but refused to teach his special method of singing; Ben Kamtzar, who refused to teach his special art of writing.[45]

In the Gemara, we are told that the sages brought experts from Alexandria (presumably from the Temple at Leontonis) who were able to bake the shewbread for the Temple, in an attempt to continue the Temple service without the house of Garmu. The foreign bakers, however, were not able to perform all the various tasks connected with the shewbread to the satisfaction of the rabbis. The sages concluded: "Everything which the Lord created He created for His honor"—meaning that God had given more ability to some than to others in order that He might be served by those whom He desired. So the house of Garmu was reinstated. However, when the sages sent for them to return to work, they refused until their wages were doubled. The Gemara then continues to tell us of a similar increase in wages in the case of the house of Avtinas, the makers of incense mentioned in the Mishnah.

This mercenary behavior of holding the Temple to ransom for a 100% rise in wages troubled the sages. They asked the house of Garmu what the reason was for their refusing to teach others, which in effect maintained their monopoly. The answer, however, was noneconomic. "We have it as a tradition that this house [the Temple] will be destroyed. We feared, therefore, that perhaps an unworthy person will learn, and will use his knowledge for idolatrous purposes." The Gemara goes on to tell us that the sons of the house of Garmu never ate refined bread, in order that people shouldn't say they were using the shewbread for their personal benefit. Similarly, the brides of the house of Avtinas never went to the canopy perfumed, and their wives had to undertake to never use perfumes, so that they shouldn't be suspected of using the incense for their personal benefit. This lack of exploitation of their monopoly status proved that the ideological argument advanced by the house of Garmu for maintaining that status was not a contrived one. So the rabbis revised the rebuke of the Mishnah and praised them [46]

Protection of the Public

The rabbis' recognition of the advantages of trade and labor associations, however, did not eliminate the need to protect the public from abuses of monopoly practices. "Protection of the public" here refers both to the general consumer and to the traders, professionals, and workers who were not members of a given union or association.

Halakhic sources required that the regulations of associations need either the unanimous approval of their members or, according to other opinions, at least the approval of a majority. The former opinion is held by the Maharam of Rothenburg;[47] the latter by the Rashba.[48] Both of these opinions would seem to solve the problem of effective minority rule so prevalent in many modern trade unions, which often become hostages, as it were, to marginal but well-organized and vocal groups.

The requirement of majority rule (or rule by representatives appointed by the majority) would seem primarily to safeguard the interests of the members of associations and unions. Yet, at the same time, the public and nonmembers needed protection against losses stemming from union monopolies.

The *Shulchan Arukh* codifies as law a discussion dating back to Talmudic times that the regulations of artisans are effective "only in those places where there is no prominent person (*adam chashuv*) appointed over the public. [According to some this had to be a Torah scholar, but others, like the Ramban, maintained that an elected neutral person was sufficient.] If such a personage is available, then their enactments have no validity and they cannot punish or fine those who do not carry them out except if they have his approval.''[49]

The gloss of the Rama, however, notes that ''such a supervisor is needed only where there is a question of losses being caused.''

The actual implementation of this halakhic requirement for some form of communal control may be seen from the statutes of the Jewish Tailors Guild of Prague in 1694: ''All disputes concerning complaints of a customer, overcharging, etc., shall be settled by the warden of the guild together with a representative of the Jewish community (appointed by the chief inspectors). In the event of the customer not being satisfied with the decision, the dispute will be referred to the *bet din*.''[50]

In some guilds, it seems that in addition to the *parnassim*, or officers elected by the members themselves, the community insisted on placing its own representatives on the executive body. So we find in the records of the Council of Medinat Lita (Lithuania) in 1686: ''Only two of the trustees of a guild may be elected by the members of the guild themselves, while the other two have to be appointed by the heads of the *kahal* [community] from amongst the members of the community.''[51]

At the same time, the economic benefits accruing to the community from the monopolies held by certain groups (made possible by the losses suffered by the ''international'' economy) were understood, as the communal leaders of Poznan in the eighteenth century acknowledged. ''It is known that the clothing industry is the foundation and the sustenance of the whole community [of Shavarzanitz, which was under the jurisdiction of Poznan]. So every enactment to the benefit of this industry and those engaged in it will receive the blessing of the council.''[52]

Unorganized Labor

The ability to force all the workers in a certain industry to join, and abide by the regulations of, a union is the major source of the economic power of organized labor. This monopolistic power is strengthened by the closed-shop principle, whereby the employer is forced to accept only unionized labor. In many cases such monopolies of labor cause economic loss both to the general economy, by keeping wages above their market value, and to unorganized workers, who would perhaps be prepared to work for lower wages or under less expensive working conditions. There are today industries in the Western world, such as shipbuilding, steel, and automobiles, which have priced themselves out of the international market as a result of unionization, with ill effects both on their national economies and on the workers themselves.

The halakhic treatment of this question has to be understood in the context of the limitations described above: viz, the need for a majority (or unanimous) vote and the supervision of an important personality or arbitrator.

Rabbi Avraham Di Buton, writing in sixteenth-century Salonika, deals with the ability of organized workers to force their agreements on others as follows:

> Regarding the question you've asked me concerning a tailor who came to your city from a neighboring village and does work at half the price fixed by the local tailors. The latter cannot force him to raise his prices [a ruling of Ibn Migas]. When the sages [of the Talmud] ruled that the people of a city or of a certain profession can force outsiders [i.e., people from another city or locals who were not part of the agreement] not to work or trade, they did not intend to cause a loss to the people of the city. Where, as in our case, the work is done for less than the ruling price, then it is not permissible to prevent it, since this causes a loss to the public.[53]

It would seem therefore that, according to this responsum, the members of a union could not enforce their wage scale or working conditions on nonworkers in those cases where the latter were willing to work at below union rates, since this is to the public benefit. Such a ruling would destroy the union's monopoly and lead to wages finding their market level. At the same time, however, we must bear in mind that where such competition would lead to a loss of livelihood, as distinct from a decline in earnings, the halakhah would support the restrictive practices of a union. This is in accordance with the general responsibility which society has for the welfare of its members. In our case, this is expressed by a responsum of Rabbi Moshe Feinstein, written in 1954 as a reply to Rabbi Joseph Eliash of Detroit.

> If the workers in a union do not represent a majority of those employed in the industry or profession, then all their decisions and enactments are worthless. Even where they represent a majority of employees in the majority of enterprises, it is not clear

whether they can enforce their authority on the minority [unorganized] workers. The latter can argue that since they do not share in the benefits of union membership (health insurance, pension plans, training facilities, etc.), there is no reason why they should be forced to accept the union's rules. At the same time, however, since the union represents a majority it can prevent the others from working on the grounds of *marufiya* and the endangering of their livelihood. This right is bolstered by the general public disapproval of strikebreaking.[54]

From the discussion on competition in the previous chapter, it would seem that union policy can be forced on outside labor in those cases where such labor destroys, as distinct from diminishing, the livelihood of union members.

The first Chief Rabbi of modern Israel, Avraham Isaac Kook, saw the issue of unionization primarily from the viewpoint of protecting the livelihood of workers. In an article published in 1933, he wrote as follows:

> In the organization of workers for the purpose of protecting their working conditions there is an element of justice and *tikun olam* [repairing the world]. Unorganized labor works for lower wages and longer hours, and this is to the detriment of the working conditions of the organized worker and causes him economic loss. Such losses can be claimed through a law suit, and therefore both the employer and the unorganized worker can be summoned to a *bet din* [rabbinic court]. Should neither of these parties agree to arbitration . . . before the *bet din*, the organized workers can use other methods approved by the courts.[55]

It must be stressed that Rabbi Kook's ruling in effect makes the power of unions, with respect to unorganized labor and the closed shop principle, subject to court approval. This is in accord with the principle mentioned above of the *adam chashuv*, which provides for public supervision either by a rabbinic personality or by an elected representative of the public.

Such public supervision would undoubtedly take into account the interests of both organized and unorganized workers as well as the effect of union policies on the consumer and on the long-term development of the economy. In this way the halakhic process would tend to strike a balance between the efficiency of the free market mechanism and the protection of the individual against the temporary effects of unfair competition or of sudden changes in market forces.

The Right to Strike

The strike represents the use of the power of a union to withhold the supply of labor from the market and thereby influence wages and the terms of employment. Without the right to strike, unions are in effect powerless to affect the price of labor. Since we have already established the halakhic conditions for labor unions, we now have to examine its attitude toward strikes.

At the outset, it must be made clear that there is no halakhic sanction for physical violence, either toward other workers or with respect to the property of the employer. "It is not permissible [for the unions who are striking] to do those things which are forbidden by the laws of the Torah. For example, one is not allowed to beat those who wish to work during the strike . . . even with the sanction [of the strike] by an *adam chashuv* it is forbidden."[56]

In order to achieve the purposes of a strike, the workers have to be able to do three things.

1. They have to cease work of their own accord. In many countries this often involves the unilateral breaking of contracts.
2. They have to prevent the employer from hiring other workers in their place.
3. They have to prevent other workers—either nonstriking members or nonunion workers—from coming to work.

It is the ability of the strikers to fulfill these conditions that has to be examined in order to determine halakhic attitudes toward the strike. Such an examination would seem to indicate that none of these actions is legal in Jewish law. The only exception, perhaps, is where a strike is called in order to force the employer to abide by the terms of the contract. Jewish legal sources view the fulfillment of all contracts, both written and oral, as basic and paramount, so that in those cases where one party refuses to comply with a contract, then the injured party may "make a law to himself." This entitles him to take unilateral action if he is able to do so.[57] In those cases where the employer has either failed to comply with a contract or wishes to unilaterally change the conditions thereof, this would give the workers the power to prevent the employer from hiring other workers and also to prevent such workers from accepting employment. Since custom regarding the terms and conditions of employment is an integral part of the Jewish labor framework, nonconformance with local custom is tantamount to breaking a written labor contract. It would seem, then, that striking in order to preserve customary amenities which are part of normal working conditions in a particular society—such as coffee breaks, shorter summer working hours, cafeteria facilities, rest rooms, and the like—would be permissible even if they were not specified in a particular contract.

Strikes for improved wages or working conditions, however, would not seem to be permissible in halakhic sources. Halakhically, the union would be required to take its case to a *bet din* or the duly elected prominent person (*adam chashuv*).

Rabbi Kook summed this up clearly:

> Irrespective of whether a strike is aimed at preserving working conditions (contracted conditions which are being renegotiated) or improving wages, etc., it is not permissible. The only way available to the workers is to call the employer to a *bet din Torah,* and in this respect they are not any different from the parties to any other form of conflict. It is possible, however, to use the strike as a weapon to force the employer to appear before a rabbinical court.[58]

There are opinions that the members of a trade association or the people of a city may keep nonmembers or nonresidents from being employed or from engaging in business even though they pay taxes. (See chapter 5.) Thus we find the *Chatam Sofer*, in Hungary, writing:

> All the regulations which [the people of the city] draw up regarding restraints on competition . . . they do not apply to those who pay the king's taxes. . . . Nevertheless . . . if the people of the city saw their livelihoods diminished they may use their influence with officialdom to prevent free entry, even though this is against the law.[59]

Both Kook's article and the responsum of the *Chatam Sofer* make some sort of public body responsible for overseeing a strike or any restraint on competition. Such a body, whether it is a *bet din* or government officials, will prevent the one-sided abuse of union power which is the crux of the problem of labor relations in modern society. The impartial arbitration envisaged by both decisions will protect the legitimate needs of union members and at the same time protect the economic interests of society. This protection is particularly important today, since much labor unrest actually affects innocent third parties—as, for instance, strikes by public sector workers in health, education, or sanitation.

It must be stressed that if a government wishes to allow unions the right to strike or to prevent the employment of nonorganized workers, it is quite free to do so. What has been discussed here is the policy evolving out of reliance solely on Jewish law.

SUMMARY

The worker–employer relationship is a contractual one similar to those existing in all other area of economic life. Nevertheless, bearing in mind the human aspects involved, the halakhah makes special provision for the protection of the worker. These provisions, however, cannot disturb the symmetry of justice, whereby the worker has obligations as well.

Aging or disabled workers have to be provided for, either by force of custom or as a result of the demands of righteousness. This is especially valid in those circumstances where the public sector—the state or community—is the employer. Workers may not be made to perform work that is hazardous to their health, even if they agree to do so.

Just as traders or manufacturers are allowed to form associations for their mutual economic protection, so are workers allowed to form unions. The halakhic sources are insistent, however, that the restrictive arrangements of unions must have the consent of an *adam chashuv*—either a prominent rabbinical personality or communally accepted figure. It is only when such arbitration is not available that such arrangements become binding—provided certain procedures to protect the public are followed.

The rights of unions are limited. While they can force their members to abide by their decisions, it is not clear that they can prevent the free entry of nonorganized workers. The use of force and the destruction of property are strictly forbidden. Furthermore, it seems that unions may strike to secure intervention by a *bet din*, but beyond that, their situation is no different from that of any other plaintiff in a normal economic dispute. The singular exception seems to be a strike called to enforce the conditions of the contract or custom.

CHAPTER 7

Money, Banking, and Interest

INTRODUCTION

Money, in all of its various forms, plays such an important role in any economy that it tends to become the central issue in every ideological or religious economic framework. Through its use as a means of exchange, people are able to buy and sell services without resorting to a barter system. As accumulated wealth, it can be invested in economic enterprises in the form of capital; alternatively, it provides loan capital and credit to other economic units.

The relationship between the supplier of money and the receiver of any form of capital or credit gives rise to important moral and ethical questions. At the same time, money as a means of exchange, whether issued by a private, individual bank, as was customary for many centuries, or by a national government, as is the case in present-day economic systems, poses similar moral questions, with regard to, say, the worth of currency, its depreciating or appreciating value.

It is not surprising, therefore, that Judaism has developed a wide range of concepts and practices to regulate the relationships created by the use of money. Although these relationships are multifaceted and complicated, our treatment in this book will be limited solely to economic aspects and will not deal with legal or other factors.

Similarly, this chapter will not deal with the many examples of rabbinic insights predating much modern economic thought. Interesting as these parallels are, they cannot be included here, since the aim of this book is to discover if there is a specifically Jewish treatment of economic issues as distinct from mere understanding of the subject. Nevertheless, two examples of such early rabbinic insight are quoted here.

Gresham's Law—that bad money (in other words, inferior, inflated currency) drives out good money—was formulated by the rabbis of the Talmud some 1,500 years prior to its formulation by Gresham.[1] In a different example, we find an understanding of the role of risk in investment. The rabbinic courts held that the value of a marriage contract to be paid to a woman, either in the case of divorce or on the death of her husband, varied in accordance with both the anticipated risk of cessation of the particular marriage and the uncertainty of general economic conditions.[2]

While the majority of such examples have, as we said, been omitted, we have included a general discussion on the role of money, since this is of great importance in determining the ethical and moral framework of credit and banking. At the same time, this chapter includes a short description of the role of money lending and banking in Jewish history. It would seem that this is essential in order to put that role in proper perspective, since it is a subject much distorted and maligned.

The establishment of Israel as an independent political entity raises some new moral issues with regard to the effect of monetary policy. Some of these questions have already been answered by halakhic authorities, and these cases will be mentioned in the text. Others, however, are still in the process of exploration and discussion, and therefore we are able only to mention them. The new element introduced by this political independence is that now, after many centuries, one has to deal with a Jewish policy that acts as an initiator of economic policy. In the past, Jews did not have control over the public purse, so that they could not determine the course of monetary policy, interest rates, and the allocation of credit. As a result, halakhic authorities had to deal primarily with legal issues between individual Jews which arose out of a monetary policy initiated by Gentile governments. In the State of Israel, however, these same authorities now have to deal with that monetary policy itself and with whether such a policy conflicts with Jewish law, and to adjudicate transactions between one Jew and another in light of that policy.

A HISTORICAL SURVEY

Although biblical sources are not very specific about the monetary system and the existence of a banking system in the independent Jewish kingdoms, nevertheless there are a number of interesting facts which may be gleaned from the texts themselves. The existence of an elaborate system of taxation, especially after the period of King Solomon, presupposes some sort of monetary system, because not all of the taxes were paid in kind or labor. Furthermore, from various passages in the Book of Kings,[3] we see that enemies of the Jewish states made a point of robbing the national treasury, including that held in the Temple. The wealth held in the Temple represented not only contributions to the religious authorities, but seems to have served also as a repository for the state and royal treasuries.

At the same time, the expansion of trade, both internal and international—such as Solomon's trade with Africa from the port of Etzion-Gever—must have also led to the wide use of precious metals, even if only on a barter basis.[4] It would seem that during the period of the first Temple the money was primarily circulated in the form of shekels—that is, by weight rather than by coinage—as we have no examples of Jewish coins of that period.

In the period of the Second Temple, we find the evolution of a monetary system, especially in the days of the Maccabean kings, who issued what are believed to be the first Jewish coins. A primary motif of these coins is the seven species with which the land of Israel is blessed: wheat, barley, grapes, figs, pomegranates, olives, and dates. (They do not bear human likenesses, on account of the biblical prohibition against making graven images.) The years after the destruction of the Second Temple saw a short-lived renewal of an independent coinage.

The expansion of international trade described in chapter 4 as well as the sophistication of internal trade during the period of the Second Temple led to a rapid development of a Jewish banking system. Once again the Temple served as a repository for charitable gifts and for tithes. It has also been suggested that the Temple seems to have served as some form of safekeeping for personal treasures, although this does not seem to be very firmly rooted in historical evidence. As a result of the taxes of the kings, there was a sizable national treasury that was used to finance economic endeavors, such as the public works pursued by Herod.

Coins of different denominations, issued by various rulers and states throughout the then known world, were brought to the Temple treasury as part of the tithes of Jews, both from the land of Israel and from the countries of the Diaspora. This medley of coinage, together with the financing of international trade, led to the development of money-changing as an important part of the Jewish economy. There were money-changers in the Temple who dealt in foreign currency and Israeli currency of different denominations. The money-changers also accepted deposits from private individuals and subsequently lent these sums to various people. This may be seen from the following Gemara where the *shulchani* (money-changer) serves as a financial agent.

> An employer gave his worker a note [check] for his wages drawn on the storekeeper [on the storekeeper's bank account] or to the *shulchani*, who delayed payment of the wages. The question then arises of the employer's liability under the Torah's law of prompt payment of wages. In this case, however, the employer is not guilty of a transgression. Rabbah maintains that despite the inability to place a biblical transgression on the employer, nevertheless the worker can claim payment direct from the employer and this is the halakah.[5]

We may see from the following commentary of Onkelos (the Aramaic translation of the Torah written in the second century C.E.) that the rabbis of that time understood the role of a monetary means of exchange. When Abraham bought the Cave of Machpelah from Ephron the Hittite, the text (Gen. 23:16) says "400 shekels of silver passed to the seller." Onkelos translates this as "were acceptable to the seller"—expressing the idea, in other words, that the basis of any means of exchange is its acceptance as such by the public. When such acceptance is withheld, as in the case of rapid inflation or drastic devaluation, alternative means of exchange develop. In the extreme case this means reverting to barter, while in less extreme cases we find a transition to other currencies.

Various halakhic decisions of that period provide records of the use of money as a major form of exchange (as explained on page 136.) Even if these decisions were subsequently altered, nevertheless they show the wide acceptance of money as a means of exchange.

At the same time, the rabbis accepted the economic role of near money—that is, goods or financial instruments, as distinct from currency, that serve as a means of payment. Debtors were allowed by the Talmudic authorities to pay their debts in kind, in those cases where the debtor had run out of cash.[6] Rav Ashi, commenting on the rule of the Mishnah that damages had to be paid in money, said that near money could also be used.[7] He also asserted that the term "near money" implies unmovable property, since chattels were considered actual money. (The word "chattels" here includes slaves and promissory notes.) We even have Rav Yani's statement that commodities can also serve as money. So the spices of Antioch are like near money, along with such goods as camels, cloths, sacks, and ropes of specific geographic areas.

Of greater importance is the rabbinic distinction between metals (such as gold, silver, and copper) as commodities and their role as a means of payment. This distinction, as well as the question of near money, will be discussed in greater detail in the section dealing with interest, since these definitions are fundamental to the halakhic treatment of interest.

These discussions in the Talmud were not meant as theoretical discourses, but rather reflected legal decisions regarding everyday business transactions involving an increasingly complex and diversified use of money in all its forms throughout the Jewish economy. Already in the Talmudic period, this economy included involvement in moneylending and banking. The following ruling shows that hire purchase (installment plan) agreements already were part of Jewish life:

> It is permissible to say to somebody hiring premises or implements, if you pay me by the month the cost will be one *sela* each month; otherwise it is ten *selim* for the year, payable now. It is forbidden, however, to make a sale in which the price is 1,000 *zuz*, but if payment is made later then the price will be 1,200 *zuz*.[8]

(The latter arrangement was seen as constituting paying interest on a loan.)

In the post-Talmudic period (after 500 C.E.), diversified financial activities became increasingly important. The Koran contains the first non-Jewish allegation of Jewish moneylending and usury.

Families such as the Netivah family rose to great prominence, both in the Jewish and Moslem worlds of Babylonia, as a result of their trading and banking activities. Such activity grew during the Crusades, and Jews were actively involved in all the financial aspects of the Moslem world.

The Crusades brought about the establishment of Jews as bankers and moneylenders, first in Western Europe and later in Eastern Europe. In England, their role was so important that special records were kept of their debtors, so that we have details regarding interest rates, the names of debtors and size of their indebtedness, and their relationship to the crown and nobility. To this day the twelfth-century house of Aaron of Lincoln, perhaps the wealthiest of the Jewish bankers in England, still stands. Nevertheless, the Jewish influence was short-lived, and toward the end of the thirteenth century Edward III called in the Italians to take the Jews' place even prior to their expulsion.

Italian Jewry's involvement in banking may be seen from the special licenses given to them; the earliest of these was that granted in the late thirteenth century in the province of Unitria. Jews remained important in this field, serving both the Popes and the secular nobility until the decline of the Italian city-states in the late sixteenth century. The first general charter of privileges granted to Jews in Poland, in the mid-thirteenth century, refers to them as moneylenders. Their role in Germany was perhaps longer and more important than in any other European country, starting in the early Middle Ages and lasting until modern times.

The source of the wealth enabling Jews to engage in banking is perhaps one of the most intriguing questions of Jewish history. It is commonly accepted that the fact that Jews were debarred from owning land, the major form of capital in feudal Europe, was the main stimulant to their holding assets in liquid form; these liquid assets then provided the basis for their financial activities. At the same time, the constant expulsion and persecution of Jews which was so characteristic of Europe, especially after the tenth century, was an added incentive to liquidity. Liquid assets, such as jewels, coins, or promissory notes, could be hidden easily, and transferred without causing severe losses.

These factors, however, should not be exaggerated: They explain why Jews kept their wealth in liquid form, not where the wealth came from. It would seem that here the major factor was the important role played by the Jew in local and international trade—at first in the countries of the Near East and North Africa, and later, in medieval Europe. The profits on international trade, especially in luxury goods, slaves, weapons, and jewelry, were exceedingly high, running into hundreds of percents.[9] This high rate of profitability also made such trade feasible despite the constant losses incurred from brigandage, piracy, etc.; the profits from one venture were often enough to wipe out the losses incurred in a number of such transactions. It was this trade which provided the funds for the Jews' subsequent involvement in moneylending and banking. This is not a specifically Jewish phenomenon; one non-Jewish example is the financing of the industrial revolution in England in the eighteenth century by means of the accumulation of profits in the preceding centuries from international trade. In our own day, the experience of the Chinese in Southeast Asia is another example of the development of a financial community from a trading one.

Irrespective of the origin of the funds available for the involvement of the Jew in financial activities, it is important to pay some attention to the reasons for that involvement. While this book cannot presume to analyze this question in detail, nevertheless it is necessary to present in a concise form some possible explanations. (It is very difficult to distinguish historical facts from views expressed in apologetic or anti-Semitic literature, and no attempt to do so will be made here.) The discussion here will be restricted to the mention of the various explanations presented for the major role of the Jew in banking, moneylending and other forms of financing.

Most of the literature on this subject has argued in defense of the Jew. Primarily the argument has been that it was a hostile society which forced the Jew into moneylending and banking. Barred from owning land, serving in the army, and other occupations, his livelihood had of necessity to be based on this occupation, from which Christians were barred because of their religious injunction against taking interest. Apologists have pointed out that actually the interest rates charged by Jews were lower than those demanded by Christian bankers.[10]

The major flaw in this argument seems to be the existence of Jewish bankers and moneylenders in the Moslem world, where the economic basis of Jewish life was not as restricted as in Christian Europe. It is true that Islam and Christianity forbade the taking of interest, but this does not seem to have been of as great importance as is commonly understood. In Islam, there existed an oral law which provided an escape clause whereby interest became legally possible. Even in the Christian world, the restriction was not as absolute as the apologists would like us to believe. First the Italians and then the Hanseatic cities of Germany, together with minor sects in France and Spain, became involved in moneylending from the period of the Crusades—this despite the Church ruling against the charging of interest.

A diametrically opposed view is that propounded by Agus.[11] According to him, Jewish initiative and entrepreneurial ability led to an involvement in the banking services needed to finance the growth in trade, both local and international, which characterized world history during and following the Crusades. This trade, together with the incipient growth of national entities (as opposed to the chaos of feudalism), provided a demand for funds and monetary assets which the Jew, in view of his international connections and cultural development, was able to supply.

It should be noted that the involvement of Jews in finance would seem to attest to their relatively high moral standing. Without this assumption, it is difficult to understand how Jews could have served as repositories of deposits or as agents for any form of banking system. Even in our day, a high moral level is essential to the conduct of monetary affairs, so that the integrity and honesty of a banking house is considered to be one of its prime assets. Furthermore, it could be argued that Jewish frugality, along with the limitations on waste and the modesty in food, drink, and clothing enforced by halakhic rulings, would automatically create a reservoir of funds that could serve as a basis for financial activities. A historical parallel may be seen in the Puritans in England, who became a basis for the banking community both because of their reputed honesty and because their modesty in everyday living released large sums of money for the purpose of finance and banking.

Perhaps all these explanations regarding the causes of Jewish involvement in banking are necessary only if one sees moneylending and taking interest as evil. If they are considered more immoral and disgraceful than any other economic activity, then we have to try to explain away the role played by the Jew in them. On the one hand, much of the uncomfortable feeling regarding this subject flows from the physical anti-Semitism caused by this Jewish activity. On the other hand, the liberal-socialist philosophy which attracted so many Jews of the nineteenth and twentieth centuries regarded the financier as an unproductive parasite. Both attitudes have permeated much Jewish historical writing. All Jewish sources, however, show that Judaism does not see anything intrinsically wrong with lending money at interest. On the contrary, it is a perfectly normal and beneficial part of economic activity, like the supply of other forms of capital. The Mosaic injunction against interest flows from a desire to place this action within the framework of righteousness, as we will discuss in greater detail in a subsequent section.

In any case, regardless of where the funds to finance Jewish moneylending and banking came from, and of what the causes of this phenomenon were, it soon became a common feature of Jewish economic life throughout Europe.

Indeed, as the economy of Europe developed and became more diversified and sophisticated, the Jewish role in banking expanded as well. In Spain, before the expulsion in the fifteenth century, Jews served not only as financiers but also as financial advisors to the crown and to members of the nobility. Perhaps the most outstanding example was Yitschak Abarbanel, a Torah scholar who served as the financial advisor to Ferdinand and Isabella of Spain. In the Germany of the fifteenth and sixteenth centuries, we find the court Jew, who was a sort of prime minister to many of the princes and dukes. His function was not just managing financial affairs but also commissioning soldiers and equipping them, and providing luxury goods and horses. In the early eighteenth century, one of these court Jews, Joseph Suss Oppenheimer, became the most powerful person in southern Germany. His attempts to concentrate political power in the hands of his patron, the Duke of Wurttemberg, led to his execution after the death of his patron. Many of the famous banking families of Western Europe in the nineteenth and twentieth centuries were descended from such court Jews as Lehman, Goldschmidt, Oppenheimer, and Rothschild.

The same intermingling of finance, trade, and other functions was evident in the Jewish economic life of Eastern Europe. A new dimension was added in these countries by the functioning of the Jew as tax collector and manager of feudal estates. Although Jews in Western Europe during the early Middle Ages had been tax collectors, the emergence of nation-states in Europe led to a phasing out of their role. Since feudalism continued to exist in Eastern Europe long after its decline in Western Europe, however, this Jewish role continued until the French Revolution and, in some places, even later.

This role of tax collector and manager of feudal estates made the Jew a middleman between the nobility and the masses. Naturally, this made him a target for the hatred and anger of the impoverished and exploited, leading to persecution and bloodshed. The Cossack uprising of Chmielnicki which devastated Polish Jewry in the seventeenth century was only one, although the most brutal, of a constant series of pogroms fueled by this role. At the same time, the holding of monopolies by Jews with respect to such common commodities as liquor, timber, and salt served to heighten anti-Semitic persecution.

One of the permanent characteristics of the Jewish banking experience in Western Europe was the high risks involved. These flowed from the pattern of persecution and expulsion, which as often as not were directly related to the Jewish role as moneylender and banker. Sometimes the persecution was a means of escaping debts, as may be seen from the description by William of Newburg of the riots in the English city of York in the late twelfth century.

> But when the slaughter of the Jews of York was over, the conspirators immediately went to the Cathedral and caused the terrified guardians, with violent threats, to hand over the records of the debts placed there, by which the Christians were oppressed by the royal Jewish usurers, and thereupon destroyed those records of profane avarice in the middle of the church with the sacred fires, to release both themselves and many others [of their debts].[12]

Whatever the reason, the Jewish role as financier and banker in Western Europe gradually declined. First, England expelled its Jews at the end of the thirteenth century. Then, in the wake of the Black Death persecution, large numbers of Jews were forced to emigrate to Central and Eastern Europe, where they soon established themselves as important financial intermediaries. By the seventeenth century, the Jews of Western Europe were, in the main, relegated to petty trade and peddling. This led to a lowering of moral standards, and so to Jewish involvement in counterfeiting, coin clipping, and evasion of debt. The Jewish Synod of Frankfurt felt it necessary to deal with these phenomena with all the power at its disposal.

It is well known how much trouble has arisen because of the wicked Jews who engage in the trade of counterfeit coins. As a result, instead of it being said, ''The remnant of Israel does no evil,'' they say ''Where is the God of this nation?'' We have therefore agreed that from this day forth, anyone engaged in such practices shall be punished. It shall be forbidden for any other Jew to marry his daughter, or to give him lodging, or to call to the Torah or to allow him to perform any religious function. This shall also apply to those who forge documents in collecting debts. . . . We have agreed that anyone who buys from one who is well known as a thief or lends a thief money or any pledge shall be punished in the manner described above. . . . Anyone who borrows money from Gentiles with the intention of failing to pay . . . them shall also be ostracized. Moreover, if he is imprisoned for such an act, no Jew will be permitted to defend him.[13]

The nineteenth century was characterized by the rapid industrialization of Western Europe, which required large sums of capital for investment and trade. This development was followed by the expansion of international trade and the building of railroads in the Americas, Africa, and Asia, which also necessitated the expansion of financial and banking services. Once again the Jew, first in Western Europe and later throughout the world, became a central figure in providing these services.

Yet, despite the growth of secularism and the political freedom gained by the Jew, twentieth century anti-Semitism continued, like its medieval forefathers, to clamor against Jewish bankers and financiers.

The centuries-long Jewish involvement in trade, credit, and banking is intimately connected with two important religious precepts: the obligation to lend money free of interest and the separate injunction against taking interest. It is to these two precepts and their ramifications that the rest of this chapter is devoted.

INTEREST-FREE LOANS

The Obligation

If [*im*] you lend money to [any of] My People, . . . you shall not be to him as a creditor; you shall not take interest from him.

The above verse in Exodus (22:24) is the basis for the positive precept of extending interest-free loans. It is interesting to point out that although the Hebrew word "*im*" is usually translated as "if," in this verse, the sages considered it to mean "when." This interpretation made giving interest-free loans a binding obligation rather than a voluntary act.

This positive commandment to lend money to a fellow Jew is one of the examples in Judaism of *chesed*, an act of loving-kindness, as distinct from acts of charity as discussed in chapter 9. These acts were considered to be obligations to which the law prescribed no limits, since *chesed* was something rendered to people primarily when they were not entitled to it. Maimonides ruled that the interest-free loan is the highest form of charity, being an expression of the biblical commandment "Thou shalt give him [the needy] support" (Lev. 25:35).[14] Charity is something one gives to the poor, whereas an act of *g'milut chesed* is one that can be directed both at poor and rich alike. To the poor person the interest-free loan represents a chance to establish himself in a craft or business, thus breaking the cycle of poverty. In the case of the rich, the interest-free loan represents a form of assistance during periods of extreme liquidity problems, thus preventing bankruptcy.

It is easy to look upon the interest-free loan commanded by the Torah as something pertinent to a primitive agrarian economy, where most financial transactions would be between a neighbor and his fellow farmer, primarily to tide one over for the next harvest. This, however, is not the way the sages saw it.

In the course of explaining the ideological basis of the mitzvot, the fourteenth-century *Sefer Hachinukh*, of Barcelona, comments as follows regarding the interest-free loan: "One who is not a pauper but who needs assistance is actually worse off than one whose poverty is public knowledge and who is used to collecting charity. If we will give [the former] assistance through the interest-free loan, he may be able to earn a livelihood and not become dependent on others [with its resulting degradation]."[15] This explanation was written at a time when the Jews, both in Spain and in other countries, were no longer farmers but were engaged in sophisticated international trade and banking.

From the earliest days of Jewish society, the interest-free loan was relevant beyond the needs of an agrarian economy and was not limited to the simple act of making small temporary loans. Irrespective of the country in which Jews lived, the sophistication of its economy, or the particular economic conditions of the Jewish community, these free loans were an integral part of the Jewish economic world. Throughout history and down to the present day, almost no Jewish community in an organized form has ever existed without the free loan as a permanent part of its communal structure.

One does not have to go back into the early history of the Jewish people in their own land to find examples of the implementation of this concept. The great Jewish migrations in the late nineteenth and early twentieth centuries, from Eastern Europe to Western Europe, the United States, South America, and Africa, can serve as an illustration of the persistence of this mitzvah. Many Jews, being poor emigrants, had neither the physical assets which could serve as collateral for bank loans, nor a personal history of financial activity sufficient to secure a credit line. In addition, Jews' illiteracy in the languages of the new countries to which they had come, and their being strangers to its social network, further militated against their being able to raise funds from the usual financial institutions.

It is quite possible that the development of Jewish economic life in trade and commerce, in real estate, or in any other economic activity would have been limited were it not for the existence of a free loan society in all of these countries. By way of contrast, perhaps one of the reasons for the difficulties which minority groups have had in establishing themselves financially today in the United States, may be that no such tradition of the free loan society exists in their cultures. Despite the centuries-old Islamic ban on interest, it is only recently that the rich Moslem countries have begun to develop the concept of interest-free loans. Until then, the objection to taking interest existed, but organized communal implementation of the interest-free loan did not.

In the State of Israel, the free loan exists as a parallel banking system. There are large public free loan societies as well as those organized by a particular synagogue, or even as a form of private initiative. The free loan societies lend money not only to their members but to the general public, usually without means tests or other questions about the purpose of the loan or the financial status of the applicant. All that is asked of the borrower is that which is required by Jewish law: namely, some guarantors who will pay should the borrower default.

The context of free loans was never restricted in Jewish law to one of duress. Such loans are not available only as something to tide one over for purposes of buying basic necessities, such as food, clothing, and shelter in a period of temporary economic distress. That is indeed one of their legitimate functions, but it is equally legitimate to borrow money from a free loan society to start a business, buy equipment, or buy a home—or for anything else, as the borrower sees fit. The free loan was never envisaged as a form of consumer protection but always as an act of righteousness, to provide people with loans for any purpose.

Security and Repayment

The rights and obligations of both lender and borrower reflect, perhaps more than any other economic transaction, the ethical and moral value structure of Judaism. There exists in this respect a perfect balance between the private wealth of the individual, his moral obligations, and his legal rights.

On the one hand, one has a religious obligation to lend his fellow Jew money in the form of an interest-free loan, since the lender is in reality only a trustee of his own wealth. On the other hand, the debtor, too, has religious obligations. He is not permitted to willfully mismanage the funds given him, nor may he spend them on riotous living. Above all, the debtor is obligated to return the loan at the date agreed upon; any deviation from this is akin to theft. This unconditional obligation to repay loans is an important concept which has implications not only in the sphere of credit, but also for many aspects of the modern economy.

In most Western economies today, the state uses selective economic intervention in order to foster its social and political aims. One of the major forms of this intervention is the granting of subsidized credit and loan capital to exporters, to provide employment of minority groups or to foster development in distressed areas.

Perhaps the case of the Israeli economy can serve as a clear example of the moral effects of a system wherein delayed payment or waiving of creditors' rights became an integral part of the economic system. In order to finance the absorption of large-scale immigration and a heavy defense burden, the new state utilized subsidized loans and cheap government credit to stimulate manufacturing, agriculture, and tourism. This perhaps made eminent sense in view of the lack of accumulated private capital. But this blanket government intervention in the capital and money markets led to the establishment of firms, on the basis not of their economic efficiency, but rather their ability to implement the socio-economic policies of the state. As often as not, these firms turned out to be white elephants, requiring large sums of public funds in order to bail them out, so as to prevent unemployment or macro-economic problems. Within a short period of time, this government policy of preventing bankruptcy and business failures became an integral part of the capital market structure. Naturally, this in turn encouraged the further establishment of inefficient firms, with a resultant squandering of public money. Furthermore, as often as not, firms did not always use the subsidized credit and loan capital for the purposes for which they were granted. All in all, this system has bred a certain immorality regarding the use of public money, over and above the economic waste involved in it.

The following discussion of the halakhic treatment of a debtor who is unable to meet his obligations may throw light on how this issue would be handled in a state run according to Jewish law.

One might argue that, since we may assume that the creditor is wealthier than the debtor, at least at this particular point in time, the former should waive his claim for repayment. This would be a meritorious deed, an act of mercy—and such was the immediate reaction of non-Jewish discussants at various forums in which I participated. However, *requiring* a creditor to do so makes him assume a responsibility for the welfare of his debtor over and above the obligations imposed on him by the mitzvah of the interest-free loan. Naturally the creditor may decide voluntarily to add an act of charity to the act of righteousness embodied in the interest-free loan, and as such this would be meritorious. To so *obligate* him, however, would be to obscure the conceptual differences between these two religious precepts. To deny the lender his money on the basis of the need of the debtor blurs the demarcation between justice and mercy which is such an important element in Judaism. It must be stressed that the community always has a definite obligation to solve the social and economic problems of the debtor; the creditor, as a member of the community, shares in that duty. Yet, justice demands repayment of loans made as acts of righteousness and not the assumption by an individual of what is a communal responsibility.

The halakhic authorities insist that, if necessary, the debtor be compelled to divest himself of his assets in order to pay back his loan. He would be left with only religious articles (*tallit* and *tefillin*) and food, clothing, and necessities for a certain period of time.[16]

This may seem to be cruel and stern, yet it has to be viewed within the Jewish framework of mutual assistance: of individuals acting beyond the demands of the law and an age-old record of communal responsibility. The same halakhic system which is so careful to protect the just claims of the creditor is as careful to protect not only the property of the debtor, but his mental and social peace as well.

The *Sefer Hachinukh* sees the above-mentioned biblical verse in Exodus, "you shall not be to him as a creditor," as expressing an obligation on the part of the lender not to demand payment when he knows that the borrower cannot repay it.[17] Nevertheless, even though one who does so transgresses a negative commandment, there is no legal way to prevent the collection of a due debt.

The inability of the debtor to pay his debt, discussed above, is only one of the risks against which the lender has to be protected. It is necessary to provide the means whereby he would be legally entitled to claim and enforce payment at the appropriate time. One of the ways to do this is the halakhic insistence that "There are three who cry out [for redress] and are not listened to [since they have brought their troubles on themselves]. They are: he who lends his money without witnesses. . . ."[18] Another method is to secure the loan by means of a pledge. In other words, the debtor hands over to the creditor an article of comparable value which remains in the latter's possession until repayment of the loan. Present-day examples of such pledges are loans where the borrower's home, machinery, inventory, etc., serve as collateral.

The symmetry of justice in Judaism demands that at the same time as we secure the creditor's loan, due attention has to be paid to the legal and moral rights of the debtor. This can be seen in all the rabbinic rulings regarding collateral. Nothing may be done by the creditor that will in any way damage the pledge or its value, even where such value is only subjective. For example, writing in seventeenth-century Austria–Hungary, Rabbi Yehoshua Falk Ha-Cohen rules that "those who argue that one may study a book (used as a pledge) in order to fulfill the mitzvah of Torah study, do so only in cases where the owner has agreed. It is not permitted to use a book without the owner's knowledge, since he may be very concerned that such use result in damage to it."[19] Pledges such as implements, which depreciate through usage, may not be used by the creditor, since the benefit derived from their use is considered interest on the loan.

Furthermore, certain assets can serve as pledges only temporarily, while others are completely beyond the reach of the creditor. So we find the Talmudic injunction that a craftsman's solitary set of tools, used as a pledge, had to be returned to him each morning.[20] This injunction was based on the biblical verse (Deut. 24:6) forbidding the taking of a millstone as security for a loan. Since millstones were essential for the crushing or grinding of wheat and barley into flour, their possession by the creditor would mean that the debtor's family would be unable to eat. A similar biblical injunction (Exod. 22:25–26) is explained by Rashi as enjoining the taking of basic necessities such as a pillow or a cloak. It was understood by halakhic authorities throughout the ages as preventing the use of all essential items as pledges.[21]

The protection afforded by the Torah to the debtor did not only extend to the goods or articles which could properly serve as security for the loan; his privacy, too, was protected. Thus, creditors are not allowed to enter a debtor's house without his permission.

The best example, perhaps, of the moral and psychological aspects of this protection of the debtor's interests is Maimonides' ruling regarding loans made to widows.[22] Maimonides writes that one may not give a loan on pledge to a widow irrespective of whether she is rich or poor. At first sight, this ruling sounds very strange. We could understand, perhaps, the exemption of a pledge in the case of a poor widow. There does not seem, however, to be much logic in not discriminating between a rich woman—whether a widow or not—and a poor one. The commentators explained Maimonides' ruling in two ways: a) Having a pledge gave the creditor certain power over the widow, which could perhaps be used for immoral purposes; and b) The widow's entering his home to constantly examine whether her pledge was still existent and in good condition would compromise her good name. Since the reasons behind this regulation are primarily those of sexual morality, it obviously makes no difference whether the widow is poor or rich.

INTEREST IN THE TORAH

The Religious Injunction against Taking Interest

The above discussion was focused on the interest-free loan as a positive religious act in Judaism. Separate and distinct from this mitzvah is the *negative* mitzvah of not taking interest, which is repeated numerous times in the Bible. In the eyes of the halakhic authorities, this repetition of the injunction against taking interest serves to compound the severity of the crime, making the participants liable on a number of different counts.[23] Even the use of two different Hebrew terms, *neshekh* and *tarbit*, both to mean "interest," is seen as reflecting the desire of the Torah to make a man liable for two transgressions from making the same single interest-bearing loan. It is interesting to see the Jewish social attitude toward interest expressed in Rashi's comment on the use of the word *neshekh* (literally, a "bite"). A snake bite is at first only slightly uncomfortable, but later increases in pain and severity. So, too, interest (*neshekh*) is at first bearable, but as the debt mounts, the debtor's suffering increases.[24]

From the Torah's viewpoint, the transgression involved in making interest-bearing loans is not limited to the lender, even though he is obviously the major factor and so bears the brunt of the responsibility. Rather, all parties to the transaction are guilty of violating religious injunctions. The lender is guilty, inter alia, of putting a stumbling block in the path of the blind (Lev. 19:14), which the rabbinic authorities always understood as referring to giving prejudiced advice to somebody or providing him with things that are to his spiritual or physical detriment.[25] Agents or other go-betweens in the transaction are considered to be guilty of the same crime. In keeping with Judaism's symmetry of justice, even the borrower is not left untouched. After all, it is his need or desire for the loan which has implicated the lender in a moral crime. Even the witnesses to the transaction, as well as the guarantors of an interest-bearing loan, are considered to have violated the injunction of "you shall not take interest from him." Without their participation, it is highly improbable that the transaction would have taken place. It is only fitting, therefore, that they share in the guilt attached to the maker of the interest-bearing loan by the Torah.[26]

Halakhic Definitions of Interest

Halakhically, there are two distinct definitions of interest, differing in both their religious stringency and their legal status. It must be pointed out, before proceeding to discuss these two types, that halakhic definitions and distinctions are not always synonymous with those made by economists. This is true in many other spheres of life—as, for example, in the case of a slaughtered animal which may be perfectly healthy ("eatable") from a biological or veterinary viewpoint, yet is declared ritually unfit to be eaten. Since what concerned the halakhic authorities was solely the tenets of the Torah, their decisions reflect those tenets and therefore become the binding Jewish "definitions" of interest.

The halakhah distinguishes between that interest forbidden directly by the Torah (*ribit m'd'oraita*) and that which is forbidden according to rabbinic law (*ribit m'd'rabanan*). Although both of them are forbidden to Jews, the religious implications of the former are more stringent.

Interest Forbidden by the Torah

The Torah is understood to directly forbid loans in which the recipient is liable to pay a known sum for the use of money. For example, Reuven lends Shimon a thousand dollars for a year on the condition that Shimon return one thousand one hundred dollars at the end of the year. This is known as apportioned interest, or *ribit k'tsutsah*.

It is important to note that since Judaism views the problem of interest from a moral-ethical viewpoint rather than according to its practical effects, it is the existence of interest itself that is important. There is no distinction, therefore, in the biblical injunction— nor in rabbinic rulings—among different levels of interest: Two percent interest is as much as a transgression as is fifty percent interest. This is in sharp contrast to the ideological pattern of modern social and economic reformers, who have directed their energies toward lowering rates of interest rather than attacking interest as such—leading in various countries to the formation of credit unions, the nationalization of banking systems, and public-sector loans at subsidized rates of interest.

Interest, as defined by the Torah, can be abrogated by the appeal of the borrower to a *bet din*. In other words, Shimon can, after the loan has been transacted, appeal to the rabbinic courts to force Reuven to waive the interest charge.[27]

Rabbinic Interest

There are an almost inexhaustible number of transactions in the marketplace which, in effect (even if not formally), constitute an interest-bearing loan. The easiest example to cite is the hire-purchase (installment plan) system. In this case, Reuven does not formally loan Shimon the thousand dollars. Rather, he sells him goods that are valued at the time of the sale at a thousand dollars and gives him sixty days credit. In exchange for this credit, Shimon will pay Reuven an additional, agreed-upon fee over and above the purchase price. Formally this is no loan, and so there is no interest. In actual fact, however, Reuven is receiving a payment in exchange for waiting for his money, which is in the economic sense considered interest. Halakhically, too, this is considered interest. Yet it is distinct from that defined by the Torah, and so is considered "rabbinic interest." The levying of rabbinic interest is forbidden, but may not be cancelled by a *bet din*.[28]

The forms that this rabbinic interest can take are far too varied for us to discuss here. Those of them which represent important examples pertinent to our own day are dealt with in a later section of this chapter on changes in the value of money. Since these economically common forms of rabbinic interest are forbidden, history has witnessed a constant battle of wits between the rabbis and the businessmen—the latter, obviously, seeking to circumvent the anti-interest regulations by means of sophisticated business transactions which disguise the loan aspect and, therefore, might appear at first sight to be permitted by Jewish law.

From a theoretical economic point of view, interest contains two elements: a time factor and an element of risk. The supplier of the money is unable to use that money for as long as the loan is operative. By extending the loan, therefore, he is losing, so to speak, the alternative use of his money in other ventures. For this loss of freedom the lender will desire to be paid. Basically, he is being paid interest for waiting to receive back his money. Furthermore, any loan, like any investment, contains an element of risk. It is possible that the debtor may not be able to pay the interest, or may not be able to pay back the loan on time, or at all. In any case, the creditor will want to be compensated for the risk involved, and the interest charged represents the creditor's compensation. The greater the risk envisaged, the higher will be the interest rate.

I must hasten to point out that it is not always easy, from an accounting or economic point of view, to determine whether the interest charged is payment for risk or whether it is simply a payment for the use of money for a specific period. In most economies, investment in government notes represents as risk-free an investment as possible, whereas extending consumer credit may be considered a high-risk venture. Obviously, within every type of loan transaction the degree of risk varies with the individual or institution concerned; we will return to this problem in the course of our discussion. At this stage, it is sufficient to point out that the halakhic definition of interest differentiates between those cases where the creditor has a share in the risk involved and those where he is paid simply for waiting for repayment of his loan. The emphasis is on the economic reality of the transaction and not simply on its formal presentation.

Before proceeding to a discussion of the implications of the religious ban on interest, it is necessary to evaluate the ideology on which it is based. Perhaps the best way to present this conceptual framework is to analyze the Torah's position on interest vis-à-vis non-Jews.

Interest vis-à-vis Non-Jews

The injunction against the taking of interest applies solely to a transaction between two Jews. It does not apply to non-Jews, so that it is permissible to lend to or borrow from a Gentile and receive or incur interest. Loans involving a corporation or bank whose shareholders or depositors are not Jewish may carry interest without transgressing either biblical or rabbinic rulings;[29] this would not apply to bank deposits by a Jew in a Jewish financial institution.[30] It is true that it has been argued that interest involving a limited liability corporation is permissible, since such corporations are separate legal entities distinct from their shareholders, so that there is no direct lender–borrower relationship. It is not at all clear, however, whether all halakhic authorities recognize the legal separation of the corporation from its shareholders regarding the prohibition against interest. Be that as it may, it is quite clear that almost all authorities follow the Mishnaic ruling permitting interest-bearing loans involving non-Jews.

> It is not permissible to receive assets [for the purpose of operating with them, e.g., sheep given to a shepherd under condition that the owner and shepherd share in the wool, lambs, and milk] with responsibility [where the full responsibility in case of theft or death of the flock falls on the receiver] from a Jew, since this is interest. [It is rabbinic interest, according to Maimonides, since the owner has no share in the risk. Other authorities, like *Tosafot*, see this as *ribbit medoraitha* as the profit accrues to the shepherd, who pays a fixed sum annually to the owner for the use of his capital.]
>
> It is permissible, however to accept such assets from a Gentile. It is permitted to borrow from Gentiles and to lend to them interest-bearing loans. This ruling also applies to a *ger toshav* [a Gentile who lives in the land of Israel and accepts the seven Noachide laws].[31]

Maimonides represents the biblical verse, "To the Gentile you may [*tashikh*] lend upon interest" (Deut. 23:21) as a positive injunction; he views the Hebrew *tashikh* as meaning "You shall" rather than "You may," so receiving interest from or paying interest to a Gentile is not something left up to one's discretion but rather a *mitzvah*.[32] We can perhaps understand his view in the light of his interpretation of the Jewish people as a chosen people. Maimonides maintains that the choosing of the Jewish people was a result of the rejection of God by the rest of creation and their adoption of idolatry. It was the failure of mankind from Adam onwards to maintain their relationship with God which led to the isolating of a specific group to carry out that which was originally given to all men. Thus, they were released from the laws of the Torah including the injunctions against receiving or paying interest.[33]

There are other commentators, like the Ramban (Nachmanides), who argued, on various grounds, that the taking of interest from Gentiles was permissible, but not obligatory. The Raivad, in his gloss on Maimonides' *Mishneh Torah*, avers that we are to understand the Torah as granting permission to lend Gentiles money at interest rather than obliging us to do so.

Rav Hiya, in the Talmudic discussion on the ruling in the Mishnah quoted above, felt that one should be engaged in moneylending to Gentiles only if there was no other occupation open to one, or only to the extent of providing a livelihood.[34]

It seems, however, that their disagreement with Maimonides was based not on grounds of morality but rather on other considerations. For instance, in the same Talmudic discussion, Ravina held that moneylending to Gentiles led to general intercourse with them and should be limited in order to prevent Jews from learning from the evil ways of the Gentile world. On the other hand, Rabbenu Tam, in the eleventh century, argued that since the Jewish–Gentile commerce was no longer limited, neither therefore should the practice of moneylending be limited.

Finally, other sources like the *Mekhilta* of Rabbi Ishmael (commenting on the parallel verse in Exodus [22:24] forbidding interest-bearing loans), argue that acts of *chesed* enjoined on the Jew, such as the interest-free loan, should be extended to non-Jews—in accordance with the principle in Jewish law that, "for the sake of peace," Jews act on various principles of righteousness and kindness in their dealing with non-Jews, even when such behavior is not biblically obligatory.

Irrespective of whether they saw moneylending as obligatory, permissible, or undesirable, the mainstream of halakhic authorities saw nothing intrinsically wrong with money earning interest. Yitschak Abarbanel, financier and rabbinic scholar in the Spain of Ferdinand and Isabella, sums up what seems to be the majority opinion of rabbinic authorities. "People make profits out of dealing in capital, wine, and corn, and there is no difference between earning profits and lending money. Why should a farmer who received [a loan for purchasing] wheat to sow not pay a percentage to the lender? This is an ordinary business transaction and a correct one."[35]

The Torah does not view interest taking as an intrinsically evil action, akin to murder or theft, or it would have forbidden it altogether. After all, those acts that are intrinsically evil are forbidden irrespective of whether they're done to Jew or Gentile. If, indeed, Judaism does not view interest as inherently evil, why, then, was interest taking (or giving) forbidden among Jews? The author of the *Sefer Hachinukh*, which is devoted to explaining the ideological basis for the commandments, seems to sum up the general opinion of Jewish authorities. Commenting on the verse "you shall not take interest from him" (Exod. 22:24), it comments: "According to the normal morality of the world one should be entitled to charge for the use of one's money. However, since the whole purpose of the *mitzvot* is to purify the Jew, [God] instructed us to give up that which is acceptable by normal moral standards."[36] (One may see as a parallel the injunction on the Jew to refrain from eating non-kosher food in order to elevate his material needs to a higher plane. The eating of such food is not detrimental, per se, and so, at their discretion, Gentiles may eat or not of it.)

Following this idea, the *Torah Temimah* (a twentieth-century commentator) writes (on Deut. 23:21) that "our refraining from taking interest from one another is similar to the regulations of many trade and other associations in which the members provide each other with special benefits. Such benefits are not available to outsiders. Yet there is nothing to prevent others from establishing similar associations and providing the same help."

It should be fairly obvious that an obligation to practice a one-way-street system of morality, whereby the Jew did not charge interest to non-Jews who themselves lent their money at interest, would be a superhuman demand and one doomed to failure. An interesting idea in this respect, which I believe to be in the mainstream of rabbinic thinking, was presented to me by Rabbi Simcha Wasserman. He argues that lending money at interest is not only not intrinsically bad but is essential to the economy. Extending interest-bearing loans is actually beneficial to the borrower, who would be worse off if these loans were withheld. The special mutual responsibility of Jews to one another obliges them to extend interest-free loans to each other even though the reward, in the form of interest, is lacking. To exact this requirement of the Jew toward all people, on a unilateral basis, would simply deprive borrowers of any loans, thus causing them hardship.

It is important to stress that even those authorities who urged Jews not to engage in moneylending at all, or only to the extent that their livelihood depended on it, did so either from apologetic reasons—to ward off non-Jewish criticism—or from a moral belief in the desirability of acts of *chesed* (kindness) toward non-Jews. They did not subscribe to the Catholic idea, based on Aristotle, that money, unlike other forms of capital, was barren: that money, unlike trees or cattle or land, could not of itself produce wealth, and therefore the suppliers of loan capital were not morally entitled to receive payment for their funds. There does not seem to be any substantial body of halakhic authorities in any period who subscribed to this opinion.

HETER ISKA

Already in Mishnaic times, some 2,000 years ago, the reality of the marketplace, the demands of international trade, and an increasingly complicated money market produced situations wherein the distinction between the loan aspect of a financial transaction and the trading aspects was not always clear. Many ventures were carried out as a form of joint venture, a primitive stage in the development of our modern joint-stock company. The partners contributed varying sums of capital for a special trading venture,and their share of the profits varied accordingly. Some partners participated actively in the transaction as buyers, sellers, or artisans, while the participation of the others would be limited solely to providing funds. There were even cases in which the active partner made no financial investment at all. In all these variations the role of the inactive partners raised a serious halakhic problem, since it was possible that they were simply suppliers of loans. The following ruling in the Mishnah presents what would seem to be the basic approach to the problem, as it has been endorsed by the authorities down to our own day.

> It is not permitted to make a joint venture with a trader [providing him with goods at market value to be sold on a retail basis] on the basis of equal shares in profit or loss. Nor may one give money to a trader to buy on one's behalf [for resale], both parties sharing equally in the profit or loss. In both cases, it is necessary to pay the trader a laborer's fee.[37]

The reason for disallowing such a venture lies in the fact that the investment actually consists of two separate sums. Half of it is a regular loan to the trader, for which he is responsible and from which he earns his profit. The other half is a deposit, on which the supplier of the funds or goods earns the whole profit or suffers the whole loss. Since the trader has no share in the profits earned by the deposit, all his risks and efforts involved in that share of the operation earn profits only for the investor, and this constitutes *avak ribit*—rabbinic interest.

In order to legalize this type of transaction, the Mishnah required the investor to pay the active partner wages. The exact definition of how these wages were to be determined is beyond the scope of our discussion. What is important is that such payment meant that the share of the investor was always to be less than half, so that some return was given to the active partner for his trouble, time, and effort.

Many forms of converting financial transactions into *iska*, or real business ventures, developed whereby the investor participated in the risks and profit in unequal proportion to the active partner. Since this was permissible even according to the rabbinic definition of interest (which was wider than that proscribed by biblical injunction), it enabled Jews to participate in international and local trade as well as in increasingly sophisticated financial ventures. While real business ventures were permissible, economic pressures often created fictitious ventures aimed solely at evading the rabbinic injunctions against interest. In order to limit abuse, the rabbinic authorities in the Middle Ages formalized the legal form under which such ventures could take place without breaking the rabbinic law against interest—the so-called *heter iska*. It must be stressed that there was no way to legalize the taking of biblical interest—viz., the earning of money on a straight loan transaction.

A partial text of a *heter iska* is reproduced here in order to acquaint the reader with its main conditions. Apart from those following from the previous discussion, there is an additional one whereby the investor could forego his share of the profits, his right to a current financial report of the transaction and other documentation, and any other claims in return for a fixed sum.

> I have received from Reuven the sum of 100 dollars to trade with for six months. . . . This money takes precedence over my own investment regarding all profits which God may give me from this venture. Half of the profit shall be given to Reuven and half shall belong to me [together with some remuneration, even token, for the borrower's trouble]. The same shall apply to the loss. As soon as the six months are over, I undertake to return the 100 dollars and Reuven's half share of the profit. . . . We have agreed

that if I wish to do so, I may pay Reuven 10 dollars in lieu of his share of the profit. In that case, he has no further claims against me, even if it be evident that there is considerable profit.[38]

All financial institutions and banks in the State of Israel operate under a *heter iska* whereby the parties to transactions become, in effect, partners to a joint venture, sharing in profits and losses. In actual fact, today the *heter iska* simply formalizes a situation which exists and is not to be regarded as a legal subterfuge. Modern banking makes the lender an investor in the firm or individual to which it grants loans, if not in the legal sense then definitely in the economic sense. The vast majority of loans, both commercial and consumer, are not made solely on the basis of collateral but are heavily influenced by the business performance or income prospects of the borrower. Any decline in the borrower's profits or income may lead to slower repayment of the debt. Sustained losses or economic problems on the part of the borrower may lead to bankruptcy—and, therefore, to the total or partial loss of the funds advanced.

In many countries, the investment of the lender is far greater than that of the shareholders, so that in economic terms the former is, in reality, an investor. In Japan, owners' equity equals roughly a quarter of the total assets of corporations; in Israel, a third. Even in the United States, where leverage is lower than in almost all Western countries, equity in manufacturing corporations equals only 50 to 60 percent of total assets. From the above, it should be clear that lenders to firms often share in the risks which suppliers of equity capital bear, so that, in effect, they are partners, even though legally they are only lenders. Any examination of the analyses made by banks, finance companies, and credit managers will show that to a large extent, such analyses are identical to these made by investors. This is perhaps the best evidence of the nature of the modern lender as, in effect, an investor.

It would seem that in a modern state run on a halakhic basis, there would exist two different monetary systems: First, a system based on the principle of *heter iska*, wherein the lender-*cum*-investor has a potential share in the risks involved, so that the interest (in economic terms) paid to him does not contravene the rabbinic definition of interest; and second, a system of interest-free loans (*g'milut chesed*) for all those cases wherein the lender definitely has no investor role, and therefore, no real risk.

In the case of various types of modern-day consumer borrowing, rabbinic opinion should be obtained regarding the necessity for a *heter iska*. The following discussion is meant only to highlight the halakhic issues involved.

Mortgage Loans

Where mortgage loans, either first or second ones, are obtained from Jews or Jewish-owned institutions, it would seem that perhaps a *heter iska* does not avail. The mortgage loan has all the legal trappings of a long-term loan secured by a lien on real estate. In such loans, payments by the borrower are simply compensation for the lender's waiting period and would seem, therefore, to be a case of *ribit m'd'oraita* (interest as defined by the Torah itself) and therefore forbidden. Since the lender faces no risk, the *heter iska* would seem not to constitute a solution.[39]

Laws or customs preventing the creditor from evacuating the householder upon default on the debt would change the situation. Lacking the ability to sell a vacant property, the holder of the mortgage now faces a real risk, since he has, in effect, made an unsecured loan; the security offered by the real estate may be worthless. The Israeli custom of demanding personal guarantees alongside the mortgage reflects the creditor's need to protect his loan.

Furthermore, however, it must be borne in mind that the real estate market in most countries is very volatile one. The mortgage holder, therefore, is faced with a risk of default and, perhaps, of not even being able to receive the amount of the mortgage from resale of the property. Furthermore, the homeowner has a profit, as it were, from this transaction in the form of living rent-free. (In the United States there is a further "profit" to the homeowner since the interest payments are recognized as tax-deductible expenses.) These two factors, the homeowner's profit and the mortgage holder's risk, would suggest that the *heter iska* necessary in such loans is simply a legal recognition of a fact of economic life.

Buying and Selling on Credit

A common feature of all modern economies is the great expansion in the buying and selling of goods on credit. This includes the business sector, in which trade credit, given and received, has always formed a major part of corporate finance, as well as consumer credit. Trade credit takes many forms. Some are formal, such as the buying of capital goods on a mortgage or hire purchase agreement, as discussed above. Others take a less structured form, as in the common practice of simply paying for one's purchases at the end of a given period. For the purposes of this discussion, the use of credit cards has not been included, since this is primarily an act of borrowing from a bank and therefore belongs to the general question of bank borrowing.

In all these transactions, obviously, a payment is made for the use of a credit facility. In economic terms, such payments are interest payments. The question to be reviewed here is whether they constitute interest according to halakhic definitions and are hence forbidden unless accompanied by a *heter iska*.

It is known that the default rate on consumer credit in countries like the United States is very high. At the same time, the security held by the extender of credit against such loans is usually not very great (compared, for instance, to that demanded for bank or mortgage loans). The halakhic implementation in such cases of *heter iska* would, again, constitute a legal recognition that there exists a business partnership, including elements of risk and profit, rather than a simple loan.

Not all credit transactions, however, involve explicit interest. Sometimes the buyer of goods or services is entitled to a cash discount provided the debt is paid within a certain period. From an economic point of view such discounts also represent interest, the interest being the sum which the supplier is prepared to pay in order to have his debt returned to him sooner than is the normal practice in that trade or industry. Many firms often imagine that the trade credit they receive is interest-free, since there is no arrangement for payment of additional sums after the usual time period current in their trade. Yet, the cash discount which they would receive if they paid before the time period is in effect the interest rate for the credit used by them. Such interest, in the form of cash reductions, is an interesting example of where halakhic definitions of interest differ from those of economists.

Thus, whereas the halakhic ruling requiring a *heter iska* with respect to credit purchases involving an interest rate is quite clear, the attitude toward cash discounting does not seem to be so. Maimonides ruled that if Reuven bought an article from Shimon for $100 and the market practice or custom was that for such goods payment could be delayed for a month at the original price, then if Shimon suggested that in exchange for immediate cash payment he would sell the article for $90, this was not to be considered interest at all.[40] Rabbi Joseph Caro, however, in his *Shulchan Arukh*, argued that such discounts would not be considered interest only where no accepted price exists.[41] In both cases, however, it seems that the halakhic sources treat cash discounts differently from extra payments for credit. Unlike the economists, who consider both to be interest, the rabbis tend to view discounts as not always constituting interest. In a discussion with a rabbinic authority, it was explained to the author that this flows from the idea that the law against interest refers only to increasing the borrower's burden; those things that reduce it do not fall into the category of interest.

Interest on Government Loans

The State of Israel poses a special problem regarding interest—one that, it would seem, has not existed for many centuries of Jewish life. In common with most governments, the State of Israel raises funds from the public, both in Israel and abroad, in the form of forced loans, Israel Bonds, and other government paper, issued for short or long terms. These government loans, issued by a Jewish state, have raised a number of interesting problems and concepts that it would seem pertinent to discuss here. Since these are clearly loans which bear interest rates, they are not permissible unless accompanied by a *heter iska*. In common with all Israeli banks, the Bank of Israel (Israel's Central Bank, similar to the Federal Reserve Bank in the United States) has issued a *heter iska* in order to enable it to serve as the issuer of such state loans. Although such is the authoritative position, as decided by the Chief Rabbinate of Israel, there have been a number of questions raised that introduce some interesting insights into the halakhic treatment of interest.

Indirect Loans

According to Jewish law, the act of making an interest-bearing loan is illegal only if it is done directly between two individual

Jews. The use of non-Jewish intermediaries in order to evade the injunctions against interest has been a very common feature of Jewish life, and the rabbinic authorities constantly had to examine such partnerships in order to separate real intermediaries from fictitious transactions. On the basis of this requirement, the question has been raised whether state loans, as well as those made between two corporations or between a corporation and an individual, fall into the category of legitimate partnerships, even though the majority of the shareholders are Jewish. Since the joint-stock company is considered in general law as a separate legal entity, independent of the assets or personalities of the shareholders, the involvement of such corporations in financial transactions seems to negate one of the requirements of halakhic interest. There is a present-day responsum by Rabbi Weiss, formerly of Manchester, now the head of the *bet din* of the *Eida Charedit* in Jerusalem, that even in such a case, a *heter iska* is required.[42]

Loans or Charity?

It has also been suggested that interest-bearing State of Israel loans are quite legal since the purpose of these loans is to provide defense and encourage Jewish immigration, both of which are akin to saving Jewish lives (*pikuach nefesh*—a halakhically paramount consideration). It is well known that halakhic authorities over the centuries not only permitted the sale of religious articles and institutions (like Torah scrolls and syngogues) in order to redeem Jewish refugees, but also allowed communities to take interest-bearing loans from Jews for this purpose. On the basis of these precedents, it is argued that the State of Israel is engaged in *pikuach nefesh*, the saving of Jewish lives, and can therefore be permitted to take interest-bearing loans without a *heter iska*.[43]

I do not know what the legal status of the following story is, but the economic history of many countries lends an element of truth to it. One rabbinic scholar told me that his father-in-law had ruled that Israeli state loans and the interest thereon were not to be considered interest, since in actual fact these were not real loans. When a loan is made to a corporation or to an individual, the two parties to the loan are equal: The one supplies funds and the other undertakes to repay them. A breach of the obligation to repay could quite easily be settled in a court of law. In the case of a state loan, however, the borrower is in a radically different position from the lender, since it is quite easy for the state to renege on public debt; such has been done in the past by more than one state, as a result of either political changes or economic difficulties. The interest payments on such loans, therefore, constitute an act of charity or a gift more than interest on a debt, since the borrower always has the power only not to comply with the interest agreement, but not to pay back even the principal. Many economists have shown that the public does indeed react to forced loans as taxes and to the interest thereon as windfall profits.

On the other hand, many religious Jews in Israel have consistently refused to accept the interest on government debt in the form of forced loans, on the argument that this is interest and that the *heter iska* held by the government does not have much validity since there is no business transaction, unless the question of a moratorium is taken seriously.

Parallels in the Private Sector

A parallel situation may exist with regard to what are in effect the forced loans made by utility companies who demand from consumers a deposit, to be kept for as long as the meter, telephone, etc., is in the hands of the user. In order for the utility not to be accused of simply defrauding the consumer, such deposits are regarded as interest-bearing loans, and from time to time the consumer will receive interest payments on these sums. If these sums are regarded as interest payments for the use of the consumer's deposits, then obviously they are not legal in Judaism, even if there is a *heter iska*. However, some public utilities in Israel have regarded them as a form of profit sharing by consumers in the corporation. As such, they may be legitimate from a halakhic point of view, even though still requiring a *heter iska*.

The Halakhic Concept of Money

Throughout the centuries and even in our day, changes in price levels and government-sponsored debasement of the currency gave rise to halakhic questions regarding interest: in the case of straight loans, *ribit m'd'oraita* (biblical interest), and in the case of business ventures, *ribit m'd'rabanan* (rabbinic interest). In either case, grantors of loans will want to be paid back in real purchasing power, while the lender will endeavor to repay according to the lower nominal value of the debt.

The question whether or not there is a problem of interest depends on the definition of money, its purchasing power and its nominal value. The halakhic treatment of money seems to be based on three concepts: its metallic content; the authority of the state; and acceptance in the marketplace.

Metallic Content

According to this idea, it is the metallic content of coins that provides them with an intrinsic value. This value will fluctuate according to changes in the amount of precious metal included in the coins. Such changes can be caused by the substitution of coins of lesser metallic value, or by debasing the metallic content of the original coinage. In our own day, the devaluation practiced by governments achieves the same purpose. Naturally, this affects the level of prices in the economy. In the days of the Mishnah and Talmud, this was a common feature of the monetary policy of the Roman emperors. Changes in metallic content were considered to produce devalued coinage (*hufchat*), while substitutions of coins of less metallic value produced "faulty" coins (*nifgam*). The halakhic treatment of changes in currency is dealt with later in the chapter.

In bimetallic economies, where coins of two different metals were used, the halakhic ruling was that for purposes of determining whether payment constituted interest, the more precious and less common metal had the status of a commodity vis-à-vis the other, more common, one. So, for example, in the Mishnah we are told that "gold coins may purchase silver coins [without any further legal acts], but silver coins cannot purchase gold ones."[44] According to rabbinic law, the mere transfer of money does not itself legally complete a sale; for that purpose a further legal act, *kinyan*, was necessary. However, the transfer of goods was sufficient to complete a transaction. Since gold, for example, was considered a "good," its transfer from one person to another was sufficient to constitute a sale, whereas in the case of silver (considered as merely money), this was not so.

The Rama, in his gloss on the *Shulchan Arukh*, writes that "in our day [sixteenth-century Eastern Europe], gold coins have the same law as those of silver [since they were legal tender], and so in respect of loans in such coins, the authorities . . . were more lenient."[45] (Silver coins, it will be remembered, were exempted from the definition of goods for purposes of defining interest.) This meant that borrowers taking loans in gold coins—now considered money, not goods—were obligated to return the same number of coins irrespective of what happened in the interim to their value.

Until modern times, metallic content remained the basis of the monetary system. Beginning in the eighteenth century, however, paper money, backed by a linkage to gold or silver, began to appear alongside coins made of precious metals. In our own day, bank notes are no longer linked to reserves of precious metals held by the state. It would seem, however, that this does not detract from their halakhic role as money, as the rabbis discerned other factors determining the value of money.

The Authority of the State

In the Austro-Hungarian Empire of some 150 years ago, the *Chatam Sofer* invoked the state's authority when he wrote the following opinion concerning the nature of the bank note from a halakhic point of view (i.e., whether it constituted money or not). "The basic qualification to be met by anything in order to conform to the concept of money flows from the decree of the King [or state] that it constitute legal tender. No one can then refuse to sell goods and accept it in return except on forfeit of his head to the King. It is irrelevant whether the article used to represent money is gold, silver, or paper."[46] Owing, then, to the authority of the state, modern bank notes have the character of money, even though a promissory note or bill receivable issued by a private individual does not. Halakhically, such a private note is simply an acknowledgment of debt and is, therefore, not money. Formerly, bank notes carried a promise by the government to issue the holder equal value in specie; this no longer appears, so that the bank note is not even a notice of debt. Nevertheless, owing to the state's authority and monopoly inherent in the issuing of bank notes, they do constitute money.

The Authority of the Marketplace

In our own day, in Israel, the Chazon Ish defined the halakhic concept of money as "anything which the people of a country accept as legal tender in order to buy and sell with or to evaluate therewith all the transactions of the marketplace."[47] The function of money, therefore, derives from the laws of supply and demand and the degree of people's confidence in the currency.

A similar approach can be found some 900 years earlier in the writings of the North African sage, Isaac Alfasi. His opinion was asked in reference to the halakhic basis for buying promissory notes. Actually, such notes do not represent real assets, since they are only an acknowledgment of debt, payment of which may or may not materialize. Jewish law does not permit the sale of assets that "have not yet been created." But Alfasi ruled that since merchants were in the habit of buying and selling such notes, they in fact turned into real assets and so could be traded (obviously at discount rates, commensurate with the risk involved).[48]

Irrespective of whether one accepts the *Chatam Sofer*'s definition of money as deriving from the law of the land or that of the Chazon Ish, as based on acceptance in the marketplace, paper notes are to be considered halakhically as money, even though they no longer have metallic or other intrinsic worth.

HALAKHIC PROBLEMS REGARDING CHANGES IN THE VALUE OF MONEY

Following the principle laid down in the introduction to this book, problems created by changes in the value of money will be discussed without attempting to provide specific halakhic answers; for that purpose, practical questions have to be addressed to the proper rabbinic authorities. The positions presented here, rather, are provided primarily as discussion points and should be viewed as such. These discussions, furthermore, will try to emphasize the economic and ethical issues involved rather than the legal ones.

For halakhic purposes a distinction is made between situations wherein prices of goods change (owing to inflation or deflation) while the currency remains nominally stable, and those in which changes in the nominal value of the currency occur (as a result of devaluation or revaluation). These two situations, therefore, will be discussed separately.

Irrespective of the cause, changes in the value of money affect us in different ways. When it rises, we require more money to buy the same "amount" of goods and services, so that we have incurred a loss in our economic wealth. On the other hand, we now need less money to pay back loans or debts incurred during a previous period; this constitutes a profit for us borrowers. However, we may find that our savings, in the form of pension funds or insurance policies, are relatively worthless, since they can no longer provide the security anticipated—so in that respect we are worse off. Obviously what is an inflationary profit to one party constitutes a loss to another.

During periods of rapid and substantial change in the value of money—reflected both in changes in the prices of some goods and services relative to others and those involving changes in overall general price levels—lenders will obviously try to protect themselves against losses flowing from such changes. One important protective device is common today in many countries: viz., linkage of loans, wages, or insurance benefits, either to the consumer cost of living index or to the exchange rate of some external stable currency. In earlier periods, similar methods were employed either through providing for payment in another currency, or by the promise of actual goods rather than currency in payment. All these arrangements are aimed at enabling the lender, investor, or worker to purchase with his earned or invested money the same "basket" of goods and services as he could have at the time of the transaction—in other words, at preserving the purchasing power of money, even though in actual fact one may be receiving a greater number of nominal monetary units than he originally disbursed or earned. The problem to be considered is whether agreements to achieve this constitute rabbinic interest, since the money amounts received by the lender/investor are greater. If so, they would be forbidden, or at least require a *heter iska*. The problem becomes more involved in those cases where no specific agreement was made but one of the parties suffers a loss and seeks compensation.

Changes in Price Levels

When prices change, the nominal value of money remains stable, but its real value, or purchasing power, has been altered. Such changes occur either as a result of natural causes, such as drought, or because of disruptions flowing from war, breakdowns in transportation, rises in wages, or other circumstances.

The halakhic problem may be stated fairly simply by reference to the following example: Reuven borrowed $1,000 at the beginning of the year—in the form of an interest-free loan, in the form of goods bought on credit at the time, or in the form of commodities to be returned at some future date. At that time, $1,000 would buy, say, a "basket" of x goods. During the year prices rise, so that now the same amount of dollars will buy only 75 percent of the same basket. Shimon now wishes to collect his debt, receive payment for the goods sold, or receive the commodities lent. If Reuven repays his nominal debt, Shimon the lender will receive only 75 percent of the purchasing power of his original $1,000, even though in terms of actual dollars he is receiving the same sum he lent. Shimon has thus lost 25 percent of his capital in economic terms. On the other hand, if we were to compensate Shimon for the decline in purchasing power of his capital, Reuven would then have to repay $1,250. The question is, does this constitute interest?

Halakhically, where no agreement to the contrary exists, changes in price levels do not have an effect on the payment of debts. So, in our case, Reuven would still have to return only $1,000, despite the rise in prices. In other words, anything over the nominal value of the debt would be considered rabbinic interest.[49]

What would happen, however, if one were to substitute goods for money, either as a loan or in the form of credit sales? In this case, one would safeguard one's investment since one would receive the same goods at the due date. Generally speaking, the borrowing of goods to be repayed in goods is not permissible. This may be seen in the discussion in the Mishnah that is an important basis for the rabbinic discussion regarding protection against changes in price levels: "A man may not say to his neighbor, 'Lend me a measure of wheat and I will return it to you at harvest time.'"[50] If, however, there was at the time of the loan a known market price (equilibrium price) for wheat, or if the borrower had in his possession a similar quantity of the goods borrowed, then such loans would be permissible, as there would be no question of interest resulting from price fluctuations; either the same goods could be bought or the borrower could return his own.

The *Shulchan Arukh* codified this law and provided a way for handling changes in the real value of money when no nominal change occurs.

> It is not permissible to lend a measure of wheat against a prom-
> ise to return a similar measure even though no time has been
> specified for its return. The same applies to all goods except sil-
> ver coins, which are legal tender and not goods. [The reason for
> this ruling is the concern that] perhaps their price will rise, and
> the borrower will thereby be returning more than he borrowed
> [and this will constitute rabbinic interest, which is halakhically
> forbidden]. In order to prevent this, they should convert the loan
> into monetary terms. Now if the goods increase in value, the
> borrower will return the value at the time of settlement. If, nev-
> ertheless, they did not make such a conversion, and the prices of
> the goods rise, then the borrower will repay their monetary
> value at the time the loan was made. If, however, they have be-
> come cheaper, then he will repay the lender the same quantity
> he had borrowed.[51]

In this and other allied rulings the halakhic emphasis is on preserving the nominal value of the debt. Increased payments to the creditor would seem to constitute at least rabbinic interest, if not interest in the biblical sense. Legal questions, such as whether the debt was for a specific time or not and whether a market price existed, affect such decisions but are beyond the scope of our discussion.

It is interesting to note that Rabbi Ya'akov ben Asher, in his codex written in fourteenth-century Spain, held, along with other authorities, that it was permissible to borrow loaves of bread, household goods, and other small, everyday items with the intention of returning similar items, irrespective of any changes in prices. Because of the petty value involved, the authorities were not concerned about the profit or loss involved in such price changes.[52] These halakhic sources did not, therefore, accept Hillel's ruling in the Mishnah forbidding, on grounds of interest, commodity loans on such a scale.[53]

Changes in the Nominal Value of the Currency

In addition to changes in the real value or purchasing power of money, we may be faced with changes in the nominal value of the currency. Such changes may take a number of forms, each one of which is handled separately by the halakhic authorities.

1. The state voids the current currency and issues a new coinage of equal value. Since the old coins are no longer legal tender, the halakhah insists that all legal obligations have to be met in the new currency. (Maimonides excepts those cases where the old coinage is legal tender in another country or district and the creditors are able to exchange them there without undue trouble.[54]

2. The Talmud describes a case wherein a new currency is of greater metallic content and has a great intrinsic value.[55] In this case, Maimonides[56] and Joseph Caro[57] rule that we have to examine the effect on price levels. If prices are lowered, then the debt has to be paid in the new coinage, after deducting the increase in value. This deduction applies also to those cases in which the price levels remain unchanged, provided the revaluation is greater than 20 percent.

Rabbi Isaac Alfasi (eleventh-century North Africa), in a ruling that was accepted by almost all the authorities, decided that the same adherence to nominal value applies in the case of debasement of the currency, so that the lender has to add back the loss.[58] Alfasi is concerned not only with the problem of interest involved when the borrower has to pay back more than he borrowed, as in the case of a revaluation; he adds another dimension, that of the robbery involved when a lender receives less nominal value than he loaned, as in the case of *devaluations*. We have already mentioned that rabbinic interest is primarily concerned with increased payments, so it is not surprising to find an individual opinion expressed in the above discussion by the Raivad that there is no interest involved when currency is devalued, and so the borrower can pay back the debt in the new currency without adding the amount of the devaluation.

3. The value of money can also change as a result of changes in public confidence or administrative regulations, as in the case of devaluations of paper currency. In 1811, the Austrian govern-

ment reduced its bank notes to a fifth of their previous value, with instructions that within a specified time, these notes would cease to be legal tender. The Chatam Sofer ruled that

> according to the halakhah, debts have to be repayed in the original bank notes as long as they are legal tender, leading to a loss for the lender. After that payment has to be made in the new notes, and the borrower will lose. However, this is according to halakhah, but since the state has made special arrangements whereby repayment of debts shall be made in new notes, these arrangements shall prevail. In these matters, the law of the land is the law [*dina d'malkhuta dina*] and so I have ruled in practice. [According to halakhic rules, the state regulations determine the resolution of all financial disputes, It seems that, even in a Jewish state, such nonhalakhic financial arrangements would generally have the sanction of law.][59]

In our own day, the Chazon Ish in Israel has ruled that payment has to be made in the nominal terms obtaining at the time the debt was incurred.[60]

Protection against Changes in the Value of Money

The rulings we have mentioned above deal with debts and loans incurred without specific agreements protecting either creditor or debtor; in those cases where such agreements exist and do not contradict the laws of interest, they apply and are enforceable. We can now proceed to examine some of the methods of ensuring such protection.

Communal Enactments

Since sudden changes in the value of money, irrespective of their cause, can cause great hardship to some of the parties involved, other moral and religious questions emerge over and above that of interest. Sometimes it is simply a matter of charity; in other cases it may seem like a case of theft. Throughout the Sephardic world—Italy, the Balkan countries, North Africa, the Middle East—we find communal enactments designed to spread unexpected losses more equitably, beyond the demands of the law.

Two examples will suffice to demonstrate the reasoning behind them and the results of their application:

Fez, Morocco (1616)

This enactment comes to supplant the previous ones and to be in force for generations to come: that in all the claims between Jews, the excess resulting from monetary changes from the time of the transaction till the due date will be equally divided between the two parties.[61]

The enactments of Fez applied only to changes in the value of money introduced by the government. These enactments were practiced throughout the communities of Morocco until our own day.

Erets Yisrael (sixteenth century)

In one of his responsa concerning the *k'tubah* (the marriage contract, whereby a woman is entitled to an agreed-upon sum of money in case of divorce or the death of her husband), Rabbi Joseph, of Trani, Italy, quotes an enactment made in the Land of Israel:

There are places where it is customary to pay the *k'tubah* and other debts on the basis of an average (between the value of the currency at the time of writing the contract and its value at maturity or payment), and this is the custom in the Land of Israel for many generations . . . this being a enactment made there to foster a spirit of comradeship and appeasement between the parties to a dispute. . . . They were concerned over the potential loss to the orphans [whose inheritance would decrease if the widow was to be paid the higher nominal value of her *k'tubah*] and to the businessmen, since many traders have been bankrupted through their losses [as a result of the currency changes].[62]

Now we may consider whether the linkage of debts to some index in order to protect against changes in price levels is to be considered interest or not. The halakhic discussion concerning this protection makes a distinction between linkage to a composite index of goods and services, like the consumer cost of living index, and linkage to a foreign currency. Our analysis will therefore have to consider each of these methods separately.

Linkage to a Cost of Living Index

On the face of it, it should be possible on the basis of the following decision of the *Shulchan Arukh* to link loans or debts to a consumer cost of living index: "It is possible to advance money [but not goods] to one's fellow on condition that the borrower will provide him with *peirot* [literally, fruit or agricultural produce] during the course of the year. The borrower will provide the goods according to their price at the time of the advance, even if at the due date their price has risen."[63]

Rabbi Ezra Basri, writing in present-day Israel, lists a number of objections to the validity of linkage of debts to the consumer cost of living index. He argues that the majority of authorities seem to uphold these objections, seeing such linkage as giving rise to an increment—and therefore as a form of rabbinic interest requiring a *heter iska*.[64]

> 1. The basis for the decision in the *Shulchan Arukh* is that the buyer/lender is to receive goods. However, the consumer index does not measure a specific good but rather a general "basket" of goods and services, some of which the lender may never use or possess, and others of which may not have an equilibrium price.
> 2. We permit advance payment for goods only in commercial transactions but not in the case of loans.
> 3. Most authorities hold that an advance payment is permitted only in the case of goods, but linkage to a consumer index is in effect payment of money, and this is not permissible. Even Rabbenu Tam, who permits de facto monetary payment, objects to an arrangement made at the beginning of the transaction whereby the borrower will repay money.

Over and above the legal arguments presented by Basri, there seems to be valid economic evidence for considering indexation as a form of interest. In an economy where inflation exists, lenders will raise interest rates in order to protect themselves against the losses caused by the eroding of their capital. The increased interest rates, caused not by a demand for funds or higher-risk borrowers but solely by the need to obtain a real return on their funds, is a free market method parallel to the legal and administrative one of linkage. Where central bank policy does not permit real interest rates, or where the free market mechanism is not allowed to operate fully, investors and lenders will resort to other forms of protection, such as linkage, or invest in commodities, real estate, objets d'art, etc.

These considerations would support those halakhic opinions according to which increments resulting from indexation are indeed a form of interest. Departing from these opinions is an argument presented by the former Chief Rabbi of Israel. Rabbi Shlomo Goren claims that the continued rapid inflation in Israel raises all price levels, and necessitates changes in the definitions involved in halakhic rulings on this subject. Under conditions of consistent three-digit inflation, he argues, money should halakhically be considered *peirot* (goods) and the products and services bought acquire the rabbinic status of "money," since it is the goods that are stable, whereas the former fluctuates. On this basis, linking debts and savings to the cost of living index, Rabbi Goren argues, is, in effect, linking the loan to a monetary base, which is what the sages considered permissible.[65] It would seem, though, from a halakhic point of view, that this argument is flawed—since, in effect, Israeli currency still serves the halakhic function of money: It is accepted by the marketplace (the definition of the Chazon Ish), and it is legal tender according to the decree of the state (the definition of the Chatam Sofer).

Mainstream rabbinic tradition would still seem to uphold repaying the nominal value of a loan and, in order to avoid rabbinic interest, require a *heter iska* for any scheme of linkage designed to preserve its purchasing power.

This insistence on the nominal as opposed to the real value of money is not based solely on considerations of interest, but flows from the discussion in the *Shulchan Arukh* of loans and debts in general. One of the classical commentators on the *Shulchan Arukh*, the *Turei Zahav*, written by David ben Shmuel Halevi in the first half of the seventeenth century, ruled that normally these have to be repaid according to their value at the time of the transaction.[66] This flows directly from the halakhic concept of money described previously. According to the halakhah, money derives its value either from the issuing authority of the state (the Chatam Sofer) or from acceptance in the marketplace (the Chazon Ish). By either definition, the value of currency binding on both parties to a transaction would be that known at the time of the transaction—viz., its nominal value.

Linkage to a Foreign Currency

Savings and debts may alternatively be linked to a foreign currency whose rate of inflation is lower, so that the purchasing power of the people in the weaker economy is protected. Halakhically this seems to be easier than linkage to the cost of living index; the sages were more wary of the interest arising out of transactions involving "goods" than of those involving money. Perhaps this was seen as a mechanism for protecting people's basic needs.

We have seen that in Mishnaic times, gold, as opposed to silver, was considered a commodity, since it was rare, it was difficult to transfer, and people preferred the silver coinage that was therefore considered money. Following this pattern of thought, in our own day foreign currencies are considered money and not goods, since it is possible, without excessive trouble, to actually obtain the foreign currency. Furthermore, people in country A are prepared to accept payment in the currency of country B, provided it is a redeemable and a "strong" one. For instance, it is reasonable to assume today that the American dollar is acceptable to merchants and investors in almost all countries. This means that it is akin to legal tender in those countries and not to a commodity, so that halakhically it would be considered money.

For example, Rabbi Moshe Feinstein, in a recent responsum from New York, ruled that the current ease of acceptance of the dollar in the State of Israel, and the fact that people there are conducting transactions in dollars, makes it halakhically legal tender.[67] Therefore, borrowing in shekels and paying in dollars in the State of Israel would not be considered as generating interest, even though the rate of exchange between the Israel shekel and the American dollar has changed substantially. Actually, the halakhic ruling requires that the loan itself should be made in the foreign currency to which it is linked. However, realizing that it is easy to acquire foreign currency both at the time of making the loan and at the time of returning the loan, the rabbis, it seems, have agreed that it is possible to overlook this technical difficulty, and even though the loans are made in the local currency and paid therein, the linkage to a foreign currency is legitimate.

There is a further halakhic difficulty, however, regarding indexation both to a foreign currency and to the cost of living index. This flows from the legal question as to whether one is allowed to undertake obligations, the full extent of which is not foreseeable in the near future. Most authorities have agreed that a man can contract an obligation to repay a debt even though the magnitude of that debt is not known at present. Maimonides, however, claims that only known obligations can be recognized.[68] Linkage in one form or another, therefore, might be doubtful from the point of view of Maimonides, because one does not know what the exact extent of the debt or investment will be. In light of modern forecasting methods, however, it is possible to argue that one can foretell the rate of inflation within the foreseeable future. Nevertheless, these same methods can foretell only some of the inflation, since in all inflation there is an unknown element that depends on government policy and hence cannot always be known at the beginning of the period of indebtedness.

INFLATION AS A MORAL AND RELIGIOUS ISSUE

Over and above the various legal questions discussed above, there are three separate moral issues stemming from inflation that would seem to be equally pertinent to religious thought.

Interest-Free Loans

Irrespective of whether a linkage to the cost of living index or to a foreign currency is considered rabbinical interest or not, it is necessary to re-examine the question of such linkage from the moral aspect of the illegal "profits" earned at the expense of the lender and the obligation to extend interest-free loans. Such analysis may recognize linkage as being morally imperative.

In a discussion that the author had with Rabbi Gifter of Telze Yeshivah the rabbi pointed out that the Torah commanded the Jew to make interest-free loans available as an act of *chesed,* which is a positive *mitzvah* independent of and distinct from the act of giving *tzedakah* (charity). Such loans are made on the understanding that the receiver will repay the loan, and in a previous section this obligation was discussed at great length. The inflationary profits earned by the recipient of an interest-free loan from the erosion of this debt, however, cause the loan to assume the character of an act of *tzedakah* and not of *g'milut chesed,* since such profits are not returned to the lender. Yet, by making an interest-free loan rather than giving the money as a gift, the lender had made his preference quite clear.

It may well be that in times of slight inflation, the giver is prepared to forego part of his loan as an additional act of charity. However, when the rate of inflation grows we are faced with a situation that could well lead to the withholding of acts of *g'milut chesed*, or in terms of the rabbinic usage, "closing the door before the lender." That is, Jews may be deterred from extending *g'milut chesed* if they realize that in real economic terms they will not receive their money back again. It is true that those authorities who see linkage as a form of interest permit such transactions when done with a *heter iska*. It is common knowledge, however, that many people do not take out a *heter iska* when making such loans, and the necessity of such a formal document may well deter them from making the loan in the first place. The suggestion made by Rabbi Gifter, therefore, was that in times of inflation, some sort of communal enactment, similar to that of the *prozbul* of Hillel, should be required. During the days of the Second Temple people stopped making loans, since they were worried that in the sabbatical year, in accordance with the biblical commandment, loans would become null and void. In order to prevent this drying up of interest-free loans, Hillel instituted a legal arrangement whereby debts were transferred to the *bet din* for collection, such enforcement being legally acceptable even during the sabbatical year.

Taxation

There would seem to be a question as to whether the Jewish government in the State of Israel, for example, has the right to create inflation. Even those economists who do not accept the theory that the predominent factor in causing inflation is the behavior of the public sector will agree that such behavior does *contribute* to inflation. Actually, inflation is a form of taxation, since the government uses a depreciated currency in exchange for the currency that prevailed at the beginning of the inflationary period. In Jewish law, as explained in chapter 8, taxation requires the agreement of the taxpayers or their representatives. Taxation through the inflationary process, however, is not a publicly declared tax, it is rather a form of secret taxation. It is true that anyone who studies government budgetary proposals becomes aware that there will be inflation in the forthcoming period. At the same time, given the level of economic knowledge of most legislators, it is doubtful that such awareness can be assumed.

However, even if legislators do understand the implications of budget proposals and are aware of the likely rates of forthcoming inflation, there is in every economy an additional, unexpected inflationary effect over and above that projected in the budget. This unknown inflationary rate, at least, would seem to constitute illegal taxation according to Jewish sources.

Furthermore, in our chapter on taxation, we will show that the levying of taxes and the allocation of the tax burden has traditionally been left to communal leaders, with the *bet din* or halakhic authority serving as a review court. A taxpayer could claim the protection of this court if he felt that the tax was not being allocated according to Jewish law. How does one determine, however, whether the burden of taxation arising out of inflation is being allocated according to Jewish law? What halakhic mechanism exists for a review before a *bet din* of this type of tax burden on the individual? Both of these questions require answers in order to meet the halakhic demand that inflation-*cum*-taxation not be akin to theft.

Finally, it has been found that the prime sufferers from inflation are the weaker members of society—the poor, the pensioners, the sick—so that Torah considerations of justice would make a rabbinic review mandatory in any case.

Morality

Inflation effects moral conduct in a number of ways:

1.   By devaluating the currency, inflation distorts the impartial and consistent value of goods, services, property, and even the injured bodily parts of people. Since the cost of damage to property or to body now becomes subjective and not easily measured, crime of all types tends to rise.

2.   Conversion of money into goods becomes essential in order to preserve one's income or wealth, thus encouraging consumption and waste. As a result, immediate gratification of the needs of the individual becomes a way of life, often at a moral and ethical cost.

3. As wages are eroded by inflation the work ethic disappears, and people try to get by with doing as little work as possible in return for a decreasing real wage. At the same time, people try to increase their borrowing, hoping to pay their creditors with a devalued currency.

4. Governments, unchecked by the discipline of a budget, find it easy to pander to the demands of the people, whether these are realistic or not. Bread and circuses, to be paid for at the expense of future generations, become the normal means of appeasing, and ruling.

5. The whole society spends a major part of its time, energy, and brain power in manipulations aimed at preserving their own real wealth, often at the expense of the less wary or more vulnerable part of the population.

Judaism has always understood that morality is not divisible. Immorality in the economic sphere, and the encouragement of immediate gratification and self-aggrandizement, soon spreads to sexual immorality and crimes of violence. We have already mentioned the teaching of the Chasidic sage, Shmuel of Sochochov, that when the generation of the flood became guilty of robbery, all the other cardinal sins—murder, idolatory, and sexual immorality—followed, which explains the rabbinic dictum that it was robbery that led to the destruction of that generation.

It is accepted halakhic philosophy that it is as necessary to legislate so as to prevent wrongdoing as it is to punish the wrongdoing. Communal regulations bolstered by the rabbinic authorities to prevent the entry of immoral people into the community, to promote modesty in consumption and in dress, to minimize gambling and law evasion, and to enforce Torah study are to be found in many Jewish communities, as we show throughout this book.

It is not merely coincidental that Keynes, the father of the concept of public sector intervention in order to straighten out the fluctuations in the business cycle, was also a member of the famous Bloomsbury Group in England. This group was a pioneer in the liberal onslaught against traditional religious and moral values. They were also opposed to any form of moral coercion or legal limitation on the rights of the individual, provided one did not damage property or hurt other people. This humanistic, liberal philosophy was transferred by Keynes to the conduct of public affairs.

Like budgetary restrictions on the individual, a metallic-based monetary unit (such as a gold standard) places severe restrictions on a government. On the other hand, deficit financing, which in the long run usually leads to inflation, enables a government to live beyond its means. Governments can then give in to all sorts of pressure groups and encourage many forms of economic irresponsibility, knowing that inflation can be used to, as it were, paper over its guilt. It is true that maintaining a fixed monetary system introduces a rigidity into the economy that may impair its efficiency, as well as its ability to solve social problems like unemployment. Yet the conflict between market efficiency and sociocultural values is resolved, in the end, according to the value structure of the society. As has been demonstrated throughout this study, Judaism is quite prepared to impair the efficiency of the market for the sake of its values, and it may well be that further halakhic study of these questions would lead to restraints on a Jewish government's right to cause inflation. Naturally, the social welfare benefits that may derive from inflation would have to be weighed against the moral costs.

SUMMARY

Basically, Judaism views credit and loans merely as other forms of investment in capital goods and treats them as such. So the sanctity of contracts, the symmetrical legal rights of all parties, and principles of trade apply. Furthermore, the operation of the market mechanism, as explained in our chapter on competition, applies here as well. At the same time, special limits are imposed on the money and capital markets. These limits, however, flow primarily from ethical and religious principles and not from an ignorance of the function of money, nor from an anticapitalist bias. Thus, in the *Shulchan Arukh* and *Arba'ah Turim*, the laws of interest are placed not in *Choshen Mishpat*, the section dealing with civil and commercial law, but in *Yoreh De'ah*, alongside the laws of family purity.

One is obligated to lend other Jews money free of interest. Such loans are to be made available for purchasing consumer goods, for investment in a business, and for financing temporary illiquidity. These interest-free loans are regarded as acts of righteousness and as the highest form of Jewish charity, since they enable the poor to break out of the poverty cycle and prevent the rich from entering it.

One is also forbidden to take interest, either as a direct payment for loans or in the course of business activities, where no risk is involved or where the activity is a disguised form of extending credit.

A legal formula, *heter iska*, has been derived whereby financial transactions are transferred into business ventures and therefore rendered permissible. In many aspects of modern banking and finance, the *heter iska* is a legal recognition of situations which, at least in economic terms, are in effect already in such ventures even though they are not considered so in the ordinary legal sense.

The role of money is understood by rabbinic sources to flow from one of two concepts: the authority of the state as the issuer of the currency, or its acceptance in the marketplace. It would seem that from these concepts stems the halakhic insistence that debts or loans be repaid according to their nominal value. Thus increments, as a result of inflation or of devaluation or debasement of currency, are seen as rabbinic interest and hence forbidden unless agreed upon in an acceptable fashion, such as through a *heter iska*. Many communities, especially in the Sephardic world, instituted regulations whereby losses flowing from changes in the value of money would be shared by both parties, not as a legal principle but as a means of achieving peace between men and limiting the social friction that often results from such changes.

CHAPTER 8

Taxation

INTRODUCTION

In any society, there are certain functions and needs that lie beyond the domain of the individual and, therefore, have to be fulfilled by the group. Naturally, the society's economic resources—the money to finance such activities—will have to come out of the incomes and property of individuals. The total ability of individuals to divert part of their wealth to the needs of the group will determine the possible magnitude of the communal budget, while the willingness of members of the group to sacrifice resources to this purpose will reflect the value structure and sociopolitical conditions of the society.

The most common method of public finance has always been the raising of funds through taxation. It should be borne in mind that irrespective of the ideological basis for taxation, its economic effect will be the same. Nevertheless, each system of taxation reflects the ideological values of the society in the rates imposed, the basis of assessment, and even the exemptions allowed various groups of taxpayers. Furthermore, it is these values which will, in no small measure, determine the degree of compliance with the demands of the tax collector.

Tax rates obviously have an effect on the degree of participation in the public budget: The higher the tax rates, the less inclined the individual will be to pay his taxes and the greater the degree of tax evasion. It has been argued that the high tax rates prevalent today in Italy, France, Israel, and the United Kingdom are the primary reason for the relatively extensive "underground economy" in these countries. At the same time, however, the rate of taxation is only one factor affecting tax evasion. When the taxpayer feels that his money is being spent wisely for the benefit of society (however that may be defined by the individual), that the tax burden is spread evenly, and that waste is kept to a minimum, then his participation in the tax burden, even if at all times unwilling, will be normal. Contrariwise, it seems that it is possible to attribute the growth of an underground economy in the United States (which has the lowest tax rates in the Western world) to the "loopholes" used by the wealthy to pay little if any tax; to documented large-scale waste in, for example, the military budget; and to the perception that the "needs" met through the federal budget are not real ones. The sociomoral structure of a society would seem, therefore, to be as worthy of examination as its tax rates. It is from that viewpoint that taxation is studied in this chapter.

Jewish societies developed a ramified system of taxation right from the outset of the nation's birth. In all centuries, whether Jews constituted an independent national sovereign entity in the Land of Israel or lived as scattered communities in the various lands of exile, the social, ethical, and religious needs of Judaism necessitated a viable source of public funds and, therefore, a tax system. This system, like any other, required decisions regarding what constitutes a basis for taxation, methods of assessment, and punishment for evasion, along with a legal structure that could arbitrate between the conflicting claims of the individual and the group. As the Jewish economy became more complicated and sophisticated, so, too, did all these mechanisms, even though the ideological basis for taxation remained the same. It is with this ideological, ethical, and legal basis for Jewish taxation that we begin.

THE CONCEPTUAL FRAMEWORK OF THE TAX SYSTEM

Collective Responsibility

Perhaps the most Jewish of the underpinnings of taxation is the now universally accepted concept of society's responsibility for the needs of its members. One must bear in mind that the welfare state, with its publicly financed education, health care, and subsidies to the poor, is only a recent phenomenon amongst other nations. On the other hand, the Jewish provision of such services through the public purse, as opposed to relying on personal charity, dates back to antiquity. It must be stressed that the financing of these services bore all the hallmarks of government activity; that they were, in fact, undertaken by autonomous communities is irrelevant. For the individual Jew, these communities had all the authority and power to tax and punish evasion that the state has today. Charity at the individual level existed, just as it does in many other religious systems. In Judaism, however, taxation was introduced as a manifestation of the concept of the rights of the community and of less fortunate individuals in the property of all the other individuals. The setting up of a tax system institutionalized these rights and made participation in communal financing obligatory in addition to the voluntary charitable acts demanded by Judaism from the individual. Irrespective of the methods chosen to finance communal needs and of the size of the communal budget, Jewish religious and legal institutions throughout the centuries maintained this vision of collective responsibility as a first principle—as axiomatic.

Jewish Ethical Principles of Taxation

Jewish law and the rabbinic authorities generally left the levying of taxes to governmental authorities (the king, town council, etc.).[1] Nevertheless, they took great and constant care to ensure that all aspects of taxation strictly adhered to Jewish ethical and moral requirements. The role of the religious courts in this respect seems to have been primarily a regulatory one, with the initiation and prosecution of fiscal policy lying in the hands of the secular authorities—application of the general principle that halakhic sources are not economic, social, or sexual manuals but rather religious and moral guides intended to regulate, and so to sanctify, man's actions.

A number of basic ethical principles can be discerned in the halakhic approach to taxation:

1. The levying of taxes has to be according to the consent of the majority of the taxpayers or their representatives. There were

often cases where minority interests were also protected, but the principle of majority rule by all the concerned parties was the predominant one.[2]

Even the king, who has in Jewish law extensive rights regarding taxation, has to consider the consent of the taxpayers. The revolt of Jeraboam ben Nevat against the son of King Solomon was sparked by just such disregard. This revolt, supported by the prophets (and, therefore, justified by Jewish law), wasn't against the king's right to tax but rather against the excessiveness of the tax burden. In his commentary on the Book of Kings, the Malbim, echoing earlier commentators, explains that the people were prepared for such a burden during the reign of Solomon in view of the economic and political benefits enjoyed under David and Solomon. The new king, however, had not provided the same level of services and, therefore, wasn't entitled to the same level of taxation.

2. The tax may not be confiscatory. This precludes taxes on wealth that does not generate income.[3]

3. Taxes may not be levied twice on the same wealth.[4] This might preclude, for example, the double taxation on profits prevalent today in many countries: The firm pays on the profits earned, and the shareholder on the dividends received. It also prevented double taxation on wealth earned in one city by residents of another.

4. In all cases of conflict between the tax authorities and the taxpayer, the usual dictum of "The claimant has to produce evidence of the debt" applied.[5] In other words, when the tax authorities claimed that someone was paying less than the amount he owed, the onus of proof was on the authorities. Conversely, a taxpayer who claimed to have overpaid had to prove it.

5. Tax evasion was tantamount to theft.[6] Such theft could be envisaged either as from other taxpayers, who would now have to pay more, or from the recipients of the funds raised by taxes, who would now receive less welfare, schooling, protection, etc. The full power of the community and its legal authorities were brought to bear against evaders.

6. The tax had to be allocated justly and equitably, according to a formula that will be discussed further on in this chapter.

7. Certain classes of citizens were exempted from taxation or entitled to reductions. These classes were not decided upon arbitrarily but reflected the Jewish value structure—thereby includ-

ing, for example, Torah scholars and those willing to go on *aliyah* to the Land of Israel (in both cases, tax alleviation was in effect subsidizing performance of a mitzvah) in addition to the impoverished.

Purpose of the Public Budget

Theoretically, the lay authorities could levy taxes in order to raise funds for whatever purpose the majority deemed fit. In the same way, assuming that the majority wished to reduce the tax burden by curtailing the services provided, they were able to do so. Nevertheless, there were certain areas which the community could not ignore and, therefore, could not refuse to fund. Funds for Torah education, feeding and clothing the impoverished, care of widows and orphans, and the redemption of captives were sacrosanct. Similarly, raising funds for building the essential number of religious institutions—synagogues, cemeteries, *mikvehs* (ritual baths)—was an obligation, not an option open to communal decision.

THE HALAKHIC BASIS FOR THE TAX SYSTEM

Although the sources do not specifically define a halakhic basis for the Jewish tax system, nevertheless it is possible to distinguish four distinct institutions which provide the legal justification for the system.

The Rights of Neighbors (*Hilkhot Shecheinim*)

Neighbors sharing common facilities or adjoining property had, under rabbinic law, the ability to force each other to finance common needs out of a joint fund. It is not difficult to understand the extension of this right to embrace municipal taxation, where all members of the community are, so to speak, neighbors.[7]

Obligations of the Citizen (*Ben Ha'Ir*)

From the earliest periods of Jewish history, popularly elected institutions of local government dealt with many aspects of life, including those which required public finance. The Mishnah tells us that the people of a city can force all citizens to participate in the financing of projects needed for the security and well-being of the town.[8] Although a year's grace was given to newcomers before they became liable for their share of municipal taxes, purchase of a house was taken as a sign of permanence, so that the buyer became a taxpayer immediately, without the period of grace.

Other instances can be brought to show that this power to tax covered other areas, such as welfare and education.

Rights of the King (Din Hamelech)

All the constitutional rights of the king in Judaism derive from the passages in the First Book of Samuel (8:11–12, 14–17) in which the prophet describes to the people what their fate will be under the king they desire. This description includes the power of taxation in kind, labor, and land.

> He will take your sons and appoint them for his chariots and to be his horsemen, and they shall run before his chariots. And he will appoint them unto him for captains of thousands and captains of fifties, to plow his ground, to reap his harvest, and to make his instruments of war and the instruments of his chariots. . . . And he will take your fields and your vineyards and your olive yards, even the best of them, and give them to his servants. And he will take the tenth of your seed and of your vineyards and give them to his officers and his servants. And he will take your man servants and your maid servants and your godliest young men and your asses and put them to his work. And he will take the tenth of your flocks, and ye shall be his servants.

The king's right to appropriate land for public use (a form of taxation even when financial compensation is made) is well founded in Jewish law and religious texts. "A king has the right to make a way or to break down walls, and one [the owner of the property or fields through which such roads, etc., pass] has no right to prevent him."[9] In other words, the king, representing the needs of the community and of the state, has the right to appropriate private land in order to satisfy these needs. This is clearly shown in the discussion among the commentators of the story of the vineyard of Navot in the Book of Kings.

Ahab approached Navot and asked him to sell him his vineyard in Jezreel; in return he would give him a better field. Navot refused. Christian popular thought, like the Levellers, saw this as a conflict between the rich and powerful king and the poor individual. Jewish sources, however, stressed that Navot was a wealthy man and a member of the council of sages. Abarbanel, in his commentary on the Bible, raises an important legal question that, he argues, confutes most of the classic commentaries. Since the king has the right to confiscate land for the public's needs, what right does Navot have to refuse to sell him the field? (After all, Ahab had offered compensation, so that it was not a question of theft.) Rashi comments that Ahab wanted the field for a *gan yerek*, a synonym for idolatry, and that this was the reason for Navot's refusal. In other words, Rashi argues that the king's anticipated immoral use was sufficient to abrogate his rights. Navot himself argued that this was an inheritance of his fathers, implying that it was not permissible to sell that which was inherited.

Abarbanel argues, however, that there is no legal basis for either of these explanations, since one is able to sell inherited land and the idolatrous use of the land is not Navot's concern. He argues that the real reason for Navot's refusal was that the purpose of the sale had nothing to do with the public good, implying that if it were an issue of his private property rights vs. the public good, Navot would have no right to refuse to sell his property. Abarbanel points out that Navot wanted the land for a garden in the town of Jezreel, while the capital of the Northern Kingdom of Israel was in Shomron, where the appropriation of private land for a public garden would serve a public purpose. In Jezreel, however, the king was a private citizen, and the purchase of land was for his own private benefit. Navot objected to the invocation by the king for his personal use of a right whose purpose was solely the improvement of the public good. In other words, if the state or public sector wishes to appropriate land, it may do so only for the public good; it may not invoke this right for personal gain.

The Law of the Land (*Dina D'Malkhuta*)

Halakhic sources recognized the obligation of Jews, wherever they resided, to obey the law of the land. The Gentile authorities, therefore, had a legal right to impose taxes on their Jewish subjects.[10] The Jewish communal authorities usually had the obligation to either implement this fiscal policy or, as often as not, to finance taxes placed on the community as a unit.

The taxes levied by Gentile rulers were not generally intended to finance the needs of the Jewish community. Sometimes they were taxes levied on all citizens, including Jews. Mostly, however, the authorities found Jews a valuable financial asset who could be tapped for all sorts of purposes, even—or perhaps especially—the private pleasures of the ruler. As often as not, these taxes were arbitrary and confiscatory—a fine placed on the Jew for his presence in a non-Jewish society.

Those taxes placed upon the whole population, Jew and Gentile, were not problematic from a Jewish point of view. It was the oppressive and discriminatory tax burdens placed on the Jewish community that raised serious questions. Maimonides ruled that in the case of an arbitrary, despotic, or illegal government (one which seized power against the wishes of the inhabitants), the rule of *dina d'malkhuta dina* (the law of the land is the law) did not apply. Yet, rabbinic authorities claimed that even here one was not allowed to evade these taxes—primarily, it would seem, because such evasion increased the burden of other members of the community and could lead to expulsion and even death.[11]

Nevertheless, it would be a distortion to claim that the ever-increasing tax burden, as well as the anti-Semitism which prompted it, did not lead to tax evasion and even to flight. The progressive excesses, from the seventeenth century on, of the Tsarist regime, which included within its borders the majority of European Jewry, made such evasion rampant and eventually brought many Jewish communities to a state of bankruptcy. And there is an interesting communal ruling which prohibited wealthy individuals from leaving the community and called upon other communities to refuse to accept them. The flight of such individuals obviously increased the tax burden of the remaining Jews—who, it can be imagined, were largely poor to begin with.

Modern Israel presents an important halakhic problem in regard to taxation. Maimonides makes a clear distinction between kings of the Davidic dynasty, whose rights flow from the *din hamelech*, and other kings, whose power flows from *dina d'malkhuta*.[12] According to this division, it would seem that the fiscal system developed by the secular Jewish state would have to rest on the same legal basis as that of non-Jewish states or of the Jewish kings of the non-Davidic dynasty. Alternatively, the fiscal system would flow from the rights of neighbors or of the obligations of *ben ha'ir.*

Irrespective of the legal source of fiscal policy, communal taxation was an early characteristic of Jewish social life and deeply entrenched in religious law. The widespread instances of Jewish autonomy in almost all periods of history brought with them a common pattern of communal taxation. It is not surprising, therefore, to find a wealth of rabbinic literature on the subject as well as communal ordinances from every country and period of Jewish history—which together present an extensive Jewish fiscal literature.

THE JEWISH FISCAL SYSTEM

From a historical viewpoint, the types of taxes used by Jewish communities and the basis on which they were calculated is extremely revealing and interesting. Since this study, however, is concerned primarily with exploring attitudes and values, only issues that reflect specifically Jewish moral and ethical factors will be considered. Generally speaking, the most widely accepted opinions will be presented. It may well be that there exist contradictory minority rulings, but it is not possible within the scope of this study to include them all.

Recording of transactions and wealth for tax purposes was widespread in Jewish communities as was the use of community tax assessers and auditors. There is evidence of the same cat-and-mouse game being played between tax collector and payer as exists in every fiscal system, with the resultant litigation and scrutiny of financial records. Some reference to these aspects will be found in the texts of responsa and communal enactments at the end of this chapter. This section, however, will be confined primarily to the effects of halakhic thought on the tax system and the mixture of ideology and pragmatism that created it.

Spreading the Tax Burden

Any society has to decide how to spread the burden of the costs of financing the public services it has decided to provide.

Generally speaking, these costs may be covered by any of the following methods, or by a combination of them:

1. Each individual is taxed on a per capita basis irrespective of his wealth or of his use of the services provided. Poll taxes paid at a flat rate are an example of such taxes.

2. The user of each service provided by the public sector pays for his use thereof. Sales taxes, excise taxes on liquor, cigarettes, and luxury goods; tolls on roads or bridges; and many water taxes are prime examples of such taxes as they are currently applied in many countries.

3. Taxes are levied according to the income or wealth of the individual taxpayer—as in, for example, the personal income tax. Such taxes are often intended to achieve a more equitable distribution of wealth as well as provide funds for the public budget.

Until modern times, taxes of the first two types provided the major share of the tax revenues of most countries. Taxes on income are a relatively new phenomenon and are largely the result of nineteenth-century social ideas.

Examples of all three types of taxes are to be found in the Jewish fiscal system: the *kroga*, or poll tax, levied in Babylon; the communal tax on meat, candles, and liquor (which were staples in almost all Jewish communities); and the taxes on income or wealth which are discussed below. It is interesting to observe that a note of progressive taxation was introduced in Djerba, an island off the North African coast, when the community laid a special tax on meat, claiming that only wealthy Jews were able to afford this luxury. It seems, however, that poll taxes and the tax on commodities were rather marginal. The major source of revenue was income or wealth tempered by a utility concept—which may be the most Jewish of all the methods discussed. The basis for much of the Jewish fiscal system lies in the following two Talmudic discussions, which although they deal with rather simple examples, nevertheless clearly lay down the utility principle of taxation.

The *Tosefta*, dealing with the case of members of a caravan who were set upon by a robber band, decided that the sum of money paid to ''buy off'' the attackers was to be allocated according to the relative share of goods owned by each partner in the caravan. The same source concludes, however, that in the case of a caravan which has lost its way in the desert and hires a guide, the cost of this guide shall be allocated on a per capita basis. The reasoning behind these two decisions flows primarily from the principle of what benefit is derived. In the first case, the danger was solely one of loss of goods, since the robbers were not bent on murder, only theft. The tax, therefore, had to be allocated on the basis of the share of goods owned, since a merchant who owned a major share stood to lose more than one who had only a few articles in the caravan. In the second case, however, everybody's life was in danger, since their blundering in the desert could lead to the death of all the members of the caravan. The guide who led them to safety benefited each one equally, since there is no way to gauge the value of an individual life.[13]

We have already mentioned that, according to Jewish law, a community has the right to force all citizens to participate in the building of a wall and city gate. Nevertheless, the question of allocating the tax burden still remains. Under the assumption that the purpose of the wall is to protect property, not life, the sages on the Talmud ruled against levying a per capita tax. A tax on wealth would seem to be most justified, as explained in the previous example. There is, however, a further example of utility to be considered. Rashi points out that houses or property closer to the wall need the protection afforded by the wall more than those further away. In other words, the benefit derived is greater the closer to the wall the house is situated. There exist, therefore, two considerations of benefit: distance from the wall and the extent of wealth owned. The rabbinic decision took account of both elements, so that those living closer to the wall paid a greater share of the tax burden than their fellow citizens of equal wealth living further away, yet at the same time they paid lower taxes than neighbors who possessed greater wealth.[14]

The Rashba, writing in thirteenth-century North Africa, claims that "this principle has been well established by previous generations: namely, that the approximation [of the taxes] shall be according to the prevention of damage [or, in other words, the degree of benefit]."[15] Perhaps the moral reasoning behind the utility principle flows from the ruling that benefiting from somebody else's money against his wishes or without his knowledge is theft. The receipt of services that somebody else has paid for would, it seems, quite easily be included in this category.

It must be pointed out that certain types of taxes, such as *tzedakah* and assistance to the poor, were automatically funded on the basis of wealth and not utility. This is not simply a pragmatic decision but rather one based on the greater moral responsibility of the rich for this type of public need. In other cases, however, reliance on the utility principle alone would not provide the public finances needed. Reality demanded a more pragmatic approach, which would place a greater burden on those who could provide the funds. It was need and not a philosophy of redistribution of wealth which led to a mixture of utility taxation and taxation on wealth. The Rashba, dealing with the funding of the *chazan* (cantor), admits that actually this should be on a per capita basis, since poor and rich alike benefit from him. At the same time, he points out that the poor are unable to contribute a pro rata share.[16] This is the pattern that is repeated in many different countries and periods: a basic premise that justice demands that each one contribute according to his benefit; considerations of righteousness, however, demanded that the rich contribute a greater proportion of the communal budget.

The Tax Base

The economic history of most countries contains many examples of a struggle between various pressure groups as to which types of wealth would be the basis for taxation. That basis is not accidental or merely pragmatic, but reflects important ideological and material biases. The distinction, for example, between capital gains tax and ordinary income tax is not an economic distinction but a sociopolitical one. So, too, in the Jewish fiscal system the tax basis is a reflection of Jewish ethical and religious concepts. Although the existence, at various times, of pressure groups striving to limit their tax burden at the expense of their fellow Jews cannot be denied, nevertheless the literary evidence shows that by and large the rabbinic authorities were able to maintain the Judaic value structure described below.

The most common method of taxing wealth was measuring equity, or the sum of a man's property of all kinds. This is very similar to taxing income, since, after all, current income is only the stream produced by capital. At the same time, however, this does not tax income derived from providing services or work.

By and large, only property which generated wealth was used to determine a taxpayer's equity. Such property included houses (other than the house in which he lived), trade debts, inventory, and farms. All such assets possessed by a member of the community were evaluated and taxed accordingly. Other forms of wealth, such as personal belongings and non-income-bearing assets, were usually not taxed, as such taxation would mean the gradual erosion of wealth and its ultimate confiscation.[17] Thus, books, one's own dwelling, and fields were exempt from communal taxation, as was a trust set up for charitable purposes.[18] Even though non-income-producing assets were, generally speaking, exempt from current taxation, most authorities levied taxes when such assets were sold. The logic behind this was that through their sale these assets became regular merchandise and, like all other merchandise, were liable to taxation.

The evaluation could be done in one of two ways: either through a declaration or through assessment by community officials. A general halakhic principle that the onus of proof falls on the claimant in monetary matters applies here, too. Since it is the public which, through its appointed officials, is claiming debts, if the community feels that a taxpayer has not made a truthful declaration, it has to prove it in a court of law. Furthermore, the tax assessors cannot say that the taxpayer should first pay according to the wealth he has declared and then they will perform their own evaluation. They have to choose, and adhere to, one of the methods, not both.

Just as the fiscal needs of a society change in scope and structure, so, too, does the structure of its tax base. Since economic conditions are dynamic, the forms of wealth held and their relative ability to yield income are in a constant state of flux. This is true, too, of the tax base in the Jewish community. Nevertheless, the principle involved of taxing only income-yielding wealth remains, even though the form of that wealth perhaps changes. One example of this may suffice to demonstrate the continuity of this principle despite changes that occur in the forms of wealth.

In Babylon during the period of the *geonim* (circa 900 C.E.), gold jewelry and similar articles were not included in the taxable wealth of an individual. This was based on the understanding that such articles constituted personal belongings and were not capital employed in generating income. Gradually, however, gold, in all its forms, became a means of storing and transferring capital, to be used later in income-generating investments. This change was caused in part by the mercantile revolution which came to Europe as a result of the Crusades, which necessitated an expanded supply of available money, and in part by the continual persecution of Jews, which required a form of wealth that could be easily hidden and easily transferred. There was also, perhaps, the added intention of evading communal taxes by investing in such non-income-creating capital. Whatever the cause of the change in the role of gold jewelry and articles, it became obvious that they were no longer simply decorative items but were in reality temporary forms of investment. So the protection afforded to non-income-producing wealth was no longer justified, and, therefore, the halakhic authorities included such items among the taxable assets of the individual. In Franco-Germany at the time of the First Crusade, Rashi allowed articles and jewelry of gold to be included in capital statements, but only at half their market value; in other communities, the custom arose of taxing these articles at 90 percent of their value.[19] In both cases, the assumption was that at least in part, they genuinely served as purely decorative articles.

It was not only the income-bearing nature of the wealth that led to its exclusion or inclusion in the tax basis. Investments with a great element of risk could not be considered as wealth for tax purposes to the same extent as secure assets. Justice demanded that if taxes were not to confiscate wealth, but only provide the community with a share of the income, then the investor's risk, of losing not only his profit but his investment capital itself, had to be considered. Obviously, risk is not a static condition but one that is affected by technological changes and sociopolitical developments. So we find that the halakhic authorities investigated the actual degree of risk involved and authorized taxation accordingly.

In Franco-Germany during the eleventh through thirteenth centuries of the Common Era, vineyards were not included in wealth for tax purposes. Rabbi Joseph Tov Elem, writing to the Jewish community of Troyes in response to their query, states that they are not allowed to tax the vineyards of their members. In that climate and at that stage of viticulture, grapes were a crop that was very susceptible to the ravages of the climate and, therefore, represented a high-risk asset. Even the agricultural implements used in cultivating this crop were included in the exemption, since taxation would obviously erode their value, too.

Following this ruling, the Maharam (Rabbi Meir of Rothenburg), some two hundred years later, reiterated the exemption. In his ruling, however, he linked the element of risk to the general principle of the nonconfiscatory nature of Jewish taxation. "Fields are, generally speaking [in medieval Europe], not articles of trading, so that their owners should not be burdened with tax as are other forms of merchandising, since in their case, the taxes will eventually erode the basic investment."[20]

In the course of time, agriculture, in general, and viticulture, in particular, became dependable and relatively secure industries, as technology improved throughout Western and Central Europe. This meant that the risk involved, while not eradicated, because of their dependence on the vagaries of the weather, nevertheless had been minimized. Clearly, therefore, there no longer existed any fear as to the confiscation of funds invested therein. This being the case, their exclusion from taxable wealth was no longer justified nor moral. So communities in Germany were allowed to tax investments in vineyards. However, since agriculture is always at the mercy of the elements, these assets were assessed at half their real value for tax purposes.[21] In Spain, where viticulture had become a stable and widely practiced economic activity, the exemption from taxes had been abolished already in the twelfth century, and vineyards were likewise included in the tax base at half their real value.

A development similar to that which occurred in agriculture, albeit historically in reverse order, may be observed with respect to the tax liability of funds invested in moneylending. In the early medieval period, when default on debts was rare and interest was seen as income earned with little risk or effort, there was no moral justification for differential treatment of such investments. Later, as Gentile borrowers found it easy to repudiate their debts, moneylending became far more complicated and fraught with greater risk. Theoretically speaking, it might have been possible to release the funds invested in moneylending from taxable wealth, but practically speaking this was impossible, since moneylending was a prime element in the Jewish economy. Mixing pragmatism with acceptance of the risk of confiscatory taxation, the halakhic authorities ruled that debts could be included in taxable wealth but the interest accrued could not.[22] Citizens were allowed to exclude from their taxable wealth bad debts, provided the rights of the claimant were transferred to the communal authorities.

TAX EXEMPTIONS

The ideological basis which determines the assets to be included in taxable wealth also determines the exemptions enjoyed. So the same Jewish value structure exempted certain types of people from paying taxes as well as certain types of investments.

It has already been noted that books owned by a Jew were exempt, since they produced no wealth and, therefore, such taxes would amount to gradual confiscation. At the same time, it should be noted that such a tax on books would discourage scribes from writing them for sale and, thus, limit their availability. In view of the centrality of Torah learning in Judaism, the rabbis could not agree to such a limitation and therefore legislated what amounted to a subsidy, through the tax exemption, for the publication of books.

The settlement of Jews in the Land of Israel has always been considered a cornerstone of Judaism. Whether one follows the dictum of Nachmanides that this constitutes one of the 613 mitzvot, or that of Maimonides, who argued that it was not a divinely ordained precept but merely something extremely desirable, such settlement has always been an integral part of Judaism. Accordingly, funds allocated by an individual for the expenses of travel to the Holy Land and subsequent settlement were partially exempted from an individual's taxable wealth.

The centrality of the study of Torah in Judaism has been discussed at length in chapter 3 of this book, so it is not surprising to find that in many communities, scholars, who had no other source of income except that accruing to them from their study, were exempt from taxation—a practice that continues to this day in regard to municipal taxes in the Israeli city of B'nei Brak.

In common with those of many other Jewish communities, the communal ordinances of Castille, in fifteenth-century Spain, granted partial exemptions to widows, unmarried orphans, and handicapped members of the community. Similarly, almost all communities exempted from taxation those whose taxable assets did not exceed what was considered a "poverty" level.

TITHING (*MA'ASER KESAFIM*)

At first glance, the concept of tithing one's income appears to be identical to that of charitable donations. A closer examination will show, however, that in actual fact tithing in Judaism is part and parcel of the tax system. It is not merely the result of the individual's kindness or goodness (even though, as explained below, the tithe *rate* may well be), but rather placed on him by Jewish custom and law. Furthermore, taxes paid to the communal or public sector budget may be deducted from the tithe in all those cases where such taxes are meant for welfare or Torah education (the purpose of tithes). It is true that the tithe is a self-monitored form of taxation. Nevertheless, its legal, religious and moral framework seems to parallel the rest of the Jewish pattern of taxation, and therefore it is included in this section.

Although halakhic authorities are divided as to the legal source of the tithing obligation—whether it is only a custom, a rabbinic decree, or of Divine origin—it is considered by all authorities to be binding today, and therefore has to affect the individual's disposable income as well as the size of the budget available to the public sector.[23]

The *Shulchan Arukh* rules that "the obligation to tithe one-tenth of one's income is only the mark of the average person. A more meritorious one is the opportunity [to give] a fifth."[24] (This 20 percent is usually considered to be an upper limit, necessary so that people won't neglect the needs of their own families in pursuit of the mitzvah of charity and thus become wards of the community themselves.)

The basis for the tithe is the income earned in that year, defined as all profits earned from business, wages, commissions, lotteries, stocks, gifts, and inheritances. (Real estate is not included in the tax base except when it is sold; the profits thereof have to tithed.) It is interesting to note that all the other taxes discussed in this section are levied either on a per capita or on an equity basis, whereas the tithe is an income tax.

Since the tithe is a tax on income and not a sales or value added tax, all expenses may be deducted provided they are not in effect part of the individual's disposable income. For example, a businessman may deduct the wages of his employees, since this is not part of his income. He may not, however, deduct an imputed wage for his own work or the wages of domestic help, or the cost of other such "perks" or benefits.[25] This is in contrast to most modern income tax practice, especially in small or family-owned firms, where owners' salaries and living expenses are legitimately charged as business expenses, even though as often as not they in fact constitute a withdrawal of profits.[26]

Furthermore, although travel expenses (including for food and drink) incurred in the process of earning profits may be deducted (even when no profit is actually earned from that trip), the deductions are limited to the normal eating habits of the individual when at home. In view of the many abuses of expense account living at the expense of the tax authorities so prevalent in all modern societies, it is interesting to quote the ruling laid down recently (1982) by Rabbi Moshe Sternbuch of B'nei Brak, Israel:

> In considering the costs of doing business or earning an income [that may be deducted before tithing], we are only allowed to consider the essential ones. If one, for example, uses luxury hotels or eats in expensive restaurants, one may not deduct these expenses [presumably one could deduct the costs of the medium-class ones]. So, too, luxury cars, bought for the purpose of exhibiting one's wealth and power, may not be included as expenses before calculating the tithe. One may deduct the costs of those cars used solely for the purpose of business; however, one is allowed to deduct only a pro rata share of cars used both for business and for private use.[27]

The same source contains another ruling which sheds light on the problem of taxation under conditions of inflation.

> The tithe is levied only on profits earned. One who has invested his money in a bank or in any savings scheme, the yield of which is less than the consumer cost of living index, actually doesn't have to tithe from it. However, for this purpose, the official government index is not to be considered, since it includes changes in the price level of luxury items as well. In calculating the profit for purposes of tithing, only the price changes in basic commodities, such as milk, eggs, bread, and chickens, may be used.

In chapter 3 we explained that Judaism views wealth as something given to man in order, among other things, that he may assist others. This assistance to others is not only a favor which he bestows, nor a free will offering given out of the goodness of his heart, but rather an obligation. The tithe is, therefore, in fact a partner in one's income. This is shown by the fact that the tithe, just like the profits of ordinary partners, is calculated on income after all involuntary payments are deducted. Such involuntary payments are restricted to those imposed on the firm and include income tax, social insurance, and sales and valued added taxes. Compulsory government loans (common, for instance, in present-day Israel) may also be deducted at the time of their imposition but have to be included when they become due.

According to Rabbi Epstein (*Arukh Hashulchan*, a nineteenth-century commentary on the *Shulchan Arukh*), all Jews are liable to tithe except those who have only bread and water. This would indicate that the obligation flows from a certain level of income.[28] There is, however, another opinion, of Rabbi V. Soloveitzick, that what counts is the needs of the individual and not merely the income.[29] For example, one earning and needing $1,000 to keep his family at a modest standard of living would be liable for at least $100 tithe if we follow *Arukh Hashulchan*; according to the second opinion he wouldn't be liable. It seems that the second opinion is in accordance with the concept that taxation shouldn't be confiscatory, while the former is based on the idea that all have an obligation to share their wealth.

TAX ENFORCEMENT

Just as in any society, the Jewish community needed the power to enforce its tax edicts in order to protect itself against tax evasion. From early antiquity, Jewish law provided the king, the *bet din*, and the popularly elected representatives with the power to use physical force and imprisonment to enforce all their decisions, including fiscal policy; this power existed even during periods of life in exile. There were, however, periods when these physical powers were not available to the community. Irrespective, however, of whether the community possessed independent police powers, there were two major factors which ensured the continuation of the Jewish tax system.

It is a well-established fact that in any society, a breakdown in the moral basis for taxation is rapidly translated into widespread tax evasion. The religious and moral teachings of Judaism, however, created an ideological climate in which the individual's obligations to the communal well-being were constantly reiterated, so that they became an integral part of him. This climate remained throughout the centuries and in all the countries of the dispersion, guaranteeing the continuation of a well-defined fiscal system.

Secondly, till the Napoleonic Wars in Europe and even later in some of the Moslem countries, the Jew as an individual had no existence outside of the community. The threat of excommunication, or even of temporary exclusion from communal life, was powerful enough to provide the discipline needed for the enforcement of an independent tax policy.

The proof of the pudding is in the eating. The existence of independent, autonomous Jewish communities from the days of the first Jewish state till the nineteenth century, financing a host of social, religious, and political activities, would have been impossible if tax evasion was rife and a general rule.

Nevertheless, it would be naive to maintain that there was no tax evasion in the Jewish world; people do not like to part with their money even though they are emotionally and intellectually convinced of the morality and necessity thereof, and Jews are no different. As with all other aspects of life, however, Judaism enmeshed the matter of taxation within a practical framework that minimized the possibilities of tax evasion.

Tax evasion can take two forms: the deliberate falsifying of returns in order to reduce tax liability, and a refusal to pay the tax levied. Jewish law consistently pursued a course that would minimize the loss of revenue to the community through either of these forms.

Jewish moral literature throughout the ages pointed out that tax evasion was akin to theft. The classical medieval Book of the Pious (*Sefer HaChasidim*) subsumes both the obligation to pay taxes and the sin of evasion within the moral structure of the Jew. This view is repeated in the vast responsa literature down to the present time, so that religious authority as well as public disapproval were placed at the service of the communal authorities.

Those authorities did not hesitate to use the two powerful punitive measures at their disposal to enforce the halakhic rulings regarding false tax declarations. These two measures—the oath and excommunication (*herem*)—were practiced by rabbinic courts from the earliest days of Jewish history. The retraction of an oath necessitated the bringing of a sacrifice during Temple times and the special dispensation of a *bet din* in later times, while the taking of God's name in vain—in this case through a false oath—was a basic prohibition of Judaism enshrined in the Ten Commandments. Conditioned by generations of these religious teachings, Jews were loath to take oaths on any subject. Halakhic sources are rich in examples of men willing to suffer economic losses rather than take an oath in order to settle their disputes. Within such a cultural structure, the power of the courts to force an oath on members of the community in order to validate their tax declarations must be recognized as a powerful weapon in the war against tax evasion.

When moral and religious pressure failed, refusal to pay a tax debt owed to the community brought with it imprisonment in many communities. At the same time, the precedents for excommunication from the community for this crime were manifold, so that the mere threat of the *herem* was as often as not sufficient to prevent massive tax evasion. It is perhaps convenient and simplistic to assume that the *herem* was a defense mechanism created by the pathetic sociopolitical conditions of European Jewry after the late Middle Ages, since the surrounding non-Jewish society's refusal to recognize the Jew as a part of society meant that he had no alternative but to obey halakhic rulings. Yet the evidence in Jewish sources is sufficient to show that the use of the *herem* predates this condition by close to 2,000 years, and that its real power lay in the desire of the individual to remain part of the Jewish people.

Comparative studies of modern economies show that tax evasion through the exploitation of legal loopholes is a very common phenomenon that requires the constant attention of the tax authorities. The same exploitation may be found in the history of the Jewish fiscal system. It has already been noted that articles of gold jewelry were not taxed at their full value. However, when in fifteenth-century Austria the use of gold and silver jewelry as a tax haven became widespread, Rabbi Israel Isserlin's halakhic ruling was that they should be taxed. He used the argument of tax evasion to include vineyards and fields in the taxable wealth.[30]

There is another modern form of tax evasion that also has parallels in Jewish sources: viz., moving one's business or one's home to an area or country where the tax rates are lower. Rich men in communities with a heavy tax burden would want to move to other Jewish communities in order to evade their responsibilities. Such a move would obviously be to the detriment of the other taxpayers and, as often as not, the whole community, since the tax base was usually very limited. The *herem* was used to prevent the migration of such wealthy citizens to other communities. For the same reason, we find the Rashba ruling that Reuven, who lived in city A but conducted his business in city B, had to pay the relevant taxes to the community of city B, since this is where his wealth was actually created.[31] In modern terms, this ruling would seem to have important implications for the problem of people living in suburbia but not sharing in the tax burden of the inner cities, where they actually earn their livelihood.

COMMUNAL ENACTMENTS

In order to provide the reader with a balanced picture of the actual, everyday operation of the Jewish tax system, a sample of the relevant literature is presented here—ranging from extracts of the communal minute books of various Jewish communities and the decisions of Jewish synods to the responsa of halakhic authorities to practical questions. Although this is only a small cross-section, the variety—in subject matter, historical perspective, and geographical breadth—would seem sufficient for our purposes.

Takkanah of Rabbenu Gershon Me'or Hagolah (ninth-century Franco-Germany)

If a contribution has been assessed against a person he may not summon the collector to *bet din* until he has either paid the tax in cash or given a pledge for its value. Even before he pays he may make a complaint, however, if he feels that his rights are being violated, until justice is done. Otherwise, a ruthless man might deprive a member of the community of his property and declare that he is collecting it as a tax.

Takkanah of Rashi (tenth-century Franco-Germany)

And each one shall give that which we have commanded the citizens of the city . . ., as has been customary from the day of the formation of our community. Each one shall give of all his wealth, excepting articles for personal use, houses, vineyards, fields, and deposits of Gentiles. [These were highly volatile and therefore could not be considered as true income-bearing investments.] Funds invested through an agent are considered to be half a pledge [on which there is no tax] and half a loan, which is part of the tax base of the agent. If one has gold or silver articles or jewelry, these are liable to tax at only half their value.

Synod of Castilian Jews (1432)

A stringent *herem* of ten curses shall be pronounced in all the communities on the Sabbath between Rosh Hashanah and Yom Kippur of each year at the time the Torah is in the ark, against any Jew who will attempt to evade the payment of taxes, or who will help others to evade taxes which they are legally obliged to pay. [The Frankfort Synod, called in 1603, explicitly separated such Jews from the community and forbade intermarrying with them or permitting them to take part in religious functions.]

Any widow or orphan [male or female] who is not married and possesses less than four hundred maravedis shall be exempt from payment of taxes. If they have more the surplus will be taxed. The same rule shall apply to the lame and the crippled.

No Jew or Jewess shall obtain any letter from the king or queen or any landlord or lady or any other influential person by which he or she may be freed from paying the taxes which the community shall impose.

A community having forty families or more shall be obliged to endeavor, in so far as possible, to maintain a rabbi who shall teach them halakhot and agadot. The community must maintain him reasonably. His salary shall be paid from the income from the tax on meat and wine and the income from the *hekdesh* [communal property], if there is any, or from the Talmud Torah [Study of the Torah] Fund.

[The following is an example of a type of indirect tax common amongst all Jewish communities throughout the centuries. Actually, this is a tax on consumption and so is similar to the sales tax prevalent in many modern economies. It is often considered regressive, since although the poor pay the same tax as the wealthy on each item, their tax rate relative to their income is greater. Many Jewish communities placed taxes on wine and meat, considered luxuries, and taxed the more common articles of consumption only as their economic situation declined.]

Whereas we saw that the hands of the students of the Torah have slackened and even the children of the primary school are idle because their parents cannot afford to pay the teachers' salaries . . . [therefore,] to provide a voluntary fund for Talmud Torah:

For every head of big cattle [cows, oxen, bulls] which is slaughtered among them and for them [i.e., for each of the communities of Castille] they shall pay five maravedis; for each calf or heifer, two maravedis; and for a sheep or goat, one maravedi; for each small sheep or goat weighing less then four arreldes, they should pay for Talmud Torah one coronado; otherwise, five pence each.

For each jug of wine sold at retail, . . . they should pay three pence per jar; if more than five jugs are sold [at one time,] two dinars [total].

Whoever makes a wedding shall pay ten maravedis; for a circumcision, also ten maravedis, as soon as the child reaches the stage where he is not to be considered any longer a *nefel* [i.e., it is likely to live] [32]

Council of Lithuania (seventeenth century)

The heads of the community shall appoint two men in their towns to be responsible for the collection of the poll tax, the taxes to the community, and the pourotne tax [levied by the state]. These men shall have the authority and power in matters of taxation to punish and to confiscate, to attach and seize goods as a pledge [in cases of nonpayment].[33]

Sugenheim Town (Germany, 1756)

[This was a community of some twelve householders.]

1.   The communal treasurer [to be elected for one year] is to be free from rendering a formal account of income and expenditures, as every householder has confidence that in this matter everyone will act in accordance with Jewish conscience and will not defraud the community.

2.   The treasurer, together with the heads of the community, shall have the power to impose the *herem* as well as fines.

3.   A majority of the residents and of those who have children to be educated shall decide upon the *chazan* [cantor, who also served as teacher and ritual slaughterer]. His wages are to be paid in part by the parents of the pupils [the utility principle], in part by taxes [righteousness or pragmatic, since it was based on wealth], and in part by a fixed per capita sum [reflecting every individual's obligation to share in the Torah learning even of other people's children].

4.   The expenses of the synagogue are to be covered by taxation, half on the basis of wealth and half on a per capita basis. [Even though everybody derives the same benefit from the syna-

gogue, a per capita tax alone would not be sufficient to cover the costs.][34]

Padua (sixteenth–seventeenth-century Italy)

[In a meeting held on the 2nd of February, 1588, the Council of the Jews of Padua appointed accountants to oversee the accounts of the community and also appointed tax assessors for the purpose of collecting taxes from the members. They described the work of these assessors as follows.]

The assessors shall evaluate every member of the community according to the following dictate of the Council: They will evaluate the capital of each member as they understand it and, also, . . . the extent of their trade and its profit. Furthermore, the assessors will evaluate the property which the members have outside the town from which they earn an income. The assessors will also investigate the extent to which the members have people working for them in such a way as to increase their incomes. They shall distinguish between those who have capital and earn from that and those who don't have capital but who earn their livelihoods from commerce or from a profession or from a trade, and they will evaluate such activities according to their expenses and income and everything will be done according to the judgment of the assessors. They can enforce an oath on the possessors of the money only once in order to discover the truth.

13th of January, 1590

We will appoint one person who will go together with Reb Shimon Sarfaty to collect donations of bread every eve of Sabbath and eve of festivals, even as it has been done until now, and they will provide this food to the poor according to the list given to them by the *parnasim* [communal wardens]. In order to prevent the confusion that has resulted in the past, the appointed persons shall keep a record of the donations given by the various householders, so as not to have to approach them a second time.

It has been decided to release the widow Breulin, the widow of Avraham Safarty, from all her debts to the community arising out of the rental of the house in which she lives at present. Furthermore, this house will be available for her as an act of mercy so that she may dwell therein for free until such time as the community will decide otherwise. [This was, in effect, negative taxation.]

Moshe Rimina, who will be marrying off his daughter next week, B' Mazel Tov, has asked for financial assistance from one of the members of the community. The latter has brought it to the notice of the community leaders, who have decided to give him eight lines [or liters of gold], half from the charitable funds and half from the general communal funds [probably taxes for communal needs as distinct from external taxes]. This decision was passed by six votes against one negative vote.[35]

Va'ad Arba Aratsot (Eastern Europe)

1661

Addressed to the leaders and officers of the communities of Askenaz [Germany and probably Austria-Hungary], their rabbis and batei din regarding the complaint of the leaders of the community of Poznan against Reb Avraham ben Rabbi Joseph Hanover:

Reb Avraham was formerly a member of the community of Poznan and one of its taxpayers. Praise to God, he was financially successful and his wealth increased greatly. However, the economic fortunes of Poznan declined, so that they were unable to bear the communal tax burden and their resultant debts. . . . Seeing this, Reb Avraham separated himself from the community and went to live in Askenaz [thereby evading his tax obligations]. Now, with the grace of God, Poznan has recovered economically. Later, [Reb Avraham] returned secretly but continues to leave periodically in order to remove himself and his wife from the community to escape from his communal obligations.

Therefore, our request to you, in all your communities, is that you treat him and all the members of his family according to the ban [herem] we have pronounced against him. This is in accordance with the halakhic ruling that one excommunicated by one community is automatically excommunicated from another. In this way, you will protect the renowned community of Poznan [from exploitation since the removal of a major taxpayer meant that the rest of the community had now to shoulder a greater burden].

You are asked to use all forms of bans and pressures against this man who has broken the communal yoke, even recourse to the laws of the Gentiles. [The restrictions against Jewish settlement in most Germanic communities of that time could only be overcome, if at all, via the consent and permission of the community.]

All this shall be done to him until he repents and returns permanently to Poznan and participates, once again, in their tax burden.

We have [also] decreed that all Jews living in the exile of the four countries [of Greater and Little Poland, L'vov Land, and Volhynia] will participate in the great mitzvah of *pidyon sh'vuyim* [the redemption of captives, in this case Jews expelled from Russia to various countries, including those of the Turkish Empire and Asiatic Russia]. On pain of being punished by the usual communal fines and bans, every Jew in all our communities will pay within one year six payments, as assessed by the community. The matter is urgent, in case the authorities expel the Jews to lands where there is no possibility of redemption. Therefore, we have appointed three notables to travel through the lands of the Council to collect immediately three payments; the remainder will be collected by the communities themselves and forwarded to us in Lublin before the fair. We will then find ways to transfer the money to the community in Constantinople.

1668

We hereby decree on the leaders of all the communities and on individuals that they may not foreclose and thereby possess property of individuals or of a group in lieu of debt or even in payment of the king's tax. Rather, the debtors will declare their assets under oath or through the *bet din*'s assessors; from the amount of these assets, the creditors will be able to realize their debts and the king's tax. We are issuing this edict in order to encourage *yishuv ha'olam* [literally, "the settlement of the world"], so that the economy shall be open to all without fear of physical attachment of their goods and property.

Concerning the evil habit which is sometimes practiced of delaying burials because of nonpayment of the burial plot: This is a desecration of the dead and constitutes a "theft of truth" both against the living and the dead. We are explicit in our objections to this practice and declare excommunication and the *herem* on its practitioners. Furthermore, we levy a fine of fifty adumim on each of the leaders of those communities which do not prevent their *gabba'im* [congregational officials] from doing this. By this edict we nullify any communal enactments or customs which have been instituted in this regard.[36]

RESPONSA AND HALAKHIC CODES

Mishnah

On the fifteenth day of Adar [the end of the winter season], the roads and the streets are to be repaired [from the damage caused by the winter rains], the ritual baths cleared [from the fungi and mildew of winter], and all the public needs settled.[37]

The Talmud Yerushalmi maintained it as a duty of the *batei din* to force the community to perform all these public works and, therefore, to finance them out of tax money. A later implementation of this ruling may be seen in the decision of the Jewish council of Padua in the sixteenth century "to add a third person to the two who were appointed in order to repair the paths and roads in the ghetto. The three of them shall keep a careful account of the expenses involved, and they will be able to draw all the required money from the community funds."[38]

Shulchan Arukh

The citizens of a town are able to force each other [even on the basis of a minority decision] to participate in the cost of building a wall and gate to the town, to build a synagogue, to purchase a Torah scroll and the books of the Bible. This applies to all the needs of the town, including the hiring of a *chazan*, the provision of hospitality for wayfarers, and contributions toward a charitable fund. To finance all those functions that the individual cannot maintain through his own resources, it is necessary for all the taxpayers to assemble so that each one can express his opinion in honesty. The decisions of the majority are binding.

One who has a courtyard [house] in another town, the townsmen of that town can force him to participate in the cost of providing drainage and water, even though he lives in another city. The costs of other services are not binding on him.

The financing of the public safety is to be the responsibility of all members of the community, including orphans [who are exempt from other types of taxes]. Rabbinic scholars, however, are exempt, since they do not need protection, as the Torah protects them. At the same time, scholars are, however, liable for their share of the cost of providing sidewalks and roads, etc. [presumably because they benefit from them—an application of the idea that it is not moral to benefit at another's expense]. In those cases where labor is provided instead of a monetary tax, the scholars are exempt even regarding roads, etc. [to preserve the dignity of scholars].[39]

Responsa of Shlomo ben Adret (the Rashba) (thirteenth-century Spain)

Question: In our community, every member is required to participate personally in the duty of night-watch. This is done in rotation, and now a dispute has arisen as to how we are to allocate participation. The poor members claim that since only the rich need protection because of their wealth, they should assume the full duty or at least a greater share.

Answer: The allocation of guard duty [a form of taxation, even if it was not paid in money] depends on the object or purpose of the duty. If the guard is provided in order to protect the community against robbers, then, obviously, the rich have to contribute more. At the same time, one has to take into account proximity to the wall. Those closer to the wall are more liable to loss and, therefore, have to pay a greater share [than those in a similar income group, but living further away from the wall]. Real estate, however, is not to be included in the tax base since it is not liable to be plundered.

If, however, the guard duty is meant to provide protection against an invading army, so that the danger is to life itself, then all should participate equally in it.[40]

Question from the Council of Majorca: Since there are people in our community who are very poor and, therefore, unable to pay the tax allocated to them, the *parnasim* wish to waive their obligation. However, we have a communal enactment which forbids the changing or rescinding of any tax regulations. How can we exempt these poor from taxes?

Answer: There are many communities whose custom it is to free from taxation those who are poor. However, in your case this is not to be done, since your ordinance forbids it. It is possible that the poor can be required to pay their share and then you can return it to them. Alternatively, their share of the tax can be allocated to all the other members of the community equally.[41]

In another responsum, the Rashba notes that in case of illness or poverty some communities grant exceptions from taxation. This is so even if the person becomes ill or poor after the tax had already been levied. If, however, the taxpayer recovers from his illness, or his economic position improves, then he becomes liable for his past debt.[42] Sudden changes in wealth were very common amongst the Jews who were engaged in international trade, since this trade was subject to the constant threat of losses from robbery or inclement weather.

The Rashba addressed himself in various responsa to the question of taxing property which is in another town or community. In reply to a number of different queries, he lays down quite clearly that the community cannot tax valuables which a member has in another community, since these had already been taxed where they were acquired; therefore, he would be paying tax twice on the same wealth.[43]

In reply to a question about taxes on the property of a minor, which was held in trust by a guardian, the Rashba's answer was "that the tax has to be advanced by the trustee. . . . When the ward becomes eighteen, the guardian can recover the taxes he has advanced. Those guardians unwilling to take upon themselves the duty of advancing the taxes have to hand over the trust to the *bet din*, who will administer it."[44]

(Some idea of the difference in tax policy between different communities or even in the same community at different times may be obtained from the responsa of the Rashba.)

> In Lerida it was the custom to tax the debtor for loans granted to him [since they produced income for him]. At a different period in the same town the creditor was liable for the tax. In that town movables were taxed at three percent of their value, immovables at one and a quarter percent and dwelling houses were tax-free. Yet, in Saragossa dwelling houses were also taxable.[45]

Responsum of Rabbi Joseph Colon (Pavia, Italy, fifteenth century)

A rabbinical assembly at Nürnberg had instructed all the communities surrounding Regensburg to come to the assistance of seventeen members of the community of Ratisbon who had been accused of killing a Christian child before Passover.

> It is lawful that the neighboring communities be called upon to contribute to the forthcoming expenses [bribery, etc., to avert the decree]. A similar case is to be found in *Baba Metzia* [108a]. Rabbi Yehudah says, "If the upper reaches of a stream dry up or are impeded by stones, the owners of the fields down river have to contribute to its restoration because they, too, need the water to

irrigate their fields. In the same way, house owners who live in the upper parts of a city have to contribute to the costs of draining the rain water if the lower parts are flooded. For although at present only the lower parts are threatened, there is a danger that the upper parts will suffer if help is not offered to the former.

And even if the surrounding communities will object, saying that the libel which has brought so much misfortune to the Jews of Ratisbon will not be brought against them formally and therefore there exists only a vague possibility of their being affected, nevertheless they are still obligated, since it is the duty of the Jews to assist one another.[46]

Rabbi Moshe Feinstein (New York, 1961)

To my esteemed friend, Dr. Eskowitz. Regarding your question of apportioning the cost of building a *mikveh* [ritual bath for women]: This has to be done, half on the basis of wealth and half on a per capita basis. This is the compromise which has been practiced over the ages regarding funds for the execution of religious precepts [Rama on *Orach Chayim*, section 53, subsection 23]. Such a compromise [between the progressive taxation principle and the poll tax concept] is necessary because we actually have two functions to finance: viz., the utilitarian performance of the mitzvah [which can be carried out cheaply] which is obligatory on all and therefore has to be financed on a per capita basis and the [enhancement of the mitzvah by] luxury or refinement [which adds to the expense] which has to be funded on a wealth basis]. . . .

There is an additional reason for this compromise, as may be seen from the ruling of the *Magen Avraham* (section 55, subsection 16) dealing with the hiring of men to complete a minyan. The poor can, after all, go to a nearby town, whereas the rich cannot leave their property or business. Furthermore, the poor [whose alternative use of time is less expensive] are prepared to go to the bother of traveling, etc., rather than spend money on the pleasure of having the minyan at hand. The wealthy, on the other hand, would rather spend the money and save themselves the travel. [Since this is a question of cost–benefit analysis,] those who have the greater pleasure [as they prefer to save the bother and travel] should pay more, i.e., the allocation of cost should be half on per capita basis [since everyone including the poor has some benefit] and half on the basis of wealth. [This arbitrary compromise is necessary as it is difficult for people to evaluate accurately the different degrees of utility enjoyed by each individual].

The Rama, in his gloss on *Choshen Mishpat,* section 163, subsection 3, seemingly contradicts the above principle with regard to the hiring of a *chazan;* here the ruling is that the cost is to be allocated on the basis of wealth alone. According to some authorities, this is an application of the principle that where a community has no set precedents for its tax policy, then one should allocate the burden according to wealth alone. It seems, however, that the question of a *chazan* is an exception since it is not a basic religious necessity; therefore the cost can be allocated on the basis of wealth only. Furthermore, there is also the element of pleasure and aesthetics in prayer [for which the rich are prepared to pay more].

With regard to the *mikveh,* however, which is an essential and obligatory precept binding on each individual, [taking precedence over the building of a synagogue and other religious requirements] the allocation of cost must be according to the compromise of half on a per capita basis and half on the basis of wealth.[47]

SUMMARY

As Judaism is a national, communally oriented religion, the community has a responsibility for the welfare of its members and a corresponding right to finance those needs through taxation over and above the individual's duty to contribute to charity.

While a community is free to choose a fiscal system and tax base, they must be reviewed by the halakhic authorities in the light of Jewish law, morality, and justice.

The utility concept is an intrinsic part of the Jewish tax system. It flows from the centrality of justice in Judaism that people cannot benefit at the involuntary expense of others, so that all those who benefit from the object of a tax have to participate in the burden of financing it.

Jews are obligated to tithe their incomes. This is not simply a charitable act, but a tax imposed in addition to the voluntary acts demanded by religious teachings.

There are certain spheres of activity that the community cannot refuse to finance: Torah education, the redemption of captives, the provision of ritual baths, synagogues, and burial grounds, and charity. Budget cuts designed to lighten the tax burden cannot eliminate them; at most they can be limited to accord with financial realities.

CHAPTER 9

Welfare

INTRODUCTION

At one time it was assumed that the only proper role of the state was the provision of a legal system and the defense of the physical security of its citizens. Education, assistance to the poor, care for the sick, etc., were regarded as the province of private or institutional charity. In the past century or so, however, the role of the state has been rapidly expanded, so that today, in most modern economies, services like public transport, educational facilities, and medical and other forms of insurance are provided by the state or by public authorities. In addition, such benefits as unemployment insurance, subsidized housing for the poor, and subsidies on essential foodstuffs have become accepted as part of the obligation of the public sector. In modern society, welfare has come to mean far more than the provision of charity—and a major portion of economic activity is devoted to the provision of security and welfare for the individual citizen.

Even a casual perusal of Jewish sources will show that right from the outset, Judaism understood that it was the community's duty to provide for the social needs of the individuals in that community. This obligation flowed from two concepts basic to the economic philosophy of Judaism: the premise that part of the wealth of individuals is given to them by the Deity in order to provide directly for the needs of less successful members of the community; and the desired creation of a religionational group. Both concepts demanded participation in the welfare costs of the community. It should be no surprise, therefore, that throughout the centuries and irrespective of which countries they inhabited, Jews have maintained a widely ramified welfare system, in its most modern sense. It is true that the Jewish welfare system differs radically from the underlying philosophy of the modern welfare state. Such differences, however, do not flow from any doubt as to the validity or necessity of such a system, but rather from basic Jewish concepts regarding the role of wealth, economic justice, the dignity of the individual, and the moral responsibility devolving on him.

THE CONCEPTUAL FRAMEWORK OF THE JEWISH WELFARE SYSTEM

Fundamentally, the provision of welfare is seen in Judaism as an act of *Imitatio Dei*—the imitation of God's ways—and as such is the mark of the Jew, who is obligated to walk in God's paths. In a Talmudic discussion, a rabbi asked how one can compare oneself to God and be so presumptuous as to assume that one can walk in His footsteps. After all, He is eternal, He is all-consuming fire, He has neither shape nor form, etc. To this, the rejoinder was that just as God is all-merciful, so man should be merciful; just as God is kind and righteous, so man should be kind and righteous; just as God is careful to look after all the creatures in His world, so should man be. Rabbi Simlai taught, the Torah begins with an act of *chesed* (loving-kindness) and ends with an act of *chesed*. As it is written at the beginning of the Torah, "And the Lord God made garments of skin for Adam and Eve and clothed them" [Gen. 3:21]; and at the conclusion of the Torah, "He [God] buried him [Moses] in the valley in the land of Moab" [Deut. 34:6].[1]

This view of acts of welfare as an imitation of God's greatness was extended to every aspect of the welfare spectrum, not just the giving of gifts to the poor. So we find Shimon Hatsadik writing in the fourth century B.C.E.: "There are three things on which the world stands: on the Torah, on Divine Service, and on acts of lovingkindness [*chesed*]."[2] The three are equally important in Judaism and equally essential for the construction of a religious and Godly nation. Acts of *chesed* were, therefore, considered to be characteristic of the Jewish people, both as individuals and as a nation.

It is not for nothing that Jewish folklore abounds with stories of the greatest men of its history performing mundane acts of lovingkindness. Moses saves the daughters of Jethro from the hands of the shepherds; Jacob rolls away the rock so that the flocks can be watered. Moses and David were shepherds, and in their conduct of this occupation, the sages saw a spiritual dimension necessary for leadership of the nation. Thus, it is written that

> Moses observed that one of the lambs of Jethro's flocks had wandered off a little far in search of water. He rebuked himself for failing to know that the lamb was thirsty and carried him on his shoulders from the spring, all the way back to the main flock. The Lord saw this and said that if Moses had such mercy in looking after the flocks of human beings, then he would be suitable for looking after the Jewish people.[3]

It is perhaps pertinent to point out that Chasidic commentary on the Bible saw this characteristic of *chesed* not only as being present in the leaders of the Jewish people but as integral to the physical formation of the Jewish nation. Thus, it is difficult to understand why Abraham sent to Aram, to the home of his family, for a wife for his son Isaac. After all, he had been Divinely commanded to leave his family and his homeland, so why renew these ties? Furthermore, the people in the house of Terach and Laban were idolators, just like the tribes who were living in the Land of Canaan. What difference did it make if the matriarchs of the Jewish people came from these idolators or from the idolators who were part of his family? In such circumstances, a lack of kinship might even be preferable.

The Chasidic master Shmuel of Sochochov points out that idolatry is an intellectual mistake, so that it is possible to teach people logically and rationally that there exists only one Deity. Good deeds and righteous actions, however, are not developed simply by intellectual training. In order for them to be ingrained in one's daily life, it is necessary to have role models in one's home and to acquire cultural and behavioral patterns characteristic of previous generations. The family of Abraham, even though they were idolators, were practitioners of hospitality and the heirs to a tradition of kindness. This may be seen in the actions of Lot, when he risked his life in extending hospitality while dwelling amongst the sinners of Sodom and in the kindness and mercy of

Laban in welcoming both Eliezer and, later on, the patriarch Jacob. Eliezer was sent, therefore, to find a wife who would be endowed with the qualities of mercy, kindness, and righteousness; after all, the problem of idolatry could be solved by education. So, too, the patriarch Jacob went to take his wives from the same source.[4]

In Judaism, however, assistance to the weaker or impoverished members of society is not simply an act of kindness, prompted by one's pangs of conscience, but rather an obligation placed on all individuals and on the community, to use their God-given wealth in the way commanded by the Deity. That obligation embraces not only assistance to the poor, the widow, and the orphan, but also the provision of communal services deemed essential for the spiritual and physical well-being of the community.

Although Judaism translated this obligation into practical religious behavior subject to legal enforcement, nevertheless the spiritual framework of mutual obligation is just as important. Some idea of this framework may be gauged from the following precepts from the ethical literature:

> Beware of oppressing other men, whether by money or by words; neither envy or hate them. Do not rely upon the broken reed of human support and do not set up gold as your hope, for that is the beginning of idolatry. Rather, distribute your money according to God's will; he is able to cover your deficit. Let expenditure of your money be of less value to you than utterance of your words. Do not set your eyes upon who is richer than you but upon one who is poorer. . . . Rejoice in your lot, whether it be large or small. Do not give less than half a shekel each year and at one time. Every month and every week give what you can. On every day let there not be lacking a small donation before prayer. When your income reaches a tithable amount, set aside the tithe. Thus you will have something at hand, wherever you would give to the living or the dead, whether to the poor or the rich. Enjoy neither food nor drink without reciting a blessing before and after. Be zealous to praise your Creator for satisfying you.[5]

> He who says, ''Mine is mine and yours is yours'' is only of average spiritual stature; other sages maintained that this is the characteristic of the people of Sodom. He who says, ''Mine is yours and yours is mine'' is an ignoramus. ''Mine is yours and yours is

yours" is the saying of a pious man. "Yours is mine and mine is mine"—This is the mark of evil.[6]

One may not withhold knowledge or evidence that may lead to a loss of your fellow man's money, as it is written, "You shall not stand upon your brother's blood" [Lev. 19:16].[7]

The involvement of the Jew in welfare programs has two distinct aspects: (a) those personal mitzvot that oblige him to tithe, to leave part of his field for the poor, to provide for the well-being of the widowed, etc.; and (b) participation in those acts of communal welfare that are funded out of tax money.

Both types of mitzvot have the same Jewish legal status as any of the so-called "religious" or "ritual" mitzvot relating to prayer, kashrut, Sabbath and festival observance, etc. Furthermore, both individual acts of welfare and participation in the communal funds are enforceable by the community and the *batei din*. This means that the negative mitzvot are punishable by a court of law in the same manner as transgressions of other negative mitzvot. For example, one is not allowed to harvest the corners of the field (*pe'ah*). If one nevertheless does so he can be flogged, which is the punishment meted out for any negative precept ignored.

In addition to enforcement by human agency, the neglect of mitzvot, both positive and negative, calls down Divine displeasure and punishment. So, welfare transgressions result in tragedy, both individual and communal.

[Pestilence increases] in the fourth year on account of the failure to give tithes to the poor in the third year [of the sabbatical cycle]; in the seventh, on account of the failure to give the tithe in the sixth; at the end of the seventh year, because of the illegal use of the produce of the seventh year [i.e., the sabbatical year, when all land must lie fallow and whatever grows on it is considered ownerless]; and at the end of the festival [of Sukkhot] every year, owing to the theft of the gifts for the poor [denial by the owners of their right to participate in the annual harvest either by barring them from the land or by not leaving sheaves, gleaning, or unharvested corners required by Jewish law].[8]

Furthermore, the honor and dignity of the recipients of welfare are to be preserved throughout. One may not insult them, or cause them to be slighted or insulted, as a result of their receiving charity. After all, Judaism taught that all men were in fact the recipients of charity and welfare from God, of Divine bounty; for Judaism viewed all wealth as being of Divine origin, and given to man for his benefit. (See chapter 3.)

The *Sefer Hachinukh,* in explaining the purpose of those mitzvot relating to the weaker members of society, points out that "it is written, 'One may not oppress the orphan or widow' [Exod. 22:21]. One must see that all one's transactions with the widow and orphan will be charitable, merciful, and tranquil. Their rights must be respected even more than would have been the case if the husband or father was alive and involved in the transaction."[9]

The Chasidic teacher Menachem Mendel of Kotsk points out that the Bible, immediately following the injunction against oppressing the orphan, uses repetitive forms of the words "oppress," "He will cry out," and "I the Lord will hear." The Rebbe explained that when an orphan complains about his oppression or his mishandling at the hands of the community, his complaint is twofold. There is the normal complaint of being hurt, but in addition to that is the cry that he is being hurt because he is an orphan, because he has no protector, because he has no father or mother to look after his interests. Since the oppression of such people is a dual one, the Deity's censure and His punishment will also be multiplied.

The existence of *matan b'seter* (giving of charity wherein the recipient and the giver are ignorant of each other's identity) and the protection of the debtor against abuse by the creditor or confiscation of his basic necessities, along with numerous rabbinic injunctions concerning the slighting of the poor, are further examples of this consideration for the feelings of the poor—a concern not always present in some modern welfare systems. At the same time, poverty carries with it no spiritual connotations in Judaism, nor is it regarded as a way of achieving sanctity. So "living on welfare" was not designed to be a way of life, nor were its recipients viewed as paragons of sanctity. There are no "poor friars" nor Sadhu begging bowls in Judaism.

Summing up opinions expressed by the sages, the Talmud tells us that "it is better for a man to flay a carcass in the market [regarded as menial labor of the lowest kind] than to be dependent on others. A man should not say, 'I am a priest, I am a great scholar—provide for me.'"[10] Maimonides continues this idea:

> The greatest of our scholars were hewers of wood, porters, drawers of water for gardens, and workers in iron and coal. They

did not ask anything of the public and when offered did not accept. A person who deserves to be helped but who refrains from public assistance even at the expense of dying in poverty and difficulty will merit that he will be able to support others. In this respect it is written, "Blessed be the man who trusted in God" [Jer. 17:8].[11]

Indeed, Jewish welfare is aimed not only at providing for the poor but also at enabling people to escape the poverty cycle by their own efforts. Maimonides considers the highest form of charity "He who supports his fellow Jew by giving him a gift or a loan, or by establishing him in a trade so that he should not need the assistance of others."[12]

And although the community is obligated to provide services for its members, at the same time all of them—including the poor—are required to participate in the financing of these services. (The poor's exemption from taxation was considered a pragmatic accommodation, not a legal right.)

Finally, despite the importance attached to welfare in Judaism and the obligation of society to actively promote such welfare, there does not seem to be in Judaism support for the concept of the redistribution of wealth that is the basis of much present-day social thinking, such as income policies. Furthermore, although we use the term welfare throughout this chapter, it is important to note that Judaism is concerned much of the time with charity, with its negative overtones for the recipient, rather than transfer payments from the public purse as a free right.

TZEDAKAH (CHARITY)

Although the English word "charity" has been used as the translation of the Hebrew word "tzedakah" in the heading of this section, it must be stressed at the outset that this translation does not convey the real meaning of the Jewish concept of giving assistance to others. "Tzedakah" has the same root as "tzedek"—justice—since acts of assistance are looked upon in Jewish thought primarily as a rectification of a social imbalance. They are not merely prompted by mercy or personal pangs of conscience, but rather constitute the fulfillment of the obligations that flow from wealth. We have seen that Judaism envisages all wealth given to an individual as a form of custodianship. One of the major purposes of that custodianship is the acts of assistance that a man is able to perform with his God-given wealth. The future of man's material success is in no small measure a reflection of his ability to measure up to the responsibilities imposed by his present wealth.

In all forms of charity, the Jew was obliged to preserve to the best of his ability the dignity of the recipient. At the same time, it was clearly understood that the shame involved has a positive role to play. The Chatam Sofer, writing in nineteenth-century Hungary, pointed out to his students that there is nothing in life that is free; everything has a cost. They rejoined that people who receive communal assistance are in effect receiving it for nothing. His answer was that their shame was the price they paid for the assistance given to them.

It is this "cost" that prevents charity from becoming an accepted and justified pattern of life. In our own day, liberal and socialist thinkers have objected to the use of the word "charity" to describe the assistance given to the poor and weak. "Welfare," to their mind, was a more correct term, since it preserved the dignity of the recipient. Almost all of the policies of the welfare state are based on this distinction. Unlike "charity," "welfare" provides free education, medical treatment, job security, and old age pensions to all irrespective of the individual's income or ability to provide for himself. All these forms of assistance often involve no financial cost to the recipient.

For example, suggestions in Israel to provide subsidies directly to the poor rather than to goods and services have been rejected by the trade unions. The latter method has been shown to lead to waste of the subsidized goods, and also to benefit many who are not really deserving or needy; nevertheless, the unions argued that subsidizing the poor directly would be insulting or demeaning. Unfortunately, the expansion of social benefits that flows from this attitude may place a burden on the public purse that it cannot bear, leading either to a breakdown of the whole welfare system or to rampant inflation.

Furthermore, when "welfare" rather than "charity" is the normative system, many of the same people who would not wish to draw on charitable funds, with their resultant stigma, see nothing wrong with "living off welfare"—since it is theirs, so to speak, as a right. This leads to a certain moral disease that encourages abusing the system or, at best, discourages efforts by individuals to break the poverty cycle. When unemployment benefits almost equal the lowest wage levels, for example, it has been found to retard re-entry into the labor force, especially when these benefits are not linked to a commensurate, if any, contribution by the worker, as in most European countries.

Judaism's view of charity, while ensuing both individual and communal care of the weak and unfortunate, militates against welfare as a way of life. Not only is there a price in the form of pride that has to be paid for receiving charity, but there are also legal obligations imposed. A poor man who receives charity is himself obligated to give some to those who are poorer than himself, while the recipient of an interest-free loan may not waste it or in any way abuse the opportunity given to him. The poor can be obligated to work in exchange for the charity given to them, as may be seen in this regulation, proclaimed by the Jewish Council of Padua on July 27th, 1603:

> It often happens that one of our fellow Jews needs assistance from a man or a woman either because of disease, God forbid, or for another reason. Even though it may be that he wishes to get this assistance for money, nevertheless, sometimes there is nobody who is available for such assistance. Therefore, we decree that all those who receive charity from the community are obligated to go if they are called by a certain individual, and they will receive each one of them a wage of one liter a day and one liter at night in addition to the food that the householder is obligated to give them. Should one of these participants refuse to go when he is called, then the *parnasim* will not be entitled to give him any charitable assistance for a full year.[13]

Perhaps the most immediate and pressing aspect of any welfare system is the provision for the basic needs of the poor. Such subsistence items have to take precedence; otherwise, people might starve to death, making other welfare provisions superfluous.

Jewish poverty relief basically centers around two concepts: the agricultural gifts commanded by the Torah and the assistance in money and kind provided for by charity. For the reader's convenience they will be dealt with separately, even though they are only variations of the same basic concepts and duties.

Agricultural Gifts

The poor have the right to participate in the Jewish farmer's harvest: the Jewish poor in accordance with the Torah and the Gentile poor *mip'nei darkhei shalom* (for the sake of peace). (It is obviously not feasible to grant by right all the poor of the world a share in the bounty of such a small entity as the Jewish farming community.) Although at first glance the effect of these gifts on the poor of a modern nonagrarian society seems to be severely limited, this is not really so. Even today, even in industrialized societies, the specter of hunger is such that mitigating it in this form would seem to retain some importance. More importantly, perhaps, the influence of the ideology underlying these gifts in shaping the attitudes of Jews toward wealth and the responsibility for each other's welfare inherent therein is as great today as ever. Similarly, the institution of gifts to the poor is based on principles that are relevant to many of the issues confronting the modern welfare state. It is this relevance, both to the concept of wealth and to the perfection of the welfare system, which, we suggest, is as important as an analysis of the role of the gifts themselves.

Halakhically, the gifts enumerated below are applicable, in one form or another, to the Jewish farmer today.

At harvest time the farmer has to leave a corner (*pe'ah*) of his field that the poor can harvest (Lev. 19:9). The amount or area of the *pe'ah* was not defined in the Torah, but rabbinic opinion required a minimum of one-sixteenth. However, if the yield is so small that this proportion is inconsequential, or if the number of poor is great in that year, the farmer is expected to leave more. In addition, sheaves, or individual fruits, left (*leket*) or forgotten (*shikh'chah*) in the fields automatically become available to the poor and the owner may not return to gather them (Lev. 19:10; Deut. 24:19–21).

Rabbinic legislation translated these precepts into practical, everyday behavior by clearly delineating the obligations and rights of both the field owners and the poor—Jewish justice insisting, here as always, on the symmetry of rights and obligations. With respect to farmers, all three injunctions have the full force of (negative) Torah commandments, transgression of which leaves one liable to corporal punishment.

At the same time, the property rights of the farmer are legitimate ones and have to be respected. So the poor may not glean or harvest the pe'ah before the harvesters have completed their work. Otherwise, they may come to be guilty of theft. It must be stressed, however, that none of these gifts are the property of the farmer owner. They are, thus, not his to dispose of to particular poor, as he may do in the case of the priestly tithes. These gifts also do not possess any sanctity like the priestly tithe.

Maimonides is careful to point out that pe'ah has to be left unharvested "linked to the ground" (even though, if it is harvested, the farmer is still obligated to give it away).[14] This involves the poor in an act designed to earn their food. The owner is not obligated, as he is in the case of tithes, to bring the gifts to the poor; rather, they are required to be actively involved in the gathering, harvesting, etc. It would seem that this has an important application in preventing the attitude of "I'm entitled" so common in welfare recipients. At the same time, it would seem to encourage poverty programs that encourage people to work while they are receiving benefits.

> Three times daily [writes Maimonides] the pe'ah is allowed to be harvested by the poor: at early morning, at midday and at the time of the afternoon service. If a poor man wishes to harvest at another time, he may not do so. Why wasn't only one time set aside? Because there are nursing mothers who require to eat at the beginning of the day; there are poor children who do not awake so early; and there are elderly poor who do not [because of their age] reach the field till the time of the afternoon prayers.[15]

This is another example of the consideration for the convenience and dignity of the poor that is a common and important element in the Jewish welfare system.

If the poor do not wish to avail themselves of the bounty offered them by the Torah, then that bounty becomes available to everyone. In the early years of the State of Israel, the mass immigration there brought with it great economic hardship, so many people could be seen gleaning in the fields. Today, however, there doesn't seem to be a demand for these agricultural gifts, even though the Jewish farmer is still obligated to provide them.

The aforementioned gifts are annual events in the agricultural cycle. In addition, the Torah demands a tithe to be given to the poor (*ma'aser ani*) in the third and sixth years of the seven-year (sabbatical) cycle. (The tithes of the first, second, fourth, and fifth years have to be taken by the owner to Jerusalem and eaten there.) These tithes can be given by the farmer to whichever poor person he wishes. They have to be separated after the gifts to the priests (*t'rumah*) and Levites (*ma'aser*) are separated; the crops are then permitted to be eaten or used for any other purpose (such as trade).

Tithes are given to the poor for their own subsistence, so they are not allowed to pay off their debts with them.[16] They are, however, able to use them for limited charitable purposes, such as a gift to another poor person; but they may not be sent out of the Land of Israel.

Some authorities view the tithing of money (*ma'aser kesafim*) as an implementation of this *ma'aser ani*. Irrespective of whether this is the case, Jews are obligated to tithe their monetary incomes, as explained in chapter 8, and this tithe is used for purposes of charity.

In addition to these gifts, the produce of the land during the sabbatical and jubilee years is available to everybody, the land itself being considered ownerless. All debts are remitted in the sabbatical year, while in the jubilee year land reverts to its original owners. (Such reversion applied only in the days of the first Temple, when the allocation of the Land of Israel among the twelve tribes was still in effect.) Although secular scholars adduce various reasons for the institutions of the sabbatical and jubilee years—such as the benefits of leaving land fallow or the prevention of accumulation of land in the hands of the few—Jewish mainstream commentators follow the *Sefer Hachinukh* in attributing important moral and ethical values to them.

Charity to the Poor

It is a positive commandment incumbent on every Jew to give charity, even as it is written, "You shall surely open your hand to him" [Deut. 15:8], and "you shall support the stranger and your brother shall dwell with you" [Lev. 25:35]. He who sees the poor begging and ignores him and does not give him charity transgresses a negative commandment, as it is written, "And you shall not harden your heart, and you shall not close your hand from your poor brother" [Deut. 15:7].[17]

This formulation of Maimonides is reflected in all the codes.

The major purpose and the highest degree of charity is, in the words of Maimonides, "to support a fellow Jew who has become poor by giving him a gift or a loan, or by forming a business partnership with him, or by providing him with a job, till he is no longer dependent on the generosity of others." In order words, to enable the poor to break out of the poverty cycle. One instrument for achieving this, the interest-free loan, has already been dealt with in detail in chapter 7. Another, which Maimonides mentions, is the obligation to provide employment to other Jews. The timeliness of this form of assistance could be seen some eight centuries later, in the pre-state years of modern Israel.

The waves of *aliyah* (immigration) between the two world wars created a serious problem of unemployment in Palestine. Arab workers were able to undercut the immigrants, who were accustomed to a European standard of living and at the same time unused to the rigors of unskilled agricultural work. One of the methods used by the labor federations to force Jewish labor onto the owners of the orange groves, a major employer at that time, was the strike. Orthodox Jewish unions joined their secular counterparts in these strikes; when Rabbi Elchanan Wasserman, one of the leading rabbinical figures of Eastern Europe, rebuked them for this, they replied that Jewish tradition required the orange growers to give preference to Jews in order that they might earn a livelihood and not become dependent on welfare.

> It is true [he replied] that it is a great mitzvah to provide a fellow Jew with a livelihood and one is obligated to do so. This obligation, however, is valid only when the loss involved is marginal. The [legal scholar] Chafets Chayim ruled that in those cases where the employer stood to lose large sums as a result of preferred hiring of Jews, he was free to hire non-Jews and save himself this loss. Since the wage difference between Jewish and Arab workers is very great, the fruit growers are not required by Jewish law or custom to give preference to Jewish workers.[18]

The rabbinic leaders who supported the demand for Jewish labor on halakhic grounds argued that Reb Elchanan was not living in Erets Israel and therefore not really cognizant of the national significance of the new Jewish settlement and its attendant economic difficulties, which should be lessened by this form of charity.

In any case, the implications of such a preference would seem to be that Jewish tradition would approve of a full employment policy aimed at breaking the poverty cycle as part of its welfare system. In addition to being the type praised by Maimonides as the highest form of charity, such employment fulfills another dictum of Jewish charity—viz., the minimizing of the shame attached to receiving support from others.

When ranking the status of different types of charity, Maimonides places the secret gift (*matan b'seter*) just below the assistance described above. Such gifts—"where the giver does not know to whom he gives and the recipient does not know from whom he receives"—save the poor from humiliation and prevent the giver from feeling pride about his charitable actions regarding specific individuals or power over them. The pride has no justification, since, after all, the giving of charity is one of the purposes for which God has given him his wealth in the first place; and the power is transitory, since "the world is like a revolving wheel: One who is rich today may be poor tomorrow."[19]

Taxation in the case of the State of Israel—where a major part of the public budget is earmarked for education and assistance to the poor, the unemployed, the sick, and the aged—would seem to fall in the category of *matan b'seter*. It could be argued that one could deduct from one's charitable obligations that proportion of one's taxes corresponding to the proportion of the Israeli budget devoted to welfare. Such an arrangement, however, would reduce the awareness of other people's suffering, the cultivation of which is a prime purpose of Jewish charity.

It is told of a *chasid* that he once asked his rebbe why the Almighty had to create rich and poor people and then command the rich to share their wealth with the poor. "Surely," he asked, "he could have distributed the wealth so that neither one would have to give, nor would the other have to receive?" In that case, replied the rebbe "how would the Jew learn to care for his fellow and share in his sorrows?" But a welfare bureaucracy has, in fact, developed in Israel, and the impersonal individual contributions to communal funds so prevalent today in the countries of the Jewish Diaspora do not answer this need.

Some years ago, the mayor of Jerusalem proposed a law outlawing begging in the streets of Jerusalem, as this was a bother and a nuisance to passers-by. The city council dismissed it, among other reasons, on account of the traditional Jewish attitude to begging. I never really understood why begging should be allowed until my first visit to New York in the early 1960s. My work there was primarily concentrated in the financial district, and for some time there was something there that bothered me without my knowing exactly what it was. Finally, it dawned on me: There were no beggars, no blind men, and no poor old men or women on Wall Street sidewalks or corners. It is true that the argument for the Jerusalem proposal was based on the assumption that society will take care of these people in a more dignified and efficient way. Irrespective of whether in actual fact this is so, there is an additional reason behind such legislation: viz., to prevent the sorrows and misery of the poor and weak from being thrust onto the everyday consciousness of the average person. In the Israeli religious kibbutz movement, for example, we found in the 1950s that even though the kibbutz gave charity as it was supposed to, our children had grown up completely unaware of the reality of poverty and suffering—an ignorance that has far-reaching effects on the moral and ethical development of a person.

Implementing *Tzedakah*

The practice of charity among Jews could never remain a matter of personal behavior, dependent on the subjective decisions of the individual, but had to become an integral part of communal life and public economic behavior. Indeed, Judaism is a communally oriented religion, more interested in creating a holy nation than in developing spiritually mature individuals. And in all aspects of behavior, Judaism has translated its precepts and teachings into concrete and well-defined practical actions that are monitored and guided by the halakhic authorities and the rabbinic courts.

These two factors helped to ensure that in those cases where an individual was inclined to shirk his charitable duties, a *bet din* could be invoked to provide the assistance needed by the poor. And the legal superstructure enabled the needs of recipients to be met in accordance with a public, unbiased allocation of funds rather than according to the subjective, personal whims of the individual.

So we find a number of halakhic rulings, communal enactments, and responsa elaborating on the public administration of charitable funds.

The communal authority for levying taxes to finance meeting the needs of the poor is clearly set out in the following ruling of the *Shulchan Arukh*:

> Every man is obligated to give charity, even the poor who themselves are recipients thereof. One who gives less than his due, the *bet din* forces him and applies corporal punishment until he pays what he has been assessed. They have the right to seize his assets for the amount of his debt to the charitable funds.[20]

It is interesting to note that the Maharsha, one of the classical commentators to the *Shulchan Arukh*, says that it is doubtful that one may take something away from a poor man who has seized it from a person who has refused to pay his assessment to the communal funds.[21]

The Talmud considered the existence of a communal charitable fund fundamental to the very existence of Jewish life. "A Torah scholar [the role model for all Jews] may not live in a town that does not possess these ten things . . . and a fund for charity."[22]

Both Maimonides and the *Shulchan Arukh* translated this dictum into part of the legal communal structure. Thus Maimonides:

> Every city which has Jews is obligated to appoint officials who are well known and trustworthy, who will go among the people during the weekdays and collect from each one what is appropriate and what has been assessed of him [by the officials of the community]. Then they will distribute a weekly ration of food.
>
> We have never seen or heard of a Jewish community which does not have such a *kupah* [fund] for charity. The *tamchuy*, however [an institution for distributing food], exists in some communities but doesn't exist in others. In the *tamchuy*, the officials collect each day from every courtyard [around which houses were built], bread and food and fruit or money [for that purpose]. They then distribute to the poor their daily needs.[23]

Maimonides also places the responsibility for contributing to the charitable funds on all the members of the community, even transients.

> One who lives in the country for three days may be forced to contribute to the *kupah,* and if for three months, also to the *tam-*

chuy. [This difference stems from the fact that only the *kupah* was a universal Jewish practice.] After six months he becomes liable to contribute, according to the tax rates imposed on the people of the city [community], to the charitable funds which provide clothing for the poor, and after nine months for the burial funds which enable the mitzvah of burying the poor dead [properly].[24]

These and other charitable funds provided basic necessities for the poor. Apart from food, Maimonides includes the obligation to provide "clothing if he is naked, household utensils if they are lacking, and a wife if he is unmarried; a husband for a woman who is unmarried."[25] The aim was to provide that which is lacking, so that such charity included a horse to ride on and a servant to precede him, in the case of a rich man who has become poor; a psychological salve for the real anguish such people suffer from. The Rama, in his gloss on the *Shulchan Arukh*, limits the fulfillment of these obligations to the communal funds; the individual has only the duty of bringing the problem to the attention of the communal authorities and to give what he is capable of. Naturally, the scope of the charitable gifts given to the poor depended on the financial ability of the community and the number of poor within that community. Even so, it was universally recognized that basic food, shelter, and clothing were to be provided.

All individuals, communities, and states have limited resources. Therefore, the halakhic sources had to provide guidelines as to what constituted basic necessities and who was eligible for such charity. Furthermore, since all welfare systems are open to exploitation, justice demanded that the individual mitzvah of charity and the communal obligation to assist the poor had to be protected from abuse. It is owing to these guidelines and to the protection mechanisms that were put in place that living off charity and welfare never became a legitimate and acceptable way of living in Judaism, as has happened in many modern welfare systems—and which tends to expand such systems beyond the ability or willingness of the society to finance them.

Maimonides limited recourse to the communal funds to those who did not have fourteen meals for the week, and the *tamchuy* gifts of daily food to those who didn't have two meals for that day. In the same way, he ruled, based on the Mishnah, that only a person who has net equity (excluding loans) of less than two hundred zuz could avail himself of the agricultural gifts discussed in the previous section.[26] It is of interest to note that Maimonides differentiates between idle and active capital in defining the status of the welfare recipient. Fifty zuz actively employed in a business disqualified a person in the same way as two hundred zuz of idle capital did. This distinction assumed that the income earned on the active capital would be sufficient to provide the poor with basic necessities.

The halakhic definitions of poverty allowed for temporary distress, or for difficulties caused by serious problems of liquidity. For instance, a person who had assets over the poverty line but who would have suffered great loss if they were sold at a bad time in the market (such as during the rainy period, when sales of real estate and farm land are sluggish) was entitled to receive *ma'aser ani* (the poor tithe) up to half of the value of his assets in order to assist him until a better season arrived. Rabbi Yitschak Alfasi (The Rif), writing in eleventh-century North Africa, held that "there are commentators who ruled that such a person was entitled to receive unlimited *ma'aser ani* until such time as it's possible to sell some or all of his assets at half their real value."[27] Similarly, permission was given to a traveling trader who had spent all his money, to avail himself of all the gifts to the poor and the communal funds. He is not required to reimburse these funds when he arrives back home, since at the time he was really poor, even if only temporarily.

The limits described by Maimonides show that Judaism approves of means tests to evaluate the validity of recourse to communal funds or other charitable institutions. This is not out of lack of sympathy for the poor, but simply an application of principles of equitable behavior. The individual and the community have the obligation to provide basic necessities, and the recipient, like any creditor, has to prove that he is entitled to them. To rule otherwise would be unjust even if it would save the poor person from the shame of convincing others that he really needs the help. Such means tests, however, are kept within certain bounds, as may be seen from the following ruling of Maimonides:

> If a poor man who is unknown to the officials [so that they do not know what his financial position is] comes and says, "I am hungry," then they are not allowed to examine him to see whether he is dishonest. Rather, they have to feed him immediately. If, however, he asks for clothing, saying, "I am naked," then it is possible to examine whether he is really entitled to charity.[28]

We do not find in the Jewish charitable system anything approaching the incomes policy of the modern welfare state. None of the halakhic authorities seem to consider *tzedakah* as an egalitarian device intended to transfer funds from the rich to the poor. Rather, they would agree with Maimonides that "it is not the obligation of the householder to enrich the poor, only to support them."[29] Furthermore, the rabbis of the Talmud had laid down a principle that was repeated throughout the centuries in various forms: "Let a man flay a carcass in the market [considered one of the most menial and degrading jobs] rather than be dependent on others."[30]

The Jewish view of charity as an obligation of the community through its fiscal policy, rather than a matter of simple individual acts of piety, is reflected in the ruling of the *Shulchan Arukh* regarding "the case of a town or community where the poor were many [so that the demand for the charitable funds was great] and the wealthy argued, 'Let them go and collect alms from the householders.' To this, the middle classes rejoined that it was not right to let them depend on alms, but rather they should enjoy the communal funds raised on the basis of taxes on wealth. The law is with the middle class demand for a tax on wealth to finance these needs."[31]

Just as important as the amount of charity distributed and the communal responsibility for the financing thereof is the *way* in which the poor are helped, both by individuals and by the community officials. Judaism places great stress on the dignity and honor of the recipient (thus, when Rabbi Yannai saw someone give charity to a poor and shy man in public, he said to him, "It were better not to have given him at all than to have given and embarrassed him"[32] —but just as much education is focused on the attitude of the givers of charity.

A *chasid* once boasted to his rebbe that even though he was wealthy he only ate the simplest of foods, and only in minimal quantities. This was meant to demonstrate his piety and modesty. The rebbe, however, rebuked him, saying, "It is not right that a wealthy man like yourself should eat so sparingly. If you eat only herring and dry crusts, then you imagine that the poor can get by with even less. I want you to eat only of the best—ducks, fish, cake and wine. Then, perhaps, you will feed the poor reasonably well."

Even when one is unable to give the poor what they need owing to one's own financial situation, the *Shulchan Arukh* ruled that "one should not grow angry with them but try and comfort them with words."[33]

Rabbi Abaye taught that there was a son who fed his father pheasants and brought death to himself in the process. A second son forced his father to grind flour in the mill and thereby assured himself a place in the world to come.[34] Rashi, commenting on this Talmudic passage, explains that the former begrudged his father the fine food he was giving him, while the second son comforted his father with kindness.

Care for the Aged, the Orphans, and the Widows

There does not seem to be any indication in Jewish sources of the existence of special institutions for looking after orphans or the aged. This does not flow from a negligence with regard to such people, or callousness regarding their situation; rather, the religious teachings and the practical mitzvot associated with them created a framework that provided for assisting them without the need for special institutions. It must be noted that in Judaism, remarriage after divorce or after the death of a spouse is considered a normal and positive action. While it is true that the rabbis understood that "the wife of one's youth" was someone special, there is no romantic concept in Judaism of remaining true to a dead spouse. The religious, social, and emotional sanction given to such second (or third) marriages made a major contribution to the proper care of orphans and widows in a normal and natural fashion, without recourse to artificial institutions.

It was always considered a great positive mitzvah to adopt or raise orphans. In those cases where there were no close relations, the community or individuals established special funds for their care or provided foster parents. The community of Padua adopted both these methods, as may be seen from the following entry in their minute book:

> Since the girl Sarale, daughter of Ya'akov Yitschak, has been orphaned both of mother and father, people of righteousness and mercy have approached R. Moshe, who has agreed to take her into his house. He will guarantee her board and lodging for four years, during which time he will also clothe her. After these four

years the community undertakes to become responsible for the child's welfare.

Not only poor orphans were the concern of the community; assistance also had to be given to the orphans of wealthy parents who were unable to fend for themselves. So the same communal records relate:

> The orphans of R. Ya'akov Yitschak Katz are now left without any guardians, since one of those appointed by the community has died in the plague and the other has left the city, and we do not have an account of the financial status of the estate. It has therefore been decided to appoint three new guardians who shall be responsible for realizing the assets of the orphans and protecting them. They are empowered to place these funds in the hands of a trustee, who will invest them so that they will grow. The appointees cannot refuse to act as guardians and are obligated to complete their task before *Shavuot,* so that they can render an account to the heads of the community and its accountant.

A further method of assisting orphans was to allow them special tax privileges, as explained in chapter 8 on taxation. This applied not only to poor orphans but also to wealthy ones, who were to be helped because of their special psychological and emotional problems.

And of special interest is the concept of *hakhnasat kalah*—the dowering of the bride in order to save an orphan or poor girl from the shame of coming empty-handed to her husband. For example, the will of Zechariah of Porto in the seventeenth century provided 18,000 scudi for dowering brides yet left only 2000 scudi for support of Jews in the Land of Israel and 4000 scudi for *pidyon sh'vuyim*—redemption of captives.[35] *Hakhnasat kalah* is considered by the Mishnah to be one of those acts of righteousness of unlimited bounds in contrast to limited concepts such as tithes.

Hospitality for the Traveler *(Hakhnasat Orchim)*

Our purpose in this chapter is to describe the provisions made for assistance to the needy or weak, so *hakhnasat orchim* has been used in its narrow sense. Actually this concept refers to a wide range of hospitable actions toward guests not necessarily needy and therefore beyond the scope of this discussion.

In the natural course of economic activity, it is necessary for people to move from one part of the world to another. There is also a specifically Jewish element to this phenomenon, in that, as often as not, Jews found it necessary to move, either because of edicts of expulsion or simply as a result of great economic or political oppression. So while refugees were a common feature of Jewish life, so, too, were transients. Some of them were poor people trying to collect funds from larger and wealthier communities; some were wealthy men engaged in international trade; and some were businessmen temporarily stranded and therefore needy.

The concept of mutual responsibility, so ingrained in Judaism, meant that the community was required to help such travelers. Such help is reflected even in religious ritual. For example, the custom of reciting *kiddush* in the synagogue on Friday night in addition to at home owes its source to the presence of travelers. Those in transit did not have a home, and therefore the question of their fulfilling the mitzvah of hearing *kiddush* on Friday night arose; so public recitation in the synagogue was introduced. (On Passover night, however, when it was assumed that even travelers would be invited to somebody's home for a seder, the festival *kiddush* was not recited in the synagogue.)

There was a long tradition of providing inns or other forms of lodging for travelers at the expense of the community. Sometimes there was a suitable building adjacent to the synagogue; sometimes the community financed private lodgings. Such was the case in Padua, where the communal records in 1578 report that "three of the *parnasim* are hereby authorized to find an owner of a restaurant or hotel who will provide lodging and food for the poor who pass through our city."

The rich traveler away from home, in strange surroundings, is often in need perhaps not of lodging, but of advice, friendship, and services; Agus, in his study of medieval Franco-Germany, points out that the commercial advice granted to the Jew by his co-religionists, along with lodging (not available even for money from a hostile Gentile environment), were primary factors in enabling Jewish participation in the expanding international trade of the period.[36] This tradition continues even to our own times. In the nineteenth and twentieth centuries, for example, emigrants moving from Eastern Europe to the New World, or to Southern Africa and Australia, were assisted by similar hospitality on the part of the Jews of Germany and England. Not all of these emigrants were penniless, so that there were elements of both hospitality and charity involved.

Important as the religious and social aspects of Jewish hospitality are, we are concerned primarily with the provisions for communal assistance to poor travelers and itinerant beggars. The general tenor of the halakhic authorities seems to be that while one is required to assist such people (primarily for moral and religious reasons affecting both giver and recipient alike), such assistance is usually limited in scope to the provision of basic needs. This was both to prevent exploitation by professional beggars and a reflection of the dictum that "the poor of one's own city have preference."[37]

The general principle for such assistance was laid down in Mishnaic times in the Land of Israel and entrenched in the rabbinic codes of later centuries.

> A poor man, passing from place to place, is entitled to receive not less than a loaf of bread [for two meals]. . . . Should he spend the night he is to receive sustenance for the night as well as bed, pillow, and blanket. If he also spends the Shabbat he is to be provided with enough for the three shabbat meals [incumbent on all Jews].[38]

The various techniques of implementing these provisions during the centuries are of limited importance; what is important is that such provisions did exist. In the Cairo geniza, for example, we find letters referring to needy travelers lodging in inns belonging to the community; one such medieval Jew writes that after suffering through a storm and throwing part of his cargo overboard, finally "through God's grace we arrived at Caesarea; however, both my clothes and goods were completely soaked. I did not find a place to spread out my things to dry. So I took domicile in the synagogue, where I stayed for five days."[39]

Some fifteen hundred years after the Mishnaic ruling, the Jews of Sugenheim Town in Franco-Germany (comprising twelve householders) included the following in their constitution:

> Since the wayfarers cannot [by Jewish law] travel on the festivals, they are to be given additional meal tickets [a system adopted early in the fourteenth century and common throughout Central Europe] for those days. Each family is to provide eight meal tickets and two additional ones for every hundred florins of capital owned by the family [a traditional mix of taxation according to capita (as a fulfillment of a mitzvah) and according to wealth]. If any of the travelers are ill and cannot be sent on, they are to be

lodged with the cantor. Should such a person die and there are no means to provide for his burial, the expense is to be borne by the communal treasury.[40]

Obviously the economic resources of a community dictated its ability to provide such services, and abuses of the system had to bring in their wake limitations. Thus, the Lithuanian Council, in 1623, limited the sojourn of beggars to twenty-four hours; in 1672, the community of Poznan, weighed down by debt, outlawed all begging by outsiders.

These limitations, however, are not surprising. What is surprising is the general pattern of communal responsibility for strangers, so consistently applied despite the nonexistence of an external political apparatus enforcing it.

Redemption of Captives *(Pidyon Sh'vuyim)*

An additional need of the Jewish welfare system throughout history—even in our own day—has been the redemption of captives. Sometimes it has been a question of individual slavery; sometimes a whole community has been held to ransom; sometimes it was a question of rescuing refugees. It is really immaterial whether the "captivity" is open and obvious or concealed behind a screen of national rights or internal policies. In our own day, Nazi Germany released Jews in return for payment, while the rehabilitation of the remnants of European Jewry paralleled the rescue of refugees and slaves in earlier periods. Arab countries and the Soviet Union still hold their Jewish communities hostage, to be released only in response to the pressure of world opinion or suitable political actions. In any case, the efforts and funds expended on the redemption of modern-day "captives" are simply a continuation of the centuries-old pattern of Jewish charity.

Funds for *pidyon sh'vuyim* take precedence over all other kinds of charity, since the captive suffers all the hardships of the poor and in addition faces the danger of death. The *Shulchan Arukh*, like the other codes, rules that "*Pidyon sh'vuyim* has precedence over support for the poor, and there is no greater mitzvah than this. Therefore, a community which has collected funds for other charitable purposes may divert them to *pidyon sh'vuyim*. [Usually, communal funds or individual donations earmarked for a specific purpose cannot be used at all for another one, or may be diverted only if permission is obtained.] Even funds raised for the building of a synagogue or materials bought for that purpose may be used for redeeming captives."[41]

Halakhic sources did not hesitate to extend the help of *pidyon sh'vuyim* even to people imprisoned because of their own behavior, such as debtors. They were considered to be in grave danger, over and above the matter of their debt and, therefore, merited the assistance of the community. Always aware of the dangers of exploitation of the wide-ranging Jewish welfare system, the same sources provided limits in this respect, as they did with respect to other aspects of charity. "One who sold himself to non-Jews, or was imprisoned by them as a result of his indebtedness or of loans extended to them—It is incumbent [on the community] to redeem them the first and second time [it happens]. However, beyond that it is not required to redeem them. [This would prevent a person from making a habit of selling himself or from making high-risk loans, since he could not indefinitely depend on the community's assistance.] [But] should there be a danger to his life, we are commanded to redeem him time after time."[42] Thus, the sanctity of life is of such overriding importance in Judaism that the obligation of *pidyon sh'vuyim* remains even though it may be exploited.

In the same chapter, Maimonides codified a ruling based on the Mishnaic discussion in *Gittin* limiting the price to be paid for Jewish captives to the market price for general captives. One is not allowed to pay excessive prices to redeem Jewish captives, since this will, it is feared, lead to the widespread and increased capture of Jews for sale in view of the high ransoms paid for them. The discussion in *Gittin* provides two possible motives behind the placing of such limits: One is that the ability of the community to fund such ransoms is limited, and the second is that mentioned above.[43] Malmonides' ruling in the spirit of the second motive has implications for individual actions in respect of redemption of captives. If the reason for limiting ransom payments is the limited communal funds, then an individual should be allowed to pay whatever price he is asked, as is the ruling in the *Shulchan Arukh*, who views this as a personal danger. If, however, we are concerned about the effects on the community as a whole, then we would have to limit even the ransom paid by individuals. Maimonides ruled that a man whose wife has been captured may not agree to an excessive ransom even if only he is bearing the cost. This shows that limits on ransom payments flow not only from a concern over limited funds but rather from fear of the increased danger to all Jews which would result from such ransoms, even if they are paid by individuals.[44]

A classic example of this concern is found in the story of the Maharam of Rothenburg. This leading scholar of thirteenth-century Germany was imprisoned in Worms by the local duke. Although the Jewish world was prepared to ransom him, the Maharam ruled that this was forbidden; acquiescing in such ransoms would lead to the wholesale arrest of Jewish leaders as a means of providing wealth for their Gentile overlords. He languished in prison and subsequently died there. After he was dead, his body was ransomed by Alexander Wimpfen, who requested that his own body should be buried alongside that of the Maharam. Today, one can still see the two tombstones side by side in the ancient Jewish cemetery of Worms.

In our own day, the State of Israel has refused to negotiate with terrorists and hijackers for the same reasons expressed by the halakhic authorities: viz., paying ransoms encourages more acts of terror.

Priorities among Captives

Like all societies, Jewish communities, no matter how wealthy, have limits on their budgets, and therefore some basis for rationing scarce funds has to be arrived at. The rationing is always done in accordance with the value structure of a particular society, so that the ranking of claims with respect to *pidyon sh'vuyim* is a reflection of Jewish values regarding religious observance, sexual morality, the value of human life, Torah knowledge, and other central concerns. The implications of this value structure apply to all forms of welfare within Jewish society, so they are discussed here in detail as they appear in the *Shulchan Arukh*.[45]

"If a person is taken captive and has assets, then they [the *bet din* and the community] sell his assets to redeem him even if this is against his will." For, according to Jewish law, one may not commit suicide (or even place oneself in danger*).

"If one is taken in captivity together with his father or his

---

* This is in accordance with the Biblical precept, "Guard your lives exceeding carefully" [Deut. 4:15]. This precept is understood by the rabbis to apply to a wide variety of dangerous habits and behaviors involving eating, drinking, occupation, etc. Some authorities, such as Rabbi Waldenberg, a present-day halakhic source of responsa on medical questions, see in it an injunction against smoking, in view of its proven relationship to cancer. We have dealt with other aspects of this aversion to risk in chapter 6 on wages.

teacher [who have precedence over others, the former because of the injunction to honor one's parents and the latter in accordance with the importance of Torah study], he has the obligation to redeem himself first." One's life takes precedence over that of others, since we are not able to judge the value of different people. In the Talmud, this principle is expressed in the discussion concerning two who are lost in a desert, one of whom has a pitcher of water sufficient to keep only one of them alive. Is he obligated to give it to the other one, as dictated by mercy or by the objection to spilling blood? Rabbi Akiva presented an opinion that became codified into Jewish law: One doesn't have to sacrifice his life for another, since the value of different lives is unknown to us.[46] (Nor is one allowed to take one life to save or cure another. Maimonides discusses a case wherein "Gentiles say to the people of a town, 'surrender one of your numbers, so that we may kill him; otherwise we will kill all of you.' [This is another form of the problem of redemption of captives.] They may not do so, but, rather, all have to allow themselves to be killed."[47]

"Women have precedence over men in the redemption of captives." Maimonides, quoting the Mishnah in *Horayot*, presents this as the order in clothing and feeding the poor as well. In marriage, too, the orphaned girl has precedence over the orphaned boy. The Talmudic sages saw the greater natural shyness and modesty of women as the reason for this.[48] However, men have greater obligations in keeping mitzvot than women, who have been released from certain of the positive commandments requiring fixed times for their fulfillment. Since the purpose of man is to fulfill as many mitzvot as possible, men would take precedence over women in those cases where there exists a distinct danger to life. Furthermore, should the captivity involve sexual danger men have preference, since male homosexuality is regarded as an abomination rather than simply an illegal sex relationship. But "one's mother has precedence over one's teacher and one's father, since her shame [at her enslavement] is greater."

Maimonides provides the following ranking where there are insufficient funds to support all the poor or redeem all the captives: priests; Levites; Israelites [i.e., everyone else]; one born of a marriage prohibited to a priest (as with a divorced woman or a convert); one whose mother is known but the father is not, one who parentage is entirely unknown, one born of an incestuous or adulterous relationship (*mamzer*). "This is only so," Maimonides continues, "where they are all equal in Torah knowledge. However, where the High Priest is an ignoramous and the *mamzer* a scholar, the *mamzer* has precedence. Whosoever is greatest in Torah learning has precedence."[49] Indeed, such is the pre-eminence of Torah scholars in Judaism that, where one's father and one's teacher are in need of ransoming, one's teacher takes precedence.

EDUCATION

Elementary Torah Education

"And you shall teach [these words of Torah] diligently unto your children, and shall talk of them when you sit in your house and when you walk by the way, and when you lie down and when you rise up" [Deut. 6:7]. This Biblical commandment to commit oneself to Torah study is a basic and far-reaching one, codified into law and translated into individual and communal action.

The codifiers of Jewish law all considered Torah study to be an obligation unlimited in time, so that all other activities became either limited in its light or were even frowned upon. Furthermore, the obligation to study Torah was considered not to be limited by one's age, knowledge, or economic or social condition. In chapter 2 of this book, we have already discussed how economic activity was regarded—and to some extent confined—vis-à-vis this restriction; here we consider the financing of the educational structure as a matter of public policy.

Some two thousand years ago, Rabbi Yehoshua ben Gamlah, a high priest during the days of the Second Temple in Jerusalem, ruled that "the community is obligated to provide elementary school teachers in every state and every province and city."[50] This codifying of ancient tradition placed this obligation squarely on the shoulders of the community, who were seen as being surrogates for parents. After all, the Jew had been commanded, as we have seen, to "teach [Torah] to your children," and according to the oral tradition "children" refers to all pupils, extending beyond one's immediate family.[51]

The power of the *Herem* (excommunication) was to be used, according to Maimonides, against communities refusing or neglecting to provide teachers and facilities for Torah education. Although the cost of such education was theoretically to be borne by the parents, financing was usually either partially or completely via taxation (wealthier parents often maintaining tutors at their own expense over and above their tax payments). It is important to note that this obligation respecting communal or public financing for Torah education is not left to the discretion of the community. While a community has, in general, the right to levy taxes for all purposes deemed fit according to its priorities, this educational levy cannot be abrogated even by majority vote. Support for Torah study flows from a higher dictate than that of majority rule—usually a guiding factor in Jewish tax law.

It is this common acceptance of public sector financing for education that has enabled the Jew to translate into reality the rabbinic legislation regarding Torah study. Obviously, the financial resources available depended on the economic status of the community. Yet, notwithstanding this budgetary limitation, Torah education and scholarship have been the hallmark of Jewish communities in all centuries and in all the countries of the Diaspora.

Adult Torah Education

Torah education was not limited to children but had to be extended to adults, in view of the obligation "you shall devote yourself to its [Torah] study" (Jos. 1:8). Fulfillment of this obligation obviously required teachers and rabbis—which brought in its wake financial burdens on the public purse.

In the days of the independent Jewish states, the Levites and the priests fulfilled this teaching function, and the community provided the funds in the form of *t'rumah, ma'aser,* and other gifts. So, too, in all later generations, the participation of the community in the support of these scholars (and the upkeep of the necessary physical facilities) remained an obvious duty.

A conspicuous expression of how such continuing adult education was a mass phenomenon, rather than one of elitist scholars in isolated yeshivot or academies, was the *yarchei kalah* of Babylonian Jewish society. Twice a year, in the months of Elul and Adar—the former preceding Rosh Hashanah; the latter, Passover—large numbers of Jews, representing a social and economic cross-section of their communities, flocked to the academies of Sura and Pumpadeetha. In the days of Rav, in the third century—when we have the first records of this institution—twelve thousand students came day in and day out to study. The students were maintained free of charge. To this day, blessings are still invoked—in the *Y'kum Purkan* prayer, composed in Babylon and recited each Shabbat—on the heads of the *Khallah* or Torah assemblies. Evidence of continuity of the same value structure lies in the revival of the institution of *yarchei kalah* in the independent State of Israel.

The existence of special *havurot* (fraternal groups) devoted, among other things, to adult education is an interesting phenomenon observable in almost all Jewish communities throughout the centuries. The fact that we have, to date, written evidence of the existence of such *havurot* only from the fourteenth century onwards is no reason for supposing that they did not exist prior to that period, since there is no historical or cultural watershed that would explain the sudden emergence, as it were, of such an institution. Be that as it may, *havurot* are to be found in a wide variety of Jewish societies, ranging from Western Europe to Eastern Europe and the Sephardic world, from late medieval times down to the present day. Many of these *havurot* left behind minute books, from which we can easily determine the extent of their activity.

The earliest record of such a society is that of the *kenesiah l'Shem shamayim* ("assembly for the sake of heaven") of Venice, at the beginning of the seventeenth century. What is remarkable is the authority to enforce the study obligation in a community that lacked the physical power usually associated with public sector activity—further testimony to the deep commitment to Torah study that has consistently characterized Jewish life.

> The *parnasim* shall have the power to order each member to come each day to study in the place designated for that purpose. . . . A member who does not come before the close of the session shall be fined two soldi. . . . In the month of Adar it shall be the duty of the *parnasim* to collect from each member two lira for the purpose of buying a gift for the rabbi as a token of love and esteem. Should there not be sufficient funds, they can assess the membership without further authorization, for an additional ducat.[52]

Financing Torah Education

The prime cost in education was teachers' salaries. In theory, the Torah was supposed to be taught free of charge; but an exception was made in the case of teaching children. This was obviously a full-time job, requiring suitable compensation. The exception was later extended by some authorities to include adult Torah education as well.

Many communities understood that there were other costs involved. So we find in the 1585 communal minute books of the Jews of Padua:

> The *parnasim* of this community have decided to allocate to the teacher of the children three great baskets of coals for heating in order to make the schoolchildren more comfortable. The money for these coals shall be raised in the following way: six liters from the "community pocket [fund]" of the Ashkenazi community, two liters from the "community pocket" of the Sephardi community.

A previous enactment of the same community had already provided for the salary of the teacher. It should be noted that the number of pupils was small, since the Jewish population itself wasn't large.

> Seeing as how the community has given the authority to three people to find a teacher who will busy himself with the holy work of the young boys of our holy congregation in Padua, they have found a suitable teacher, Rav Elchanan ben Rav Avraham, and therefore the committee has decided to apportion for the above-named teacher of the five pupils, ten liters a month. The community will have to raise this money in the following ways: The *parnasim* will have to go on Tuesday and Wednesday to raise funds from the Ashkenazi and the other synagogues in Padua. An additional two liters are levied on the Ashkenazi congregation, to be provided from its general funds, while one liter is to be provided from the general funds of the other congregation. In the future, all donations on behalf of the school resulting from the sale of "honors" of the Torah [i.e., the honor of being called up to the reading of the Torah in the synagogue] will be devoted to this purpose. Any shortfall in these sums will be made up from the general sale of honors in the synagogue.

In all other communities, similar legislation existed. Such communal financing was seen as an additional service provided, over and above the obligation of the parents.

It should be pointed out that in addition to the obligations arising out of legal codes or communal enactments, Jewish law accorded great importance to the role of custom in creating financial obligations in many spheres, including that of education. In those communities where it was customary to give presents to the rabbis and teachers, or to support them in any way, individuals could be forced to participate in such assistance even if it went beyond that required by rabbinic or communal legislation.

The importance accorded the financing of facilities for public Torah education may be seen in this ruling of the *Shulchan Arukh*:

> The charity of supporting poor boys in the study of Torah or of giving to the needy sick is more important than the maintenance of a synagogue. Charity funds given for a synagogue or a cemetery may be diverted for the needs of [an adult] house of learning or a school even against the will of the donor, except in those cases where the needs of the school are being met satisfactorily.[53]

Maimonides had earlier ruled that "it is permitted to sell a synagogue in order to erect a house of study, since one has to ascend in the scale of holiness."[54]

The problems of tenure and of differential pay for effective and ineffective teachers continue to plague most modern educational systems. In most countries, unions have today secured for the teaching profession a great measure of job security, so that it has become extremely difficult to fire teachers, even when they are not very good or when the results they obtain are not satisfactory. It would seem that Jewish law and practice in this respect stand in contradiction to the status accorded educators in most present-day societies.

Joseph Caro, in the *Shulchan Arukh*, authoritatively lays down that if a community finds a more qualified teacher, then it is permitted to remove the present one from his post. (This is one of the exceptions to the rule that one party cannot abrogate an employment contract.) Furthermore, competition between teachers and rabbis was actively encouraged, according to the dictum "The jealousy of scribes [scholars] increases wisdom."[55] Even those authorities who opposed competitive practices in general agreed to a relaxation of such barriers in the case of teachers and rabbis. Obviously, this competition, which applied equally to the publishing of religious literature, stimulated the dissemination of Torah studying. In effect, the reduced "earnings" of the incumbent scholars and authors subsidized, as it were, the spread of Torah learning.

The weekly oral examination, either by parents or by the local rabbi, became widespread in many communities. Such examinations enabled the community to monitor the progress of pupils. It is interesting to note that at least one community linked the wages of teachers to the results of these examinations. A statute by one of the Jewish communities in Moravia provided that payment of salaries was to be made each week after the examination by the rabbis of the community; those teachers whose classes had made no progress were deemed not entitled to any remuneration, on the basis that they had not accomplished their work.

Notwithstanding the encouragement of competition and the demands made on teachers, care was given to preserve the dignity of the teacher.

Joseph Caro laid down a regulation that communities were not allowed to pay teachers' salaries and rabbis out of the general charity funds, because this would make the rabbi or teacher a welfare recipient rather than an important functionary of the community.[56] And given the importance of education, communities endeavored to attract great scholars to settle in their midst, offering not only direct salaries but also other forms of financial assistance. Freedom from certain forms of taxation has already been dealt with in chapter 8. Economic support for rabbis often took the form of preferential treatment, such as buying goods from their stores in preference to others, or allowing them to have a monopoly on the sale of certain articles. In this way, the dignity of the educator was preserved and at the same time, the community was participating in his upkeep.

Aside from the way in which the costs of Torah education were covered by the public sector, notice should be taken of the wide ramifications, both social and cultural, of the Jewish emphasis on Torah education. The prestige of a community was determined, inter alia, by the number and caliber of the scholars it produced and by the quality of its educational facilities for children—so much so that a man was not allowed to dwell in a town or community that did not provide Torah education for its children. A man was expected to make every effort to obtain Torah scholars as sons-in-law, and the wealthy members of the community, even though they exerted tremendous influence as a result of their wealth, nevertheless understood that there was a competing source of power, prestige, and status: the scholars.

Secular Education

Until this point, our discussion has centered around the provision of Torah education. However, the question of the provision of a secular education, and the degree to which the community is obliged to fund such an education, has to be discussed if a complete picture of the public sector role is to emerge. My own research has not shown any definitive or authoritative halakhic ruling in this respect. What follows is an attempt to gain a sense of Jewish attitudes toward communal education of this sort. (It should be noted, however, that such attitudes may be substantially a reflection of attitudes drawn subconsciously from other cultures.) The communal implementation of these attitudes in municipal or national legislation—for example, in Israel—would require an authoritative rabbinic responsum.

The parental obligation to provide an education or training that will enable a child to earn an honest and productive livelihood is clearly stated in the Talmudic dictum "A man is obligated to teach his son a trade. Whoever does not do so teaches his son to become a brigand."[57] This encompasses non-Torah knowledge as a means of earning a livelihood; the problem of secular studies not related to this purpose is beyond the scope of this book (as is the issue of community-subsidized perpetual Torah study, as in the *kolel* system).

Viewed from the aspect of public finance, the question arises whether this parental obligation is to be extended to the communal or public sector at the local or national level, as is the case with Torah education. Is the communal purse automatically obliged, irrespective of the wishes of the citizens, to finance such education? The halakhic sources seem to contain differing opinions.

Although the codes repeat the Talmudic dictum mentioned above regarding a parent's responsibility, they do not consider this a communal responsibility.[58] Furthermore, it would seem that there is a basis for allowing citizens to absolve themselves from any participation in non-Torah education if they wish to do so (a freedom denied in the case of Torah study). According to the Talmudic sages, "Neighbors in an alley cannot prevent one of them from establishing a school for teaching Torah to little children."[59] The sages understood that such a school would cause economic damage to the neighborhood, through a noise factor, and an increase in littering, etc. These factors constitute a cost to the neighbors, yet the rabbis ruled that incurring this cost is part of the obligation of every Jew to provide Torah education for Jewish children, both his own and others. In the *Shulchan Arukh*, a contrary decision was reached regarding the cost of secular education. "Members of a courtyard can prevent each other from establishing a school which teaches secular subjects. [The Rambam, on the Mishnah, specifically mentions arithmetic and geometry.] They can claim that the noise, etc., of the children is a burden to them [and they are not obligated to suffer it]."[60] From this it would appear that there is no moral or religious obligation devolving on members of the Jewish community to provide for the secular education of children. Obviously, as explained in chapter 8, a community is free to decide to provide such education and to force its members to pay for it, even if this means a majority imposing its will on a minority. Such an option, however, derives from the rights of the community, which is something completely different from a Torah obligation, where the decision is taken out of the hands of the communal policy makers.

At the same time, the discussion of the sages on the *parah adumah*, the red heifer, seems to lead to a different conclusion. There is a ruling in the Torah (Deut. 21:1–8) that if a corpse was found in a field, the leaders of the nearest community as well as national representatives were obligated to bring a heifer and to make a confession that they were in no way involved in the shedding of this blood. The rabbis ask in astonishment, "Can we imagine that the leadership of the Jewish community was responsible for the shedding of this blood?" So the discussion perforce centers around the community's responsibility for the social infrastructure that made possible such a terrible crime as murder. Communal leadership is responsible because it did not, in the words of the Talmud, provide for the stranger, thus forcing him to have to go out and attempt to steal in order to survive, such attempted theft leading either to his own death or to the death of the potential victim. However, it is possible that the murderer was a member of the community. Since he not given a proper education and preparation for a productive life he turned to brigandage, and it was this brigandage that resulted in the murder of the corpse before them—and for this the leaders *were* responsible.[61]

Such a notion, along with the attitude toward full employment discussed in a previous section of this chapter, would seem to indicate the necessity of public financing for secular and vocational training. The absence of a definite halakhic ruling, however, leaves the issue of public financing, in a Jewish state, for universities and technical schools an area still be be resolved.

SUMMARY

Assistance to the weaker members of society is an obligation placed on the individual and on the community, so that its financing falls both on the public purse, through taxation, and on voluntary donations. Such assistance encompasses the provision of communal services to enhance both the physical and spiritual well-being of the recipients.

At the same time, there does not seem to be in Judaism automatic support for the notion of the egalitarian distribution of wealth which is the basis of many present-day welfare systems. Rather, the aim of welfare, in Jewish terms, is to provide a means of breaking the poverty cycle or of preventing a descent into poverty. In other cases, Jewish welfare is meant only to provide basic necessities or to achieve economic justice, not economic equality. This leads to restrictions on the degree of public support for welfare.

Although acts of welfare are considered to be characteristic of the Jewish people, poverty carries with it no spiritual connotations, nor is it regarded as a way of achieving sanctity. On the contrary, there is a strong tradition militating against being dependent on others or on the communal purse—and an element of shame is seen as properly attaching to such dependence. Living on welfare, in the modern sense of transfer payments from the national treasury, is not respectable in Judaism.

CHAPTER 10

Environmental Issues and the Public Good

INTRODUCTION

The welfare of all the citizens of a community, irrespective of their economic status, is affected by factors over and above those dealt with in the previous chapter. Such factors as their health, their physical surroundings, and their security are all as much a part of the communal welfare as is the care of the poor and the unfortunate, or the Torah education of children and adults. Just as Judaism sees charity and education as legitimate objects of communal or public financing, so, too, does it view these factors. In this chapter, we will discuss the environmental welfare, so to speak, of the Jewish community under three main headings: the damage inflicted by one individual on another; public health; and town planning.

From an economic viewpoint, these sorts of issues involve a determination of the value of preventing damage or promoting the communal welfare, on the one hand, vis-à-vis the potential benefits to be derived from the undisturbed production of goods and services. So an entrepreneur planning to establish a new plant has to consider the ecological costs borne by the community or by certain individuals (e.g., neighbors of his plant) as part of the overall cost of erecting his plant and producing his goods.[1] Society, for its part, has to consider the potential benefits accruing from such a plant—in the form, say, of new jobs, or the increased availability of goods or services—over and against the damages caused by pollution to the air or water, or disruption to the peace of mind of the community.

Similarly, it may be perfectly obvious from a humane point of view that sick people should be provided with suitable medical attention, and that every effort should be made to prevent illness from affecting the healthy members of the community. At the same time, the question arises as to who is to bear the cost of these health care services. Are they to be placed solely on the individuals concerned, as a private matter, or considered as a communal responsibility, to be met from public funds? In other words, it is necessary to compare the material benefits accruing from economic activity with the social cost involved.

There is, however, a further point to be considered, which may be far more important than the cost–benefit analysis we've referred to. There is a moral and ethical dimension involved in preventing damage to other people's persons or property—or, for that matter, even to one's own person or property. Sometimes the conception of such damage in purely economic terms tends to obscure this aspect of these environmental issues—yet it remains an important part of our value system. When one is not allowed to damage one's own property, let alone that of another, or one's own body, let alone that of another, it constitutes a recognition that man's property rights are limited. Such an outlook on life accepts that there are factors in the world over and above man's right to private property and to the creation of material goods, even in a legitimate manner. Thus, it is possible to argue that economic growth not only is limited by the cost of preventing pollution or by the depletion of economic resources, but should also be limited by the need for man's spiritual and religious growth. Even if no damage is done to other men, it may be preferable to limit economic growth to the provision of necessities alone, however these may be defined, so that man does not despoil God's world and waste its resources.

A CONCEPTUAL FRAMEWORK

Whether environmental issues are seen in terms of a cost–benefit relationship alone or in the context of spiritual limitations on growth, the treatment of these issues must be undertaken within the conceptual framework existing in Judaism in this regard, which may be summarized as follows:

1. Man dominates the world as an administrator responsible for its well-being. The sages in the Midrash tell us that "When God created Adam he led him past all the trees in the Garden of Eden and told him, 'See how beautiful and excellent are all My works. Beware lest you spoil and ruin My world. For if you spoil it there is nobody to repair after you.' "[2]

2. One is not permitted to do damage to another's property, either directly or indirectly, even if there is a profit to the other involved. The payment of monetary compensation is only a compensation offered after the act; it does not justify it.

3. One is obligated to make efforts to protect other people's property and persons, even where the damage is caused by other parties, by negligence, or by forces of nature.

4. Private property rights exist in Judaism, but they are not sacred. Religious observances, the needs and welfare of other men, and the concept of public welfare all limit individual rights.

5. One is not permitted to do damage to one's own body and is required to take all necessary steps to keep it from harm. In view of the communal nature of Judaism, it is clear that such responsibility extends to the health of other members of the community as well.

6. The physical beauty of the world can enhance one's religious thought, and the enjoyment thereof is conducive to man's spiritual development. After all, all the physical aspects of creation attest to the greatness of the Creator.

7. Economic growth is not an end in itself. It helps to provide for man's material needs—which are only one, even if a major one, of his needs. Therefore, we must make a definite distinction between an economic system that provides necessities and one that provides "luxuries." It is true that the dividing line between these is subjective and difficult to define. Nevertheless, the Jewish value structure necessitates such a division. The growth of the economy would then be limited as far as luxuries are concerned. After all, there is no limit to man's material needs, since "he who loves money will never be sated of money" (Eccl. 5:9). Rabbi Eliezer taught, "Envy, lust, and [the desire for] status push man out of the world."[3]

There is a story in the Talmud that Alexander the Great came to a country in Africa and they provided him with a set of scales. In one pan was a skull and in the other heaps of gold, silver, jewels, and precious stones. The pan with the skull outweighed the other one. More treasures were added, but the skull still outweighed them. Then Alexander took some dust from the earth and put it in the sockets of the skull's eyes, finally closing them. Now the treasure outweighed the skull. Only in death are man's material desires satisfied.

The sources at our disposal—the halakhic codes, the responsa literature, and the communal enactments of various Jewish communities—will enable us to see how this conceptual framework was translated into action. This will provide some guidelines as to the relevance for present-day living of Jewish values regarding environmental issues.

In this area of environmental welfare, there is a perpetual struggle between unbridled individual freedom to do with one's body and one's property whatever one would like, and the common good. This being the case, Judaism's guidance would seem to have pertinence not only for Jews but for all human beings.

PROXIMITY PROBLEMS BETWEEN INDIVIDUALS

Perhaps the simplest problem in what we call environmental welfare is a conflict between two individuals or groups of individuals arising from the economic restraints placed upon us by the proximity in which we live. If space, light, air, water, etc.—our environmental resources—were all unlimited, then there would seem to be no possibility of conflict between the activities of one person or group of persons and the property or personal rights of others. There would simply be enough space and everything else to enable everybody to do exactly as they please without any harmful consequences. The problem arises since there is a limitation on all these factors, which means that if one person, say, builds a factory or performs some other economic act, it may affect the welfare or property of other individuals, producing a clash of interest. Our problem may be summed up as follows: Given the scarcity of environmental resources, the utility or benefit that one person derives from some economic act is at the expense of a loss, material or otherwise, on the part of others.

Such a loss may be inflicted by one's property, by oneself, or by employees. Rabbinic terminology classifies all these as damages caused by neighbors. In a Jewish legal context it is quite irrelevant whether such damages are caused by economically motivated firms, by individuals' gratifying some ecological or aesthetic need, as in the case of landscaping and home improvement, or even by simple vandalism. Halakhic sources are clear that one may not cause damage to another's person or property either through one's own person or through one's property or employees.

The *Shulchan Arukh* codifies many laws dealing with the damages of the Talmud.[4] Those tractates are devoted to a detailed discussion of the four major categories under which rabbinic law dealt with this subject. Naturally, anyone personally involved in any capacity in a case of damages should consult a relevant halakhic authority. We cannot digress here for a full legal treatment of the subject; for our purposes, it is sufficient to adduce only a few examples to show how rabbinic literature made men responsible for damages they caused.

To begin with, man is considered liable for any damages caused by him directly, even without intent or unconsciously (as, for instance, in his sleep). Regarding damages caused by property, the Mishnah categorized them into four groups, each one reflecting a distinct characteristic. Thus, the ox represented two categories of damage caused by living creatures, through grazing, or walking. The biblical example of one who digs a pit and thereby causes damage to others represented all forms of inanimate objects; fire typified damages magnified or spread by natural forces.[5]

During the ensuing discussion in the Talmud, the sages held a man responsible for damages caused by him even in areas that are not his private property. For example, they held that one who digs a pit in a public thoroughfare—likened by modern halakhic authorities to an equally inanimate parked vehicle—would be liable for any damage resulting therefrom, even though the road does not belong to him and therefore the damage didn't occur within his jurisdiction.

The same source points out that some types of damage are caused by objects propelled by natural forces, such as wind or water. Obviously such forces are not subject to ownership by the individual, and therefore he should not be held responsible for the loss involved. Nevertheless the Mishnah placed liability on an individual who set an object in motion (sparks from an anvil, chips from the felling of wood) even if the final damage was spread by natural causes. In our own day this would seem to apply to the pollution of the atmosphere or water through industrial wastes.

Disturbing the tranquility, infringing on the airspace, or obstructing the view of a neighbor were also seen as inflicting damage, albeit of a nonphysical nature. We have already mentioned in the previous chapter an example of this in the realm of education. There we showed that neighbours could prevent the establishment of a secular school, since it increased the noise and dirt in their vicinity, thus disturbing their peace and interfering with their normal activities.

The Mishnah sums up very succinctly what was later adduced in all the codes as the basic formula for solving problems arising out of damages. A factor common to all forms of property is that they have a tendency to cause damage, and you, the owner, are expected to prevent such damage. Should damage occur you are liable to payment.

Later in our discussion we will see that the injured party sometimes has the option of accepting the presence of damages or environmental obstacles in return for payment. He is able to sell some of his rights, as it were, to the party causing the damage. The halakhah recognizes the possibility that it may be cheaper for the one causing the damage to pay damages than to involve himself in the cost of removing the obstacle altogether or operating his business in such a way as to reduce noise or pollution or other forms of damage. Nevertheless, the majority opinions in the rabbinic sources see the provision of monetary compensation as secondary, compared with the moral injunction of not causing damage. Thus, Maimonides rules that where an animal in search of pasture enters into other people's fields or vineyards, the owners of these fields must warn its owner three times, irrespective of whether, as yet, any damage has been done. If the animal's owner does not prevent future entry, the owners of these fields have permission to slaughter it according to the laws of ritual slaughter, the carcass belonging to the owner, who has to remove it. This is because a man is not permitted to do damage on the assumption that he will be able to pay for what he has caused, since it is forbidden to cause damage.[6]

The Raivid, in his gloss on the codex, wishes to limit Maimonides' injunction as follows:

> In the discussion in the Talmud [that is the basis for the decision] it refers only to goats who are about to be slaughtered and therefore have been allowed to go without a shepherd. In that case the owners of the fields, or the injured parties, have the right to carry out the law as it is stated by Maimonides. If, however, a person has a whole flock or herd of sheep and cattle it is not permissible to slaughter the whole lot, but the owners are required to pay if they have done any damage, even without any warning.

It would be reasonable to assume that the reason behind the Raivid's opinion is that the damage done to the injured party is relatively small compared with the benefits received from the development of the cattle. This may be seen also from the willingness of the animals' owner to pay for it. We might, out of considerations of efficiency, support such an arrangement; but the *Shulchan Arukh* rules with Maimonides that one is not allowed to cause damage on the assumption that one will escape with a monetary fine. The moral and ethical issues involved in causing such damage take precedence over efficiency.

At the same time, morality demands that the property rights of the injured party and the injunction against causing damage be limited in those cases where the complaint of the injured party borders on selfishness or rests on an unwillingness to help his fellow man. It may well be that the forgoing of a certain right, even where it is acknowledged by all authorities to exist, may cause only very slight inconvenience to the injured party, whereas the gain to the other party is really very great. In such a case, for the injured party to refuse to accept any compensation would be denying assistance to his fellow man. This refusal to do another person a favor is considered by the rabbis to be characteristic of the people of Sodom. One such example is the Talmudic discussion wherein we are told that "a man should not spill his well water as long as there are others who need it."[7] In other words, I am required to conserve my water because there are others who may derive a benefit from it. It is true that legally the well water belongs to me, so that I may do with it as I please. However, by invoking my property right I am preventing somebody from enjoying a benefit without causing myself any loss. Another example of this is the story in Genesis of Rivka, when she drew the water for

Eliezer. The rabbis tell us that she was careful not to waste the water she had drawn from the communal well, even though this involved physical hardship for her, since it involved pouring the water back into the trough. These are examples of the rabbinic dictum of "One has a benefit and the other does not suffer a loss." Great stress is laid in Jewish economic behavior on countering "dog in the manger" attitudes.

This idea is closely allied to the notion of *bal taschit,* according to which a man is not permitted to vandalize or destroy even his own property, let alone that of another, since other people might be able to benefit from it. Even though the owner has an explicit and defensible right in his property, the concept in Judaism of man being a mere guardian of his economic assets makes such destruction immoral. The sages saw such waste as an act of rebellion, a rejection of God's role as the creator and master of the world; hence, "He who tears his clothing, breaks his utensils, or scatters his money in anger should be in your eyes as if he had served idols."[8] The biblical paradigm of *bal taschit* is to be found in the laws against destroying trees bearing edible fruit in time of war (Deut. 20:19). It is interesting to note that the discussion centers around trees that are owned by the enemy; all the dictates of war would seem to overrule such moral considerations. Nevertheless, we are halakhically required to refrain from needlessly destroying fruit-bearing trees, since one is destroying the products and creation of the Lord, who is responsible for giving man his sustenance. The rabbis extended this injunction to include all useful items; in our day, the inefficient use of fuel would be considered a transgression of *bal taschit. Bal taschit,* it should be noted, is also relevant in the case of ownerless property, as may be seen from the story of Hezkeyahu, who, in anticipation of the siege of Jerusalem, closed up the spring of the Gichon, much to the displeasure of the rabbis.[9]

It must be stressed that one person's forgoing of his rights in order to do another person a favor is morally correct only when slight inconvenience or minimal damage, which can be easily rectified, is caused to the property of the injured party. Where such damage is major or irrevocable, the first individual's property rights are paramount.

In the responsa of the Rashba we find the following answer to a question regarding the prevention of smoke causing damage to other neighbors.

> The *chachamim* [sages] of the Talmud said that one has to remove
> a furnace which causes smoke and therefore damage to neigh-
> bors. This, however, refers only to constant or excessive smoke,
> such as that which is produced by industrial furnaces. [This in-
> junction to remove a furnace that causes damage would seem
> highly relevant to the ecological problems caused by "smoke-
> stack" industries such as steel and coal.] It does not apply to the
> smoke created by the normal activity of a household. Were this
> not the case, nobody would be able to build a house and make a
> fire beneath his food.[10]

In other words, there exists a concept of damage caused by the
normal activities of people, without which it would not be possible to continue any kind of human activity. In such a case the
property rights of other individuals will have to be abrogated.

The same is true in a variety of other circumstances. Thus, we
are told in the Mishnah that

> a tree has to be removed from the proximity of a water storage pit
> [since the tree, through its roots, extends into the neighbor's
> field and prevents him from digging wells for his water]. But
> Rabbi Yossi said that even when the pit [is dug] before the tree [is
> planted], it is not necessary to destroy the tree, since this one
> digs within his own property and another plants within his own
> property.[11]

The *Shulchan Arukh* and other authorities ruled according to
Rabbi Yossi.[12] At first sight it would seem that Rabbi Yossi permits
each person to do within his property whatever he wants, without
considering the effects on others. This would absolve one from
many liabilities that the halakhah imposes on him, however, and
therefore cannot be accepted. The commentators and legal authorities explained, though, that Rabbi Yossi accepted that the
matter of the other's welfare exists, but that in this case there is another consideration. The *Tosefta* explains that Rabbi Yossi's argument is based on the concept of the common good and its max-
imalization.[13] The sages who insisted on the destruction of the
tree argued that *yishuv ha'olam*—the development of the world—is
based on the existence of water pits and therefore they have preference. To this Rabbi Yossi countered that "just as in your case
you consider the water pits essential to *yishuv ha'olam,* I regard the
trees as essential to the welfare of the world." In other words, it is
not solely the personal benefit of the tree owner that is important
here, but the contribution of his tree to the general welfare which
overshadows the right of the owner of the water pit.

The same basic problem was addressed to the Rosh, Rabbi Asher ben Yechiel, in early fourteenth-century Spain. His answer understands Rabbi Yossi's opinion from a different perspective than that of the common good. He accepts limitations on the property rights of the injured party in a case where it is possible for the latter to have the injury rectified easily, without incurring any real, substantial damage, and at the same time benefitting the other party. His treatment, however, is closely allied to the general dictum of the Talmud that in cases where one has a benefit and the other doesn't suffer any loss, we can force the latter to do certain acts (i.e., of *chesed*).

> *Question:* Concerning two neighbors dwelling in apartments one above the other, and the gutter [in their time, more correctly, the material that was used to protect the walls against rain and wetness] has been damaged. Now, every time Reuven, the dweller in the upper apartment, washes his hands or uses water in another way, the water drains into the apartment of Shimon, causing him damage. Who should repair the damage?

The Rosh answered as follows:

> *Answer:* This case is similar to the case discussed in the Talmud concerning the owner of the tree whose roots damage the water pit on the adjacent property. In line with the halakhic opinion which accepted Rabbi Yossi's decision that it was not necessary to destroy the tree, we have ruled that the dweller in the lower apartment, Shimon, has to repair the pipe of the wall, since the damage done was not direct, but rather the water would accumulate and would gradually seep into the bottom apartment. Even Rabbi Yossi would have agreed that if the damage was direct, then Shimon would have a claim against Reuven. In our case, the normal, everyday activities of Reuven cannot be removed to another place. It is not possible for him to live without using his water, and after all Shimon can very easily rectify and repair the pipe so that water won't enter his apartment. Regarding the case of the water pit and the tree dealt with by Rabbi Yossi, it would seem that the reason behind his decision is that the water pit can be moved very easily. The same benefit can accrue to the owner of that field irrespective of where he places his pit, and therefore it is not fair to force the owner of the tree to cut down his tree, which represents a permanent loss, simply because the pit owner is not prepared to move his water pit.[14]

A more modern example of this same principle of forcing an injured party to forgo his right to damages—where, in this case, it

is not possible for the party causing the damage to earn his livelihood in any other way—may be seen in a responsum of the Chatam Sofer, writing in nineteenth-century Hungary. The issue is
made clearer when we consider the language of the rabbi in his in-
quiry to the Chatam Sofer:

> A man in our community died and left a house to his three sons.
> Two received the upper portion of the house, and one received
> the lower portion. Now, one of the dwellers in the upper portion
> of the house wishes to sell brandy in bottles in order to earn his
> livelihood. The lower dweller in the house wishes to prevent this
> because of the noise and other problems caused by customers
> who use the common courtyard of the house. The *Shulchan
> Arukh* has ruled that it is possible for them to prevent the estab-
> lishment of such a business, just as in the case of the one who
> wishes to open a store in a common courtyard; the other owners
> of the common property can prevent it. However, I did not de-
> cide in this way, because it seems to me strange that one can pre-
> vent a person earning his livelihood by selling liquor from his
> house. . . . This led me to rule that they cannot prevent him
> from opening such a business. After all, if he is not able to earn
> his livelihood in this way, he will be, God forbid, dependent on
> the public purse. We know that in those cases where the rabbinic
> law is not clear, we follow local custom. In this community it has
> become accepted that the owners do not use their right to pre-
> vent people from earning their livelihood in this way. Since,
> however, there seems to be a clear contradiction between this
> decision and that of the *Shulchan Arukh*, I'm asking for your
> opinion.

The Chatam Sofer, in his answer, agreed to allow the brother
to conduct his business in the house. He relied on the principle
"that those things that are not possible to do in the marketplace
[an area zoned for commercial enterprises and industrial under-
takings] we have to agree to permit, even though it causes damage. Otherwise, we are preventing many people from earning
their livelihood."[15] It seems that this is not a case of the person
who caused the injury merely increasing his profits; else we could
assume that the sages wouldn't allow it. What we are dealing with
here is the complete negation of a source of income, since it would
not have been possible to conduct the business elsewhere. The
ruling of the *Shulchan Arukh* preventing the establishment, in a
noncommercial area, of a shop concerns a different situation, because after all that shop can be moved to a different place. We see
a similar discussion in the Mishnah, where people were not al-

lowed to prevent a craftsman from using a grindstone in his house, or to impede an artisan whose craft necessitates noise, such as a person who works with a hammer.[16] These are all things that cannot be done elsewhere, and therefore were permitted.

We shall return to this discussion in the following section, which deals with the far more complex problems caused by proximity and scarce resources at the communal level, which involve conflicts between the livelihood of individuals and the welfare of the community. These are what we really refer to when we talk about *ecological* problems.

PROXIMITY PROBLEMS BETWEEN INDIVIDUALS AND SOCIETY

In the case of conflicts, arising out of scarce resources, between individuals and the community, the issue is again one of costs vs. benefits, but the problem of allocating costs and measuring benefits is far more difficult than in the case of damages between two individual parties. It must be reiterated at the outset in a Jewish economic system the community, either at the local or communal level (when there is an absence of political independence) or at the national level, has rights to the property of the individual. Individual property rights are in many respects limited and abrogated by Jewish law when this is in the communal interest. Such interest, however, is not only economic. It includes all those aspects of life, such as religious needs, education, and welfare, in which the Jewish community has a mutual responsibility for its individual members. The idea that all Jews are responsible for one another applies in the field of ecology as well.

In the course of economic development there often occurs a clash of interests between the benefits of such development and the costs of increased pollution, smog, noise, etc. The issue in these cases is the welfare of the community, which has to consider the cost of limiting such development or of preventing the damages associated with it. In view of Judaism's vision of creating a sociopolitical entity at both the local and national levels, such issues form an integral part of the halakhic system, to be enforced with the full power of the rabbinic courts.

The community's right to expropriate land or other property for the communal good has already been discussed in chapter 8 on taxation. Benefits to the community are seen as outweighing the costs, monetary or otherwise, to individuals. It is not surprising, therefore, to find a ramified form of urban planning in Jewish sources, whereby the entrepreneur is forced to establish or relocate his firm where he will not cause damage to the community. Halakhic sources insist on the removal of dangerous industries or firms, whether the danger envisaged is physical (when health is affected), or aesthetic (when, e.g., the scenery is impaired). The sources quoted below reflect some of the trends in halakhic sources throughout the centuries regarding the safeguarding of the interests of the community.

At the outset it must be pointed out that sometimes the conflict between the ecological benefit of the community and the damages caused by certain industries or firms involves considerations over and above the economic cost to the individual owners of such firms. Satisfying the former, for example, may cause local unemployment or lead to a rise in the cost of living for the community. In such cases, who is to foot the bill? This perhaps is the real problem, from an economic point of view, underlying what are loosely termed ecological problems in the modern world.

We find in the Mishnah the following rabbinic ruling: "It is necessary to remove [from the confines of the village] the permanent threshing floors [because of the chaff], cemeteries, tanneries [because of the stench], and kilns [because of the smoke]."[17] Not only were the firms engaged in these industries to be removed from a residential area, but they were to be relocated so that natural factors like water and wind would not bring these harmful effects to the area concerned.

In halakhic sources, such pollution was termed "the damages of smoke and bad odors." These damages were regarded by the rabbis as being of special seriousness because they do harm to the body.[18] We have observed in the previous section that although the halakhic sources accepted the idea that it is possible for the individual to set aside his opposition to a plant that is causing him damage in exchange for a monetary consideration, this did not apply when the damage was to one's health. In respect to such damage the individual does not have the right to cause injury to himself or to allow such injury in exchange for the compensation he would receive from the owner of the polluting plant or enterprise.

Sometimes, at the time of the establishment of polluting plants the neighbors make no protest and it might be argued that such silence should be understood as acquiescence in their presence. The rabbinic authorities accepted, however, that the neighbors could still claim their rights to the removal of such plants at a later date, contrary to normal legal procedures.

For instance, Rabbi Daniel Estrosa, writing in sixteenth-century Italy, issued the following ruling regarding such a case.

> The question you have addressed to me concerning the butchers who have bought from the neighbors the right to build an abattoir has reached me. I understand that the butchers have already established such an abattoir and have commenced to operate it. At the outset it would seem that because they have purchased this right from the neighbors, the neighbors have given their consent to its construction and may not be allowed to retract their consent. However, we see that all the authorities argue that, with regard to damages of smoke and bad odors, a man is not really able to bear them, and therefore we may suppose that even if one agreed at the beginning we may not see this as forgoing their rights in the future. They agreed at the outset, since they thought they would be able to live with the damage. However, now, when they see and smell it in practice, they see that they cannot do so. Even if, as in our case, they actually sold this right, they may retract their consent, and therefore the abattoirs have to be closed.[19]

The *Shulchan Arukh* ruled that the neighbors could rescind their consent only when no formal sale of their rights had been considered.[20]

The correction of ecologically damaging factors through expropriation by the community of private land presents an additional area of conflict, over and above the monetary value of the land. There exists a constant danger of exploitation of the public purse on the part of the private owner. Such exploitation may take the form of price gouging or of protected negotiations at public expense. Both these forms of exploitation are possible since public officials tend to have a more casual attitude to public money than to the expenditure of their private funds.

It seems that this is not a modern phenomenon at all. We find a rabbinic treatment of it, some two thousand years ago, which takes into account both the exploitative nature of the individual and the impersonal, casual attitude toward the management of public funds.

The Mishnah tells us that "it is incumbent to remove the tree from a town [because it is more pleasant to the town to have an open landscape in front of it], and if the tree was there before the town was established, it is to be cut down and monetary compensation paid."[21] The Gemara then goes on to explain why we first force the owner of the tree to cut it down and then pay him compensation. After all, the owner could claim that "as long as you don't pay me my compensation, I will not cut down the tree." The Gemara rejects this argument since the collection and distribution of funds for public purposes often tend to be "neither hot nor cold," that is, without the efficiency and activism associated with private finance. Rashi sums this up in his commentary, when he writes that "if we will have to wait until all the money will be collected from the townspeople for this purpose, the tree will remain forever, since the members of the town rely on each other to see to the collection of such funds." (This would apply also to the distribution of these funds.) The owner of the tree is happy to go along with this, since his tree remains.

It must be pointed out, however, that over and above the economic considerations involved in ecological cost–benefit analysis, there is a moral element involved. By insisting that enterprises that harm the public have to be removed, we are asserting a moral and religious framework that regards such governmental interference as legitimate. Without this moral context the industrialist will feel that his personal rights are being arbitrarily abridged for the benefit of others. In the Torah scheme of things, the Jew is educated to understand that the public has rights in his property, and therefore his own property rights are necessarily and consistently limited.

Although legislation pertaining to ecologically dangerous industries applies to all countries in which Jews live, nevertheless, the main emphasis in such legislation was on the Jewish settlement in the Land of Israel. This should be seen not only as flowing from the obvious understanding that living in their own country gives Jews the right and ability to legislate their own economic affairs in accordance with Torah law. It is primarily a reflection of the sanctity of the Land of Israel, and of the desire of the religious authorities throughout the ages to encourage Jewish settlement there as a means of raising the religious consciousness of both the individual and the community.

And so the rabbinic codes are replete with injunctions protecting the physical assets of the Land of Israel and its people. We find that one may not, according to the Mishnah, "raise small animals in the Land of Israel [meaning sheep and goats, whose manner of grazing destroys the fields and causes soil erosion]. . . . Nor may a man raise a dog [who tends to bite and frighten people with his barking. It is interesting to note that special reference is made to pregnant women, who may lose their babies as a result of such fright]. It is not permissible to spread nets to enable the capture of birds, unless these are removed from the city thirty measures.'' (Such nets or snares, if set up close to the city, would entrap the birds of the townsmen.)[22] In all these cases the owner of the damaging element cannot in any way buy from the townsmen a waiver of their rights against such an injury. Furthermore, we see that in regard to Jerusalem, special care is given to ecological considerations. Jerusalem is singled out because of its sanctity, the proximity of the Temple, and its high population density. The Talmud did not allow garbage plants and kilns to be erected within the city: the former because they attract vermin and therefore spread disease, the latter because they pollute the air with their smoke. Rashi adds that kilns were forbidden in Jerusalem because their smoke would blacken the walls, and this would be a disgrace to the nation as a whole.[23]

A society desires to protect not only its physical environment but also the general quality of its life as determined by its value structure. This may lead to restrictions on forms of entertainment or on the rights of citizenship. In chapter 5, we discussed the right of townsmen to prevent settlement in their town on economic grounds if this would increase competition. We saw there that many authorities, especially those of the Sephardic world, were opposed to such legislation. All authorities, however, are agreed that is possible to prevent the entry of new citizens into a town when this will have a morally and religiously detrimental effect on the town. This is shown both in the halakhic codes and in the minute books of the various communities. Thus:

> In the year 1266, the community of the Jews of Canterbury [England] . . . have come to the resolution and bound themselves by oath that no Jew of any other town than Canterbury shall dwell in the said town to work without our permission. However, no liar, improper person, or slanderer [the latter being of special importance in medieval times, since much persecution arose from the slanders and misinformation supplied by Jews to the Christian world] may settle in our town.[24]

In a much later document, we have a reiteration of the right of the community to prevent moral detriment by restricting the entry of "evildoers." In the responsa of Rabbi Chaim Palache, of eighteenth-century Turkey, we find the following:

> I have been asked concerning Reuven, who had a courtyard for sale. A missionary has requested to buy this courtyard for an inflated price, and the neighbors have protested. Reuven has said to them, "I am willing to sell my courtyard to you for whatever the missionary has given me, so that I should not lose out on my money." The point is that the missionary will make a school that will entice the young of the house of Israel to learn the Bible according to his way. The question is whether the neighbors have the ability to prevent Reuven from selling. And my answer is yes and that, strictly speaking, Reuven should lose the money he would have received. However, since this is so [that he is required to bear the loss flowing from the difference between what he was paid by the neighbors and the market price], the community is obligated to help Reuven minimize his loss by means of the public funds. In the past I have carried out a similar positive action. We have bought a courtyard from a Gentile prostitute and sold it at a loss to an upright Jew. The monetary loss we then covered from the public fund, because it is incumbent on all Israel to help, even as it is written, "And you will destroy the evil in your midst [Deut. 13:6]."[25]

All too often, even where there is physical damage involved, the economic welfare of the community would be seriously harmed by the removal of an offending plant or industry. If the damage envisaged is one that causes bodily harm, as distinct from inconvenience or irritation, the economic loss is not allowed to take precedence over the paramount concern for the safety of human beings. This may be seen from the case, discussed in chapter 6, of an individual worker who wishes to endanger himself in order to increase his income. The rabbis taught that since man's need for economic growth is unlimited, we cannot allow him to endanger his life, even though he himself is willing to run the risk, in order to increase his income.

Where, however, the conflict is between communal economic suffering and inconvenience or physical unpleasantness, we find that the halakhic authorities were prepared to permit such inconvenience. After all, were this not done, the community would be threatened with extinction, or at least severe privation.

We are assuming here, of course, that there is no alternative site at which to place a given plant. Should such an alternative exist, all the authorities agree that the factory or industry should be located so that the damage is removed. Furthermore, it should be noted that, according to all halakhic authorities, the owner of a plant has to take as much care as possible to see that damages are kept to a minimum.

Writing in sixteenth-century Turkey, Rabbi Shlomo Cohen ruled in a responsum as follows:

> The damage caused to the townspeople by the vats used by the dyeing industry is extremely great and has to be considered as similar to that of smoke and bad odors. However, since the textile industry is the main basis for the livelihood of the people of this town, it is incumbent on the neighbors to suffer the damage. This is an enlargement of the principle that where a person is doing work that is essential to his livelihood and that it is not possible to do elsewhere, the neighbors do not have the right to prevent it.[26]

Rabbi Shimon Morpurgo, writing in seventeenth-century Italy, saw this bias in favor of economic welfare as a temporary phenomenon necessitated by the distortions introduced by Jewish history.

> It is forbidden to erect industries that are harmful and necessary to remove those that already exist, so as to protect the people of the city. However, in this country, since we are closed in and separated into a special Jewish quarter, which is narrow and insufficient for our needs [the reference being to the ghettos, which were first created in Italy], this injunction to move the offending obstacles is one that the community cannot stand up to.[27]

It may be understood from this that in normal conditions, in an independent Jewish state, it should be possible to plan things in such a way that sources of ecological harm will be removed. The community, being independent, should be able to allocate land and other resources in such a way as to provide for the common good, this being the yardstick according to which ecological obstacles are considered in halakhic sources.

Until now our discussion has centered around the restrictions placed on individuals from harming other individuals or from clashing with the public good. The halakhah, however, went a step further and required of individuals and the community active steps to ensure the health and well-being of human beings over and above the prevention of damage.

Notwithstanding this, the responsum of Rabbi Cohen regarding the vats would seem to indicate that where eradicating ecological damage means destroying the basis of the community's economy, then the halakhic sources would allow the source of that damage to remain. In the case of a single factory whose closing would cause large-scale unemployment, it may be assumed, although I have not been able to find a halakhic decision on this matter, that the solution would be to close it and support the workers out of communal charity. Where the ecological damage is minimal or causes only loss of wildlife, etc., then perhaps the factory should remain. This would be in accordance with the idea that everything in the world was created to serve man. These decisions would apply only where there is no alternative site, where no serious threat to health exists, and where all steps have been taken to keep the damage to a minimum

URBAN PLANNING

We have already seen that industries or personal property representing a danger to the members of a town may be forced to close down or relocate if it is not otherwise possible to prevent such damage. We have also learned that stores and factories can be relocated out of residential areas. Both these options provide a halakhic framework for urban planning.

There is, however, a further provision regarding urban planning which, it would seem, has ramifications for what is probably the most important issue involved in contemporary environmental problems: viz., striking a balance between urban growth and the ecological needs of society.

Land is one of the most important of all economic resources, and its intelligent allocation forms the basis of all healthy economies—while its misuse often dooms societies to poverty and hunger. In most developed countries, an intelligent balance between the competing needs of housing, industry, agriculture, and the amenities of health and recreation is the aim of economic policy.

The Torah requires the maintenance of a green belt around each walled city, as we learn from the laws regarding the cities that were given to the Levites [Lev. 25:34]. Each walled city had an area of 2,000 square cubits around it; the inner 1,000 were called *migrash ha'ir*—the city common—and were reserved for the animals and social amenities of the citizens. The other 1,000 (or 2,000, according to Maimonides) were reserved for their fields and vineyards. The biblical text tells us that the *migrash ha'ir* cannot be sold, and the Talmud explained that this means that the city common cannot be rezoned. In other words, the fields and vineyards cannot be converted into a common, nor can the common be turned into an agricultural area or, by being built upon, become part of the city. No one generation has the right to dispose of its natural resources simply as it deems fit, without handing over to future generations the same possibilities it inherited from the past.

Rabbi Hirsch, in his commentary on the Torah, goes on to say that these laws, together with the Jubiliee year (whereby every fifty years, land reverted to its original owner), preserve the balance between urban and rural development. Since only houses within walled cities could be sold permanently, and the "common land" represented a green belt that could not be encroached on, urban expansion would be limited. Any growth in population or mobility that necessitated the construction of homes, factories, and offices would need to be managed by constructing a new city, with its own fields and common land. This prevents the growth of megalopolis and its resultant traffic snarls, pollution, and alienation.

Such laws constitute important restraints on the economic development of society. Given Judaism's view of the role of economics, discussed in chapter 3—as a means to ensure man's existence, but not as an end in itself—it would seem that such restraints are easy to understand in a Jewish religious context. In that chapter we saw that it was considered necessary for the individual to restrain his consumption, both in order to allow time for Torah study and in order to maintain a modest standard of living. Such modesty is seen as a means of "educating" man's urge for material goods—itself a form of the *yetser harah,* or evil inclination. The same principles apply to society as a whole. Thus, economic growth should be limited to providing "essentials," and restraint should be reflected in the use and exploitation of scarce resources, such as land, oil, air, and water.

PUBLIC HEALTH

In the Torah there are a number of injunctions based on a twofold ideology: the prevention of illness and the removal of "unclean" things from areas of human habitation. "You shall carry a spade with your weapons and it shall be when you sit outside you shall dig therewith a pit that will cover your excrement, and your camp shall be holy" [Deut. 23:14]. The temporary quarantine and purification of garments, utensils, and houses prescribed in Leviticus was aimed both at eradicating the physical results of spiritual deficiencies and at preserving the physical health of the community. All the laws of *Tumah*—impurity—which required expulsion from the community and purification before re-entry [e.g., Lev. 15:2–23; Numbers 19:7–22] served the same dual purpose.

In the same way, the Talmud, the halakhic codes, and the rabbinic literature all include the discussion of health problems, nutrition, and preventive medicine as part of the religious pattern of life. Man, created in God's image, is required to care properly for his body and is enjoined against harming himself or others through neglect of that body.

This side of Jewish law, interesting as it may be, is beyond the scope of this book. We are concerned here with the economic costs of health and medicine and how they are to be covered. Such costs may be divided for convenience into two groups: those flowing from damages caused to the body, and those associated with medical care, doctors, hospitals, etc.

Damages to the Body: The Responsibilities of Individuals

Special place is given in the context of damages to the prevention of damage to the human body. Here, in addition to the economic loss caused by the loss of limbs or by death itself, there are obviously also moral and psychological costs, both to the individual and to society. Halakhic sources are careful to translate even these costs into monetary ones, since a human court would not be able to inflict punishment commensurate with the moral or psychological damage. Thus, "an eye for an eye, a tooth for a tooth" [Lev. 24:20], has always been understood by the Oral Law to mean *monetary* compensation, as defined in the following Mishnah:

> He who damages his fellow man bodily is liable to pay for five types of damages: namely, damage [a monetary assessment of the physical damage done]; pain [payment for the pain incurred on account of the injury]; medical costs; enforced idleness [as a

result of the sickness or damage done]; and shame. [It is an affront to human dignity for a man to have been involved in the kind of situation in which the damage resulted.][28]

Such damages are enforceable in a *bet din* just like any other damages. The legal conditions for when these various types of damages have to be paid are beyond the scope of this study. All that we are interested in here is that the cost of committing damage to the human body is clearly placed on the person causing the damage and includes not only the amount of the actual physical damage done.

Furthermore, a man is required to make certain investments in his property so as to prevent it from causing physical harm to other individuals when they are within its confines. The *Shulchan Arukh* is quite clear and emphatic on this obligation.

> It is a positive commandment for a man to make a fence around his roof, as it is written in the Torah: "And you shall make a fence on your roof [in order to prevent somebody from falling from the roof]" [Deut. 22:8]. He who does not make such a fence disregards this positive commandment and is also guilty of violating the negative commandment "And you shall not spill blood in thy house" [Deut. 22:8]. And so it is with every obstacle [even in a public thoroughfare] that is liable to cause damage to the human body: It is a positive precept to remove it [stones, garbage, even seemingly harmless items] and to do so diligently. It is written in the Torah, "And you shall surely pay heed and beware."[29]

One is not permitted to do damage to one's own body and is required to look after it, since it is a gift from God. Therefore one has the responsibility to refrain from bad habits or from placing himself in danger for the sake of sport or thrills or pleasure, in accordance with the biblical injunction "You shall surely guard your lives very carefully" (Deut. 4:15). On such grounds, for example, cigarette smoking has been forbidden by some present-day halakhic authorities.[30] Even those who question this ruling hold that it is forbidden in public places, since it damages others.[31]

Judaism's treatment of damage caused by one individual to another does not rest only on the necessity for monetary compensation and for the removal of the cause of damage, irrespective of whether it is to another's (or one's own) body or to his property. Great lengths were taken, both in the moralistic literature and in the legal codes, to inculcate in the Jew a duty to prevent damage, even when such damage was not caused either by him or by his property. The halakhic sources stressed that it is a man's duty to prevent his neighbor from suffering loss or from undergoing pain or physical suffering. This is in contrast to many modern societies, wherein people are taught to mind their own business and so to refrain from interfering when others are being caused financial damage or bodily harm. The collective responsibility of Jews for one another, which has been stressed throughout this chapter, makes such an attitude impossible.

We find the following ruling in the *Shulchan Arukh*.

> He who sees his neighbor drowning or being attacked by robbers or by wild animals and is able to save him himself, or to hire others to do so, and did not do so; or if he heard people plotting against his neighbor to do him harm or to inflict damage on him and did not inform his neighbor; or even one who is able to comfort his fellow man for his agony or sorrow and does not do so with words—whoever does all these and similar things is guilty of transgressing the biblical commandment "You shall not stand upon thy brother's blood" [Lev. 19:16][32]

It is interesting to note that this positive religious obligation of the Jew to save others is to be carried out even at the expense of killing the pursuer, irrespective of whether the latter's purpose is sexual assault or bodily harm.

The demand of Jewish sources that one act to protect others is not only concerned with the prevention of bodily harm. The *Sefer Hachinukh*, the thirteenth-century Spanish study of the reasons behind the mitzvot, explains the biblical commandment in Exodus "And if you see the donkey of your enemy straining under its burden, . . . you shall surely help him" [Exod. 23:5]: (As to the scriptures saying a donkey, it does not mean a donkey specifically, but any beast. It is only that scripture spoke of what is the usual purpose of a donkey—for carrying burdens.) "It is a religious duty to help unload a man laden with a burden as well. Furthermore, even if he suffers only the loss of his goods and possessions, it is a religious obligation for us to take pity on him. At the root of this precept lies the purpose: to teach our spirit the quality of compassion, which is a noble trait of character. [A fortiori,] There is no need to say that a duty lies on us to take pity on a man who is suffering physical pain."[33]

Medical Care: Communal and Individual Obligations

The provision of medical care is considered an essential part of Jewish religious living, since the saving of a life (*pikuach nefesh*) takes precedence over many religious obligations. For example martyrdom is limited to the 3 cardinal issues of idolatry, bloodshed, sexual immorality except in times of general persecution. In other circumstances *pikuach nefesh* takes precedence. There is no question in Judaism that a man may, and should, avail himself of the services of a physician for medical care: the rabbis understood that God had enabled the doctor to perform his services, making him a human agency for His healing powers. So a city that did not have a doctor was considered by the Talmudic sages to be unfit for a Jew to dwell in. The medical profession has always been highly regarded by Jews, and many great rabbis throughout the ages and countries of Jewish settlement have been medical men.

What concerns us here, however, is how the services of physicians were to be financed. Basically the physician's work was considered to be a service that was to be provided free of charge; after all, it was an obligation placed on the doctor by a Divine source. A parallel may be drawn with the obligation to teach Torah without charge.

It should be obvious, however, that this was not an economically sustainable system, and therefore permission was given physicians to take money. However, the authorities insisted that payment was not for the specialized knowledge of the physician, but solely for his time.[34] Even if this makes no practical difference, it at least puts the cost of medical services in a light different from that of other services provided by professionals. This argument was used against doctors in a recent strike in Israel. It would seem, however, that since doctors in that country are not members of a free profession, but are primarily employees of the sick funds or of the state, they are essentially in the position of all the civil servants.

The fundamental question with which the Jewish sources are concerned is the medical costs of the poor—since the wealthy are able to provide for these services, just as they do in the case of other goods or services they desire. Halakhically, a Jewish community or society can, if it wishes, legislate free medical care for all; it cannot, however, escape its obligation to provide for the medical needs of the poor, even if it so desires. If, for example, the State of Israel decided to change its present publicly financed medical system to one based strictly on self-insurance, it may be assumed that halakhic authorities would require the state to bear the cost of insurance premiums for the poor.

Writing to his physician son Samuel, the medieval Jewish physician Yehuda Ibn Tibon provides a guide for a personal solution to this problem that was typical of many Jewish doctors. "While you take your fees from the rich, heal the poor gratuitously. The Lord will requite you."[35]

There is a halakhic opinion that the *bet din* can force a doctor to treat poor patients free of charge if there are no other doctors available.[36] Irrespective of this, the councils of many communities made decisions providing for public financing of medical care. In Padua, in 1585, we find the following decision of its council: "It is decided to raise further funds in order to provide for the medical care of Shimon Levi Ginzberg. This shall be done both from the funds raised by [the *parnas*] on every Tuesday [from the members of the various synagogues]; and also further funds are to be raised from the general charity funds of the community."[37]

It must be borne in mind that communal funds for medical care and hospitalization could be used only for those types of medical services approved of halakhically.

So, since abortion, for example, is not permitted except in cases of danger to the mother's life, we may assume that no sanction would be given for public financing for abortions for other reasons. At the same time, communal responsibility would seem to be axiomatic for children born to women who, in a non-halakhic framework, might have sought abortion as a solution. The Council of Padua, meeting in 1587, took note of the situation of Golda Ashkenazi, who had just given birth to a son whose father was unknown, and they decided as follows.

> It has been brought to our notice that the child born recently is to be brought to the synagogue, since the mother says that the congregation has the obligation to provide for its sustenance or to seek out the father of the son in order that he should have a name and in order that there shouldn't, God forbid, be a tragedy and the loss of a soul in Israel. Therefore, we have decided that the *parnasim* have the authority to undertake everything that

is necessary in this matter, both to enforce whatever decision they should come to, and also to spend such funds as may be necessary to attend to it.[38]

A further example of the use of communal funds to cover the costs of medical care is contained in an enactment of the community of Cracow, in sixteenth-century Poland: "Regarding a domestic who became ill, the employer is required to pay the costs of hospitalization up to a period of two weeks. If she requires further treatment, the costs are to be shared equally between the employer and the employee for a fortnight. After that, all the costs are to be borne by the communal charitable funds."[39]

The above enactment describes the sick domestic as being hospitalized in the "*hekdesh*." This is a reference to the communal hospital, maintained by the community. It is interesting to note that "*hekdesh*," a term originally used to refer solely to the funds provided for upkeep of the Temple, came over the centuries to refer to the hospice maintained by many Jewish communities throughout the Diaspora. The hospice often served a dual purpose: that of an inn for travelers and that of a hospital for the poor, both local and transients. From Josephus Flavius we know of the synagogue erected in Jerusalem by Theodotos, son of Venettenos, which served also as a hospital and inn for needy travellers.[40] In Talmudic days we hear of the *cheder hashayish*—the room of marble—as a place for the care of the sick. In 1373 the Nürnberg Memor book describes the bequest of Samuel ben Natan Ha-Levi of 50 pounds to the *hekdesh*.[41] In 1765, we learn that there were 18 patients in the Vilno *hekdesh*.[42] Writing in Saloniki in the seventeenth century, Samuel di Medina addressed one of his responsa to the problem of the erection of a joint hospital by four different Balkan communities.[43]

From a discussion in the Talmud we also learn of communal doctors paid for out of public funds, whose job it was to assess the bodily damage done to claimants in cases of accidents or physical violence.[44] These doctors also measured the degree of physical endurance of those sentenced by the *bet din* to flogging.[45]

The phenomenon of publicly financed hospitals continues to be a feature of Jewish communal life down to our own day. Such hospitals absorb major portions of the welfare funds, for example, of Jewish communities in the United States.

Effective medical care, however, not only involves the cost of a physician and hospitalization, but also requires a support system to alleviate the effects of illness on the peace of mind of the sick person and on the family unit. Modern medicine recognizes such a support system as an intrinsic part of communal health care and therefore expects home care and personal counseling to be funded either by the patient's health insurance or by the state. Such supports have always been part and parcel of the Jewish welfare system.

The following ruling of Maimonides shows this support system to be legally binding and not just desirable.

> It is a rabbinic commandment, incument on all, to visit the sick . . . and this may be done many times in the day . . . except in those cases where it is a bother to the sick. He who visits the sick removes part of his illness and eases his situation. He who does not visit the sick, it is as though he has shed blood. [Since visitors took care of all the patient's needs, by refraining from such visits, one is harming the patient, perhaps even fatally.][46]

Maimonides goes on to rule that visiting the sick is an act of righteousness performed with one's body, and thus without legal limit in its fulfillment (in contrast to monetary acts of righteousness, which the sages had limited to 20 percent of one's wealth). He sees the visiting of the sick as a fulfillment of the Torah's commandment "You shall love your neighbor as yourself" [Lev. 19:18].

This support system, like most moral and ethical injunctions in Judaism, is not left to the choice of the individual, to be observed or not according to his degree of religiosity. The community saw it as one of its obligations to force individual members to assume responsibility for visiting the sick, either through taxes or by personal effort.

The Jewish commuity of Avignon, in southern France, passed a statute in 1558 that obligated the entire community to visit and nurse the sick. In accordance with Jewish concern for modesty and sexual morality, strict segregation was insisted on, so that men visited men and women visited women patients. Those in charge of the charity funds of the community determined by lot the rotation of the members, and those who did not perform their duties were fined accordingly.

Alongside the communal enforcement of the duty of visiting the sick, there existed *hevrot* (associations) in almost all communities throughout the centuries, who were either devoted solely to the medical support system or included this among their functions. Those devoted solely to the medical support system were in theory voluntary, but the Jewish value system and peer pressure meant that the individual was often left with little choice.

The second type of *hevrot* were sometimes part of the trade and mercantile associations to which we referred in chapter 6 on wages and labor. (These guilds and associations had the communal power to force all those engaged in that particular trade to belong and therefore may be regarded as an arm of the public sector.) The charter of the Jewish Shoemakers Guild in Zaragoza (fourteenth-century Spain) describes this aspect of members' obligations.

> Likewise if any of the aforesaid brethren falls sick, the officers of the Benevolent Society shall visit him twice a week on Mondays and Thursdays, and if [the member] needs money or a loan requiring security, they may lend him up to five solidi from the treasury of the society. If it happens that the officers of the society see that he is in need, the said officers shall give him from the said treasury two dinarii for each day [of his illness]. Also, all the brethren shall be obliged to visit the said ill member every Saturday, and whoever fails to do so shall pay one denarius [for each missed visit].[47]

Even a society that accepts responsibility for providing medical care, in whatever form and scope, is faced with the problem of rationing scarce medical resources, such as expensive drugs, hospital space, and sophisticated machines. Obviously if these facilities are available as needed, there is no problem. Unfortunately, however, in real life scarcity exists, and therefore an answer has to be provided.

The discussion of this problem in a Jewish legal context would seem to be based on a number of basic halakhic principles regarding the value of life and the necessity to guard it. There is the Talmudic discussion, to which we have referred before, regarding two people who are stranded in a desert and have only enough water to keep the owner of the water alive. Should he drink it himself; should he divide it equally (and then both will die); or should he nobly give it up to keep the other alive? Halakhically, the ruling of Rabbi Akiva was accepted as binding—viz., that the owner of the water is required to keep himself alive, since ''your life takes precedence.''[48] Maimonides rules that one may not take one life in order to save or cure another.[49] This is based on the Talmudic ruling that one is not permitted to give in to a demand that the Jews hand over one of their members to be killed, or the enemy will kill them all.[50]

These basic principles have been applied by contemporary halakhists to cases involving the allocation of scarce medical resources, such as replacing one patient by another in dialysis treatment or apportioning intensive care units. Rabbi Waldenberg, writing in present-day Jerusalem, rules that the basis for such allocation is medical criteria, so that, for example, those with a potential for cure are preferred over the incurable. In the case of drugs, the question of ownership enters into the decision. If the drugs are private property, the owner, in accordance with Rabbi Akiva's view, is not required to give them up, even if he is incurable. Where the drugs are public property, then they should be divided among the equally sick, even if they only prolong life temporarily; there is always the possibility of Divine intervention, or of new medicines being developed in the meantime.[51]

SUMMARY

Man's economic needs have to be understood within the framework of his role as an administrator, responsible for the well-being of the world and its natural resources. So economic growth cannot be achieved through damage to another's property or health nor through harmful exploitation of natural resources, even when these are legally within one's possession. The physical beauty of the world is a valuable enhancement to religious thought and contributes to man's spiritual growth.The property rights of the individual are limited by the demands of religious observance, the welfare of other individuals, and the public welfare. Even one's own body is not one's exclusive property, and so one is required to take all necessary steps to preserve it from harm. Such responsibility extends to the bodily health of other members of the community.

There is a moral and ethical dimension involved not only in desisting from damaging property, but also in actively preventing such damage.

These limitations on the property rights of the individual mean that economic growth is not an end in itself but only one of man's needs. A distinction would have to be made in a Jewish economy between the provision of necessities and the pursuit of luxuries, even though the dividing line is not always a clear one.

Glossary

Arba'ah Turim: literally, "Four Rows"; codex by Rabbi Ya'acov ben Asher (1269–1340)

bet din (pl., *batei din*): rabbinic court operating on the basis of Jewish religious law

Chasidism: religious mass movement which swept Eastern Europe in the eighteenth century and continues to maintain large concentrations in all present-day Jewish communities

chesed: acts of lovingkindness, usually undeserved or nonreciprocal

din: a Jewish legal decision

Erets Yisrael: proper name for the biblical Land of Israel, irrespective of the actual borders of Jewish states at particular periods of history

Gemara: codified commentary on and discussion of the Mishnah by the Rabbis of Babylon and the Land of Israel, compiled first in Tiberias in the fourth century and later in Babylon in the mid-fifth century

genizah: repository of remnants of religious books, ritual objects, and communal and halakhic records

halakhah: literally, perhaps, "road"; the collective literature of rulings of Jewish written and oral law, as defined by and in accordance with, authoritative rabbinic rulings within the clearly defined principals of Jewish law. These rulings constitute an all-embracing legal system covering man's actions, both collective and individual, in all fields and facets of life

hasagat g'vul: literally, "removing a landmark"; but used generally to denote certain forms of encroaching competition

herem: excommunication from the community, either for trans-gressing communal edicts or for not obeying the rulings of a *bet din*

heter iska: formalized legal arrangement creating a partnership between borrower and lender, so as to prevent transgression of the prohibition against taking interest

m'd'oraita: literally, "from the *Torah*"; refers to laws having their source directly in the Torah

m'd'rabanan: literally, "from the rabbis"; refers to rulings and enactments of the rabbis as distinct from those obligations flowing from the Torah itself

Midrash: conceptual framework of Judaism written in the form of a rabbinic commentary on the books of the Bible

Mishnah: six orders authored by R. Yehuda Hanasi, in the sec-ond century C.E., to codify the authoritative opinions of the oral law

Mishneh Torah: fourteen-volume codex of Jewish law compiled by Maimonides (the Rambam, from the initials of his Hebrew name, R. Moses ben Maimon)

mitzvah: commandment that the Jew is obliged to obey, or good deed performed

ona'ah: theft through price coercion

Pinkas: minute book of Jewish communities, containing the en-actments and decisions of the autonomous Jewish councils that regulated life throughout most of the Jewish world until the nineteenth century

responsa: rabbinic decisions, from all the countries of Jewish set-tlement and from the ninth century C. E. down to our own day, issued in response to questions submitted to them in the area of religious and ritual behavior and civil, commercial, and criminal law

Reuven, Shimon, Levi: used in rabbinic discussions to refer to the individuals in the particular case examined

Shulchan Arukh: literally, "prepared table"; major codex of law compiled by Rabbi Joseph Caro in the Land of Israel in the six-teenth century

Talmud: Babylonian and Jerusalem texts of Mishnah and Gemara

Tanach: Hebrew name for the Old Testament based on the initials of the three major components

Torah: narrowly defined as the written law contained in the Five Books of Moses; loosely used to describe all the books of the Bible and sometimes even the entire scope of Jewish religious learning

Va'ad Arba Aratsot: Council of the Four Lands: autonomous Jewish council of Greater Poland, Little Poland, Lvov Land, and Volhynia

Notes

Chapter 1. Introduction (pp. 1–10)

1. W. Sombart, *Jews and Modern Capitalism* (New Brunswick, N.J.: Transaction Books, 1982).
2. Max Weber, *Sociology of Religion* (Boston: Beacon Press, 1964).
3. R. H. Tawney, *Religion and the Rise of Capitalism* (London: Pelican Books, 1962).
4. A. S. Lieberman, quoted in A. Wolfson, "Jewish Cultural Sources for the Israeli Welfare Ideology," *Journal of Welfare and Social Security Studies*, November 1977 (Hebrew).
5. B. Borochov, *Nationalism and the Class Struggle* (New Brunswick, N.J.: Transaction Books, 1984).
6. A. J. Toynbee, *A Study of History* (New York: Oxford University Press, 1961).
7. *Mishneh Torah* (Maimonides); *Arba'ah Turim* (Ya'akov ben Asher); *Shulchan Arukh* (Joseph Caro).
8. L. Finkelstein, *The Pharisees* (Philadelphia: Jewish Publication Society, 1960).
9. E. Rivkin, "Judaic Economic Tradition," in Symposium on Religion, Economics and Social Thought (Vancouver, B.C.: Fraser Institute, 1982).
10. Y. Lieberman, "Elements in Talmudical Monetary Thought," *History of Political Economy*, Summer 1979; A. Levine, *Free Enterprise and Jewish Law* (New York: Ktav, 1980).
11. Talmud Bavli, *Baba Metzia* 42a.
12. R. Coase, "The Problem of Social Cost," *Journal of Law and Economics*, September 1960, 1–44.
13. Y. Lieberman, "Origins of Coase's Theorem in Jewish Law," *Journal of Legal Studies*, June 1981.

Chapter 3.   The Challenge of Wealth (pp. 25–60)

1. Mishnah, *Avot*, chapter 6, mishnah 4.
2. Talmud Bavli, *B'rakhot* 35b.
3. Mishnah, *Avot*, chapter 3, mishnah 21.
4. *Mishneh Torah, Hilkhot Talmud Torah*, chapter 3, halakhot 7, 10.
5. *Ibid.*
6. Ben-Sasson, *Jewish History in the Middle Ages* (Tel Aviv: Dvir, 1959), 65 (Hebrew).
7. Lev. 26; Deut. 27, 28.
8. Talmud Bavli, *Chagigah* 9b.
9. S. R. Hirsch, *Commentary on the Bible*, on Deut. 18: 1–3.
10. The *Kuzari*, part II, 45–50.
11. *Kad Hakemach* (Jerusalem: Mossad Harav Kook, 1961).
12. I. M. Bunim, *Ethics from Sinai*, chapter 4, mishnah 1 (New York: Feldheim, 1974).
13. *Hayom Yom-Lubavitch* (Kfar Chabad, 1972), entry for 4th of Av.
14. Rashi on Deut. 32:6.
15. Mishnah, *Avot*, chapter 5, mishnah 10.
16. Abarbanel on Gen. 3, 4, 11.
17. *Akedat Yitzchak* on Gen. 11.
18. *Migdal Oz*, 80c.
19. Talmud Bavli, *Sanhedrin* 24b.
20. *Mishneh Torah, Hilkhot G'neivah*, chapter 6, halakhot 8–11.
21. L. Finkelstein, *Jewish Self-Government in the Middle Ages*, Takkanot of the Rhine Communities, enactment 12 (New York: Feldheim, 1964).
22. *Shem Mi Shmuel*, Parshat Balak (Israel: Nezer, 1949).
23. *Shem Mi Shmuel*, Moadim Sukhot (Israel: Nezer, 1969).
24. Talmud Bavli, *Baba Kama* 30a.
25. *Mishneh Torah, Hilkhot Shecheinim*, chapter 12, halakhot 5, 13, 14.
26. Talmud Bavli, *Ketuboth* 103a, *Baba Bathra* 12b.
27. *Kli Yakar.*
28. *Sefer Hachinuch.*
29. *Sefer Hachinuch*, Mitzvah 332.
30. Deut. 26: 1–11.
31. *Shmoneh Perakim*, chapter 6.
32. Malbim, Commentary on the Bible Exod. 20.
33. *Shulchan Arukh, Choshen Mishpat*, section 348.
34. *Guide to the Perplexed*, part 3, chapter 41.

35. Mishnah, *Baba Kama*, chapter 9, mishnah 5.

36. Tosaphot, *Baba Kama* 103a, also Rosh, chapter 7, 21.

37. Talmud Bavli, *B'rakhot* 35a.

38. Talmud Bavli, *Sanhedrin* 108b.

39. S. R. Hirsch, *Commentary on the Torah*, Gen. 6, 11.

40. *Shem Mi Shmuel*, Parshat Noach (Israel: Nezer Tel Aviv, 1949).

41. Talmud Bavli, *Gittin* 45a.

42. *Shulchan Arukh, Choshen Mishpat, Hilkhot G'neivah* 358.

43. D. Karfi, ed., *Va'ad Kehilah Kedosha Padua* (Jerusalem: Ha-Akademia Haleumit, 1973).

44. Takkanot of Frankfurt, in L. Finkelstein, *Jewish Self-Government*, sections 7/8.

45. M. C. Luzzato, *Mesilat Yesharim*, chapter 21.

46. *Sefer Hachinuch* on Lev. 25:14.

47. Mishnah, *Baba Metzia*, chapter 14, mishnah 10.

48. Talmud Bavli, *Baba Metzia* 6lb.

49. Mishnah, *Baba Bathra*, chapter 3, mishnah 10.

50. *Mishneh Torah, Hilkhot G'neivah*, chapter 8, halakhah 20, upholding Rami bar Chama in *Baba Bathra* 89a. See also *Hilkhot Sanhedrin*, chapter 1, halakhah 1.

51. *Shulchan Arukh, Choshen Mishpat, Hilkhot G'neivah*, section 358.

52. Takkanot of Corfu, in Finkelstein, *Jewish Self-Government*, enactment 12.

53. *Misheh Torah, Hilkhot Rotzeakh*, chapter 12, halakhah 12, based on Mishnah, *Avodah Zarah*, chapter 1, mishnah 7.

54. *Mishneh Torah, Hilkhot Mechirah*, chapter 10, halakhah 4, based on *Baba Bathra* 40B.

55. *Shulchan Arukh, Choshen Mishpat, Hilkhot Mekach u Memkar*, section 222.

56. Mishnah, *Baba Bathra*, chapter 2, mishnayot 11, 12.

57. Mishnah, *Baba Kama*, chapter 7, mishnah 7.

58. Talmud Bavli, *Baba Bathra* 2b.

59. Maimonides, *Guide to the Perplexed*, part 3, chapters 39–40.

60. Talmud Bavli, *Baba Metzia* 49b.

61. Talmud Bavli, *Baba Metzia* 47b.

62. Talmud Bavli, *Sanhedrin* 92a.

63. *Shulchan Arukh, Choshen Mishpat, Hilkhot Mekach u Memkar*, section 204, subsection 4.

64. Mishnah, *Avot*, chapter 5, mishnah 10.

65. Malbim, Commentary on the Bible.

66. Talmud Bavli, *Baba Metzia* 30b.
67. *Shulchan Arukh, Choshen Mishpat, Hilkhot Mekach u Memkar*, section 237, subsection 1.
68. Talmud Bavli, *Kiddushin* 59a.
69. Talmud Bavli, *Sukkah 49b: Shulchan Arukh, Yoreh De'ah*, section 93, subsection 11.
70. Exod. 22: 20–21; Exod. 23: 4–9; Lev. 19: 9–10, 33–34; Deut. 16: 20.
71. *Mishneh Torah, Hilkhot Malveh u Loveh*, chapter 2, halakhot 1, 2.
72. David Shochet, *Jewish Law and Decision Making* (Philadelphia: Temple University Press, 1979).
73. See Codex Justinian I: 5, 21; 9, 2; 8–9, repeating the code of Theodosius, which allowed the Jews their own special courts. In Western and Central Europe this was continued by the rulers of the Holy Roman Empire, down to its dissolution at the beginning of the nineteenth century.
74. *Va'ad Kehilah Kedosha Padua*, ed. D. Karfi.
75. Synod of Castilian Jews, section 3, L. Finkelstein, *Jewish Self-Government*.
76. *Mishneh Torah, Hilkhot De'ot*, chapter 5, halachot 9–13.
77. Talmud Bavli, *Pesachim* 49a.
78. *Mishneh Torah, Hilkhot De'ot*, chapter 5, halakhah, 2.
79. Takkanot of the Rhine Communities, enactment 17, L. Finkelstein, *Jewish Self-Government*.
80. Synod of Castilian Jews, enactment 11, L. Finkelstein, *Jewish Self-Government*.
81. *Pinkas Va'ad Arba Aratsot*, enactment 90, ed. Israel Heilperin (Jerusalem: Mossad Bialik, 1954).

Chapter 4. The Economic History of the Jews: An Overview (pp. 61–82)

1. Ruth 2 and 3; Judges 9, from where we learn that the farmers lived in villages and went out daily to work their lands. The exhortations of the prophets (Isaiah 5: 8; Hosea 5: 10; Rashi on Amos 2: 3) against the practice of "joining" land to land reflects a traditional objection against plantations, while the institution of the jubilee year (Lev. 25: 8–24), which called for the return of land to its original owner, provided a legal brake against the creation of great estates.
2. Y. Yadin, *The Head of Those Kingdoms* (State National Books, 1979).
3. Exod. 22: 2; Deut. 15: 0. The high value of slaves alluded to in Exod. 21: 32 indicates their scarcity. The law against returning slaves to their owners (Deut. 23: 16) and the injunctions against discarding

women bought for marriage (Exod. 21: 7–11) and against the ill-treatment of slaves (Exod. 21: 26–27; Lev. 25: 39–43) made slave-owning an unattractive investment.

4. Proverbs 31: 24.

5. I Kings, 6, 7.

6. II Kings, 24: 14–16.

7. I Kings, 15: 18; II Kings, 12: 19; 24: 13.

8. Amos 3: 15; 5: 11.

9. Proverbs 28: 8; Psalms 15.

10. I Kings, 10: 14–15.

11. Exod. 22: 24–27; Lev. 19: 13–16.

12. Mishnah, *Terumot*, chapter 7, mishnayot 5, 6, 7.

13. I Samuel 8: 11–20.

14. Judges 4: 10; 6: 34, 35; I Samuel 11: 7–8.

15. I Kings 12.

16. Isaiah 1: 22; Jeremiah 5: 26–28; 17: 22; 22: 13; 34: 8–16.

17. Avi Yonah, *Bimei Roma U. Bisantium* (Jerusalem, 1947) (Hebrew).

18. Talmud Bavli, *Baba Bathra* 21b, *Baba Metzia* 77a.

19. Talmud Bavli, *Sukkah* 51b.

20. Mishnah, *Baba Metzia*, chapter 3, mishnah 11.

21. Mishnah, *Baba Metzia*, chapter 5.

22. Talmud Bavli, *Baba Bathra* 3b, 8.

23. Talmud Bavli, *Sanhedrin* 17b; *Baba Bathra* 10b, *Baraita*; see also *Tosafot* there. Re education, see *Baba Bathra* 21a, *Shabbat* 119b.

24. Talmud Bavli, *Shabbat* 63a.

25. Josephus, *Antiquities of the Jews*, vol. XIV, pp. 10, 12, 235; Codex Theodosius I: 1, 10; XVI: 8, 10; Codex Justinian I: 9, 8, 15.

26. C. Braddock, *Portrait of a People*, part 2, chapter 1 (New York: Judaica Press, 1967).

27. S. D. Goiten, *A Mediterranean Society*, vol. 1. (Berkley: University of California Press, 1967).

28. M. N. Adler (translator), *Itinerary of Benjamin of Tudela* (New York: Feldheim, 1964).

29. A. Yaari, *Iggerot Erets Yisrael* (Jerusalem: Jewish Agency, 1943).

30. J. Jacobs (ed.), *Jews of Angevin England* (Farnsworth, U.K.: Gregg International, 1970), p. 71.

31. Irving A. Agus, *Heroic Age of Franco-German Jewry* (New York: Bloch, 1969).

32. S. Aris, ''The Jews in Business,'' *Sunday Times* (London), 1972.

33. *Ibid.*

34. M. Reich, The Economic Structure of Modern Jewry, in *The Jews*, L. Finkelstein, ed. (New York: Harper, 1948). See also M. Gross, *Economic History of the Jews*, part 7, chapter 10 (New York: Schocken Books, 1976).

Chapter 5. Competition, Prices, and Profits (pp. 83–125)

1. Talmud Yerushalmi, *Baba Metzia*, chapter 5, halakhah 1.
2. Chapter 4, halakhah 9.
3. Talmud Bavli, *Taanit* 19b.
4. *Ibid.*
5. Mishnah, *Kiddushin*, chapter 4, mishnah 4.
6. Gratain Decretum, part 1.
7. Thomas Aquinas, *Summa Theologian.*
8. Talmud Bavli, *Baba Metzia* 40b; *Baba Bathra* 4a, *Menachot* 7a.
9. Talmud Bavli, *Baba Bathra* 91a.
10. *Mishneh Torah, Hilkhot Mekhirah*, chapter 14, halakhah 4.
11. Talmud Bavli, *Baba Bathra* 91a. See Rashi and Tosafot.
12. *Ibid.*
13. *Mishneh Torah, Hilkhot Mekhirah* chapter 14, halakhah 3.
14. *Bet Yosef, Choshen Mishpat*, section 231, subsection 23.
15. Talmud Bavli, *Baba Bathra* 90b.
16. *Mishneh Torah, Hilkhot Mekhirah,* chapter 14, halakhah 6, extending only this restriction. See *Shulchan Arukh, Choshen Mishpat*, section 231 for a wider application.
17. Talmud Bavli, *Baba Bathra* 90b.
18. Mishnah, *Hulin*, chapter 5, mishnah 4; Talmud Bavli, *Hulin* 83a.
19. Talmud Bavli, *Taanit* 22a.
20. Mishnah, *Keritut*, chapter 1, mishnah 7.
21. *T'shuvot Ha'tsemach Tsedek*, section 28.
22. Talmud Bavli, *Baba Bathra* 89a.
23. Talmud Bavli, *Yoma* 9a.
24. *Mishneh Torah, Hilkhot Mekhirah*, chapter 14, halakhot 1 and 2. See *Bet Yosef, Choshen Mishpat*, section 231, subsection 28 for a slightly different definition of basic goods.
25. Rashi, *Yoma* 83a: *Menuchot* 77a; also Rashbam, *Baba Bathra* 90b, 91a.
26. Synod of Castilian Jews, quoted in L. Finkelstein, *Jewish Self-Government in the Middle Ages* (New York: Feldheim, 1964).
27. *Pinkas, Va'ad Arba Aratsot*, enactment 563 and others.
28. *Pinkas, Va'ad Kehilot Lita*, enactment 712.

29. Talmud Bavli, *Baba Metzia* 58b.

30. *Mishneh Torah, Hilkhot Mekhirah,* chapter 13, halakhah 4, based on the Baraita, *Baba Metzia* 51b.

31. Mishnah, *Baba Metzia,* chapter 4, mishnah 3.

32. Responsum of R. Meshullam, Genizah Fragments, Oxford University Library.

33. Mishnah, *Baba Metzia,* chapter 4; mishnah 9.

34. Y. Lieberman, *Economic Thought in the Talmud* (Israel: Bar Ilan University, 1973) (Hebrew).

35. A. Levine, ''The Just Price Doctrine in Judaic Law,'' *Dine Israel,* vol. 8, 1978.

36. A. Levine, *Free Enterprise and Jewish Law* (New York: Ktav, 1980).

37. *T'shuvot HaRosh,* section 1, subsection 7; see also *Piskei Din shel Bet Hamishpat,* Tel Aviv, file 444.

38. Talmud Bavli, *Baba Kama* 115a.

39. *T'shuvot Bayit Chadash,* section 65, based on Mordechai, *Baba Metzia,* paragraph 77b; Rama, *Shulchan Arukh, Choshen Mishpat,* section 227, subsection 7.

40. Mishnah, *Baba Metzia,* chapter 4, mishnah 12.

41. *Mishneh Torah, Hilkhot Mekhirah,* chapter 18, halakhah 4; *Shulchan Arukh, Choshen Mishpat,* section 228, subsection 18; the Tur, *Choshen Mishpat,* section 228, subsection 17, 6–17.

42. *Sho'el u Meishiv,* part 1, section 20.

43. Talmud Bavli, *Kiddushin* 29a.

44. Talmud Bavli, *Baba Bathra* 21b.

45. *Mishneh Torah, Hilkhot Shecheinim,* chapter 6, halakhah 8; Tur and *Shulchan Arukh, Choshen Mishpat,* section 156, subsection 5.

46. Talmud Bavli, *Baba Bathra* 21b, and Rashi there; Rabbenu Tam in Tosafot, on *Kiddushin* 59a.

47. Talmud Bavli, *Baba Bathra* 21b.

48. Rif (Alfasi) and Rosh on *Baba Bathra* 21b; *Shulchan Arukh, Choshen Mishpat* 156, subsection 11; Tosafot, *Baba Bathra* 22a. The Semag on *Baba Bathra,* section 20, however, ruled against some of the exceptions.

49. Ibn Migas, *Chidushin Baba Bathra* 21b. See also Meiri, *Baba Metzia* 40b; Rosh, *Baba Metzia,* section 16; and the Tur, *Choshen Mishpat,* section 231, subsection 26.

50. *Lechem Rav,* section 216.

51. *T'shuvot Maharshdam, Choshen Mishpat,* section 259; see also *T'shuvot Mabit,* part 3, section 31, for a similar ruling.

52. Talmud Bavli, *Baba Bathra* 9a; for additional examples see *Tosefta, Baba Metzia,* chapter 11, halakhah 12; Vilna Gaon, *Choshen Mishpat* section 231, subsection 28.

53. Sifré, Deut. 19: 14, codified as law in *Mishneh Torah, Hilkhot Geneiva,* chapter 7, halakhah 11; *Shulchan Arukh, Choshen Mishpat, Hilkhot Gezeila,* section 376, subsection 1.

54. Talmud Bavli, *Sanhedrin* 81a; *Kiddushin* 59a.

55. *Minchat Yitschak,* part 2, section 94.

56. Talmud Bavli, *Sanhedrin* 59a; *Mishneh Torah, Hilkhot Melakhim,* chapter 10, halakhah 9; *Tosefta, Baba Kama,* chapter 7, halakhah 3. *Tosefta, Baba Metzia,* chapter 11, halakhah 13; *T'shuvot Maharam Mi Padua,* section 41; *Sefer Chasidim,* section 931; *T'shuvot HaRama,* section 10.

57. Talmud Bavli, *Baba Bathra* 22a.

58. *Pinkas, Va'ad Arba Aratsot,* enactment 677.

59. *Shulchan Arukh, Yoreh De'ah* section 236, subsection 1.

60. *Pitchei T'shuvah, Shulchan Arukh, Yoreh De'ah, Hilkhot She'uvah,* section 236, subsection 1.

61. *Ibid.*

62. *Pinkas, HaKesheirim shel Kehilat Poznan,* 1621–1835, *Takkanot* 282, 283, 296, 553.

63. Avnei Nezer, *Choshen Mishpat,* section 28.

64. Ohel Ya'akov, section 65.

65. *T'shuvot Maharshdam, Choshen Mishpat,* sections 228, 296.

66. For a fuller treatment see L. I. Rabinowitz, *Herem Hayishuv* (London: Goldston, 1945).

67. *Pinkas Padua,* enactments of 1583.

68. Responsa of the Sages of Rome, *Bet Ha'otzar,* vol. 1, 57–58.

69. Mordechai, *Baba Bathra* para 517.

70. *T'shuvot Maharam of Rothenburg,* section 883.

71. Rosh, quoted in the Tur, *Choshen Mishpat, Hilkhot Mekhirah,* section 166.

72. Quoted in *Or Zarua,* part 1, section 115.

73. *T'shuvot HaRashba,* section 132.

74. Rama, *Choshen Mishpat,* Nizkei Shecheinim, section 156, subsection 5.

75. *Pinkas, Medinat Lita,* enactments 45–46, 202, 505, 516, 600, 642.

76. V. H. Vogelstein and P. Rieger, *Geshicte der Juden in Rom* (Berlin: Mayer and Mueller, 1895/6).

77. Talmud Bavli, *Baba Bathra* 25a.

78. Rama, *Shulchan Arukh, Yoreh De'ah,* section 145, para 22; *T'shuvot Chatam Sofer, Orech Chayim,* section 130; *T'shuvot Maharil Weil,* 106a; *T'shuvot Harav Mintz,* section 89.

79. Mordechai, *Baba Bathra,* para. 514; also, *Bet Yosef, Choshen Mishpat,* section 156, subsection 3; Rama, subsection 5.

80. Talmud Bavli, *Kiddushin*, 29a.
81. *T'shuvot Maharik*, section 132.
82. Tosafot, Talmud Bavli, *Kiddushin* 59a.
83. *Responsa of Maharam of Rothenburg* (New York: I. Agus, 1972), p. 56.
84. *T'shuvot HaRadbaz*, part 4, section 54.
85. *T'shuvot HaBach*, section 60.
86. *T'shuvot Ma'amar Mordechai* section 11.
87. *T'shuvot Bet Ephraim, Choshen Mishpat*, section 27.
88. *Machaneh Ephraim, Choshen Mishpat*, part 2, section 46.
89. Iggrot Moshe, part 2; *Choshen Mishpat*, section 38.
90. *Shulchan Arukh, Choshen Mishpat, section 156, subsection 4.*
91. *Chatam Sofer, Choshen Mishpat*, section 79.
92. *Piskei Din shel Batei HaDin HaRabbanim*, Tel Aviv, 1957.

Chapter 6. Wages and Labor (pp. 126–158)

1. M. Wisnitzer, *A History of Jewish Crafts and Guilds* (New York: Jonathan David, 1965).
2. Talmud Bavli, *Baba Metzia*, 76b–77a. See also Meiri, *Baba Metzia*, 77; Tur, *Shulchan Arukh, Hilkhot S'khirut Poalim*, section 334.
3. *Netivah*, Nisan 5693.
4. *Mishneh Torah, Hilkhot S'khirut*, chapter 9, halakhah 4.
5. *Mishneh Torah, Hilkhot Avadim*, chapter 1, halakhah 7.
6. Mishnah, *Baba Metzia*, chapter 7, mishnah 1.
7. *Choshen Mishpat, Hilkhot S'khirut Poalim*, section 331, subsection 1.
8. *Shulchan Arukh, Choshen Mishpat, Hilkhot S'khirut Poalim*, section 337, subsection 1–20.
9. *Mishneh Torah, Hilkhot S'khirut*, chapter 12, halakhah 3.
10. *Mishneh Torah, Hilkhot B'rakhot*, chapter 2, halakhah 2.
11. *Mishneh Torah, Hilkhot S'khirut*, chapter 11, halakhot 1–2.
12. Deut. 24: 15. See *Sefer Chinukh*, mitzvah 230 for elaboration; see also Talmud Bavli, *Makkot* 15a.
13. Talmud Bavli, *Baba Kama* 7a.
14. *Mishneh Torah, Hilkhot S'khirut*, chapter 9, halakhah 10. See comments of Maggid Mishneh.
15. Mishnah, *Baba Metzia*, chapter 9, mishnah 12.
16. Mishnah, *Sh'vuot*, chapter 7, mishnah 5.
17. Talmud Bavli, *Baba Metzia* 112a, as explained by Rashi.
18. *T'shuvot HaRashba* 20 (attributed to the Ramban). Also reproduced in the *Bet Yosef, Choshen Mishpat*, section 188.

19. Rama, *Shulchan Arukh, Choshen Mishpat*, section 333, subsection 5.
20. *She'erit Yosef*, section 77.
21. *T'shuvot Maharil Weil*, section 1288.
22. *Shekalim*, chapter 5, halakhah 1. Cf. *Mishneh Torah, Klei Mikdash*, chapter 7, halakhah 14.
23. *Ruach Chayim*, section 333, subsection 4.
24. M. Balaban, *Yaarbuch de Judisch-Literarishen Gesellishaft* (Frankfurt: Kaufmann, 1929), col. 11, p. 101.
25. *Mishpatei Uzziel*, part 3: *Choshen Mishpat*, section 4.
26. Mitzvah 482.
27. *Piskei Batei Din Harabaniim*, Haifa, 1963.
28. *Ziknei Hadayanim, Torah V'Hamedinah*, vols. 9–10.
29. Mordechai, *Baba Metzia* 24b, section 257. See also *Shakh*, commentary on *Shulchan Arukh, Choshen Mishpat*, section 259, subsection 3.
30. *Pinkas Kehilat Poznan*, Regulation 189.
31. *T'shuvot Tashbetz*, part 1, section 64.
32. *Tsits Eliezer*, part 2, section 26, subsection 9.
33. *Divrei Chaim*, part 2, section 59.
34. *Mishneh Torah, Hilkhot Melachim*, chapter 1, halakhah 7.
35. *Yoreh De'ah*, section 245, subsection 22.
36. *T'shuvot HaRashbah*, part 1, section 300.
37. *Tsits Eliezer*, part 2, section 26, subsection 1.
38. *T'shuvot Israel Mavrona*, section 134.
39. Talmud Bavli, *Baba Bathra* 8b. See also *Tosefta, Baba Metzia*, chapter 11, halakhah 23.
40. *T'shuvot HaRashba*, part 4, section 185; part 5, section 125. See also Meiri, *Baba Bathra* 8b; Rosh, *Baba Bathra* 9a.
41. *Mishneh Torah, Hilkhot Mekhirah*, chapter 14, halakhah 10.
42. *Mishpatei Uzziel*, part 3: *Choshen Mishpat*, section 42.
43. *Iggrot Moshe*, part 2, *Choshen Mishpat*, section 59.
44. *Tosefta, Baba Metzia*, chapter 11, halakhot 24, 25, 26.
45. *Yoma*, chapter 3, mishnah 11.
46. Talmud Bavli, *Yoma* 38a.
47. *T'shuvot HaMaharam*, section 968.
48. *T'shuvot HaRashba*, part 5, section 125.
49. *Choshen Mishpat*, section 231.
50. Wisnitzer, *Jewish Crafts and Guilds*, pp. 110–113.
51. *Pinkas Medinat Lita*, enactments of 1686.
52. *Pinkas Kehilat Poznan*, enactments of 1770.

53. *Lechem Rav*, section 216.
54. *Iggrot Moshe*, part 2: *Choshen Mishpat*, section 59.
55. *Netivah*, Nisan 5693.
56. *Iggrot Moshe*.
57. *Mishneh Torah, Hilkhot Sanhedrin*, chapter 2, halakhah 12.
58. *Netivah*, Nisan 5693.
59. *T'shuvot Chatam Sofer, Choshen Mishpat*, section 44.

Chapter 7. Money, Banking, and Interest (pp. 159–208)

1. Mishnah, *Baba Metzia*, chapter 4, mishnah 1.
2. Talmud Bavli, *Ketubot* 10a.
3. II Kings 16:8.
4. I Kings 9: 26–28; 10: 2, 10; 14–22.
5. Talmud Bavli, *Baba Metzia* 112a. See also ruling in *Shulchan Arukh, Choshen Mishpat, S'khirut HaPoalim*, section 339, subsection 10.
6. Talmud Bavli, *Baba Kama* 7a.
7. Talmud Bavli, *Baba Kama* 14b.
8. Talmud Bavli, *Baba Metzia* 65a, b.
9. L. J. Rabinowitz, *Jewish Merchant Adventures* (London: E. Goldston, 1948).
10. Israel Abrahams, *Jewish Life in the Middle Ages* (London: Temple Books, 1969), pp. 262–3.
11. I. A. Agus, *The Heroic Age of Franco-German Jewry* (New York: Bloch, 1969).
12. Joseph Jacobs (ed.), *Jews of Angevin England* (Farnsworth, England: Gregg International, 1970).
13. Reproduced in L. Finkelstein, *Jewish Self-Government in the Middle Ages* (New York: Feldheim, 1964).
14. *Mishneh Torah, Hilkhot Malveh u Loveh*, chapter 1, halakhah 1.
15. Mitzvah 56.
16. *Shulchan Arukh, Choshen Mishpat, Hilkhot Halva'ah*, section 96, subsections 23–25.
17. Mitzvah 67.
18. Talmud Bavli, *Baba Metzia* 75b. See also *Mishneh Torah, Hilkhot Malveh u Loveh*, chapter 2, halakhah 7.
19. *Me'irot Eineiyim, Choshen Mishpat*, section 72, subsection 4.
20. Talmud Bavli, *Baba Metzia* 113a, b.
21. *Mishneh Torah, Hilkhot Malveh u Loveh*, chapter 3, halakhot 5–6. See also *Shulchan Arukh, Yoreh De'ah*, section 96, subsections 6–18.
22. *Mishneh Torah, Hilkhot Malveh u Loveh*, chapter 3, halakhah 1.

23. *Mishneh Torah, Hilkhot Malveh u Loveh*, chapter 4, halakhot 1–2.

24. Rashi on Exod. 22:24.

25. See Rashi and *Sefer HaChinukh*, Mitzvah 232; *Mishneh Torah, Hilkhot Rotzeah u Shmirot Hanefesh*, chapter 12, halakhah 14.

26. *Mishneh Torah, Hilkhot Malveh u Loveh*, chapter 4, halakhah 2.

27. *Shulchan Arukh, Yoreh De'ah*, section 161, subsection 5.

28. Mishnah, *Baba Metzia*, chapter 5, mishnah 21; *Mishneh Torah, Malveh u Loveh*, chapter 6, halakhah 1; *Shulchan Arukh, Yoreh De'ah*, section 161, subsection 5.

29. *Sho'el u Meishiv*, part 3, section 31. See Rama, *Shulchan Arukh, Yoreh De'ah*, section 160, subsection 16.

30. Minchat Yitschak, part 3, section 1; part 4, sections 16–18; Iggrot Moshe, Yoreh De'ah, part 3, sections 40–41.

31. Mishnah, *Baba Metzia*, chapter 5, mishnah 6.

32. *Mishneh Torah, Hilkhot Loveh u Malveh*, chapter 5, halakhah 1.

33. *Mishneh Torah, Hilkhot Avoda Zara*, chapter 1, halakhot 1–3.

34. Talmud Bavli, *Baba Metzia* 70b–71a.

35. Abarbanel on the Torah, Deut. 23:21.

36. Mitzvah 66.

37. Mishnah, *Baba Metzia*, chapter 5, mishnah 4.

38. *Laws and Customs of Israel*, part II (Pardes), pp. 145–49.

39. *Vay'chi Yosef, Dinei Ribit L'Halakha* (Monsey, N.Y.: Weiss, 1984).

40. *Mishneh Torah, Hilkhot Malveh u Loveh*, chapter 8, halakhah 2.

41. *Yoreh De'ah*, section 173, subsection 1.

42. *Minchat Yitschak*, part 3, section 1; part 4, sections 16 and 18.

43. Y. Halevi B'eri, *Torah u Medinah*, vols. 5–6, pp. 296–301, based on *T'shuvot Maharam Shick, Yoreh De'ah*, section 158.

44. *Baba Metzia*, chapter 4, mishnah 1.

45. *Yoreh De'ah*, section 62, subsection 1.

46. *T'shuvot Chatam Sofer, Yoreh De'ah*, section 134.

47. *Choshen Mishpat*, section 16.

48. Alfasi, Talmud Bavli, *Baba Kama* 104b.

49. Talmud Bavli, *Baba Kama* 96–97.

50. *Baba Metzia*, chapter 5, mishnah 9.

51. *Yoreh De'ah*, 162a, subsection 1.

52. *Ibid.*

53. Mishnah, *Baba Metzia*, chapter 5, mishnah 9.

54. *Hilkhot Malveh u Loveh*, chapter 4, halakhah 12; *Shulchan Arukh, Yoreh De'ah*, section 74.

55. Talmud Bavli, *Baba Kama* 97b–98a.

56. *Mishneh Torah, Hilkhot Malveh u Loveh*, chapter 4, halakhah 11.

57. *Shulchan Arukh, Yoreh De'ah*, section 74.

58. Rif on *Baba Kama* 35a.

59. *T'shuvot Chatam Sofer, Yoreh De'ah*, section 134; *Choshen Mishpat*, sections 58, 62, 74, 166.

60. Chazon Ish, *Choshen Mishpat*, part 1, section 154. As a result, perhaps, of the consistent inflation in Israel there is a voluminous modern literature in Hebrew on both price changes and currency value changes. The reader is referred to the bibliography.

61. *Kerem Haimar, Takanot* 89–91.

62. *T'shuvot Maharim, Even Haezer*, section 2.

63. *Yoreh De'ah*, section 175, subsection 1.

64. Rabbi E. Basri, *Dinei Momanot*, section 5, chapter 7 (Jerusalem: Reuven Mass, 1974).

65. Rabbi Goren, Hatzofe, November 1982.

66. *Shulchan Arukh, Yoreh De'ah*, section 60.

67. *Iggrot Moshe, Yoreh De'ah*, Part 3, section 37.

68. *Mishneh Torah, Hilkhot Ishut*, chapter 23, halakhah 17; also *Hilkhot Mekhirah*, chapter 11, halakhot 16 and 17. See *Kesef Mishneh* in both places and the *Shulchan Arukh, Choshen Mishpat*, section 207, subsection 16, for a different opinion.

Chapter 8. Taxation (pp. 209–241)

1. Rashbam, Talmud Bavli, *Baba Bathra* 54; See also *T'shuvot Maharshdam, Choshen Mishpat*, section 408.

2. *T'shuvot HaRashba*, part 7, section 108; part 4, section 175.

3. *T'rumat Hadeshen*, section 342.

4. *T'shuvot HaRashba*, part 5, section 178.

5. *Maharshdam, Choshen Mishpat*, section 442.

6. *Mishneh Torah, Hilkhot G'zeilah v'Aveidah*, chapter 5, halakhah 11; based on Talmud Bavli, *Nedarim* 28a; *Shulchan Arukh, Choshen Mishpat*, section 2, citing the Rif; see also *T'shuvot Maharshdam*, section 453.

7. Rama, *Choshen Mishpat*, section 176, subsection 25.

8. *Baba Bathra*, chapter 1, mishnah 5; discussion in Talmud Bavli, 7b–8b.

9. Mishnah, *Sanhedrin*, chapter 2, mishnah 11.

10. *Mishneh Torah, Hilkhot G'zeilah u Aveidah*; chapter 5, halakhot 11–12; *T'shuvot Maharam mi Rothenburg*, section 106; *Tur, Shulchan Arukh, Choshen Mishpat*, section 369. It is interesting to note the placing of this ruling by Maimonides in his section dealing with the laws of

robbery as well as those dealing with the rules of kingship. Rabbi Kook, in *Mishpat Cohen*, section 148, extended this to include Jewish state authority even where there is no longer a king.

11. *Baraita, S'machot,* chapter 2, halakhah 9. See however *Mishneh Torah, Hilkhot G'zeilah u Aveidah,* chapter 15, halakhah 14.

12. *Mishneh Torah, Hilkhot M'lakhim,* chapter 1, halakhot 8–10; see however dissent of the Raivid there.

13. *Tosefta, Baba Metzia,* chapter 7.

14. *Talmud Bavli, Baba Bathra* 7b; see Rosh and Nimukei Joseph there, who reproduce the opinion of Ibn Migas. The Chazon Ish, commenting in *Baba Bathra* 4, section 7, following the reasoning of the Rama, arrives at a similar conclusion albeit the utility flows not from benefit derived but rather from the fact that the houses closer to the wall cause the area enclosed by the wall to be expanded in the first place.

15. *T'shuvot HaRashba,* part 3, section 401.

16. *T'shuvot HaRashba,* part 5, section 15.

17. *Mordechai, Baba Bathra,* section 481; also *T'rumat Hadeshen,* section 342.

18. *Shulchan Arukh, Choshen Mishpat,* section 163, subsection 3; see also *Bet Yosef,* same section, in reference to charitable funds, and *T'shuvot Maharam mi Rothenburg,* section 941, referring to books. Responsa attributed to Maimonides, section 84, taxed real estate and books at a quarter of their value.

19. *T'rumat Hadeshen,* section 342; also Rama, *Choshen Mishpat,* section 163, subsection 3.

20. *T'shuvot Maharam mi Rothenburg* 941; reproduced also in *Mordechai, Baba Bathra,* section 481.

21. *T'rumat Hadeshen,* section 342.

22. *Ibid.*

23. *T'shuvot Chatam Sofer, Yoreh De'ah* 231; *Tsits Eliezer,* volume 9, section 1, chapter 3. See also commentaries on the *Shulchan Arukh:* Bach, *Yoreh De'ah,* section 331; Taz, subsection 32; and Shach, subsection 136, who question the source of this monetary tithing, or the Vilna Gaon, *Yoreh De'ah* 249, subsection 2, who finds a source in the Talmud Yerushalmi, *Pe'ah,* chapter 1, halakhah 1, or Mordechai, *Perek Hagozel,* who finds a bibical source for tithing.

24. *Shulchan Arukh, Yoreh De'ah,* section 249.

25. *Bet Din shel Shlomo, Yoreh De'ah,* section 1, based on the *Chavot Yair.*

26. M. Tamari, ''Non-Divided Forms of Profit Withdrawal,'' *Economic Review* (Jerusalem: Bank of Israel, 1969).

27. *Am HaTorah* (Tsirei Agudat Yisrael of America), vol. 2, no. 5, 1982–83.

28. *Arukh HaShulchan*, section 248.

29. Quoted in *Am HaTorah*, vol. 2, no. 5.

30. *T'rumat Hadeshen*, section 342.

31. *T'shuvot HaRashba* 664, 788; see also *Maharik, Tur, Choshen Mishpat*, section 157. However, many authorities ruled that taxes could be levied on wealth held in other places—for example, Rama, *Choshen Mishpat*, section 163, reflecting the *Maharil, T'rumat Hadeshen*, etc.

32. L. Finkelstein, *Jewish Self-Government in the Middle Ages* (New York: Feldheim, 1964).

33. S. Dubnow, *Pinkas Hamedinah* (Berlin: Ayanot, 1925).

34. Quoted in Jacob R. Marcus, *The Jew in the Medieval World* (New York: Harper and Row, 1938).

35. D. Karfi, ed., *Va'ad Kehilah Kedosha Padua* (Jerusalem: Ha'akademia Haleumit Lemadaim, 1973) (Hebrew).

36. I. Heilperin, ed., *Pinkas Va'ad Arba Aratsot* (Jerusalem: Mossad Bialik, 1954) (Hebrew).

37. *Shekalim*, chapter 1, mishnah 1.

38. *Pinkas Padua*.

39. *Choshen Mishpat*, section 163, subsections 1–3.

40. *T'shuvot HaRashba*, part 3, no. 382.

41. *Ibid.*, part 5, no. 220.

42. *Ibid.*, part 1, no. 887.

43. *Ibid.*, part 1, nos. 664, 789; part 3, no. 379.

44. *Ibid.*, part 4, nos. 67.

45. *Ibid.*, part 1, no. 891, part 5, no. 182, part 3, no. 196.

46. *T'shuvot HaMakarik*, no. 4.

47. *Iggrot Moshe*, part 2: *Choshen Mishpat*, section 80.

Chapter 9. Welfare (pp. 242–277)

1. Talmud Bavli, *Sotah* 14a.

2. Mishnah, *Avot*, chapter 1, mishnah 2.

3. *Midrash Rabbah*, Exodus 3:1.

4. Shem mi Shmuel on *Parshat Chayei Sarah*.

5. Rabbenu Asher; in Israel Abrahams, ed., *Hebrew Ethical Wills* (Philadelphia: Jewish Publication Society, 1954), pp. 119–25.

6. Mishnah, *Avot*, chapter 5, mishnah 13.

7. *Sifra*, Leviticus 19:16.

8. Mishnah, *Avot*, chapter 5, mishnah 12.

9. *Sefer Hachinukh* on *Parshat Mishpatim*, mitzvah 65.

10. Talmud Bavli, *Pesachim* 112–13.

11. *Mishneh Torah, Hilkhot Mat'not Aniyim*, chapter 10, halakhot 18, 19.

12. *Ibid.*, halakhah 7.

13. *Pinkas Padua*, 1603.

14. Commentary on the Mishnah, *Peah*, chapter 1, mishnah 1.

15. *Mishneh Torah, Hilkhot Mat'not Aniyim*, chapter 2, halakhah 17.

16. *Or Zarua, Hilkhot Tzedakah*, section 11.

17. *Mishneh Torah, Hilkhot Mat'not Aniyim*, chapter 7, halakhot 1–2.

18. A. Sorasky, *Reb Elchanan* (Art Scroll History Series) (New York: Mesorah Publications, 1982), p. 277.

19. Israel al-Nakawa, *Menorat Hamaor* (Lamp of Illumination).

20. *Shulchan Arukh, Yoreh De'ah*, section 248, subsection 1.

21. Maharshdam on *Yoreh De'ah*, section 249, quoting from Machane Ephraim, *Zechiyah V'Matana*, section 8.

22. Talmud Bavli, *Sanhedrin* 17b.

23. *Mishneh Torah, Hilkhot Mat'not Aniyim*, chapter 9, halakhot 1–3.

24. *Ibid.*, chapter 9, halakhah 12.

25. *Ibid.*, chapter 7, halakhah 3.

26. *Ibid.*, chapter 9, halakhah 13.

27. *Rif*, Talmud Bavli, *Baba Kama* 7b.

28. *Mishneh Torah*, chapter 7, halakhah 6.

29. *Ibid.*, halakhah 3.

30. Talmud Bavli, *Pesachim* 112–113.

31. *Yoreh De'ah, Hilkhot Tzedakah*, section 250, subsection 5, based on responsum of the Rashba.

32. Talmud Bavli, *Hagiga* 8a.

33. *Yoreh De'ah*, section 249, subsection 4.

34. Talmud Bavli, *Kiddushin* 31a.

35. S. W. Baron, *The Jewish Community* (Philadelphia: Jewish Publication Society, 1945), p. 332.

36. I. Agus, *The Heroic Age of Franco-German Jewry* (New York: Bloch, 1969).

37. *Shulchan Arukh, Yoreh De'ah, Hilkhot Tzedakah*, section 251, subsection 3.

38. Mishnah, *Peah*, chapter 8, mishnah 7.

39. S. D. Goiten, *A Mediterranean Society* (Berkeley: University of California Press, 1967), pp. 320–21.

40. Jacob R. Marcus, *The Jew in the Medieval World* (New York: Harper and Row, 1938).

41. *Yoreh De'ah, Hilkhot Tzedakah*, section 242, subsections 1 and 2. See also *Shakh* and *Taz*.
42. *Mishneh Torah, Mat'not Aniyim*, chapter 8, halakhah 13.
43. Talmud Bavli, *Gittin* 45a, Mishnah and Gemara.
44. *Mishneh Torah, Hilkhot Ishut*, chapter 15, halakhah 19.
45. *Yoreh De'ah, Hilkhot Tzedakah*, section 242.
46. Talmud Bavli, *Baba Metzia* 62a.
47. *Mishneh Torah, Hilkhot Y'sodei HaTorah*, chapter 5, halakhot 5–6.
48. Talmud Bavli, *Ketubot* 67a.
49. *Mishneh Torah, Hilkhot Mat'not Aniyim*, chapter 8, halakhot 17, 18.
50. Talmud Bavli, *Baba Bathra* 21a.
51. *Sifré, Parshat Va'etchanan*.
52. N. Goldman, *Life-Long Learning among Jews* (New York: Ktav, 1975).
53. *Yoreh De'ah, Hilkhot Tzedakah*, section 249.
54. *Mishneh Torah, Hilkhot Tefillah*, chapter 1, section 4.
55. Talmud Bavli, *Baba Bathra* 25a.
56. *Shulchan Arukh, Yoreh De'ah, Hilkhot Tzedakah*, section 249.
57. Talmud Bavli, *Kiddushin* 29a–30a.
58. *Mishneh Torah, Hilkhot Shabbat*, chapter 28, halakhah 5. See also *Maharshdam*, Talmud Bavli, *Kiddushin* 30a.
59. Talmud Bavli, *Baba Bathra* 21a–22b. See also *Mishneh Torah, Hilkhot Shecheinim*, chapter 6, halakhah 12.
60. *Shulchan Arukh, Choshen Mishpat*, section 156, subsection 1; Maimonides' commentary on the Mishnah, *Baba Bathra*, chapter 2, mishnah 3.
61. Mishnah, *Sota*, chapter 6, chapter 9; Talmud Bavli, *Sota* 45b. See also Rashi on *Sota* 46b; Talmud Yerushalmi, *Sota*, chapter 9.

Chapter 10. Environmental Issues and the Public Good (pp. 278–306)

1. R. Pigou, *The Economics of Welfare* (London: Macmillan, 1960).
2. *Midrash-Rabbah, Kohelet*, 713.
3. Mishnah, *Avot*, chapter 4, mishnah 21.
4. *Choshen Mishpat, Hilkhot Nizkei Shecheinim*, sections 153–156.
5. *Baba Kama*, chapter 1, mishnah 1.
6. *Mishneh Torah, Hilkhot Nizkei Mamon*, chapter 5, halakhah 1.
7. Talmud Bavli, *Yevamot* 11b.
8. Talmud Bavli, *Shabbat* 105b.
9. Talmud Bavli, *Pesachin* 56a.
10. *T'shuvot HaRashba*, part 2, section 65.

11. *Baba Bathra*, chapter 2, mishnah 11.
12. *Choshen Mishpat*, section 155, subsection 32.
13. *Tosefta, Baba Bathra*, chapter 1, halakhah 8.
14. *T'shuvot HaRosh*, section 108, subsection 10.
15. *T'shuvot Chatam Sofer, Choshen Mishpat*, section 92.
16. Mishnah, *Baba Bathra*, chapter 2, mishnah 3.
17. Mishnah, *ibid.*, Mishnahot 8 and 9. See also *Shulchan Arukh, Choshen Mishpat*, section 155, subsections 22 and 23.
18. *Chidushei HaRamban, Baba Bathra* p. 23, 59. See also the Ritva and Rama.
19. *Magen Giborim, Choshen Mishpat*, section 38.
20. *Choshen Mishpat*, section 155, subsection 36.
21. Mishnah, *Baba Bathra*, chapter 2, mishnah 7. Talmud Bavli, *Baba Bathra* 24b. See also Rama, *Shulchan Arukh, Choshen Mishpat*, section 155, subsection 22.
22. *Baba Kama*, chapter 7, mishnah 7.
23. Talmud Bavli, *Baba Kama* 82b. See also *Mishneh Torah, Hilkhot Nizkei Mamon*, chapter 5, halakhah 9; and *Shulchan Arukh, Choshen Mishpat, Hilkhot Nizkei Mamon*, section 409, subsection 2.
24. J. M. Rigg, ed., *Select Pleas, Starrs, and Other Records from the Exchequer of the Jews* (London: Quaritch, 1902), pp. 35–36.
25. *Ruach Chaim*, section 7, section 4.
26. *T'shuvot Maharshach*, part 2, subsection 98.
27. *Shemesh Tzedakah, Choshen Mishpat*, section 34, subsection 11.
28. *Baba Kama*, chapter 8, mishnah 1.
29. *Choshen Mishpat, Hilkhot Shmirat Hanefesh*, section 427.
30. *Assia* 35, Jerusalem, pp. 10–15.
31. *Iggrot Moshe, Yoreh De'ah*, part 2, section 49; part 7; *Choshen Mishpat*, part 2, section 18.
32. *Choshen Mishpat, Hilkhot Shmirat Hanefesh*, section 426.
33. *Parshat Mishpatim*, Mitzvah 80.
34. *Shulchan Arukh, Yoreh De'ah*, section 336, subsection 1. See also *Taz* and *Shakh*.
35. F. Kobler, ed., *Treasury of Jewish Letters*, vol. 1 (Philadephia: Jewish Publication Society), pp. 156–64.
36. *T'shuvot Mei Ahavah*, part 3: *Yoreh De'ah*, sections 336, 408.
37. *Pinkas Padua*, enactments of 1585.
38. *Pinkas Padua*, enactments of 28 June 1587.
39. Cited in M. Balaban, *Yaarbuch der Judisch-Literarishen Gesellishaft* (Frankfurt: Kaufmann, 1929).

40. Josephus Flavius, *Antiquities of the Jews*, vol. XIV, chapter 7.

41. Quoted in S. Baron, *The Jewish Community* (Philadelphia: Jewish Publication Society, 1945), vol. II, p. 329.

42. *Ibid.*, vol. III, p. 210.

43. *T'shuvot Maharshdam, Orach Haim* 20, and *Yoreh De'ah* 207–9.

44. Talmud Bavli, *Sanhedrin* 78a.

45. *Ibid., Makkot* 22b.

46. *Mishneh Torah, Hilkhot Eivel*, chapter 14, halakhot 1–5. See also Talmud Bavli, *Nedarim* 40a.

47. Reproduced in N. Wisnitzer, *A History of Jewish Crafts and Guilds* (New York: Jonathan David, 1965).

48. Talmud Bavli, *Baba Metzia* 62a.

49. Mishneh Torah, *Yesodei HaTorah*, chapter 5, halakhot 5–6.

50. Talmud Bavli, *Ketubot* 51b.

51. *Tsitz Eliezer*, part 9, sections 17 and 28.

Bibliography

The following bibliography is presented in order to provide the reader with material for further study and research. Of the vast responsa literature only two modern halakhic authorities are included, since they are the primary sources of legal decisions on ongoing economic issues. The historical and social works listed are included because they provide valuable source material. The reader is reminded, however, that it is extremely difficult and perhaps impossible for the authors to free themselves from their particular religious or social philosophy. This means that the reader should acquaint himself with the viewpoint of the authors regarding halakhic, economic, and historical sources in order to evaluate the biases introduced.

Books

Abrahams, I. *Jewish Life in the Middle Ages*. New York: Atheneum, 1969.

Adler, M. N. transl. *Itinerary of Benjamin of Tudela*. New York: Feldheim, 1964.

Agus, I. *The Heroic Age of Franco-German Jewry*. New York: Bloch, 1969.

_____. *Rabbi Meir of Rothenberg*. New York: Ktav, 1970.

Assaf, S. *Tekufat Ha-Geonim Ve Sifrutah* (in Hebrew). Jerusalem: Mossad HaRav Kook, 1955.

Baron, S. *The Jewish Community: Its History and Structure to the American Revolution*. London: Greenwood Press, 1973.

Basri, E. *Dinei Momanot* (Laws of Money) (2 vols., in Hebrew). Jerusalem: Reuven Mass., 1974.

Ben-Sasson, H. *Toldot Am Yisrael B'yemei Habeinaiim* (Jewish history in the Middle Ages, in Hebrew). Tel Aviv: Dvir, 1959.

Blau, Y. *Sefer Brit Yehudah* (banking and interest, in Hebrew). Jerusalem: Y. Blau, 1979.

Bloom, H. I. *The Economic Activities of the Jews of Amsterdam in the Seventeenth and Eighteenth Centuries*. London: Kennikot Press, 1982.

Chażan, R. *Medieval Jewish Life*. New York: Ktav, 1976.

Davis, M. D., ed. *Hebrew Deeds of English Jews before 1290* (Facsimile of 1883 ed.). Farnsworth, England: Gregg International, 1972.

Eidelberg, *T'shuvot Rabbenu Gershon Me'or Hagolah* (in Hebrew). New York: 1955.

Elon, M. *Yesodot BaMishpat HaIvri* (in Hebrew). Jerusalem: Keter, 1975.

Epstein, I. *Studies in the Communal Life of the Jews in Spain*. New York: Hermon Press, 1968.

Finkelstein, L. *Jewish Self-Government in the Middle Ages*. New York: Feldheim, 1964

Fischel, J. M. *Jews in the Economic and Political Life of Medieval Islam*. New York: Ktav, 1969.

Goiten, S. D. *Letters of Medieval Jewish Traders*. Princeton, N.J.: Princeton University Press, 1973.

_____. *A Mediterranean Society*. Berkeley, Calif.: University of California Press, 1967.

Goldman, N. *Life-Long Learning Among Jews*. New York: Ktav, 1975.

Heilperin, I., ed. *Pinkas Va'ad Arba Aratsot* (in Hebrew). Jerusalem: Mossad Bialik, 1954.

Hertzog, I. M. *Main Institutions of Jewish Law*. London: Soncino, 1967.

Israel, J. *European Jewry in the Age of Mercantilism*. London: Oxford University Press, 1985.

Jacobs, J., ed. *Jews of Angevin England*. Farnsworth, England: Gregg International, 1970.

Jung, L. *Human Relations in Jewish Law*. New York: Jewish Education Committee, 1967.

Karfi, D., ed. *Va'ad Kehilah Kedosha Padua* (in Hebrew). Jerusalem: Ha'akademia Haleumit Lemadahim, 1973.

Kisch, G. *The Jews in Medieval Germany*. New York: Ktav, 1970.

Klein, I. *Responsa and Halachic Studies*. New York: Ktav, 1975.

Lamm, N. *The Good Society*. New York: Viking Press, 1974.

Levin, M. *Iggeret R. Sh'ria Gaon*. Haifa: M. Levin, 1921.

Levine, A. *Free Enterprise and Jewish Law*. New York: Ktav, 1980.

Maimonides, M. *Hakdamah LePeirush HaMishnah*. Jerusalem: Mossad HaRav Kook, 1980.

Marcus, J. R. *The Jew in the Medieval World*. New York: Harper and Row, 1938.

Meidel, Y., and S. Ash, eds. *Pinkas Kehilat Berlin* (in Hebrew). Jerusalem: Reuven Mass, 1963.

Parkes, J. W. *The Jew in the Medieval Community*. New York: Hermon Press, 1976.

Poliakov, L. *Jewish Bankers and the Holy See*. Littman Library of Jewish Civilization. London: Routledge & Kegal Paul, 1983.

Rabinowitz, L. I. *Social Life of the Jews of Northern France in the Twelfth–Fourteenth Centuries*. London: Edward Goldston, 1938.

_____. *The Herem Hayishuv*. London: Edward Goldston, 1945.

Rigg, J. M., ed. *Select Pleas, Starrs, and Other Records from the Exchequer of the Jews*. London: Quaritch, 1902.

Rotenburg, S. *Toldot Am Olam* (in Hebrew). Jerusalem: Rotenburg, 1973.

Schimmel, S. *The Oral Law*. New York: Feldheim, 1971.

Schreiber, A. M. *Jewish Law and Decision Making*. Philadelphia: Temple University Press, 1979.

Shohet, D. M. *The Jewish Court in the Middle Ages. Studies in Jewish Jurisprudence*. New York: Hermon Press, 1974.

Shulweis, J. *The Jew in the World of the Renaissance*. New York: Judaica Press, 1973.

Silberg, M. *Talmudic Law and the Modern State*. Ed. M. S. Wiener. Los Angeles: Burning Bush Press, 1973.

Starr, J. *The Jews in the Byzantine Empire*. Farnsworth, England: Gregg International, 1969.

Warhaftig, M. *Dinei Avodah Bamishpat Ha'Ivri* (Labor Legislation in Jewish Law) (2 vols., in Hebrew). Jerusalem: Moreshet, 1969.

_____. *Dinei Chozim Bamishpat Ha'Ivri* (Law of Contracts in Jewish Law, in Hebrew). Jerusalem: Machon Harry Fischel, 1974.

_____. *Dinei Matbeia Bamishpat Ha'Ivri* (Coinage and Money in Jewish Law, in Hebrew). Jerusalem: Machon Harry Fischel, 1979.

Warhaftig, Z. *Hachazaka Bamishpat Ha'Ivri* (Laws of Possession, in Hebrew). Jerusalem: Mossad Harav Kook, 1974.

Waxman, M. *A History of Jewish Literature*. New York: T. Yoseloff, 1960.

Wisnitzer, S. *A History of Jewish Crafts and Guilds*. New York: Jonathan David, 1965.

Yechiel Nissim Da Pisa, *Banking and Finance among the Jews in Renaissance Italy*. Trans. G. S. Rosenthal. New York: Bloch Publishing Company, 1962.

Zipperstein, E. *Business Ethics in Jewish Law*. New York: Ktav, 1983.

Responsa

Iggrot Moshe (Rabbi Moshe Feinstein, New York) (6 vols.)

Minchat Yitschak (Rabbi Yitschak Weiss, Jerusalem) (7 vols.)

Journals

HaTorah V'Hamedina (Torah and State) (in Hebrew) (Tel Aviv: Moreshet).

Journal of Contemporary Halachah (New York: Yeshiva University).

Journal of Jewish Social Studies (quarterly). (New York: Conference on Jewish Social Studies).

Sidrat Mechkarim B'Mishpat HaIvri (research series in Jewish law) (in Hebrew) (Jerusalem: Misrad Hamishpatim).

Index